GENRE, AUTHORSHIP AND CONTEMPORARY WOMEN FILMMAKERS

GENRE, AUTHORSHIP AND CONTEMPORARY WOMEN FILMMAKERS

Katarzyna Paszkiewicz

EDINBURGH
University Press

Edinburgh University Press is one of the leading university presses in the UK. We publish academic books and journals in our selected subject areas across the humanities and social sciences, combining cutting-edge scholarship with high editorial and production values to produce academic works of lasting importance. For more information visit our website: edinburghuniversitypress.com

© Katarzyna Paszkiewicz, 2018

Edinburgh University Press Ltd
The Tun – Holyrood Road
12 (2f) Jackson's Entry
Edinburgh EH8 8PJ

Typeset in 10/12.5pt Sabon by
Servis Filmsetting Ltd, Stockport, Cheshire

A CIP record for this book is available from the British Library

ISBN 978 1 4744 2526 1 (hardback)
ISBN 978 1 4744 2527 8 (webready PDF)
ISBN 978 1 4744 2528 5 (epub)

The right of Katarzyna Paszkiewicz to be identified as author of this work has been asserted in accordance with the Copyright, Designs and Patents Act 1988 and the Copyright and Related Rights Regulations 2003 (SI No. 2498).

CONTENTS

List of Figures	vi
Acknowledgements	viii
Introduction: Impossible Liaisons? Genre and Feminist Film Criticism	1
1. Subversive Auteur, Subversive Genre	34
2. Repeat to Remake: Diablo Cody and Karyn Kusama's *Jennifer's Body*	60
3. Hollywood Transvestite: Kathryn Bigelow's *The Hurt Locker*	100
4. Genre in the Margins: Kelly Reichardt's *Meek's Cutoff*	134
5. Genre on the Surface: Sofia Coppola's *Marie Antoinette*	173
6. What a *Woman* Wants? Nancy Meyers's *The Intern*	209
Afterword: Desperately Seeking Wonder Women	254
Bibliography	264
Index	286

FIGURES

2.1	Jennifer's jaw as *vagina dentata*	79
2.2	Jennifer as a popular girl	85
2.3	Needy's gaze	86
2.4	Postfeminist regime exposed	89
2.5	The brutalised Final Girl	91
2.6	Becoming-monstrous: Needy at the hotel	93
3.1	Eye and vision come under critical scrutiny in *The Hurt Locker*	109
3.2	James as the heroic figure in the untamed landscape who asserts mastery over the environment	113
3.3	All eyes are on James	116
3.4	The violence of the gaze	120
3.5	Dilated temporality: the Western trope made eerie	122
3.6	Guns as metaphor for cameras: meta-cinematic reflection on the war film	123
4.1	The gendered organisation of space: men withdraw to deliberate over the course, while women look on from a distance	146
4.2	The duel of the gazes	149
4.3	Sheer duration: superimposed images in *Meek's Cutoff*	153
4.4	Flat affect and underperformed emotions	161
4.5	Haptic inhospitability of the land(scape)	166
5.1	Luxurious footwear in *Marie Antoinette*	180
5.2	The abundance of shoes and accessories in *The Bling Ring*	180
5.3	Orlando as a frosted blue cake	189

5.4	Marie Antoinette blends and disappears into the ornate floral-patterned wallpaper	190
5.5	Marie Antoinette's direct mode of address	191
5.6	The palace is destroyed, but Marie Antoinette (temporarily) escapes punishment	197
6.1	*The Intern*'s central couple: Jules and Ben	222
6.2	What men want: bromantic protagonists in *The Intern*	224
6.3	Jules's eyes track up to the top of the skyscraper in front of her, she then looks to Ben, communicating her unease about the forthcoming interview	234
6.4	Ben invades the feminised space of 'pink girlhood'	243
6.5	Happy to be lost in another world: Ben shedding a tear over Gene Kelly and Debbie Reynolds's performance of 'You Were Meant For Me'	246

ACKNOWLEDGEMENTS

I would like to thank all those who have supported me during the long research and writing process. I wish to thank my friends and colleagues at the University of Barcelona, whose approaches have helped me shape my own and who have supported me in many ways, especially my superb research mentors, Helena González and Marta Segarra. Without their encouragement and guidance, this book might never have existed. For various forms of support over the years it took to complete this book, I thank Elena Losada, who continues to inspire me in all sorts of ways. I am also grateful to Cristina Alsina, Rodrigo Andrés, Francesco Ardolino, Isabel Clúa and Joana Sabadell, who helped at different stages and in different ways. Thank you for your kindness and friendship.

Along the way I have been honoured by the generous suggestions of people I respect and admire, which have certainly propelled the project forwards. I benefited especially from my research visits to the University of Melbourne and the University of Pennsylvania. I thank Barbara Creed, Karen Beckman and Timothy Corrigan for this opportunity and for a warm welcome. Many colleagues have shared feedback on my work at the Society for Cinema and Media Studies and Doing Women's Film History and Television conferences, as well as other meetings over the years. I sincerely thank my friend Dawn Hall, who helped with ideas and encouragement. I am also grateful to Christine Gledhill and Christina Lane for inspiration and support, and to Patricia White, who generously shared her manuscript, *Women's Cinema, World Cinema*, with me, and from whom I learnt so much.

ACKNOWLEDGEMENTS

This research builds on my earlier study on women filmmakers and genre, developed as my PhD thesis (*Rehacer los géneros: mujeres cineastas dentro y fuera de Hollywood*, Icaria, 2017), and has evolved in dialogue with the contributors to my co-edited book collection *Women Do Genre in Film and Television* (Harrod and Paszkiewicz eds, Routledge, 2017). My heartfelt thanks to Mary Harrod, my collaborator in the latter and long-time interlocutor, who has read and graciously commented on each of the chapters of the present volume. This book is much better than it would have been without her input and suggestions. I am also grateful to Deborah Jermyn for her generous feedback on Chapter 6 and my research on Nancy Meyers in general. I am also indebted to Linda Badley and the anonymous peer reviewers for their excellent and enormously helpful feedback on my proposal, and I wish to sincerely thank them. Many thanks as well to Eloise McInerney for her help with and invaluable comments on Chapter 1. I also want to thank my editors Gillian Leslie and Richard Strachan, as well as Eddie Clark and the whole team at EUP, and the copy-editor Elizabeth Welsh, for their interest and suggestions, for their professionalism, efficiency and understanding. My special thanks to my dear friend, Andrea Ruthven, who proofread my manuscript and provided invaluable insights to this project. Thank you for asking the right questions and supporting me in many ways during the long process of writing. You were a frequent sounding board who kept my spirits high.

My friends have provided me with great support. Among them, I especially thank Marta Font, Julia Lewandowska, Laura López, Aleksandra Malicka, Eva París-Huesca, Maribel Rams, Lola Resano and María Teresa Vera Rojas.

Finally, I would like to express my wholehearted gratitude to my parents, Jola and Zbyszek, and to Gaspar for their unfailing love throughout the years. Gaspar, who happens to be an astute critic and splendid editor, made suggestions on earlier drafts of this book – for this, I am truly thankful.

INTRODUCTION: IMPOSSIBLE LIAISONS? GENRE AND FEMINIST FILM CRITICISM

I don't think I've read the words women and film and feminism in the same sentence as much in the last few months since *Thelma and Louise* rocked the culture nearly two decades ago.

(Dargis 2010a)

Kathryn Bigelow's success at the 2010 Academy Awards, when she became the first woman to receive an Oscar for Best Director for *The Hurt Locker* (2008), has renewed scholarly and critical interest in women's filmmaking and the position of female directors within Hollywood, as illustrated by *The New York Times* film critic Manohla Dargis's comment above. The controversies surrounding Bigelow's historical win, as Dargis suggests, can be compared to those that emerged from the critical reception of *Thelma and Louise* (Ridley Scott, 1991), a generic amalgam of the Western, the buddy film and the road movie – three genres traditionally codified as male – and which significantly features two female leads. At the time of its release, Scott's film sparked considerable debate regarding its political value for feminism, often being read as a radical revision of Hollywood's conventional representation of woman's place in the domestic sphere (Tasker 1993: 134–9).

In spite of Dargis's enthusiastic response, *The Hurt Locker*, a war film about an Explosive Ordnance Disposal (EOD) team deployed in Baghdad, centred on the representation of US soldiers (of which all are male in the film), has not generated similar consensus on its significance in relation to feminist politics. While many commentators in the mainstream press celebrated the filmmaker's triumph as a female director working in a predominantly male industry – in the vein of Barbra Streisand, who famously announced that 'the time has come', just before declaring Bigelow the winner of the Best Director category during the awards ceremony – the event also provoked a fair number of hostile responses, which emanated in part, and perhaps perplexingly, from feminist circles. In a frequently quoted *salon.com* article on *The Hurt Locker* provocatively entitled 'Kathryn Bigelow: Feminist Pioneer or Tough Guy in Drag?', Martha Nochimson (2010) famously accuses Bigelow of 'masquerad[ing] as a hyper-macho bad boy' to earn the respect of the cinematic industry, dubbing her not the 'Queen of Directors', as Quentin Tarantino referred to Bigelow when she received the Directors Guild of America Award, but the 'Transvestite of Directors'. Clearly frustrated by the institutional sexism in Hollywood, Nochimson regrets the cultural marginalisation of the chick flick, observing that the industry is 'so hobbled by gender-specific tunnel vision that it has trouble admiring anything but filmmaking soaked in a reduced notion of masculinity' (2010).

In hindsight, it is evident that Bigelow's history-making win has not resulted in an increased number of women directors in the commercial film sphere, as Melissa Silverstein, author of the blog *Women and Hollywood* that advocates for gender parity across the US entertainment industry, denounces in her piece 'What Bigelow Effect?' (2012). The general disappointment is confirmed by statistics on the paucity of women directors in mainstream productions: according to Martha M. Lauzen's annual 'Celluloid Ceiling' reports released by the Center for the Study of Women in Television and Film at San Diego State University, in 2016 women accounted for only seven per cent of directors in the top 250 domestic (US) grossing films. Within this body of work, women were most numerous as producers (twenty-four per cent), followed by editors (seventeen per cent), executive producers (seventeen per cent), writers (thirteen per cent) and cinematographers (five per cent) (see Lauzen 2017). These results are even lower than in 2008 – the figures quoted by the mainstream press during the 2010 Academy Awards build-up – when women accounted for nine per cent of directors, the same percentage Lauzen measured in 1998 (see Lauzen 2009). Significantly, these low figures also translate into a lack of industrial recognition; to date, Bigelow remains the only woman in eighty-eight years to have been awarded an Oscar for directing.[1] The Academy's exclusion of women from its most prestigious category is overwhelming and attests to, in a wider sense, numerous obstacles that exist for women filmmakers working within the mainstream realm notoriously dominated by men.

While it is not my intention to herald Bigelow as an exception to the norm – a discourse reproduced over and over in critical debates concerning her Academy Award win and which overshadows a wide range of women filmmakers making movies in a variety of contexts worldwide – I contend that her triumph is relevant for feminist criticism, as it urges us to interrogate if, and to what extent, 'the time has come' for women filmmakers, especially those working within popular formats in the major film industries, such as Hollywood. *The Hurt Locker*, and its controversial reception, seems to be a stimulus for, but also a symptom of, a series of transformations in political, theoretical and commercial conceptualisations of women's cinema,[2] even if the film's focus on masculinity and combat means it does not, at first sight, appear as such.

Bigelow's interest in depicting male subjects and her work in 'male' genres like the action film, the Western and the war film is not automatically transgressive in terms of feminist politics; yet, what is striking about the reception of *The Hurt Locker* is how often the critical voices focus on this apparently unique conflation of gender and genre only to single out Bigelow's reactionary stance. Writing for *The New Statesman*, journalist and documentary filmmaker John Pilger (2010) complained: 'How insulting that a *woman* is celebrated for a typically violent *all-male war movie*' (emphasis added). Even more noteworthy is the considerable resistance from some feminist critics, such as Nochimson – a resistance that is likewise firmly embedded in the generic substance of the film, its commercial nature and Bigelow's gender. In this sense, Nochimson's remarks are a useful starting point from which to think about what happens when women make genre films in Hollywood. While they rightly point to a series of discourses which delegitimise those women filmmakers who direct what tend to be stereotypically defined as 'women's films' – the critic mentions such directors as Nancy Meyers and Nora Ephron – at the same time they turn out to be particularly problematic: how do we identify the 'masculine' filmmaking that the journalist so overtly condemns and what are the wider repercussions of framing Bigelow's unprecedented triumph in the industry as a betrayal of women and of feminist politics?

Bigelow has always been an uneasy figure for feminist criticism, precisely because of the 'male' genres she chooses to engage with in her filmmaking; for some scholars, this choice confirms her transgressive credentials, while others see it as solid evidence of sexism throughout the industry, which unfairly elevates Bigelow over other women filmmakers who engage in genres culturally codified as 'female'. The widespread feeling that Bigelow betrayed women (and, by extension, feminism) by not representing them in her films[3] is closely linked to the long-standing categorisation of genres by gender and supposed gender-to-gender identification, together with the underlying assumption that being a man or a woman is simple, self-evident and invariable, and that film genres employ a single gender address, for which reason they can be easily classified as 'male' and 'female'. This cultural, critical and industrial gendering of genres often has decisive implications for women's film practice: Martha Coolidge, for instance, has complained that she has been repeatedly denied the opportunity to direct big-budget, high-profile action movies: 'About 90% of what comes my way are 10 different kinds of breast cancer stories, 10 different kinds of divorce stories [. . .]. I do those. I care about them deeply. But one does want to do more' (in Wallace 1997). Lauzen's reports also confirm this tendency: women are most likely to work in the romantic comedy, documentary, and romantic drama genres, and least likely to work in the horror, action, and comedy genres (Lauzen 2010). The pervasive idea that some genres are more 'suitable' for women filmmakers (and audiences) potentially restricts them to a narrow set of forms defined by presumably feminine interests – home, romance and personal life; it also risks dismissing or uncritically celebrating those filmmakers who choose to work in the 'male' genres, while, at the same time, underestimating the dexterity of those women who opt for forms culturally coded as 'female', and thus perceived as less artistic (see Chapter 1).

This debate also indexes the persistent lack of consensus on the definition of 'women's cinema', not only in regard to the process of culturally gendering film genres, but also the slippery notion of female film authorship. Needless to say, the term 'women's cinema' has long been debated in feminist film theory. As scholars have shown (Colaizzi 2001; Zecchi 2011), the possessive in the syntagm might ambiguously point to the gender of the filmmakers – and, in this sense, it would become a category of 'authorship', itself a contested term in feminist studies – or to that of their audience. Melodrama, for instance, has been traditionally conceptualised as a genre that appeals to women – that is, a product explicitly addressed to female viewers and associated with a set of features (sensitivity, sentimentality and emotionality) that tend to be ascribed to both the films themselves and their spectators. The parameters of 'women's cinema' are invariably open to discussion: is it cinema (only) for women? Is it cinema that expresses 'female' aesthetics? Or, perhaps, is it a cinema that is guided by feminist activism? The first two designations are underwritten by essentialist suppositions about women; 'feminist cinema' is also a limiting concept, since 'neither is the entire cinema directed by women necessarily feminist, nor is the entire feminist cinema directed by women' (Zecchi 2011).[4]

As film scholar Patricia White observes: 'While some might find the term dated to the analog era of second-wave feminism, the discursive terrain referenced by women's cinema is still very much at stake' (2015: 3). This is immediately clear in the discursive circulation of Bigelow's oeuvre. If the term is invoked in reference to genre, then Bigelow's film practice seems to challenge whether she belongs in this category at all – or at least this is what Nochimson's comments suggest. The fact that she is concerned with supposedly 'male' genres, and that her films are situated much closer to 'commercial' cinema than feminist film practice, traditionally understood in opposition to 'the mainstream', as Joanne Hollows (2000) aptly demonstrates, contributes to the frequent exclusion of her name from studies on women filmmakers. If Bigelow belongs to women's cinema at all, it is perhaps only if we use the term to refer to the person who makes a film, which takes us back to the issue of authorship. However, this framework also proves to be problematic for many reasons, not least of which is that it engages with the discourse of exceptionality. Bigelow's oeuvre is often described in authorial terms, which are rarely applied to other directors in Hollywood, such as Nancy Meyers or Nora Ephron. 'Bigelow is a fascinating figure from an auteurist perspective in part because she, like the Hollywood directors initially lauded by the *Cahiers du cinéma* critics who promulgated such criticism, makes her signature visible in commercial films, genre products', observes Patricia White (2015: 3). Undoubtedly, the genres that she employs and the authorial performance that pivots on these same genres factor heavy in this exaltation. Such branding of Bigelow as a strong personality along conventional auteurist lines turns out to be particularly uncomfortable for feminist scholars who for decades now have been challenging the concept of auteur as incorrigibly compromised by patriarchal interests, ideology and practices – a questioning which has re-emerged with force in the postfeminist period since the 1990s, due to its complex redefinitions of gender roles 'legitimated' under neoliberal individualism.[5] This reticence has also been closely bound up with the collective and industrial nature of film production, as well as with fear of what Judith Mayne has famously dubbed the 'dreaded epithet' of essentialism (1990: 90).

Despite these difficulties, and after 'decades of embarrassed deconstruction' (Grant 2001: 123) that have almost completely sidestepped the issue of female authorship, several scholars have more recently begun to reclaim women's agency in the realm of filmmaking; yet, this reclaiming seems to have affected only some practitioners. While directors such as Chantal Akerman, Sally Potter, Jane Campion and Claire Denis have been the subject of numerous detailed monographs,[6] few analyses have considered the significance of women's contributions to mainstream genre filmmaking. At the time of writing, Bigelow herself has been the subject of only one book-length study dedicated to her oeuvre (Jermyn and Redmond 2003). Directing popular films in 'male genres', which feminist criticism has traditionally rejected as hopelessly complicit in patriarchal ideology, and working in relation to the 'hegemonic' centre rather than in the sphere of art or independent cinemas, validated as spaces in (supposed) opposition to commerce, has a lot to do with this omission.

Genre, Authorship and Contemporary Women Filmmakers addresses all of these issues: the growing visibility of the public personas and authorial images of female filmmakers; the blurring of the borders between commercial and independent cinema and gendered discourses of (de)authorisation that operate within each sphere; the distinction between 'male' and 'female' genres and the cultural value accorded to them; the issues of authorial subversion within genre cinema and popular culture in a wider sense; and the context of postfeminist media culture, and the importance of gendered genre address. Building on Patricia White, who 'borrow[s] the spotlight the Oscars shed to suggest that the publicity the event represents – red carpet reportage as a highly visible sign of the very publicness of cinema – remains crucial for feminism to tap and to incorporate' (2015: 3), the aim of this book is to look *at* and look *beyond* the exception, exploring women filmmakers working at the heart, and the penumbra, of Hollywood. While White's remarkable contribution zooms in on the dynamic intersection of feminism and female-authored world cinema (mainly art-house and independent), significantly departing from US cultural imperialism – or even pulling 'notions of core and periphery out of orbit' (2015: 4) – I am more interested in those filmmakers who are placed in the spotlight specifically in the American context, but whose contribution to genre cinema has arguably not received sufficient scholarly attention. It is not my intention to reinforce US cinema's hegemonic status in global media culture, but rather to interrogate the conditions and possibilities of these filmmakers' discursive visibility, as well as giving them the kind of detailed consideration and recognition they warrant.[7]

With these objectives in mind, the book offers five in-depth case studies of films by contemporary filmmakers, which have been perceived in the critical discourses as genre films: *Jennifer's Body* (2009) as a horror film, directed by Karyn Kusama and written by Diablo Cody, *The Hurt Locker* (2008) as a war film, directed by Kathryn Bigelow, *Meek's Cutoff* (2010) as a Western, directed by Kelly Reichardt, *Marie Antoinette* (2006) as a costume biopic, directed by Sofia Coppola, and *The Intern* (2015) as a (non-)romantic comedy, written and directed by Nancy Meyers. Notwithstanding the challenges authorship holds for feminist studies, I argue that all of these filmmakers can be situated as skilled 'genre auteurs'. Given that film texts and authorial images are conditioned by a series of factors in constant transformation, and thus should be analysed within specific historical and sociocultural moments, I seek to put women filmmakers in context, offering an examination not only of their films, but also of the representation of their public personas in the various discursive frameworks which contribute to the construction of their authorial figures (film reviews, interviews and scholarly criticism, among others) and which raise a number of intriguing questions that are crucial to rethinking the notion of women's cinema.

The films analysed in these pages have been produced over the last ten years and they constitute, to my mind, a substantial contribution to contemporary genre cinema. However, claims about women's penetration of genre in US productions need prefacing with acknowledgments of the breathtaking diversity and expansiveness of contemporary women's film practice worldwide. In this context, I agree with Patricia White when she asserts that 'full accounting for this realm of cultural production became impossible and probably inadvisable' (2015: 11). In fact, any chronicling of women's film practice in a broader sense risks reproducing essentialist notions of women's cinema that have plagued studies on this concept from its inception. Therefore, rather than providing an overview of generic production by women in a wider sense, I focus on a very limited selection of films, and on a particular historical moment, for the sake of offering a comprehensive analysis of the case studies. As mentioned before, I do not aim to reinforce the opposition between the dominant system and 'the rest of the world'; I believe that the study of genre production outside the US context requires other tools of analysis, which would bring much needed attention to cultural and linguistic specificity, as well as enable determinations regarding the extent of connection or disconnection from hegemonic film culture – or challenge this distinction altogether.[8]

One of the criteria for my selection was what I dub, drawing on Janet Staiger (1992; 2000), the 'event' of the film,[9] with a particular emphasis on discourses that have enabled the visibility of these works: *The Hurt Locker* in the context of the 2010 Academy Awards ceremony and its polemical reception following its success across several categories; *Jennifer's Body* in the shadow of the backlash against its screenwriter Diablo Cody and its subsequent reclaiming by female horror cinema fans; *Meek's Cutoff* and its widespread critical acclaim in international film festivals, while at the same time being on the receiving end of vitriolic attacks from Western enthusiasts; *Marie Antoinette*, praised by some for its 'pretty' look and carefully composed imageries, while disparaged by others as excessively concerned with frivolity and superficiality and thus as inferior in comparison to more 'serious' historical biopics; and, finally, *The Intern*, read against the background of Meyers's opulent lifestyle and her privileged position as a part of Hollywood aristocracy, used to justify her perceived lack of credibility as a director. The reception of these films speaks volumes about not only the processes of devaluation of their authors – for example, by absorbing the filmmakers' biographical details into the critics' reading strategies – but also the relevance and ideological implications of the convergence of gender and genre thrown into relief in most interpretative frameworks.

All of these filmmakers stand out discursively as authors in reference to gender and genre, regardless of critical or scholarly attention and productive output. Some of the directors under discussion have produced a significant number of 'genre' films,[10] while others have only directed a couple. They work in different contexts of production – in terms of sectors, budgets, visual resources and themes – to say nothing of their authorial performances, which show varied articulations of agency in relation to femininity (or masculinity) and creativity. As already mentioned, Kathryn Bigelow is usually associated with 'muscular' film practice and 'male' genres – mostly thrillers,

Westerns, science fiction and horror cinema. Although she began her career in the independent sector, her recent productions are largely considered to be 'mainstream' – even if, as I will show in Chapter 3, this classification is not entirely accurate. Individually, Diablo Cody and Karyn Kusama are associated with independent filmmaking, but the outcome of their collaboration is a horror film produced with a relatively big budget in a Hollywood studio. Kelly Reichardt and Sofia Coppola are now consolidated auteurs in indie cinema, although they certainly do not occupy the same position within this sector, if only by virtue of the budgets they usually handle. The work of the former is emblematic of so-called slow cinema and associated with small-scale productions; while she is predominantly read through the discourse of independence, only apparently oppositional to the generic nature of commercial productions, Reichardt, similarly to Bigelow, tends to return to Hollywood genres codified as 'male' – in particular, the Western and the road movie. Coppola's film style, on the contrary, adheres to the girlish chic and 'feminine' aesthetics, which is recurrently read as going beyond the merely generic. Her methods of financing and distribution, as well as authorial persona, have allowed her to carve out a niche in the masculinist domain of Indiewood (Lane and Richter 2011). Finally, Nancy Meyers, the most commercially successful filmmaker addressed in this volume, works at the forefront of Hollywood and perhaps best illustrates the figure of the popular auteur. She is extremely skilful at handling big budget films and generating major box office returns. Her generic pedigree is unquestionable: she has mastered the conventions of the romantic comedy, and in this sense her brand is positioned at the other end of the spectrum from Bigelow, who makes 'films about men'. The intersection of genre, authorship and women's cinema, as it plays out in the critical circulation of their films, as well as their shared interest in the productive use of genericity and the tropes of popular culture and in problematising the category of gender in their films, holds all these filmmakers together.[11]

The genres with which each of the films engage were a predominant concern when choosing those to be analysed. Considering that romance and melodrama have traditionally set the terms for feminist engagement with women directors of genre, the book starts with a discussion of the genres not immediately associated with 'women's sensibilities'. My intention is not to dismiss these preoccupations, nor elevate the filmmakers who are interested in 'male' genres over women directors who are perceived to make 'films about women', but rather to scrutinise the value accorded women's versus men's forms and, indeed, to question this very demarcation.

Both war movies and Westerns are 'the generic sites that are in some fundamental way *about* masculinity' (Tasker 2017: 111 [emphasis in original]) and thus provide an extraordinarily fruitful space for exploring gender and power relations. Since the inception of genre theory, the Western has enjoyed a privileged position – at least as far as the US film culture is concerned.[12] Although there are several studies on the representation of women in this genre (Cook 1988; Modleski 1998; Dyer 2007), the Western has been primarily associated, in both scholarly and critical discourses, with masculinity and male directors.[13] The same is true of the war film, which has precipitated countless analyses of the codes of masculinity, violence and male vulnerability, primarily for white men, also in films directed almost exclusively by men. Yvonne Tasker (2017: 111), one of the feminist scholars who opened the line of research into the 'male genres', observes that war films and Westerns share many similarities in terms of iconic images and central tropes: male mobility (the physical movement of the hero or scenes of action, combat and pursuit), moral and physical strength (the soldier's sacrificial heroism or the command of nature associated with the Western hero) and the motif of frontiers (that mark the mobility of the masculine hero). As she importantly points out, also referring to action cinema, 'although these genres have long been understood as culturally conservative, tending to support a racial and gendered hierarchy that privileges white masculinity, scholars have nonetheless found considerable complexity and ideological nuance at work across [these genres]' (Tasker 2017: 112).[14] Given the historical context in which this book was written – at a time when the US boasts implication in several international conflicts – and an immense popularity of war films and Westerns, the inclusion of these genres seems particularly apt. In Chapters 3 and 4 I will show how Bigelow and Reichardt engage with tropes such as movement, paternalism and duty to acknowledge both continuities and differences with these popular imaginaries.

Horror cinema is yet another genre from which women have historically been excluded, both industrially and through film criticism. There are good reasons for bringing it into discussion: horror seems to have taken over from the Western as the genre most written about by scholars in recent years (Jancovich 2002). Furthermore, it has been of crucial importance to feminist, postcolonial and queer studies, albeit (or perhaps owing to) its low status in popular culture. As with pornography, the genre was traditionally the object of substantial aesthetic criticism and the target of moral concern and calls for censorship.[15] Nevertheless, in subsequent years it has become vital for feminist revisions of the notion of film identification, which significantly questioned the monolithic and totalising view of the spectator that had long permeated film studies. Interestingly, even though this genre has occupied a rather privileged position in feminist film theory, horror films authored by women have received little critical attention. Chapter 2 seeks to examine the multiple reasons behind this oversight, as well as to address tensions in the discursive circulation of films by the very few women who have gained a certain amount of visibility.

In contrast to the previously mentioned genres, costume drama and romantic comedy have both been historically associated with 'female' forms.

Significantly, they have also been accused by feminist critics of promoting attitudes and values which are detrimental or disempowering for women, such as idealising heteronormativity, and which foment patriarchal oppression. Seen as inherently formulaic and/or as offering a nostalgic, apolitical view of the past, the two genres have generally sat at the lower end of cultural hierarchies of taste and, thereby, auteur studies – although costume drama, as part of the wider panorama of heritage cinema, has sometimes been argued as embodying more 'artistic' purposes in these debates. Significantly, several feminist scholars rehabilitated these narratives as a productive site for women to explore their life experiences, and their struggle over the revisionist nature of these female-oriented forms has resurfaced in the postfeminist context and concentrated around the phenomena of chick flicks, as discussed in Chapter 6. Again, with some notable exceptions, these genres tend to be addressed predominantly in reference to male-authored texts.

In each of the chapters, I seek to interrogate the varied and complex approaches to genre as materialised in the films under discussion, in order to address more fully their textual and contextual specificity and historical inscription. In doing so, I attempt to strike a balance between a detailed textual analysis of the films in the context of the genre's development and the discourses that structure the production and reception of women's filmmaking within broader frames of reference. In particular, I look at specific discourses that have enabled the popularity of these filmmakers in recent years, such as genre auteurism, 'female' versus 'male' genre divisions, authenticity (as opposed to the 'falsity' of industry produced films), exceptionalism, family connections, a privileged position in the industry and so on. The rationale of my method stems from Catherine Grant's useful insights on women's cinema and women's film authorship (2001), in which she postulates 'a broader examination of "elite" and other forms of cultural agency and agent-hood available under patriarchy to particular women at particular times and in particular places' (2001: 124). Grant convincingly argues that although the textual analysis of films has always been an important tool for feminist film theory, it must be supplemented by consideration of institutional questions, of production, distribution and critical reception, especially if we are to address female authorship. She proposes to analyse women's authorial performances through Judith Butler's conceptualisation of gender, not as 'a stable identity or locus of agency from which various acts follow; rather [as] an identity tenuously constituted in time, instituted in an exterior space through a *stylised repetition of acts*' (Butler 1988: 519 [emphasis in original]). In engaging with this idea, I likewise stress this concept of agency to highlight the ways that contemporary women filmmakers take advantage of the space they reclaim or are ceded under particular circumstances.

The turn to 'context' in the studies of female authorship is evident in feminist writing over the last two decades, as epitomised by publications including

Christina Lane's *Feminist Hollywood* (2000), Shelley Cobb's *Adaptation, Authorship, and Contemporary Women Filmmakers* (2015) and Patricia White's *Women's Cinema, World Cinema* (2015), although with different goals and different conclusions. My contribution to these studies is to combine this approach to authorship with genre theory, which privileges a multiplicity of voices *in* and *between* texts, and to stress the centrality of this multiplicity in the meaning-making processes.[16]

This perspective is dictated by an interest in delving into a field seldom explored to date. Traditionally, feminist analyses of films made by women tended to centre on experimental or art-house cinema, in the wake of early feminist cine-psychoanalysis and its indictment of classical Hollywood cinema. This might have been the main reason why women's film practice has been associated with forms and modes that go beyond the 'mainstream language' of generic conventions. Given the reputation of Hollywood, as well as the worldwide film industry, for being male dominated, on the one hand, and the perceived co-implication between genres and the reinforcement of negative stereotypes, on the other, for many decades genres were studied in terms of ideologically problematic (mis)representation. Although it is beyond the scope of this book to map the extensive history of women's film practice and feminist criticism in its entirety, it could be argued that from its inception Anglophone feminist film criticism focused on two principal issues: how Hollywood represented women in popular genres, and how women filmmakers might transform these representations (Gledhill 2012: 2). The latter critical strand led to various conceptualisations of women's cinema as 'counter-cinema', conceived as oppositional to Hollywood's practices and, more generally, to popular film.[17] According to Laura Mulvey, who in her 'Visual Pleasure and Narrative Cinema' famously defended 'passionate detachment', which would help destroy 'the satisfaction, pleasure and privilege of the "invisible guest"' ([1975] 1989b: 26), avant-garde film practice, with its focus on innovation and ruptures, as well as strategies of defamiliarisation and self-reflexivity, is the most suitable model for women's cinema. In another piece, 'Film, Feminism and the Avant Garde', she wrote:

> An important aspect of avant-garde aesthetics is negation: a work is formed, or driven to adopt a particular position, by the very code itself of the dominant tradition that is being opposed. These works tend to be read, achieve meaning, in the reflected light of the aesthetics they negate. (1989a: 123)

Mulvey's early postulate that women's film practice should be, above all, negative has led to far-reaching consequences for feminist film studies and contributed to the creation of a feminist canon formed by 'formalist' directors, such as Chantal Akerman, Maya Deren, Germaine Dulac, Marguerite Duras and Sally Potter. Even those scholars who reclaimed visual pleasure and narrative cinema for feminist ends – including Teresa de Lauretis, who famously reconfigures these debates by thinking about the specificity of women's cinema as a problem of text and address, that is, 'who is making films for whom, who is looking and speaking, how, where and to whom' (1987a: 135)[18] – reinforce, rather than disrupt, this canon in their selection of film texts.[19]

Mulvey's model of counter-cinema, although most influential, was not the only one that was circulating in the early years of feminist criticism. Already in the 1970s and before the publication of 'Visual Pleasure and Narrative Cinema', Claire Johnston developed her own concept of counter-cinema, based not on the aesthetics of negation, but of 'infiltration': the elaboration of feminist discourse within Hollywood forms. If Johnston ([1973] 2000a) coincided with Mulvey in her rejection of 'sociological' models in favour of structuralist methodologies – according to both scholars, women's cinema should alter first and foremost the language of cinema, by means of denaturalisation and estrangement, which would deconstruct the prevalent iconography of femininity and underscore the artificiality of these images – she was much more interested in popular genres than in art cinema, which she criticised for its reliance on myths of women: 'There is no doubt that the films of Agnès Varda are reactionary', she famously proclaimed (2000a: 32).

As her own references to women directors in studio-era Hollywood – in particular, Dorothy Arzner and Ida Lupino – illustrate, instead of rejecting hegemonic models, women filmmakers can use them and change them from within, articulating an internal critique of sexist and bourgeois ideology perpetrated by Hollywood. This process of the unmasking of stereotypes – which underscores their status as construct – does not necessarily have to be stripped of pleasure. In fact, Johnston embraces a counter-cinema as a political tool and as entertainment (notions she refuses to see 'as two opposing poles with little common ground'), but also a sort of projection:

> In order to counter our objectification in the cinema, our collective fantasies must be released: women's cinema must embody the working through of desire: such an objective demands the use of the entertainment film. Ideas derived from the entertainment film, then, should inform the political film, and political ideas should inform the entertainment cinema: a two way process. (2000a: 32–3)

As White astutely observes in her assessment of this essay, in contrast to Mulvey's contemporaneous embrace of 'the destruction of pleasure as a radical weapon', Johnston's model of counter-cinema anticipates a current postfeminist climate of the 2000s, which is 'much less suspicious of pleasure than was the cultural feminism of the early 1970s' (2015: 9). It also legitimates the elaboration of feminist discourse from within generic conventions, looking forward to the postmodernist preoccupation with appropriations, revisions and pastiche, as well as, as I shall suggest later, appearing prescient with regard to the film theory's recent concern with affect as an essential part of film viewing, which accompanies, or even questions, the more distanced modes of spectatorship.

Johnston's call to embrace the collective fantasies released in Hollywood genres was already taken up by feminist criticism in the mid-1980s. With film theory's 'discovery' of melodrama as a space for feminist appropriation and the dramatising of women's perspectives, many scholars shifted their attention from the denaturalising devices of 'oppositional' cinema to the narrative potential of the so-called popular 'women's genres', such as soap operas (Modleski 1982; Geraghty 1991; Kuhn 1994; Brunsdon 1997; Ang 1985), melodrama (Gledhill 1987; Gaines 1990; Williams 1998) and romance fiction in a wider sense (Radway 1984; Stacey 1994; and others), focusing on the positive role such narratives might play in women's lives – although these genres, as already mentioned, were approached predominantly in relation to films made by men. When it comes to screen narratives directed by women, feminist film criticism has tended to limit the scope of study to film genres typically codified as 'female' (aimed at the female audience and/or which placed the heroine at the centre of the narrative); the proliferation of publications on chick flicks over the last decade serves as a good example of this critical framework. As Mary Harrod observes in reference to this trend, the increasing prominence of female fan cultures severely challenges some of the assumptions underlying the female/male generic divisions, but 'it is true that melodrama and romance remain over-privileged sites for feminist scholarship about films made by and especially for women' (2016: 56).

In an attempt to depart from this tendency in feminist studies to privilege and/or recover particular genres, and from the pervasive discourse that often reduces women's cinema to chick flicks, here women's film authorship will be explored differently. I take an approach that associates women's film practice with a range of genres and different production contexts, pointing to the implications of female filmmakers adopting forms traditionally codified as 'male' – or, rather, whose gender address and alignment are not self-evident or which are even sometimes perceived to be inimical to feminism – such as horror, war film and the Western, as compared to women working within the more traditionally 'female' genres of costume drama and romantic comedy. As Christine Gledhill observes, when women

> use the tropes of power associated conventionally with the masculine – they do more than challenge binary gender labels attached to genres.

> [. . .] they begin to open up the indeterminacy of gender itself, refusing socially mandated boxes of gendered being and recognising the fluidity of identification and responses to screen fictions. (2018: xiii)

The analysis accords priority not just to assessing these filmmakers' incursion in, or skilled 'interpretation' of, Hollywood's genres, but also to dislodging the enduring assumption that women, both as filmmakers and as viewers, are more inclined to choose nominally female-orientated forms. As I will show later, most of these films, even those perceived as belonging to 'female' genres, do not fit in well with earlier models of women's cinema, albeit for different reasons, and this explains why they tend to be neglected in feminist canons (monographs or other scholarly writings on women's film practice). In Deborah Jermyn's words (who writes on Nancy Meyers), they 'tick none of the boxes that have overwhelmingly preoccupied feminist film criticism, a scholarly enterprise which has, for cogent strategic, political reasons, primarily attended to women filmmakers positioned somehow outside "the mainstream"' (2018: 60).

Redefining the parameters of women's cinema is imperative, not only because of the growing visibility of female directors in the commercial global media sphere, but also because in recent years their filmmaking practice has been increasingly exploring new directions. In the US context, not only Kathryn Bigelow, but also Sofia Coppola, Nancy Meyers, Nora Ephron, Mary Harron, Kimberly Peirce, Catherine Hardwicke, Patty Jenkins and many others have made commercially impactful films across a wide range of genres. Women's greater penetration of mainstream audio-visual production is attested to by the recent increase in publications on the topic. Articles and book chapters on women genre filmmakers are suddenly beginning to flourish as evidenced by: Tasker and Atakav (2010) on *The Hurt Locker*; Badley (2016) on genre and independent women filmmakers, such as Debra Granik, Courtney Hunt and Kelly Reichardt, who incorporate melodrama and reappropriate mainstream 'male' tropes; and four chapters in Christine's Gledhill's volume *Gender Meets Genre in Postwar Cinemas* (2012) on women-authored genre films, such as horror and film noir (E. Ann Kaplan), boxing and teen picture (Yvonne Tasker), costume drama (Samiha Matin) and the autobiographical documentary (Lucy Fischer).[20] These publications were followed, soon after work on this book began, by several published and forthcoming monographs: Fiona Handyside's *Sofia Coppola: A Cinema of Girlhood* (2017), Deborah Jermyn's *Nancy Meyers* (2017), Dawn Hall's forthcoming *Refocus: The Films of Kelly Reichardt* and Mary Harrod's forthcoming book on the heightened genericity and pastiche in contemporary women's filmmaking in Hollywood. Previously overlooked filmmakers are also receiving attention in edited collections, such as that on Amy Heckerling (Smith and Shary 2016), followed by calls for contributions to two others – on Mary Harron and Doris Wishman – all from Edinburgh University Press' 'Refocus' series. Women working in genre film and television in non-directing jobs, such as screenwriters, performers or even female viewers who rewrite texts via fanfiction and fanvids[21] – a highly pertinent area of study, given women's habitual exclusion from directorial roles – are also starting to attract a lot of attention (see Harrod and Paszkiewicz 2018).[22]

This book seeks to interrogate some key issues raised by this recent upsurge in research activity focusing on women's cinema, by engaging specifically with the reformulation of women's film authorship in genre in the US context. Film genres are relevant for feminist criticism because, as Christine Gledhill has argued, they 'constitute switching points between media and society' (2018: x). She further explains:

> They constitute public sites where cultural stereotypes and ideologies are put into play in order to generate dramatic conflict. While a film genre's engagement of topical discourses and ideologies serves to create frissons of recognition, these discourses and ideologies are reshaped to the specific purposes and conventions of the genre that draws on them. Generic fictions then circulate these back into the social sphere, reformed as aesthetic and perceptual experiences. (2018: x)[23]

As a critical tool, genre provides a particularly productive site from which to think about women's participation in cinema, film authorship and the cultural politics of gender (especially in terms of the status of the woman author or her lack of status). It is useful not only because it offers the opportunity to interrogate hierarchies of value that are both generic and gendered, but also because it presents a strong challenge to traditional auteur criticism, which tends to give little attention to the audience or other texts as sources of meaning. In Chapter 1, I argue that, even though genre was initially introduced into film studies as an alternative to auteurism, throwing both concepts into productive tension is extremely fruitful for discussing the issues of female authorship. What I want to suggest is that genre analysis tells us not just about the kinds of films women filmmakers make, but also about the cultural work of producing their authorship. Building on Gledhill's influential volume *Gender Meets Genre in Postwar Cinemas*, which asks 'how does gender get into genre, and what does genre do with it?' (2012: 1), I wish to modify this question and claim a major role for female authorship in current film culture, asking: what does genre do with women filmmakers, and what do they do with genre?

As far as genre theory and criticism are concerned, I am indebted to Steve Neale's (2000), Christine Gledhill's (2011) and Jane Gaines's (2012) publications, which foreground the role of generic repetition (with a difference) and its dynamic of expectation. In contrast to previous conceptualisations of genre (as formula, structure or myth), concerned with the search for its essential or defining features, the above scholars understand genre as process rather than end product. As I will show in Chapter 1, this concept of genre makes room for other participants beyond the texts themselves and provides a more dialogical approach to women's film practice.

Women's Cinema as Genre Cinema

This volume explores the possible tensions that arise from the intersection of gender, genre, authorship and women's cinema, starting from the fundamental premise: women's cinema is not simply a collection of films defined by their authors' (or their spectators') gender, but rather a complex discursive space, where historical and cultural processes that have erased or marginalised women's input from mainstream audio-visual productions and their interpretation converge. Instead of essentialising the difference, I understand the phrase 'women's cinema' as regards its strategic function – that is, as a culturally specific product, and one that is always changing in time and space (Colaizzi 1995: 11). As Alison Butler asserts in her discussion of the concept, 'the distinctiveness of women's filmmaking is therefore not based on an essentialist understanding of gendered subjectivity, but on the position – or positions – of women in contemporary culture' (2002: 22). Butler's book, *Women's Cinema: The Contested Screen*, which addresses a wide variety of women's film practice across different cinematic traditions – genre in mainstream Hollywood cinema, experimental film and world cinema – can be inscribed in the so-called 'intertextual' turn in studies on women's cinema, initiated by Johnston and developed within a number of publications since the late 1980s (Fischer 1989; Mayne 1990; Mellencamp 1995; Modleski 1998; Lane 2000). These studies, as Butler herself asserts, 'define women's cinema in terms of relations of intertextuality with hegemonic cinema traditions' and emerge as 'a response to the dilemmas [. . .] whether to conceptualise women's art as an alternative cultural heritage or to situate it within pre-existent traditions and whether to view the work of women artists as gendered or androgynous creation' (2002: 18).[24]

It is such an approach that guides this study of women's genre cinema. In particular, Butler's consideration of women's cinema as 'minor cinema', adapted from Deleuze and Guattari's (1975) concept of the minor – a cinema produced by a marginal group, but written in the language of majority as an alternative to the negative aesthetics of counter-cinema and its radical challenging of the dominant language – is particularly apt here, as it allows for a reconsideration of women's film authorship and the 'major' language of film genres. According to Butler, 'the plurality of forms, concerns and constituencies in contemporary women's cinema now exceeds even the most flexible definition of counter-cinema. Women's cinema now seems "minor" rather than oppositional' (2002:

21). Drawing on Meaghan Morris, Butler traces a number of correspondences between the notion of the minor, as theorised by Deleuze and Guattari, and Johnston's model of counter-cinema – that is, cinema produced by women *within* the Hollywood system and its cinematic codes:

> A minor literature is not 'marginal,' it is what a minority constructs *in a major language*, and so it is a model of action from a colonised position *within* a given society. In this it differs from theories that propose, like Laura Mulvey's early work in film, to found an alternative system. (Morris in Butler 2002: 20 [emphasis in original])

Butler explains her argument: 'Women's cinema is not "at home" in any of the host of cinematic or national discourses it inhabits, but [...] is always an inflected mode, incorporating, reworking and contesting the conventions of established traditions' (2002: 22). Interestingly, then, these 'minor' uses of the 'major' language, conceived as a strategic infiltration, can be produced in both mainstream and experimental film practice; further, the concept of 'minor cinema' destabilises this very dichotomy altogether, because 'to call women's cinema a minor cinema [...] is to free it from the binarisms (popular/elitist, avant-garde/mainstream, positive/negative) which result from imagining it as a parallel or oppositional cinema' (2002: 22).

While I embrace Butler's account of the plurality of contemporary women's cinema – and, to be sure, most of the films explored in this book could be addressed in relation to different 'major' contexts (national cinema, international art film, auteur cinema, independent cinema and so on) – in this project I will narrow my use of the concept to the 'major' language of generic conventions and its possible 'minor' uses. Building on Deleuze and Guattari, the central premise is that women's generic production as a minor cinema is not marginal, but rather designates what the minority constructs in a major language.[25] I will not make a case, then, for a shared thematic or aesthetic difference of women's cinema as genre cinema, but rather focus on the ways in which the work of contemporary women filmmakers arises in intertextual dialogue, and not in isolation, to established genre traditions. According to Deleuze and Guattari (1975), there is an energetic force that stimulates appropriations and connections in minor literatures, which undoubtedly reflects the intertextual character of women's genre practice studied in this volume.

This model helps to challenge the existence of an exclusively 'female' language, for even if we are born in a country with its own major literature, we can adopt the revolutionary attitude of a minor language, 'to be a sort of stranger within [one's] own language' (Deleuze and Guattari 1975: 48). Minor language does not emerge from a condition determined by birth, but rather from a strategy resulting from a disadvantaged position. Most importantly, the major language itself should not be viewed as essence, a fixed mould, against which one should rebel: 'Even when it is unique, a language remains a mixture, a schizophrenic melange, a Harlequin costume in which very different functions of language and distinct centres of power are played out, blurring what can be said and what can't be said' (1975: 48).

As we shall see later, this concept of the major language resonates well with the functioning of the genre, which is also overwhelmingly flexible and highly productive. Understanding genre not as a fixed formula but as a dynamic site of a continuous remaking opens up space for rethinking women's film practice beyond the 'negative' model of counter-cinema. Therefore, rather than asserting that women filmmakers act 'against' genre, I set out to determine if (and to what extent) they reappropriate its crucial features: repetition and the viewers' expectations.

Contemporary Genre Auteurs

In keeping with its theoretical and methodological emphasis, the book is organised according to the different genres and auteurs it addresses. The first sections of each chapter look at the filmmakers' brand authorship, their position in the contemporary global film sphere and the promotional and critical discourses surrounding the film under discussion – all of which structure the production and reception of women's film practice in a broader sense. Before moving on to the films themselves, it is vital to explore methodological and theoretical questions that arise from approaching women's cinema as genre cinema – namely, genre and authorship, two concepts that are notoriously difficult to define. Thus, Chapter 1, 'Subversive Auteur, Subversive Genre', sets the scene for the case studies that follow in Chapters 2 through 6 by introducing a theoretical revision of auteur theory as a gendered concept, as well as reconceptualisation of women's cinema and women's film authorship in relation to genre theory. It starts by raising several questions: is the much-debated concept of auteur equally applicable to female filmmakers, and if so, how, and in what cultural and industrial contexts? Is women's film authorship distinctive in its politics, aesthetics or industrial methods? And, finally, in relation to popular genre cinema, does the female filmmaker 'transcend' the industrial form in the way that the male auteur is said to 'transcend' genre?

The first section of this chapter briefly explores the gendering of the *politique des auteurs* and discusses the implications of the 'death of the author' for feminist criticism. It then goes on to consider new approaches to film authorship, which offer a more dialogical, 'interactive' relationship to wider film culture than the previously discussed perspectives. The author is understood here as a discursive entity, another text to be read, both constructed by, and the constructor of, his/her public persona.

As with auteur theory, I argue that the concept of film genre is a complex one for the woman filmmaker and, by extension, for the feminist film scholar. If, traditionally, genres and generic repetition are associated with the reinforcement of stereotypes and/or with 'feminised' mass culture, this raises the question of how women filmmakers might intervene, linked with the problematic search for female/feminist/authorial 'subversion' of genre cinema. My purpose is to challenge a set of assumptions about genres, beginning with the essentialist misconception that genres are static and unchanging – an assumption repeatedly called into question in the context of postmodernity, which reinforces the revisiting and reworking of past forms and discourses. I also look at the ways in which genre is often opposed to a supposedly non-generic 'high' art practice, even by those who write in praise of Hollywood (male) directors to reclaim their films for serious critical appreciation, which indicates the pervasiveness of the conventional conceptions of genre. In addition, I focus on how traditional ways of thinking about genre are closely related to the problematics of women's film authorship. The remainder of the chapter builds on Jane Gaines's (2012) argument on the interchangeability of the critical categories 'women' and 'genre', and the question of feminist subversion of mainstream forms.

If, as Gaines (2012) suggests, instead of 'violating', 'transgressing' or 'subverting' the formal dictates of the industrial genre (that is, instead of 'going against genre'), some women filmmakers 'go with genre', this might be particularly so in the case of horror cinema. As I argue in Chapter 2, although horror was considered the arch enemy for early feminist criticism, given the association of generic repetition with the reinforcement of stereotypes, as well as high doses of violence against women, it was later acknowledged as a productive site of contestation and reimagining. The analysis of *Jennifer's Body* demonstrates precisely this point. I begin by discussing the marketing of *Jennifer's Body*, in order to show how those in charge of film distribution and publicity used the director's and writer's gender as a promotional tool, and how the filmmakers themselves might have determined certain feminist and postfeminist readings of their film. These readings are contextualised within Diablo Cody's broader self-promotional activities and her commercial auteurism (Corrigan 1991) and raise several questions about what is at stake when women practitioners make horror films and the implications should a filmmaker self-identify as a feminist filmmaker. The chapter then offers a close examination of *Jennifer's Body* by rethinking the theories of Barbara Creed (1993) and Carol Clover (1992), which rely on psychoanalytic models of film spectatorship and identification, and by inscribing the film within the wider context of teen movies and postfeminist media culture, making room for reflection on female spectatorial pleasures.

Chapter 3 moves to the combat film, offering an in-depth study of *The*

Hurt Locker as an Iraq war movie. As already argued, Bigelow represents a *cause célèbre* for feminist criticism in terms of her apparent abandonment of her earlier experimental work for mainstream narrative fiction, her presumed subversion of Hollywood gender types and genres, her refusal of both feminist and gendered identities, and her 'capitulation' to the supposedly masculinist action genre. Bigelow's work thus puts into tension the conjunction of women filmmakers, genre, authorship and the questions posed by feminist film criticism – issues dramatised by her nomination for the Best Director Oscar in competition with her former husband's sci-fi film, *Avatar* (James Cameron, 2009). By examining these tensions, the first part of this chapter raises several methodological questions about the role of critical response in the discursive circulation and reception of women's films. In contrast to the readings that regret the lack of female characterisation or that place the film within the realist realm of signification – considering Bigelow's aesthetics as a documentary gesture that transmits an accurate description of warfare – I will explore the director's self-aware and metageneric approach to filming. Drawing on genre criticism in relation to war films and the Western, bearing in mind that Bigelow clearly cross-fertilises between these two forms, I will show how individualised heroism, conventionally expressed in the visual display of the Hard Body, is undercut by constant meta-cinematic reflection. While framing it within Bigelow's authorial signature, the chapter argues that *The Hurt Locker* participates in the contemporary war film format, conceptualised by Robert Burgoyne (2013) as a 'body genre', concluding that the film creates an explosive tension between abstract, mythical masculinity and the singular, material body at risk.

In view of the historical co-implication of popular genres and the Hollywood film industry, it might be expected that the latter should be at the vanguard of women's genre filmmaking. Yet women directors who draw on genre cinema might, in fact, be proportionally more numerous in American independent cinema. US-based indie filmmakers, such as Debra Granik, Courtney Hurt and Nicole Holofcener, are making increasingly significant inroads into genre filmmaking. One such director who works with forms that draw in various ways on popular genres (in particular, the Western and the road film) is Kelly Reichardt. Chapter 4 asks, thus, what it means for a woman to use a popular genre in an independent filmmaking context. The first part of this chapter shows how Reichardt's authorship and biographical legend are constructed in close relation to the processes of legitimisation of independent cinema, conceptualised discursively in opposition to Hollywood (and genre). While the boundaries between mainstream and indie cinema are breaking down in both postmodernist practice and theoretical thinking, they frequently persist in journalism. This case study is particularly revelatory, as it proves how, 'no matter how much the director of an independent film might be romanticised via auterism's "cult of the artist," her film is always a product of a broader economic and ideological context' (Lane 2000: 29). Drawing on the burgeoning scholarship on independent cinema, the chapter focuses specifically on *Meek's Cutoff* (2010) – a Western film which was incorporated into the auteurist discourse of resistance towards genre and exceptional individual achievement. Indeed, *Meek's Cutoff* seems to be diametrically opposed to the example of the use of genericity by women directors as studied in Chapters 2 and 3, since it offers a radical revision of the Western genre conventions and of the Wild West mythologies. However, even if it drastically negates them, especially in terms of filmic time and affective materiality of the images, it also draws on the productive potential of generic logic based on variation within reiteration. For example, there is no doubt that the director acknowledges generic norms in her representation of masculinity and femininity, but at the same time she plays with these expectations, working out the past forms to stage permutations for future imaginings.

Chapter 5 offers a further perspective on the use of genre in the American independent filmmaking context, by centring on Sophia Coppola's *Marie Antoinette* (2006). Coppola, one of the most visible indie directors in recent years, is clearly embedded in the commerce of auteurism (Corrigan 1991), as she actively participates in constructing her public image and in branding her films by providing them with a recognisable identity. Building on existing scholarship on the filmmaker as illustrative of the new critical paradigm in studies of women's film authorship, I will look at the promotional and critical discourses surrounding her films to trace the various processes of authentication and de-authentication of Coppola as an auteur (family connections, the privileged position in the American film industry, her filmmaking style marked by a focus on flat affects and the mise-en-scène's surface details, as well as her interest in postfeminist/neoliberal femininity which has divided critics, especially with her 2013 feature film, *The Bling Ring*). In my exploration of Coppola's authorial status, I shed light on the issue of genre, arguing that her engagement with familiar conventions is far more complex than current analysis of her work has acknowledged. This is particularly evident in the case of *Marie Antoinette*, a film which has been read variably as a costume drama and/or as a historical biopic. I start my discussion by pointing to the traditional dichotomy between female-centred, 'feminine' costume dramas and 'masculine' historical films, analysed in detail by Christopher Robé (2009). I then move on to the demarcation proposed by Dennis Bingham (2010), between the male and female biopic, seen by the author as 'essentially different genres' (2010: 13), with their own ideologies and conventions. In establishing a dialogical relationship between biopic and costume drama scholarship, I will centre on self-conscious devices deployed in Coppola's film, which are mobilised, I will argue, not *against* but *through* a logic of a feminised consumerist culture. My intention is not to reject the supposed 'feminising' aspects of the costume drama or to masculinise them in framing the film as a 'self-conscious' biopic, but rather to investigate the gender anxieties that underlay the labelling of genres by film criticism.

The last chapter focalises on Nancy Meyers, arguably the most successful woman filmmaker of all time. Bar some notable exceptions, Meyers's status, as well as her career trajectory as a female filmmaker, has gained surprisingly little scholarly attention. This chapter analyses her directorial brand as unique in contemporary American cinema, and addresses how this brand influences the reception of her films. In doing so, it shows how the carefully composed mise-en-scène and the portrayal of privileged women protagonists, present in all of her films, contribute to a critical alignment between director and her oeuvre, and at the same time how they are used to demonstrate Meyers's lack of credibility as a director (a reading strategy which often impacts other women directors, such as Sofia Coppola). This analysis is framed within the broader discussions of auteurism, the generic conventions of the romcom and the so-called feminisation of mass culture, as well as the cultural, critical and industrial gendering of genres.

The remainder of the chapter offers an examination of *The Intern* (2015), situating the film within the context of the development of the romantic comedy. If, as Stacey Abbott and Deborah Jermyn astutely observe, 'love itself is a dynamic condition that develops and transforms throughout the different stages and milestones of a relationship, so too is the romantic comedy a living, breathing entity within cinema' (Abbott and Jermyn 2009: 8), then *The Intern*, a romcom that brings friendship, and not romance, into the spotlight, is a perfect illustration of this. In terms of its critical reception, the film has been dubbed as 'a romantic comedy without the romance', and it indeed draws on several of its generic conventions – for example, on bromantic elements which allow for a rethinking of the gendering of genres. The detailed analysis of the film reveals Meyers's self-reflexive strategies – rich discursive histories engendered by the presence of stars Robert De Niro and Anne Hathaway, among others – that invoke issues of central importance in this book: the question of female authorship in a male-dominated film industry, and the heritage and evolution of genre in the Hollywood context. I will argue that Meyers evokes the affective pastness of the romcom, while revitalising it with contemporaneity; to quote Deborah Jermyn: '[S]he does this not merely to [...] suggest to audiences that she is "being meta" as a marker of certain distanciation from the genre', but rather to 'embrace the genre, to pursue and indulge and tinker with the genre's conventions' (2017: 94). The chapter concludes by observing how the seemingly conservative terrain of contemporary romantic comedy can bring to light questions that disrupt such traditional interpretations, highlighting that these disruptions are already present in the generic. Rather than being rare examples of a subversive 'counter-cinema', all of these films show the potential advantages of conceptualising women's cinema as genre cinema – understood as a 'constellation' of cultural, aesthetic and ideological materials – which facilitates a more inclusive range of possibilities than those allowed by the traditional readings based on reductive models of social 'reflection' or 'misrepresentation' (Gledhill 2012: 4).

Gendered Genre Trouble

Genre provides the conceptual space where the issues of texts and aesthetics – the traditional concerns of film theory – as well as those of industry, audiences and culture, central concerns of sociology and cultural studies, can be pursued (Gledhill 2011: 221). As many scholars have noted, 'discussions of genre are always also discussions of spectatorial address' (Harrod 2016: 53). If a new challenge for feminist criticism is to produce a more complex map of women working in, and in connection with, Hollywood, implying the need for a shift in the agendas and methodologies adopted (Cook 2012: 40), then one of the most pressing issues, and one that is highly relevant to this project, is the exploration of the ways in which the discursive split between male and female culture is produced, and the destabilisation of it by means of examining particular examples of women's films. The gendered implications of the mode of address are particularly significant, as we shall see, in the context of female authorship.

In some ways, perhaps somewhat paradoxically, one of the most influential forces in shaping critical attitudes to 'female' genres is feminist film criticism. The move to reclaim popular culture – and, in particular, 'female' forms – was a turning point in feminist studies, which arose, as Tasker argues, from the desire of 'having it all' and as an outcome of 'the cocktail of popular pleasure and radical culture that emerged in the feminist cultural criticism of the 1980s' (1991: 91). This is precisely when the phrase 'gendered genre' began to circulate widely: soap opera, romance and melodrama were conceived as 'female' because they are seen to be addressed to women and/or they construct a subject position that is identified as female – a supposition supported by extratextual discourses, such as marketing devices, as well as reference to textual strategies, including narrative and mise-en-scène, that construct a world in which women are presumably constituted (the family, the personal, the domestic and so on).

Referring to John Fiske's studies on television, Tasker points to some of the pitfalls of this formulation. Fiske has constructed a divide between 'female television' (genres that resist narrative resolution, focus on women and are watched mainly by women) and 'male television' (action-based genres with narrative closure, which focus on men and are viewed by an assumed male audience). This approach raises several problems, for example, the still enduring supposition that only female-oriented forms can be useful or interesting for women and feminism. How can we think about 'non-feminine' genres and the wide variety of filmic pleasures that they offer to their female audiences? Although at first sight some genres seem to attract specific audiences, this reasoning is a double-edged sword. It is highly significant, for example, that female viewing pleasures are primarily conceived in emotional terms (and associated with genres such as melodrama or romantic comedy), while male pleasures, often disguised as 'universal', are spread along a much broader spectrum: visceral pleasures (action film, horror cinema, pornography and war movies), cerebral pleasures (film noir, crime fiction, thriller, postmodern genre mixing), pleasures of counter-reading (B-movies) and the pleasures of cult cinema (the Western, auteur cinema).

The gendering of genres is an ideologically loaded issue; thus, it is not easy to provide an exhaustive account of the discourses that are at stake here. These divisions are never neutral, as they are embedded within a much longer history of taste formation, in which hierarchies of values are constructed along the lines of gender (as well as other power relations, such as those associated with sexuality, age, race and class). These debates extend well beyond the scope of this book, but I want to emphasise how the homogenising of the public in terms of gender is based on a prejudice against popular culture itself, traditionally marked as feminine. Not coincidentally, genres such as the musical or melodrama – which are genres that tend to be reclaimed not only by women, but also by LGTB and queer interpretative communities (Dyer 2002) – have historically been overlooked by auteur theory or film criticism, being associated with 'feminine' sensibilities or taste, and dismissed as possessing little or no aesthetic value.[26] Horror cinema, in turn, has been traditionally linked to men due to its focus on violence and, often, misogyny – and thereby rejected by some feminist scholars, while valued positively in authorial studies largely dedicated to male directors (Alfred Hitchcock and David Cronenberg are only a few examples of this phenomenon).

This divide has been questioned in many ways by feminist film theory, especially in reference to melodrama. For example, as Jermyn convincingly argues, while action cinema and melodrama[27] are currently 'oppositionally gendered', their mutual concern with excess, both in regards to acting and narrative, suggests nevertheless many affinities (2003: 132). In the same vein, Janet Staiger (2011) points in her analysis of *Casino Royale* (Martin Campbell, 2006) to an evolution of action cinema in terms of an increasingly marked tendency towards 'tears'. On the other hand, in a number of John Ford's classical Westerns, 'the expressive use of music and mise-en-scène to heighten emotional affect can only be described as melodramatic' (Cook 2012: 31). According to Pam Cook, 'the choices facing the Western hero, between love and duty, family life, and a wanderer's existence are not that different from those encountered by women's picture heroines' (2012: 31). Finally, Steve Neale has famously demonstrated through a historical investigation of US trade press from 1920 to

1950 how the label 'melodrama' was not always associated with women, but was initially used to refer to action-sensation dominated subgenres, assumed to be addressing male audiences (1993: 69), which remarkably complicates its subsequent association with the domestic realm. William McClain remarks in reference to Neale's study:

> The creation of genres in critical discourse, and the assertion of authority over them, must first and foremost be seen as a Foucauldian move to create knowledge and thus simultaneously to assert power, authority, and control over textual interpretation and a field of textual objects. As such, film critics claim the power not only to describe the genre but also to legitimate changes to its character and canon. (2010: 54)

The opposition between 'male' and 'female' genres stems from a set of assumptions regarding the representation of men/women, different spectatorial pleasures and, above all, the issue of film identification. However, the supposition that it is possible to locate a single specific mode of address – not only in terms of gender, but also class, race, ethnicity, age or sexual preference, and so forth – can no longer be taken for granted. As Pam Cook has demonstrated, social subjects do not necessarily align themselves according to these categories, but they are likely to occupy other, opposing positions. She suggests that 'the invitation to the cinema is based on the promise that spectators may experience the thrill of reinventing themselves rather than simply having their social identities or positions bolstered' (2012: 33).[28]

Identification might not necessarily take place between viewers and characters of the same 'sex' (or other difference markers); indeed, our experience of cinema can bypass the issues of identification altogether, as phenomenologically informed film theories, based on the notions of embodiment and that of 'the haptic' – Deleuze's term for the tactility of vision – have widely demonstrated. Feminist film theory has greatly benefited from this new interest in affect, sensorium and the non-representational, since it helped transcend oversimplified models of identification and cognition. In the mid-1990s, and crucially inspired by Vivian Sobchack's *The Address of the Eye: A Phenomenology of Film Experience* (1992), scholars started to focus on the material and sensual aspects of viewing, 'thinking about film through such notions as the lived-body (applied to both film and spectator), the embodied and synesthetic nature of perception, the reversibility of perception and expression, and the material and sensuous operations of the technological film apparatus' (Del Rio 2008: 2). As evident in books by Giuliana Bruno, Patricia Pisters, Anna Powell, Steven Shaviro, Laura Marks and Jennifer Barker, which attempt to reconsider the film image from a non-representational angle, this new path in film theory opens up interesting possibilities for thinking about gender and film experience. In seeking to overcome the paradigm of representation, most of these scholars question some of the major assumptions of psychoanalytic film theory – in particular, its theoretical reduction of the viewing experience to gaze, frequently associated in feminist film theories with controlling, patriarchal looking. Building on Maurice Merleau-Ponty's phenomenology, Sobchack states that 'we do not experience any movie only through our eyes. We see and comprehend and feel films with our entire bodily being, informed by the full history and carnal knowledge of our acculturated sensorium' (2004: 63).

Following Sobchack's influential work on the affective dimension of film viewing, scholars like Barker and Marks have questioned the representational paradigm in favour of a somatic, embodied or tactile perception. They are both interested in the embodied materiality of film experience as a key component in cinematic affect, mobilising the notion of the haptic,[29] which supposes that viewers might abandon themselves corporeally to the flow of images on screen. For Marks, haptic images, which appeal to a complex multi-sensory perception – in contrast to optical images, which are based on a clear separation and control – collapse the distance between the viewer and the image, creating a form of mutual contact (2000: 124). While Marks is interested in experimental film practice, Barker (2009) includes popular texts in her analysis, such as Buster Keaton's physical comedies or the Wile E. Coyote and Road Runner duo from the Looney Tunes and Merrie Melodies series of cartoons. In her thought-provoking account of the film experience as a tactile interaction between film and viewer, Barker extends the notion of haptic visuality and considers it on three overlapping levels: the skin, the musculature and the viscera. Film experience goes far beyond our identification with characters, as we 'respond to whole cinematic structures – textural, spatial, or temporal structures' (2009: 74). Barker explains her reasoning: 'Our bodies orient and dispose themselves toward the body of the film itself, because we and the film make sense of space by moving through it muscularly in similar ways and with similar attitudes' (2009: 75).

The focus on affective and bodily spectatorship has also been pivotal to studies on genre cinema. Linda Williams's (1991) work on horror, melodrama and porn films, and the kind of spectatorial pleasure they produce (terror, pathos and sexual excitement respectively), has effected a major shift in genre theory, as it explored not only the genre's system and structure, but also its effects on the bodies of spectators. In her groundbreaking essay 'Film Bodies: Gender, Genre, and Excess', Williams briefly mentions other genres that address the senses or engage the body in an affective manner, such as musicals, slapstick comedies and thrillers – and we could also include here action films, war films or, in fact, any other popular form. Notwithstanding some obvious differences, Williams's understanding of the affectivity in certain genres connects in many ways with the phenomenological notion of embodiment, as postulated by Sobchack: they both emphasise the often intimate relation between the film and the body viewing (or experiencing) the film.[30]

While extremely useful as a critical tool, the line of thought focused on affects and bodily responses that are generated by the narratives, the characters or the film body is not without its problems. As Mary Harrod (2016: 54–6) astutely observes, many of these theorisations are applied by feminist scholars to women-authored experimental, art-house cinema, prioritising films that offer 'feminine' qualities such as emotion and embodied experience, confirming, rather than destabilising, the binaristic logic on which a conception of gendered spectatorship rests – the centrality of Jane Campion's oeuvre in these studies is a particularly evident example of this tendency.[31] Most importantly, however, they overlook women filmmakers' and women viewers' concerns with more conscious cognitive pleasures, such as, for example, reference-spotting, culturally associated with male viewing practices. Rather than simply reversing these poles, Harrod makes a persuasive case for bypassing the 'brain-body' dualism, arguing that 'genres appeal to both domains and that female filmmakers have recently been drawn to genre films that are at once highly over-determined or reflexive and yet highly affecting' (forthcoming). In her illuminating reading of the work of Amy Heckerling, Harrod shows how

> the tactical pairing of narratives designed to elicit affect with extreme referentiality – one possible definition of the genre film – demands reading in terms of a move to blur the boundaries between intellectual and bodily engagement, thus contributing to the erosion of the categories of cognition and affect. (2016: 68)

Not only does she consider how female-authored films may lead to the erosion of these (always gendered) epistemological categories, but she also sets out to question 'the very status of the category of epistemology – as divorced from embodied, affective sentiment: a realm which has traditionally been gendered feminine' (2016: 58). She explains: 'Specifically, there can be no "masculine" realm of cerebral pleasures into which women incur if the Cartesian severing of affect and emotion from cognition is challenged' (forthcoming).

The view that female-authored films appeal only to the emotions, latent in any process of the gendering of genres, has already been questioned by Roberta Garrett (2007) in her study of self-reflexivity in recent 'chick flicks', on which Harrod also draws. Even though Garrett does not address the issue of female authorship, several of her case studies are directed by women filmmakers, both from popular and art-house cinema spheres: Nora Ephron, Sharon Maguire, Sally Potter and Jane Campion, among others. Garrett's central premise is that what distinguishes the new female-orientated cycles of 'the woman's film' from the previous ones is the integration of aesthetic, formal and thematic concerns that she identifies as postmodernist, which are often used not against a more emotional address of these films, but 'to ameliorate the sentimentalism and feminine naivety associated with older female-identified forms' (2007: 7). These postmodernist features include, among others,

> anti-realist distancing devices (such as characters directly addressing the camera, abrupt shifts in character or location), metagenericity (the playful, self-reflexive mixing of well-known generic formulas) and the frequent references to either past or contemporary film and television shows and popular culture which were becoming ever more prevalent in post-classical cinema. (2007: 5)

Garrett points to how many of these features are associated with male-orientated cinema (which she also dubs 'nasty', because of its explicit depictions of violence), exemplified by the work of cultish indie directors such as David Lynch, Quentin Tarantino, Martin Scorsese, David Fincher, Oliver Stone and Mary Harron (in particular, her *American Psycho*, 2000), as well as mainstream action movies, such as the *Die Hard* series. As Garrett convincingly argues: 'At the other end of the cinematic spectrum, female-orientated genres are still haunted by the hopelessly uncool figure of the dim-witted, impressionable female viewer' (2007: 7).

I similarly take as a starting point Garrett's observation that the self-consciousness of chick flicks, traditionally associated with affective intensity and female viewers' over-engagement, tends to be critically overlooked by film criticism. As will be discussed in Chapter 6, this is particularly true in the case of mainstream directors working in the realm of the romcom, such as Nancy Meyers; despite the obvious play with generic self-awareness and intertextuality, critical responses to her films tend to underscore their imitative, clichéd and even patronising nature, rather than focusing on their self-conscious features. Where I do not necessarily agree with Garrett, however, is regarding her assertion that what she labels as 'male-orientated' postmodernist cinema does not offer the emotional saturation or moments of intimacy associated with female viewing pleasures. Garrett argues that:

> The standard features of postmodernist cinema – irony, narrative self-consciousness and allusion, are associated with the more cerebral, distanced, 'masculine' pleasures of reference spotting than the overengagement which is closely bound to the cultural perception of female viewing pleasure. In addition to the ironic address of cultish postmodern films, moments of emotional engagement tend to be brief and fleeting in male-orientated postmodernism. (2007: 7)

As I will show in my analysis of horror cinema in Chapter 2 and the genre of war films in Chapter 3 – conforming to Harrod's model of 'heightened genericity', which she finds both pervasive today and particularly prevalent in female-authored genre films – both cases draw on 'heightened intertextuality' and 'revel in their own constructed-ness' (Harrod 2016: 56), while also offering moments of intimacy and an intense emotional saturation. This is not to claim that these films are automatically innovative solely on the basis of the gender of their authors, or that these women filmmakers are transgressors of genre paradigms. On the one hand, Garrett's account of the proliferation of self-reflexive practices in both female-authored and male-authored texts across Hollywood and independent filmmaking cautions us from interpreting such strategies as inherently subversive. On the other, as Linda Williams's work in the field implies, all genre films promise an affective engagement, if with varying degrees, so it is hardly exclusive to women's genre filmmaking.

All of the films studied in this volume mobilise, then, the cerebral pleasures of reference-spotting historically seen as the purview of male viewers (Garrett 2007: 7), which are never divorced from affective intensity and the filmic pleasures these genres offer. In *Jennifer's Body*, the critique of historical gender and power relations in horror cinema, carried out through an overwhelming referentiality to previous texts, is enhanced by, rather than in competition with, the affective power of the genre. In *The Hurt Locker*, the blend of the self-reflexive mixing of well-known genres with visceral filmmaking, which enables sensorial immersion in what is represented onscreen, highlights what Harrod has aptly dubbed 'discourse's status as highly fake yet our experience of it as "real" and/or affectively meaningful' (2016: 63). Reichardt's use of the Western cinematic conventions and Wild West mythologies, in turn, exceeds the limits of representation and identification with characters towards the phenomenological realism and the materiality of haptic viewing. In *Marie Antoinette* the metafictional take on history is linked to an ideological critique of the patriarchal construction of marriage and motherhood, which is carried out in line with, and not against, the modes of affect and embodied memory already present in period films. 'The convergence of fakery and feeling', as discussed by Harrod (2016: 65) in reference to Heckerling, is perhaps most fully apparent in *The Intern* – in particular, in its representation of romance. The viewer's engagement 'is likely to come not just from spotting specific references but also, in large measure, from appreciating a generalised sense of familiarity' (Harrod 2016: 51).

In sum, this book argues for the consideration of genre and gender as a flexible recombination that enables the dissolution of borders and enlargement of cinematic experience beyond the restrictive confines of identification. In order to analyse how cinema engages emotions or stimulates affective responses, I will frequently question the traditional paradigm of vision typical of 'apparatus theory', and emphasise the importance of affect and experience in film spectatorship, as analysed by phenomenological and Deleuzian film theories. This is not to dismiss the importance of more conscious moments of reference-spotting; in fact, I concur with Harrod, who states that these two types of response are frequently indistinguishable – a critical position which interestingly recalls Mulvey's 'passionate detachment' ([1975] 1989b: 26), provided that we understand it as a powerful balance of paradoxical opposites.[32] I believe that these approaches are helpful because they challenge our previous comprehension of how films engage us and potentially contribute to the expansion of a reflection on the complex formulations of women's cinema, intimately bound up with the historical gendering of genres.

Therefore, instead of locking women filmmakers into a segregated gender sphere defined by 'women's culture', I argue here for the mutability of gendered identities and question the oversimplified notion of gender-to-gender cinematic identification – a typical assumption underpinning the categorisation of genres by gender. This questioning is important and pertinent for thinking about women's film authorship, since, 'by positing that popular cinema is more ideologically open, and processes of identification more fluid than has previously been imagined, it suggests that opportunities for resistance are more available than the opposition between "dominant cinema" and "counter-cinema" allows' (Cook 2012: 33). An increased focus on gender fluidity in cinematic identification might help redefine women's cinema in terms of an exclusive address to female spectators and offer new perspectives on how women explore the aesthetic and imaginative power of genre – seen as a catalyst for, rather than a restriction on, the possibility of cultural engagement and thus ideological intervention. Instead of arguing for the subversive nature of these texts, however, I suggest throwing them into Gledhill's 'feminist orbit' (1994: 121), even if it is more than likely that not all of the filmmakers discussed in this volume will be seen as feminist. 'Such criticism is not concerned with progressiveness or reactionariness of the text, but with tapping its cultural energy, making it productive for feminist debate and practice' (in Lane 2000: 26). Building on this model, which presupposes that 'meaning is neither imposed, nor passively imbibed, but arises out of a struggle or negotiation between competing frames of reference, motivation and experience' (Gledhill 2006: 114), this book does not purport to offer a feminist theory of genre, but rather it seeks, through feminist readings, to put forward a methodological reflection on genre and women's film authorship that might prompt new avenues of inquiry and enable a fuller understanding of women's place in, and contribution to, the film industries.

Notes

1. Since the first Academy Awards in 1929, only four women have been nominated for the Best Director Oscar: Lina Wertmüller (*Seven Beauties*, 1975), Jane Campion (*The Piano*, 1993), Sofia Coppola (*Lost in Translation*, 2003) and Kathryn Bigelow (*The Hurt Locker*, 2008).
2. As also postulated by Patricia White (2015), who similarly opens her book with the Bigelow example, although with different aims.
3. Historian Claire Potter stated that Bigelow, similarly to Kimberly Peirce, director of the war drama *Stop Loss* (2008), has become successful by promoting herself as a woman director who 'knows men' (Potter 2010). The search for female characterisation in Bigelow's movie recalls the long-standing debate over the 'images of women' initiated in the 1970s, when feminists working in the social sciences addressed how women were represented in the 'content' of media production, and when it was postulated that female stereotypes should be replaced by 'positive' images of women. See Joanne Hollows's (2000) critique of this research paradigm.
4. All of the translations from Spanish are mine.
5. Not unlike the term 'women's cinema', the issue of 'female authorship' has an equally long and complex history in feminist criticism. I elaborate on this in Chapter 1.
6. According to Deborah Jermyn (2014), Sally Potter has been the subject of two monographs and Jane Campion seven. Claire Denis has another seven dedicated to her work and Chantal Akerman four (see Harrod and Paszkiewicz 2018).
7. In fact, the exclusion of women filmmakers from both mainstream cinema and critical discourses has not always been total. Women were involved in making films in Hollywood from its inception, but they were marginalised when cinema shifted from art to industry. Historical precedents to women's current work in genre cinema are notably acknowledged by Johnston ([1975] 2000b), Gaines (2012), Zecchi (2014) and Mayne (1994), among others.
8. As Patricia White argues: 'Scholarship and teaching in this expansive field [...] require flexible, comparative methods' – for example, those provided by 'multicultural, postcolonial, and transnational feminist theory that foregrounds questions of power, relationality, and intersectionality' (2015: 12).
9. In order to analyse discourses of reviewing, I adopt the context-activated reception theory proposed by Staiger (1992), which focuses on the historically constructed interpretative strategies and tactics which spectators bring to the cinema.
10. For the distinction between *film genre* and *genre film*, see Chapter 1.
11. There are, of course, precedents to this phenomenon. As Judith Mayne (1994) argued, similar discourses appeared in the 1920s with Dorothy Arzner, who made genre films in the classical Hollywood studio system.
12. This is because, arguably, the Western represented the starting point of genre criticism in film studies, particularly evidenced by Robert Warshow's and André Bazin's critical essays, published during the 1940s and 1950s.
13. Even though the Western typically centres on male protagonists, many films do feature female characters – for example Joan Crawford's saloon owner in *Johnny Guitar* (Nicholas Ray, 1954). These films have been frequently framed in terms of either female masculinity or long-standing figurations of tough femininity (see Tasker 2017).
14. Assumptions about the inherently conservative nature of these genres persist in contemporary scholarly writing about them. Lisa Purse's comments in her discussion of *The Hurt Locker* illustrate this tendency: '[T]he question remains whether the action film, with its reliance on simplifications of notions like heroism and

justice, its often conservative representational hierarchies and its inexorable progress towards a thrilling, spectacular expression of the hero's mastery over clearly identifiable foes, will ever be able to accommodate adequately the complexities of the post-9/11 world' (2011: 168).
15. For example, it was argued that the slasher subgenre encourages viewers to identify with the killer and his violence, rather than with the female victims. It was observed that the most terrifying attacks are always perpetrated against women – in particular, those who are sexually active (Wood 1986: 197).
16. See also Cobb (2015: 10–11). The benefits of bringing women, authorship and genre itself into dialogue are multiple, and will be discussed in more detail in Chapter 1.
17. In fact, early feminist criticism that emerged in the 1970s developed two different approaches: the so-called 'positive images' criticism and the psychoanalytic approach associated with Laura Mulvey.
18. What is more, de Lauretis argues in her 1980 account of women's cinema that we need to unpick the oppositions between 'Hollywood vs independent, avant-garde vs classical, entertainment vs political, alternative vs mainstream cinema' established in early cine-psychoanalysis (1990: 6).
19. This tendency can also be traced in E. Ann Kaplan's *Women and Film* (1988), Lauren Rabinovitz's *Points of Resistance* (1991) and Anneke Smelik's *And the Mirror Cracked* (1998), as well as the more recent Sophie Mayer's *Political Animals* (2016) and Kate Ince's *The Body and the Screen* (2017), among many other examples.
20. Tania Modleski's chapter on appropriating the Western in *The Ballad of Little Jo* by Maggie Greenwald, included in *Old Wives' Tales and Other Women's Stories* (1998), is an important precursor to these publications.
21. The practice of fanvid refers to women 'rewriting' mainstream narratives – notably, cinematic ones – through online editing practices (see Coppa 2018).
22. Earlier publications should also be acknowledged here – see, for instance, Francke (1994) on screenwriters, or Haskell (1974) and Stacey (1994) on film stars.
23. As Gledhill explains: 'This becomes abundantly clear in the pleasure that can be derived from nineteenth-century fictions or their contemporary media adaptations, which mobilise for their dramatic potential social ideologies and moralities we no longer believe in. The Victorian ideology of "true womanhood", for example, provides the stimulus for deviant passions and piquant feelings' (2018: x).
24. Here, Butler references Lucy Fischer (1989: 2–24) and her detailed account of the significance of intertextuality and remaking for feminist film practice.
25. Taking into consideration the scarcity of women working as directors in Hollywood, we could also talk about 'minority' in quantitative terms, although it is not a requirement according to Deleuze and Guattari.
26. Although there are some notable exceptions – for instance, Douglas Sirk and his 'authorial revision' of melodrama (Klinger 1994: 1–35). A more recent example is Damien Chazelle's musical *La La Land* (2016), nominated for fourteen Oscars and read in critical discourses through the lens of authorial subversion (the film was considered a nostalgic and highly self-reflexive revisiting of classical Hollywood cinema).
27. Christine Gledhill, for her part, has considered melodrama as a mode underpinning Hollywood's genre system, attached to both 'male' and 'female'-gendered genres, from Westerns to 'woman's film' (1987: 34, 13).
28. This idea was already explored by the late 1980s, when feminist film theory started to examine the issue of cross-spectatorial identifications and/or the pleasures to be derived by female viewers from the nominally male genres, such as science fiction,

film noir, horror and action films (Clover 1992; Tasker 1993; among others). As Roberta Garrett observes in her useful overview of early feminist criticism, the period saw much scholarly interest in 'a slightly wider range of roles that were beginning to be inhabited by the female figure in popular cinema' (2007: 3), such as lawyers, investigators and new action heroines in films including *Aliens* (James Cameron, 1986) and *Terminator 2: Judgement Day* (James Cameron, 1991). These generic reworkings that place women in conventional male roles seem 'compatible with the theoretical shift away from gender/text identification into notions of spectator cross-identification and the disintegration of the anti-popular, avant-garde project of women's cinema' (Garrett 2007: 52).

29. It is worth clarifying that while Sobchack's and Barker's projects draw mainly upon Merleau-Ponty's phenomenology in their exploration of the corporeal dimensions of cinema, Marks's focus is on both phenomenological and Deleuzian theories.

30. We could extend this comparison to feminist studies on the affective qualities of melodrama (Modleski 1982; Ang 1985; Williams 1991; Gledhill 2011; Gaines 2012, among others).

31. It should be noted, however, that the majority of 'contact theory' scholars challenge the perception of these qualities as essentially 'feminine'. For instance, Laura Marks considerably resists the identification of the haptic with femininity (in reference to viewers and filmmakers), conceptualising it as a strategy shared with 'an underground visual tradition in general' (2002: 7).

32. Similar to Harrod's, my approach privileges textual analysis, even if I frequently refer to reception contexts of the films under discussion. Eugenie Brinkema (2014) has recently observed that discussions of cinematic affect have been divorced from those of textuality for too long. In reference to this assertion, Harrod underlines 'the inseparability of processes of textual signification and embodied address when it comes to film analysis' (2016: 65). She also correctly detects the challenges of this endeavour, as for all attempts 'to return the question of affect to formal analysis, the usual challenges of describing subjective experiences are multiplied when considering film and other texts as a whole or in their intertextual relay' (2016: 65).

1. SUBVERSIVE AUTEUR, SUBVERSIVE GENRE

> Perhaps it is that we have learned to love our hegemonic fantasies – the more hegemonic the better – and not only to consume but also to critique because the pleasure of analysis is in finding the 'shred' of something, of anything remotely utopian, in the most crudely escapist entertainment.
>
> (Gaines 2011: 111–12)

Auteur

Any reference to female auteurs – especially those perceived to be working within the so-called 'mainstream', whether in terms of the financial parameters or use of more 'conservative' forms – runs the risk of reproducing a pre-structuralist, romantic discourse, according to which the auteur is an empirical being able to transcend industrial, commercial or even collective limitations, in order to individually 'author' her films in transgressive and innovative ways. This conceptualisation of film authorship, along with the category 'auteur cinema', is mainly associated with a series of publications that appeared in the French magazine *Cahiers du cinéma* in the 1950s, according to which a film director is an individual agent who controls the entire creation process of the film. Referring to this concept of film authorship, John Caughie remarks that the intervention and critical revolution of the *politique des auteurs* ironically involved the simple installation of a figure that had dominated the other arts for a long time: the romantic artist, who is individual and self-expressive (1981: 10). According to Caughie:

> Within its distinguishable currents [...] auteurism shares certain basic assumptions: notably, that a film, though produced collectively, is most likely to be valuable when it is essentially the product of its director [...]; that in the presence of a director who is genuinely an artist (an auteur) a film is more than likely to be an expression of his individual personality; and that this personality can be traced in a thematic and/or stylistic consistency over all (or almost all) of his films. (1981: 9)

It is no surprise that feminist film theorists, much as the literary critics before them, did not readily adopt these tenets. The defenders of the avant-garde film practice criticised auteur theory for its almost exclusive focus on commercial cinema, which left little space for the exploration of experimental filmmaking – the field that boasted the highest number of female directors from the 1970s onwards. Conceiving authorship in terms of coherence, recurring themes and 'authorial' obsessions that are manifested throughout a film career raises another problem: few women, at least in the context of Hollywood or mainstream cinema, have been able to produce a sufficiently extensive body of work, making it difficult to reflect on their authorship through examination of their 'recognisable style' or 'personal obsessions'. Moreover, many feminist analyses have expressed ambivalence towards the language used by those who championed 'auteur cinema', pointing to the phallocentric character of metaphors such as the *caméra-stylo* and showing how the concept of the auteur as an individual genius is determined by certain assumptions relating to gender, class and race; indeed, it is no coincidence that those granted this status are white, middle-class men.[1] Analysing the male-centredness of auteurism, Angela Martin (2008) argues that the critics writing for *Cahiers du cinéma*, for instance Jacques Rivette, infused the term 'auteur' with a set of notions such as 'self-expression', 'youth', 'violence', 'virility' and 'rage'. However, these were often incompatible with the practice of many female directors and with the feminist tenet that the personal is political, which is very different from the *Nouvelle Vague*'s call for a personal self-expression (2008: 129).

Another key problem emerging from auteur theory is the assumption that out of all the people who work on a film (screenwriters, producers, directors of photography, editors and so on), only the director can be the auteur. Cinematographic production, especially in Hollywood, is a collaborative and industrialised process involving a large number of practitioners, and the opportunities for exercising authorial control over a film are often extremely limited. When there are so many artists involved in the making of a film, up to what point can it be considered the product of a singular, individual agency? To what extent can the collaborative character of industrial filmmaking allow us to speak of auteurs? Christina Lane (2000: 46), for example, poses the following question in relation to *Thelma and Louise* (1991), a paradigmatic text for feminist film criticism: in addition to the director, Ridley Scott, should we not also consider the co-producer (Mimi Polk), the screenwriter (Callie Khouri) and the film stars (Susan Sarandon and Geena Davis) as equally responsible for the creation of meaning, especially given the potentially feminist content in the film? Furthermore, it is important to highlight that the romantic conception of the film auteur especially erases the presence of women who, due to a series of historical, economic and cultural circumstances, have had greater access to the positions of writer, editor and costume designer than to that of director.[2]

One of the main reasons for the mistrust towards auteur approaches is the chronological coincidence of feminist film theory, not so much with the creation and development of auteur theory, but rather with structuralist and post-structuralist paradigms. In the mid-1970s – just as some female critics were beginning to denounce the absence of female directors in the arena of cinematic production, and were actively promoting films made by women at numerous film festivals – structuralist and post-structuralist thinkers declared auteur theory obsolete. In short, both the glorification of the auteur by the *Cahier du cinéma* critics as well as the author's supposed death – which can ultimately be viewed as two sides of the same coin with regards to the exclusion of women from both empirical histories and authorial pantheons – created numerous obstacles for the conceptualisation of women's film authorship.

If, on the one hand, feminist scholars were conscious that the supposed death of the author was highly problematic because it occurred at a particular historical moment when marginalised groups were starting to reclaim their subjectivity (Braidotti 1991), at the same time they continued to regard with suspicion the 'elitist' and 'masculine' conceptualisations of the author that were developed over subsequent years. It would seem that the benefits for feminist theory of raising the question of female authorship in relation to the contribution of women to cinema were even less evident than in the case of literary authorship (Grant 2001: 114), which translates into a surprising lack of theoretical works on female directors, at least in the first decades of feminist film criticism. Making reference to this issue, Judith Mayne (1990) speaks of the spectre of essentialism, which she claims has haunted feminist criticism since its beginnings:

> While virtually all feminist critics would agree that the works of Germaine Dulac, Maya Deren, and Dorothy Arzner (to name the most frequently invoked 'historical figures') are important, there has been considerable reluctance to use any of them as privileged examples to theorise female authorship in the cinema, unless, that is, such theorising affirms the difficulty of women's relationship to the cinematic apparatus. This reluctance reflects the current association of 'theory' with 'antiessentialism'. (1990: 90)

According to Mayne, assumptions about a 'female tradition' or 'female canon' in debates about women directors are highly problematic and generate significant concern about a regression towards an essentialist theory of subjectivity, which instates itself in opposition to the traditional (masculine-oriented) view of the auteur. While recognising these difficulties, though, Mayne defends authorship as a viable method for thinking about the cinematic practices of women: 'The notion of female authorship is not simply a useful political strategy; it is crucial to the reinvention of the cinema that has been undertaken by women filmmakers and feminist spectators' (1990: 97).

Despite the highly problematic character of the concept of authorship in cinema, feminist film scholars – at least in the Anglophone studies – have more recently followed the path trodden by Mayne, defending the necessity to adopt this notion as a useful and necessary category and proposing diverse frameworks through which to rethink the validity of the female author as a hermeneutic key. They hold that, instead of a theory about the death of the author, what we need is a new theorisation of authorship, one which is not based on a somewhat naïve concept of the female auteur as an autonomous genius who creates aesthetic objects outside of history, and one which does not diminish the importance of the different forms of agent-hood in women's responses to historical developments. This is the central argument of Catherine Grant (2001), who, in her article 'Secret Agents: Feminist Theories of Women's Film Authorship', poses a thought-provoking question: maybe, in their approach to women's film authorship, feminist film theorists have been 'overly anxious about the wrong kind of "essentialism"'. In situating the author as a fictional figure within the text, this text has been constructed as an ideal essence, removing whatever ties it to the 'social and historical outside' (2001: 121). Contemporary female authorship, according to Grant, cannot be approached solely through 'formalist' methodologies, as these ignore the importance of the context of production, distribution and reception of films. She proposes, thus, that we consider various aspects of female directorial 'authors' as agents: '[F]emale subjects who have direct and reflexive, if obviously not completely "intentional" or determining relationships to the cultural products they help to produce, as well as to their reception' (2001: 124). In order to speak about the interventions of women as cultural producers and their sociocultural reception in wider terms, Grant and other scholars – such as Susan Martin-Márquez (1999) and, more recently, Barbara Zecchi (2014) – consider agency through the optic of Judith Butler's positing of gender, as a 'reiterative or re-articulatory practice, immanent to power, and not a relation of external opposition to power' (Butler 1993: 15). As Grant concludes, women's agency can finally 'be subjected to analysis in the form of its textual, biographical traces, alongside more conventionally "legitimate" activities for feminist cultural theorists, such as applying theories to "primary" literary and film texts in formal "readings"' (2001: 123).

Despite the fact that the notion of 'agency' or 'agent-hood' implied in these analyses might be questionable – precisely from the point of view of the post-structuralism that these theorists are, to varying degrees, attempting to displace – their propositions open up a way to reconsider authorial perspectives and methodologies in relation to films directed by women. Grant suggests that, instead of shifting attention from formal structures and the style of film texts, we should broaden our ideas about what constitutes a 'primary text' in film studies and widen the scope of those texts employed to theorise about female authorship. In other words, this means examining not only the films and the 'facts' of the director's life, but also interviews, film reviews, academic studies, photographs and press materials, which enable the much more complex understanding of the multiple mediations operating in the creation and imagining of the authorial figures of female directors. Breaking down the earlier text/author impasses necessitates the adoption of more rigorous methodologies for 'interactional' and 'intersubjective' analyses of women's film authorship, suggests Grant.

Needless to say, this way of thinking about film authorship is not entirely new and can, for example, be traced back to David Bordwell's (1981) concept of biographical legend, which implies taking into consideration the creation of the director's public persona in their films and interactions with cinematic institutions, through interviews, statements and press conferences, as well as to the concept of the auteur as a 'commercial dramatisation of self [and] as the motivating agent of textuality', developed by Timothy Corrigan (1991: 108). Corrigan points out the paradigm shift in auteur theories which occurred over the course of twenty years, from 1960 to 1980 – from authorship understood as a mode of production to authorship understood as a way of watching and consuming films.[3] Corrigan analyses auteurism 'as a *commercial* strategy for organising audience reception, as a critical concept bound to distribution and marketing aims that identify and address the potential cult status of an auteur' (1991: 103 [emphasis in original]). Thus, the author whose death Barthes declared in 1967 is reborn a few decades later as a star whose public image is constructed in negotiation with the repertoire of cultural narratives, and who can also regulate the readings, fantasies and pleasures of spectators, favouring a form of consumption which does not necessarily include the viewing of the films.

Similarly to Grant, then, Corrigan attempts to reconceptualise the practices of auteurism in terms of strategies of social agency, describing the author in relation to the conditions of cultural and commercial intersubjectivity – a social interaction which is very different to the intentional causality or textual transcendence of the auteur. He explains it thus:

> In the cinema, auteurism as agency [. . .] becomes a place for encountering not so much a transcending meaning (of first-order desires) but the differ-

ent conditions through which expressive meaning is made by an auteur and reconstructed by an audience, conditions that involve historical and cultural motivations and rationalizations. (1991: 105)

Women filmmakers do not escape this phenomenon and might even benefit from it. Directors like Kathryn Bigelow, Sofia Coppola and Lena Dunham have turned themselves into a commercial brand, an intertextual sign which is read and constructed through diverse sources, including advertising, press articles, interviews, directors' profiles, blog entries, Facebook and Twitter posts and so on. Although Corrigan focuses on male filmmakers such as Francis Ford Coppola, Alexander Kluge and Raoul Ruiz, his approach can be applied to women filmmakers, as they also construct themselves, and are constructed through, the marketing strategies typical of the film industry, which regulate the reception of their authorial images and their works. However, an analysis of female authorship can generate different questions to those raised by Corrigan, given that women have not had the same relationship with the film industry as men. As Corrigan observes:

In line with the marketing transformation of the auteur of the international art cinema into the cult of personality that defined the film artist of the seventies, auteurs have increasingly become situated along an extra-textual path, in which their commercial status as auteurs is their chief function as auteurs: the auteur-star is meaningful primarily as a promotion or recovery of a movie or group of movies, frequently regardless of the filmic text itself. (1991: 105)

Corrigan's concept of 'the auteur-star' might not necessarily apply to the discursive circulation of all women filmmakers' public personae studied in this volume. As I argue in the following chapters, rather than the position of 'the auteur-star', the type of visibility that Diablo Cody, Sofia Coppola and Nancy Meyers enjoy grants them the status of a 'celebrity director' – a term that connotes a 'representational structure' framed by a person's 'private life or lifestyle' (Handyside 2017: 19). Drawing on Diane Negra and Sue Holmes, Fiona Handyside usefully reminds us that 'given that the celebrity is structured through an emphasis on lifestyle, and it is women who are primarily associated with the domestic and the private, celebrity culture is itself gendered' (2017: 19).

In the context of co-optation of film authorship by film commerce, the relationship between women filmmakers and the 'voluntarist and Romantic understanding of the agency of film authorship as encapsulating the possibilities for expression of an (especially male) artist's "personality"' (Grant 2001: 114) is complex. In the context of shared genericity and sociality, which, after all, lies at the heart of all expressive forms, the question of the nature of women's authorship and agency, pursued in this book, raises even more difficult challenges. On the one hand, there is the apparent incompatibility between film authorship and genre, which is closely bound up with the cultural distinction between auteur cinema and genre filmmaking. As Christine Gledhill puts it:

> [T]he notion of authorship as encompassing a coherent and singular body of work, attributable to the imagination of a unique individual director, cannot be squared with the socially generic forms through which all makers create or with the collective, albeit hierarchical, conditions of nearly all media production. Nor can it be squared with the media industries' answerability to diverse external interests – including financing, state regulation, marketing, distribution, exhibition and publicity, not to mention their dependency on audiences. (2018: xii–xiii)

On the other hand, there is an apparent incompatibility between the two theoretical approaches, as auteur theory privileges individual creative power over a film, while studies of film genres emphasise the repetition of industrial formulas, adjusted to the expectations of the audience. In this sense, Corrigan's idea of the auteur as a 'commercial dramatization of self' (1991: 108) is particularly relevant for a study of popular women filmmakers, because understanding authorship as a function of the cultural industries suggests an interesting equivalence with the concept of film genre. For its part, genre studies can help rethink Corrigan's understanding of film authorship, which at certain points seems to reveal 'voluntarist' tendencies with regards to the interventions of auteurs, downplaying the importance of other creators of meaning.

Although, as observed by Christine Gledhill (2011: 222), genre was introduced in film studies as an alternative to auteur theory – considered by some as inappropriate for the study of popular cinema and the mass entertainment industry – the two perspectives are interconnected rather than opposing. Most critical discussions that engage with Hollywood cinema and film genres position themselves – at least initially – in relation to debates about film authorship which, notwithstanding the post-structuralist critique, have been central to film criticism since the 1950s. For some critics, genre offered a tool capable of elevating certain auteurs within the commercial realm of Hollywood, which before the 1950s had been marginal to film studies. For others, it was an opportunity to question notions of creativity and individuality inscribed in the authorial figure and focus on mass fictions and what they 'reveal about society, resulting in analyses of genre films in terms of myth and ritual, or as "reflections" of mass consciousness' (Gledhill 2011: 222). The relationship between the auteur and film genres is much more complex than might appear at first glance and demands more detailed examination.

Genre

> As soon as the word 'genre' is sounded, as soon as it is heard, as soon as one attempts to conceive it, a limit is drawn. And when a limit is established, norms and interdictions are not far behind: 'Do,' 'Do not' says 'genre,' the figure, the voice, or the law of genre.
>
> (Derrida 1980: 56)

It is intriguing to observe the devaluation of the category of 'genre' over the course of history. Terry Threadgold points out that prior to the advent of Romanticism, genre was associated with literature, while cultural forms such as pamphlets, ballads or romances – what we might call 'popular culture' – were 'not only *not* literature, but also *not* generic'; they 'escaped the law of genre [and were] seen as a kind of anarchic, free arena, unconstrained by the rules of polite society and decorum, by *genre* in fact' (1989: 121–2 [emphasis in original]). For his part, Steve Neale also observes that most modern notions of genre come from Romanticism, which was characterised by a hostile attitude towards the formal rules. This hostility was directed towards the supposed routine and impersonal character of genres, which were seen as a threat to the creativity, originality and individuality of the author.

> In consequence, the element of repetition inherent in all genres was stressed, along with the allegedly simple – or simple-minded – nature of the conventions, meanings, structures and characters they were held to embody or contain. While genre texts were more or less 'all the same', conventions were thought of as clichés, meanings as transparent and impoverished, structures as formulae, and characters as one-dimensional stereotypes. (Neale 2000: 195)

Subsequently, repetitive patterns started to become associated not so much with 'the law of Culture, but with the law of the market' (2000: 20); for this reason, genre is today linked with commercial, industrial art that is mechanically produced, much as it is in the film industry, especially in influential and popular film industries, such as Hollywood.

This understanding of genre is closely intertwined with definitions of Hollywood cinema, and there have been a number of differently articulated attempts to disentangle these terms. For instance, Thomas Schatz (1981: 16–18) suggests that we should distinguish between *film genre* and *genre film*: on the one hand, all films participate in – rather than belong to – one or more genres, according to Jacques Derrida's theory;[4] on the other, some critics talk about genre films to refer to works created in Hollywood, and in this second instance the perception of genre is often influenced by the hostility towards the industry. Similarly, there is a terminological correspondence between genre cinema, popular cinema and commercial cinema: genre films are popular and therefore more profitable for the major studios, which capitalise upon previous box office successes by exploiting already existing, successful and proven formulas.

Genre is today seen as the key to commercial production and remains separate to artistic practice, which is supposedly 'non-generic' (Gledhill 2011: 222). The opposition this premise created between 'genre cinema' and 'art cinema', which (although highly debatable) is still alive in contemporary discourses on the cultural value of popular forms, rests on the figure of the author and, more concretely, on the latter's ability to avoid generic formulas or else creatively manipulate them. Andrei Tarkovsky's rejection of popular genres is particularly revelatory; the Soviet auteur vigorously opposed reading his film *Solaris* (1972) as science fiction:

> Any talk of genre in cinema refers as a rule to commercial films – situation comedy, Western, psychological drama, melodrama, musical, detective, horror or suspense movie. And what have any of these to do with art? They are for the mass consumer. Alas, they are also the form in which cinema exists now pretty well universally, a form imposed upon it from outside and for commercial reasons. There is only one way of thinking in cinema: poetically. Only with this approach can the irreconcilable and the paradoxical be resolved, and the cinema be an adequate means of expression of the author's thoughts and feelings. The true cinema image is built upon the destruction of genre, upon conflict with it. And the ideals that the artist apparently seeks to express here obviously do not lend themselves to being confined within the parameters of a genre. (Tarkovsky [1986] 2012: 150)

Robert Warshow argues, in reference to this opposition between 'high' art and genre on which Tarkovsky's comments clearly rest:

> Genre art, in this account, can never reach the heights of greatness because its creators are too tied to artistic precedents and are therefore not 'original'. The countervailing argument asserts that genre creativity is defined by exactly that manipulation of past motifs to create a new work. ([1954] 1999: 609–10)

The conception of genre based on a negative perception of the repetition is generally shared by both detractors and defenders of Hollywood cinema: '[T]hose who wrote in praise of Hollywood's genres often found themselves using the same epithets and concepts as those who did not' (Neale 2000:

195). This was the case, for example, with the creators of the *politique des auteurs* – a generation of French critics who had grown up surrounded by commercial US film culture and who wanted to assert its value. Andrew Sarris (1968), who brought these ideas to the United States as 'auteur theory', held that some directors who take risks and fight against the standardisation of the Hollywood system manage to maintain their coherent style or 'individual signature'. According to Sarris (1981), critics should concentrate on three criteria for recognising an auteur: technical competence, a recognisable personality and an 'interior meaning' that is extrapolated from the tension between the personality of the auteur and the material with which he works. This final criterion locates us again in the field of film genres, whose limitations can be understood as resistance of the material Sarris refers to. Paradoxically, through being so conventional, genre cinema creates even more opportunities for the inclusion of individual signatures on the part of authors. It is precisely the conventionality of Hollywood production which enabled Sarris to elevate American auteurs above European auteurs. In relation to this claim, Robert Stam – citing Jim Hillier – highlighted the paradox that representatives of the *politique des auteurs* admired North American cinema, where the imposed restrictions on production are greater than anywhere else, without recognising its more admirable feature: '[T]he genius of the system, the richness of its ever-vigorous tradition, and its fertility when it comes into contact with new elements' (Hillier in Stam 2000a: 88).

Many of these film auteur approaches share a tacit assumption with regards to the definition of genres: they *really* exist, and are separated by clearly defined borders that can be identified without great difficulty.[5] In addition, a relationship of authority (in sum, property and control) is assumed between the auteur and film genres, understood as formulas which are bound to be transcended.[6] The notion of genre as a formula,[7] which can be identified across several publications on both mass-culture theory and auteurism, alludes to particular uses of this term in scientific discourse to describe a 'procedure', whereby certain elements are joined together in an established order so as to produce a predetermined and invariable result (Jancovich 2002: 10). This conceptualisation of genre as ruled by strict combination patterns, executed in order to achieve a final product that is easily classifiable and marketable, is linked to a specific way of understanding popular culture – and Hollywood cinema in particular – which brings us irrevocably to the thinkers of the Frankfurt School.

Theodor W. Adorno and Max Horkheimer's (1979) aesthetic and political condemnation of genres and mass culture in general is well known; they denounced not only the trivialisation and superficiality of cultural products, but also the passivity of the masses, who become conformist and are easily manipulated. Robin Wood ([1977] 2012: 79–80),[8] for his part, connected film genres with a series of values and assumptions which were reinforced by classical Hollywood cinema and its formulas: capitalism (the right to property, personal initiative); work ethic; marriage (legalised heterosexual monogamy) and family as a validation of capitalism and work ethic in a society dominated by men; nature as agrarianism (virgin earth like the Garden of Eden); nature as wilderness (civilisation is built through the subjugation of the Indians); progress, technology and the city; success and wealth; the Rosebud syndrome: money is not everything, money corrupts, the poor are happier ('a very convenient assumption for capitalist ideology; the more oppressed you are, the happier you are' [2012: 80]); the United States as a country where everyone is, or can be, happy and where all problems are capable of being resolved *within* the current system (which might require the occasional reform, but never a radical change). Wood points to two ideal figures who emerged from this list of ideological contradictions: the ideal man (the virile adventurer, the invincible man of action) and the ideal woman (wife and mother, perfect companion, who maintains house). Given that the ideal man and the ideal woman are together a somewhat 'incompatible' pair, each one has its shadow: the respectable but boring husband/father and the erotic woman, fascinating but dangerous, who ends up betraying the hero.

In the same vein, Judith Hess (1974) claimed that genres serve the interests of governing elites, helping to maintain the status quo. Hess accused genre films of temporarily alleviating the anxieties awakened by social and political conflicts, dissuading the audience from any kind of action emerging from the tensions generated by these conflicts. Film genres stimulate a feeling of satisfaction, grief or reassurance, but never call for rebellion, and oppressed groups naïvely accept the simplistic and reactionary solutions they are offered. Three important features make these solutions appear viable, according to Hess: genre films almost never depict current social problems in an explicit way; these problems are not usually situated in the present moment; finally, the society in which the story takes place exists only as a background, and it is the individual characters who confront the problems that present themselves in the film. In this way, the public is discouraged from developing any kind of critical attitude towards contemporary society and are induced to confine themselves to the realms of fantasy.

In conclusion, within this strand of criticism, which is sometimes called 'ideological' (Altman 1999: 29), genre (seen as conservative in theme and style) serves the interests of the dominant ideology, which uses prefabricated narrative formulas to sedate the audience, creating an illusion of reality. Each of the distinct film genres is characterised by its own ideological conflicts and 'illusory' ways of resolving them, although, ultimately, they all serve the same objective: to put the audience to sleep and reinforce hegemonic messages. According to various studies, science fiction dramatises the intrusion of 'others'

– for example, in the cinema of the 1950s, which brought the tensions of the Cold War and the accompanying fear of nuclear threat into relief; gangster films produced during the first half of the twentieth century represented a series of contradictions derived from the American dream; the musicals of the 1930s shaped the escapist fantasies during the Depression; Westerns promoted patterns of 'tough' masculinity, usually associated with the armed conflicts of the United States; finally, the film noir of the 1940s and mid-1950s was claimed to be a symptom of the social and sexual upheavals provoked by the end of the Second World War, the return of men to their homes and their subsequent drive to return women to the realm of the domestic. This last genre, film noir, has been of particular importance for feminist criticism, which has produced numerous analyses of the *femme fatale* and her role in the fragmentation of the middle-class family structure (Haskell 1974).

Although these studies, which address a broad selection of films to grasp historical conjuncture, might sometimes be interesting and useful for feminist criticism, it is not productive to limit oneself to these conclusions and ignore textual and contextual specificity when it comes to analysing concrete films. As Christine Gledhill rightly observes: 'Despite complex theories of ideology and subjectivity developed in the 1970s, the notion that mainstream films can be correlated with their social contexts still draws on more or less sophisticated models of textual "reflection"' (2011: 221). Thus, she finds the 'picture conjured of a huddle of producers, scriptwriters, and assorted film-makers planning how to make the next film noir direct its female audience back to their kitchen sinks' largely 'improbable' (2011: 221). This line of reasoning gives rise to a series of questions, especially with regards to the passive nature of the audience. Are film genres made popular through influence of the studios – for example, through the employment of targeted promotional strategies – or is it the audience which makes them popular and guarantees their continued existence? In addition, many of these theorisations are based on an assumption that genre is a simple repetition of the mould, when, in fact, variation is a key element in its operation (Neale 2000). More precisely, given the central role of repetition with difference, it is impossible to constrain the notion of genre to a totalising, all-powerful formula.

From this understanding of genre as a formula (and film authorship, which is situated at the opposite end of the spectrum), we can deduce a number of reasons for which genre films directed by women – produced within an industry dominated by economic profitability and characterised by a supposedly predictable, conservative aesthetic with 'little artistry' – is an area that has barely been visited by feminist criticism until now. In its first stage, feminist film theory almost never identified itself with genre theory, or auteurism, but focused above all on radical criticism of Hollywood fictions, drawing on textually orientated concepts such as ideological interpellation and subjectivity.

The association of film genres with the 'bad dream factory', or a pedlar of ideologically contaminated fantasies (bourgeois, capitalist, patriarchal), orientated towards mass consumption (Gaines 2011: 106), predominated in film studies of the 1970s and 1980s, inspired in large part by psychoanalysis and Althusser's notion of ideology:[9]

> Here, the dreams we dreamed in the dark theatre were never our own, and they turned against us even as we claimed them as deeply personal secret wishes. [. . .] These wishes were always 'hegemonic fantasies', dreams that, although they seemed to be ours alone, actually served our masters, whether those masters were the husbands of traditional wives or the owners of the means of production. (Gaines 2011: 106)

This perspective expresses, implicitly or explicitly, a series of assumptions about film genres, which, in a nutshell, are conceived of as a series of formulas that support existing power structures and patriarchal society. Hollywood is responsible for producing entertainment products which serve such reactionary ends, according to the negative pronouncements of the Frankfurt School. However, Jane Gaines challenges this view, recuperating the concept of hope as theorised by Ernst Bloch – another Frankfurt theorist who remained in the shadow of Adorno and Horkheimer. The latter thinkers are regularly quoted in studies on the entertainment industry, which, throughout the decades, revitalised the 'bad factory' metaphor. Bloch's theory, in turn, is that of a '*good dream-factory*', 'theory of the longing for change, for world-transforming revolution, and therefore [. . .] a theory *for* the mass audience' (Gaines 2011: 107, 110 [emphasis in original]). Instead of understanding the utopian as regressive nostalgia – as postmodernist critics, such as Fredric Jameson (1979), later did – Bloch foregrounded the forward movement of hope, which is 'precise and action-oriented' (Gaines 2011: 107). Gaines raises questions about the utility of this concept as a tool of analysis:

> What would it mean to put 'hope' back into the model of analysis, back into critical theory? Since this question sounds a bit naïve as phrased, let us ask if we could substitute 'hope' for 'politics', coming closer to Bloch's meaning. [. . .] Bloch's 'world-improving dream' is not exclusively about social upheaval but about upheaval in the accompanying realm of fantasy. (2011: 112)[10]

This postulate resonates with Claire Johnston's insistence that politics accompanies pleasure in the entertainment film. If fantasy, as Judith Butler argues, 'is what allows us to imagine ourselves and others otherwise' (2004a: 29), then the benefits of exploring feminist potentialities involved in its realm are multiple.

Genre theory, in particular, has much to offer feminist criticism, because it constitutes an alternative to individualist notions of the traditional auteur positioned as the only begetter of this dream-making and because it expresses the tensions of inheritance versus originality. The 'auteur versus genre' approach has been significantly revisited by film theory inspired by De Saussure's linguistic structuralism and the works of Vladimir Propp and Claude Lévi-Strauss. Following the former's distinction between *langue* (the structure of language) and *parole* (the individual speech act), a number of critics (Buscombe 1970; Kitses 1969; Wright 1975, among others) demonstrated that genre operates as a structure, or a myth, based on a set of binary oppositions, and that films can be seen as individual speech acts, whose meaning depends precisely on these structuring oppositions.

While, at first sight, the notion of auteur moves into the background in these publications – given that linguistically oriented scholars seem to have little interest in films as the expression of the creative will of individual auteurs – it certainly does not disappear, and its relationship with genre becomes even more intricate.[11] Robert Stam refers to this framework as *auteur-structuralism*, which 'saw the individual author as the orchestrator of trans-individual codes (myth, iconography, locales)'. He adds that *auteur-structuralists*

> highlighted the idea of an auteur as a critical construct rather than a flesh-and-blood person. They looked for hidden structuring oppositions which subtended the thematic leitmotifs and recurrent stylistic figures typical of certain directors as the key to their deeper meaning. (2000a: 123)

Interestingly, in contrast to French critics, for scholars such as Kitses auteurs were not obliged to rebel against genre. Genre was not considered 'an empty vessel breathed into by the film-maker [but] a vital structure through which flow a myriad of themes and concepts' (Kitses 1969: 26). Therefore, instead of seeing genres simply as formulaic narratives against which filmmakers defined their authorial personality, Kitses considered them a repertoire of cultural materials on which the filmmakers drew, and something which was as limiting as potentially enabling. Although often perceived as outdated,[12] these considerations raise compelling questions about the issue of subversion and the gendered aspects of authorial relation to genre and mass culture in a wider sense.

Subversion

The model of artist as genius, who questions the status quo and swims against the ideological currents of popular culture, is a gendered concept – clearly marked as masculine – as numerous scholars have shown (Huyssen 1986;

Modleski 1998). Jim Hillier demonstrates (1993: 129) that the language used to talk about directors and their filmmaking practices finds its metaphors in spheres which are traditionally seen as masculine, such as sport or the Far West. In Hollywood, successful films are often talked of as home runs, and 'maverick director' is a phrase used to denote artists who rebel against the system. Leslie Felperin traces the origins of this phrase to a Texas rancher named Sam Maverick, who was famous because he refused to mark his animals. Felperin observes that this term – which was applied to filmmakers such as Sam Fuller or Robert Altman, but never to a female director – denotes 'manly whiff of tobacco, whisky and the dusty road' (in R. Williams 2001: 29), an image that places us directly inside the mythology of the Western.

The invariably 'masculine' character of the auteur's personality and, implicitly, the film genres in which this personality can fully express itself, are thrown into relief in this extract from an editorial in the magazine *Movie* (1962), which dedicated a special issue to the work of Howard Hawks:

> When one talks about the heroes of *Red River*, or *Rio Bravo*, or *Hatari!* one is talking about Hawks himself. The professionalism of his heroes is shared by the director. They get on with the job without any unnecessary nonsense. So does Hawks. He can say what he wants to through actions, because his is a cinema of action. No need, then, to start playing hide-and-seek with the camera, which is there to capture the actions, not to interpret them. Hawks uses his camera simply to do a job, just as his heroes would use a gun or a lasso [. . .]. He communicates very directly through his personality. Finally everything that can be said in presenting Hawks boils down to one simple statement: here is a man. (Andrew 1962: 7)

Although Hawks worked across many film genres – for example, in comedies such as *Gentlemen Prefer Blondes* (1953) and *His Girl Friday* (1940) – the editors emphasise his status as an action director, which ties in well with the requirement for a director-author to possess a strong and individual personality, marked by values such as 'vigour', 'simplicity' and 'sincerity'. Yvonne Tasker, in her analysis of the editorial, elucidates that 'camera, gun, and lasso are drawn together in a notion of the right tools for the right purpose, each without fussiness or frills' (2010: 220). Characteristics that culturally codify 'a true man' and 'a true auteur' are thrown into the same frame of reference. Importantly, the quotation also displays certain assumptions with regards to acceptable 'auteur' genres, which, unsurprisingly, tend to be culturally codified as masculine, such as the Western or action movie.

It has been widely demonstrated that in the mythology of the Far West, women have a more 'maternal' or 'civilising' function. In the same way that the maverick must escape from civilisation – symbolised by 'feminine' values like home, family or domesticity – in order to maintain his 'outsider' status, the maverick-auteur must struggle against the limitations of the big studios who try to domesticate him and subjugate his individual talents. The Hollywood system tends to be conceived of as a threatening form of mass culture, a concept which has been associated with femininity. In 'Mass Culture as Woman' (1986) Andreas Huyssen famously traces the concurrence between massification and commercialisation of literature in the late nineteenth century and the increased visibility of the female public, showing how popular culture was discursively feminised in opposition to the more 'authentic' modernist art, which was marked as masculine. Male fear of the masses became inextricably linked to male fear of women, which, for Huyssen, resulted in 'the persistent gendering as feminine of that which is devalued' (1986: 53). As he asserts, modernism, permeated by patriarchal thought and misogyny, positions itself against bourgeois values and presupposes that the work of art should be experimental, that it should be the expression of an individual mind as opposed to a collective, and that it should remain separate from the feminine spheres of mass culture and daily life. Huyssen analyses the theories of Clement Greenberg and Theodor Adorno, concluding that 'for both critics, mass culture remains the other of modernism, the spectre that haunts it, the threat against which high art has to shore up its terrain' (1986: 56).

If we apply these ideas to genre cinema, it is not surprising that, in order to be considered a true auteur, a filmmaker should rewrite generic conventions and, above all, include a 'personal signature' in his work, as set forth by Andrew Sarris. The metaphors Sarris uses are particularly revelatory: he employs the word 'forest' to refer to Hollywood, which connotes conformity and repetition rather than diversity and variation. According to Sarris, the directors can be compared with trees, and the true auteurs with 'the topmost trees' (1976: 240): 'The auteur theory values the personality of a director precisely because of the barriers to its expression. It is as if a few brave spirits managed to overcome the gravitational pull of the mass of movies' (1976: 247). Sarris simultaneously rebukes the so-called 'forest critics' (as opposed to 'tree critics') for rejecting Hollywood filmmakers and for not allowing the possibility that some directors can create great works of art within the limitations of the system:

> The forest critic cannot admit even to himself that he is beguiled by the same vulgarity his mother enjoys in the Bronx. He conceals his shame with such cultural defence mechanisms as pop, camp, and trivia, but he continues to sneak into movie houses like a man of substance visiting a painted woman. (1976: 241)

His commentary points towards the feminisation – and possible racialisation – of popular culture, as it is the 'mothers of the Bronx' who openly enjoy

Hollywood products. In this light, despite its revisionist nature, Sarris's auteur theory shows itself to be a hostile reaction against popular culture, discursively embedded with femininity. True auteurs who work within generic conventions do not produce films that are simply entertaining or popular, but ones which continue to question, challenge or subvert these rules, opposing the system like fearless cowboys, persistently displaying their strong personality and determination to rebel against mass culture and impose their interpretation on commercial, generic products.

If a director is skilled enough, he can even transform 'prohibited' genres like melodrama and romance into something more valuable than mere products for 'weepy' women. This was the case with Douglas Sirk, who (supposedly) distanced the effects of the 'feminising' aspects of emotion and dignified melodrama through 'ironising devices, deployed to undercut what are described as the hollow sentimentalities derived from a feminised consumerist culture' (Gledhill 2011: 236). According to Barbara Klinger, he was considered a 'progressive auteur', because he apparently rewrote the generic conventions in order to question the values of a society obsessed with consumption. For example, it was argued that his use of mise-en-scène was strategic, as it enabled him to subvert the meanings of a film and critique bourgeois ideology. Working within the constraints of what were seen as the deeply conservative narrative and formulaic generic conventions of the woman's film, the auteur managed to introduce 'art' into mass culture codified as feminine, incorporating a rationalisation or even 'masculine' condemnation (Klinger 1994: 1–35). Klinger posits theoretical problems arising from such a designation of texts or auteurs as progressive, challenging this type of 'rupture criticism' that praises films according to how they adhere to or depart from dominant expressions of ideology. She argues that the critical investment in designating 'counter-cinema' or 'progressive cinema' is based on restricted formulations of what constitutes 'classic' textuality, or classical Hollywood cinema, against which the progressive practice tends to be defined.

The 'progressive authorship' within 'female' forms is markedly gendered, as it rarely applies to women's film practice in scholarly writings and critical discourses. While a man uses the 'reactionary' forms to his own subversive ends, if a woman creates within genres considered as 'female', she cannot be more than a (re)producer of standardised formulas (as I will show in Chapter 6 on Nancy Meyers). This discourse of de-authorisation also affects women's literary authorship in the neoliberal context, as argued by Nattie Golubov. Although, as Golubov demonstrates, the 'masses' are probably less threatening than in the nineteenth century, the claim that an increased visibility of women has mitigated the association between mass culture and femininity seems too precipitated (2015: 37). Golubov shows that in the case of acclaimed writers (and some Nobel Prize winners) such as Doris Lessing, Toni Morrison, Nadine

Gordimer, Wisława Szymborska, Herta Müller and Alice Munro, in addition to female-authored popular genre texts such as *The Hunger Games*, critics tend to dismiss both these works and their authors, because, 'despite their commercial success among predominantly female readers, this is a "feminine" literature, a simple "trash" like *Fifty Shades of Grey* or *Twilight*' (2015: 38). Golubov's analysis of the figure of the woman writer as a celebrity, as merchandise in cultural, transnational industries, is illuminating, as it explores the dichotomy implicit in Roland Barthes's work – between a bourgeois writer and a modernist writer – which has become particularly problematic for feminist criticism, as it links women with mass culture, passivity, consumerism and reproduction, rather than artistic creation.

In this framework, women's authorship, especially in popular forms codified as 'female', points to a complex terrain, that traces a correlation between their creativity (or lack of thereof) and the consuming/viewing practices of the presumed female audience, associated with deficient taste levels; this is a new facet of an old idea that devalues women as writers or readers: they are incapable of writing or reading real literature and 'naturally' inclined to 'low' forms, which are, furthermore, the ones which tend to be highly lucrative. Isabel Clúa observes in her examination of the discursive circulation of *Twilight* (2008) that this cliché is common place in both misogynist attacks and some of the feminist responses to this type of literature (2011: 38).[13]

Indeed, the roles available to women in relation to artistic processes are that of passive and voracious consumers, almost never auteurs. The language that devalues their incursion into popular culture, whether as filmmakers or fans, deserves closer attention. Richard Dyer shows how the terms related with pastiche – which bears many affinities with the workings of genre itself, for 'to be aware of a work as being of a particular genre is perforce to be aware of it as an imitation of an imitation' (2007: 4) – are predominantly of culinary derivation: 'Given pastiche's low cultural status it belongs with terms from the predominantly feminine arena of domestic practice rather than the rather more masculine one of sexual prowess' (2007: 5). The word pastiche comes from the Italian 'pasticcio' and is used to mean a pie, which 'mixes things together such that the identities of the different ingredients remain largely intact, albeit modified by their interaction and by being eaten all together' (2007: 9–10). A number of other words used in the same way as pastiche also have culinary and domestic meanings: mélange, mishmash, patchwork, cannibal art, just to give a few examples (2007: 9). Although, as I will show in Chapters 5 and 6, these metaphors particularly affect 'female' genres, they can occasionally also relate to the nominally 'male' forms – for example, to qualify non-American Westerns, such as spaghetti Westerns, Sauerkraut, Paella, Camembert, Chop Suey, Borsch and Curry Westerns, or even Hollywood Westerns, which used to be dubbed 'oaters' (Fraylin in Dyer 2007: 102). Instead of rejecting these food terms, Dyer reclaims them for political ends, because they 'suggest a much more inclusive aesthetics'; 'they involve skill and labour, savouring and satiation' (2007: 5).

This model of art based on imitation or repetition of pre-existing materials raises suggestive questions about subversion and authorship in female directors whose work is inscribed within popular genres. If we define genre not as a formula but as a process or shared space of change and negotiation, whose strength lies in the reiteration of certain elements and in the play with the expectations of the public, what kind of figurations of authorship could we begin to reflect on? As Klinger indicates (1986), the disturbance is already written into the Hollywood system (with the very genre that regulates this process), and any analysis which ignores it risks slipping back into a series of simplifications and reductions.

It is in response to these concerns that Jane Gaines, in her text 'Genius of Genre and the Ingenuity of Women', significantly revisits the assumptions that cement the binomial author-genre. In her previous works, Gaines had already put forth a radical criticism of the concept of author – for example, in her essay 'Of Cabbages and Authorship', which, she divulges, she originally conceived of as 'Disbelieving in Authors', making reference to Dyer:

> If believing in authorship (in film) means believing that only one person makes a film, that that person is the director, that the film expresses his/her inner personality, that this can be understood apart from the industrial circumstances and semiotic codes within which it is made, then I have never believed in authorship. (Dyer cited in Gaines 2002)

Gaines, the founder of the Women Film Pioneers Project – which is a project that at first glance is based on the notion of traditional authorship – seems to contradict herself when she proclaims that she is a 'confirmed anti-auteurist' (2002: loc. 1864). Without abandoning the feminist commitment to champion innovative women as vehicles of historical restitution, Gaines distances herself completely from the romantic notion of individual authorship. At the same time, she raises an important issue: when a female director is said to 'author' a genre film, does she 'transcend' the mould in the same way as the male auteur is said to do in Hollywood? (2012: 16). She then she asks a further question: is the genre subversive, or is it the author? (2012: 22).

Feminist film theory has never resolved the confusion between the textual critique performed by the auteur and so-called 'auto-critique', performed by the film, as Gaines demonstrates by looking at a number of examples from the history of cinema (2012: 21).[14] She links this confusion with the preponderance of traditional definitions of genre as a collection of negative restrictions on artists, whose artistic expression is supposedly constrained by a series of conventions. When the auteur encounters a genre, they are expected to 'transcend' its formal and industrial dictates (2012: 19).

Forty years ago, Janet Bergstrom already argued in relation to 'progressive' readings of Dorothy Arzner's work that 'gaps, fissures, ruptures' are integral to the operation of classical style (1979: 27). Klinger (1986), on the other hand, questioned the notion of the 'progressive' Hollywood genre, scrutinising various utopian readings of film noir, 1950s melodrama, exploitation films and 1970s horror films – genres which supposedly subvert the system 'from within'. Some of the features of 'progressive genre' include: a pessimistic worldview, a narrative structure emphasising ideological contradiction and the refusal of narrative closure, as well as stylistic self-consciousness as opposed to Hollywood's typical realistic illusionism (1986: 80–3). As she argues, rupture, irony and excess have always been constitutive features of the classical Hollywood genre. The question of generic/systemic evolution and of genre's relation to classical narrative is also posed by Dyer (2007) in his discussion of the Western. In interrogating invention and self-awareness as defining features of 'progressive' texts, Dyer examines André Bazin's much cited analysis of 'superwesterns' like *Shane* (George Stevens, 1953), in which Bazin assumed that in such films there was 'something extra to the Western which was not there in its original state of innocence' and in doing so, he evoked 'a very common trope of genre criticism, the positing of an age [...] when a given genre existed in a pure, uninflected form' (Dyer 2007: 118). But, as Dyer states, bar some early examples, today 'all Westerns know they are Westerns, [and they] are in this sense self-aware' (2007: 118).[15]

Generic repetition and the expectation of the public – two key categories for reflecting about genre – open up new interpretive trajectories in thinking about films directed by women. While the majority of previous theories focused on similarity as a main feature of genre (which, as I have indicated, converted it into something inherently static), Gaines (2012), following Steve Neale (2000), affirms that genre is best understood as a process. This process is characterised not only by repetition and sameness, but also by difference and change, which are crucial for understanding the way the genre works: not all texts belonging to the same genre are the same, because if this were so, there would not be enough difference to produce viewer pleasure.[16] Difference and invention can be seen, thus, as instances of the system's indispensable operation. Any break from tradition, or its continuation, is firmly entrenched in the Hollywood cinema itself. For Neale, genres operate 'not [...] as forms of textual codifications, but as systems of orientations, expectations and conventions that circulate between industry, text and subject' (1980: 19). This dynamic and processual conception of genre, based on the idea of 'repetition with difference', which holds that the law (of genre) persists thanks to its continuous transgressions, brings us inevitably to Deleuze: 'In every respect, repetition is a transgression.

It puts law into question, it denounces its nominal or general character in favour of a more profound and more artistic reality' (1994: 3).

In her 'generous theory of popular film genres', Gaines also turns to Deleuze, proclaiming:

> Rather than thinking of the rule-boundedness of genre, we are encouraged by this formulation to think of genre as rule-breaking. With transgression, especially after queer theory, increasingly seen as politically productive, we can thus understand genre rules as meant-to-be-broken and genre pleasures as shared historical refeeling, only enhanced by anticipation of echo and imitation. Here lies the very genius of genre. (2012: 19)

Gaines thus proposes to question the traditional 'locus of genius': 'The director and the actors step into the genre which, like a ready-made, takes over and generates the work we have historically designated as "theirs"' (2012: 27). This more dialogical approach to authorship, which opens up multiple potentialities in thinking about women's film practice, shares many commonalities with recent developments in adaptation studies. Once viewed as 'the appropriation of meaning from a prior text' (Andrew 1984: 97), adaptations have more recently been seen, in line with poststructuralist theory, in terms of a more general intertextuality: as 'tissues of anonymous formulae, variations of those formulae, conscious and unconscious quotations, and conflations and inversions of other texts' (Stam 2000b: 64). This view has been particularly productive for reconfiguring women's film authorship, as Shelley Cobb's (2015) recent 'conversational' approach to the practice of adaptation in contemporary films made by women demonstrates. The foregrounding of the metaphor of conversation, instead of transmission, also resonates with Dyer's (2007) take on pastiche, which is 'social and sociable':

> It is social: it always accepts and indicates what is really the case in all cultural production, that it exists by virtue of the forms and frameworks of meaning and affect available to it; it acknowledges itself as being in the realm of the already said. It is also sociable: in acknowledging where it comes from, it is comparable 'to the game of adaptation and half-echoing that goes on all the time in a conversation'. (Bromwich in Dyer 2007: 179)

Dyer's work on pastiche is indicative of a marked shift in genre theory, especially in terms of valorising emotional knowledge, which combines affect and cognition.[17] The pastiche of earlier genre films might 'create a certain kind of world and feeling' (2007: 176) – that is, make us feel as we once did all over again. The pastiche is where our past and our present come together and, crucially, 'the historical feelings' (Gaines 2012: 19), felt historically, are shared, not individual, according to Dyer.

These proposals not only highlight the collective character of cinematic production, overlooked by most auteur theories, but also the active role of the audience, which participates in a cultural negotiation of shared thoughts and feelings. Equally, they help to dismantle the idea that cinema produced by women is (or should be) opposed, or resistant, to a set of monolithic conventions or constructs, often becoming an enemy of feminist criticism: genre cinema, commercial cinema, popular cinema or the Hollywood system. These constructs serve both to locate women's cinema or feminist film on the opposite side of the spectrum and to conceptualise women working within film genres as transgressive, obliged to subvert or negate some of genre conventions. Thus, while in this book I defend the work of female creators in popular forms, within and on the margins of the Hollywood system, recognising the sociopolitical importance of their access to the means of cultural production, I contend that it is imperative to confront the essentialist vision implied in the concept of 'women's cinema', shifting the emphasis from the directors as authors or the text as the origin of meaning towards considerations regarding the wider publicness of cinema's generic worlds – that is, in the words of Teresa de Lauretis, 'who is making films for whom, who is looking and speaking, how, where and to whom' (1987a: 135).

Gaines's propositions – which are evocative, but also radical when compared with other writings on women's film practice – create a series of problems as far as the analytical method is concerned. In attempting to designate a number of female directors as genre auteurs, what would their particularity consist of if we were obliged to question their agent-hood or intentionality with regards to the transgressions that take place, and which – as Gaines seems to suggest – happen not because of them, but due to generic, cultural and historical processes? Or, thinking back to Johnston's ([1975] 2000b) work on Dorothy Arzner, if the discursive disjunctures in her films are not a product of her specific positioning as a female director, then why should it matter whether there are female directors at all? In Nancy Miller's words, in response to Foucault's 'What is an Author'?, in which the French philosopher imagines a world 'without need for an author' (1984: 118–20): 'Only those who have it can play with not having it' (1988: 75). And, as Sue Thornham adds, 'after all, the subject who is dispersed through the "unauthored" text is as universalised a subject as the author who is seen to transcend it' (2012: 28).

Rather than remove the women filmmakers as authors from their position in the genre-author-audience triangle, perhaps it is more useful to underline the culturally constructed nature of their authorial figures and the stories which circulate about them, thus situating them within complex discursive networks in which the creators themselves also have multiple ways of impacting the reception of their works. Mary Harrod neatly observes in her examination of the aesthetics of pastiche in the work of Richard Linklater: 'There is something ostensibly paradoxical about an auteurist study of a practice which, in referring to works by other authors, downplays the significance of the single creative vision' (2010: 22). Rather than 'espousing any notion of the director as transcendental auteur', her method of analysis 'comes closer to a Barthesian relocation of the author in the reader' (2010: 22), focusing on pastiche (and we could easily extend it to genre) as an act of interpretation. The acts of both reading and interpretation encompass not only films, but also authorial images. Indeed, I would suggest that one cannot be read and interpreted without the other. Building on Raymond Williams, Gaines suggests asking not only 'what did this author do to this form?', but 'what did this form do to the author?' (2012: 26). Following on from this question, we could further ask: what did the genre do to the (female) author?

Despite all discussion thus far, it could be argued that this book has slipped into the pre-structuralist 'romantic' discourse of the individual author: a number of female directors work within and against dominant traditions, transcending industrial limits to individually 'author' their films in innovative ways. Without a doubt, this project boasts a degree of utopian thinking and hope in terms of its political vision – in the conception of Bloch (1986), as 'ultimately a practical, a militant emotion, [which] unfurls banners' (Bloch in Gaines 2011: 107) – since one of the main objectives is to reposition female filmmakers as artists *and* skilful 'adapters', who manage to make impactful genre films despite the discrimination and numerous obstacles they encounter in an industry governed by men. Thus, notwithstanding Gaines's (1992) warnings that we must be mindful of 'the tendency to automatically ascribe transgressiveness to films [...] when made by women', I will draw upon a wide range of terms such as 'revision', 'rewriting' and even 'departure', while always taking into account the constant tension between an 'intentional'[18] subversion by the directors and the subversive power which is implicit in generic repetition and the multiple possibilities of reading by the public. In other words, while I claim these filmmakers as auteurs, I also acknowledge the conventional forms they use as 'the locus of genius', praising the 'ingenuity of the narrative and iconographic structure, a structure itself incorporating the director[s] and [their] audience' (Gaines 2012: 17). If the analysed films can be constituted as 'subversive' representations at all, they are not so because of a radical break in form. Building on Neale and Klinger, who recognise disequilibrium and difference as a vital component of the overall system itself, I prefer to see these films as part of an economy of variation rather than rupture.

In a similar way, when I refer to 'traditional', 'conventional' or 'classical' texts, I am aware that these labels involve a certain generalisation and universalisation, which also brings us back to outdated definitions of art, cinema and culture, removing the marks which characterise the diversity of cultural products. These categorisations are employed here as critical tools that serve to detect differences within the repetition – although, undoubtedly, these concepts also exist in critical discourses focusing on the works or their authors, just as they form part of the expectations of the audience and, in this way, play an important role in the dynamic of repetition and difference. Ultimately, instead of making a priori assumptions about subversions in films made by female directors or calling up a series of essences in order to lay bare binary oppositions between 'patriarchal' texts and 'feminist' texts, I will – following the intertextual paradigm of minor cinema outlined previously – pull the examined films into productive tension with the different cultural forms and film traditions. The objective is not to declare women's uses of popular genres as necessarily progressive or subversive – since such claims cannot be proven from textual readings or even audience research (Gledhill 2018: xiv). Gledhill argues, building on Gaines, that

> ideologies are not the endpoint of film genres, but the beginning of their dramas. Their development and where they end is not necessarily controlled from the starting point, but, under the command of a genre's store of re-combinable and re-accentable conventions, they may veer in unanticipated directions, the more so as these provoke the imaginations and ingenuity of the makers. (2018: x)

The chapters that follow will demonstrate that the women filmmakers being studied not only undo genre,[19] but also mobilise its productive potential, reappropriating its fundamental features, repetition and fulfilment – or rupture – of the public's expectations, which offer 'the possibility of generative surprises, twists and new combinations' (Gledhill 2018: xiv). The constant oscillation implicit in the with-against genres dynamic (Gaines 2012), which ranges from denaturalisation, reappropriation, genre mixing and excess, can appear in varied ways and to different degrees in directors who create in diverse industrial contexts. It is not the same thing to work in a big Hollywood studio (Cody and Kusama, Coppola, Meyers) as it is to independently shoot a Western that circulates around international film festivals such as Sundance (Reichardt) or to make a film about the war in Iraq that is mainly financed outside Hollywood, even if it is later distributed by a major studio (Bigelow). For this reason, and as each chapter will detail, I stress the diversity of ways in which women filmmakers create new combinations out of generic materials in a variety of production and reception contexts, analysing the degree of difference in repetition, without converting women's cinema into yet another homogenising, totalising and monolithic construct.

Notes

1. This critique could be readily compared to feminist perspectives on literary and artistic authorships – in particular, in publications that reflect on the conditions under which values associated with creation, such as exceptionality, singularity, individualism, unity, anteriority, authenticity, solitariness and originality, emerge. On the other hand, as Aina Pérez and Meri Torras remind us, we could trace a number of correspondences between these values and a construction of the disembodied subject associated with Platonic and Cartesian traditions (2015: 9).
2. Not surprisingly, women have been awarded Oscars for roles typically considered 'feminine': costume designers, such as Edith Head (who holds the record for most Oscar wins by an individual woman: eight), and editors, such as Thelma Schoonmaker – a frequent collaborator of Martin Scorsese.
3. See also Neale (1981).
4. According to Derrida (1986), no text or discursive instance can escape the generic, since all texts or articulations can be placed in specific contexts, therefore they can be labelled or categorised according to genre definitions.
5. This idea has been questioned by a number of scholars, such as Tudor (1973), Altman (1999) and Neale (2000).
6. See, for example, Robin Wood's study on George A. Romero's *Night of the Living Dead* (1968), praised by the critic for the ways in which the director 'systematically undercuts generic conventions and the expectations they arouse' (Wood 1986: 114–15). Horror film is seen as conventional and predictable, but the presence of the auteur enables the subversion of the formula.
7. See, for example, Cawelti (1976) or Schatz (1981), among others.
8. Wood's text, 'Ideology, Genre, Auteur', was originally published in 1977 in *Film Comment*.
9. This negative perception of genre is also visible in the earlier, so-called sociological strand of feminist criticism, in which Marjorie Rosen's *Popcorn Venus* (1973) and Molly Haskell's *From Reverence to Rape* (1974) are frequently mentioned. The objective of these studies was to denounce stereotypical images of women in Hollywood, associated with the industry produced, formula-based genres. Haskell criticises, for example, the 1940s and 1950s film noir, as it offers extremely 'negative' images of women: it infantilises them, demonises them or converts them into exuberant sexual objects. As an exception to these harmful representations, Haskell considers some examples of the woman's film – in particular, characters interpreted by Katharine Hepburn, Joan Crawford and Barbara Stanwyck, actresses that created strong and independent heroines, and in this way propitiated alternatives to negative models. Following this line of argument, the objective of women's cinema would be to promote 'real' or 'positive' images of women, to influence positively on their audiences and prevent them from adopting the negative models. As many critics have noted, this model is not without problems, such as the issue of referentiality of the 'female types' it analyses, as well as the subjective and highly mutable notion of positive images. Although widely questioned, the 'images of women' paradigm was crucial in establishing the second phase of feminist research on cinema, which shifted its interest from images of women to the gendered nature of film viewing and its ideological implications.
10. While Gaines concludes by urging us to look for the dreams generated beyond Hollywood and the West, she argues that sources of hope can also be found at the heart of the US film industry.
11. Critics such as Kitses or Wollen never rejected the idea of auteur, but rather treated it as one of the codes, and not the point of origin – and these arguments were soon

followed by poststructuralists who famously announced the death of the author (Barthes [1967] 1984), to be replaced by the workings of the text and its relation to ideology and to the subject formation. Michel Foucault's ([1969] 1984) 'What is an Author', in turn, replaces the author as an originator by the author as a variable and complex function of discourse.

12. Similarly to the previous notions of genre as a formula, the concept of structure – that is, the supposition that a body of work can be related because of specific binary opposition – has been dismissed as essentialist. These critics remain obsessed with the search for what Andrew Tudor (1973) has referred to as factor X – whether it is a myth or a deep structure of underlying oppositions – which implies not only identifying genres, but also policing borders between them: deciding which films are *really* Westerns or horror movies, and which are not.
13. In fact, this cliché is perhaps one of the main reasons for the surprising lack of critical interest in feminist scholarship in analysing Meyers's oeuvre, as will be discussed in Chapter 6.
14. For example, Gaines discusses the so-called 'E category', developed by Jean-Louis Comolli and Jean Narbonis (1971), which was used to denote popular films capable of subverting their own ideological schemas. 'In retrospect, one wonders if the methodology of ideological critique, originally developed for popular genre films, was not in this moment gradually and imperceptibly moved into auteur criticism, where it remains today', observes Gaines (2012: 16).
15. However, as Dyer clarifies, most films 'just get on with the job of being Westerns. A few make self-awareness part of their concern' (2007: 118).
16. More recently, Deborah Jermyn has stressed an ongoing overemphasis on formulaic repetition, specifically in the context of the romantic comedy, presumed to bar the genre from making any social comment; she argues: '[L]ike all genres, rom-com had to keep bringing new inflections to bear to avoid becoming stale' (2018: 61).
17. In contrast to Fredric Jameson, who famously dubbed pastiche 'blank parody', a reactionary 'speech in a dead language' (2000: 204), Dyer focuses on its aesthetics potentialities and political progressiveness.
18. As Dyer observes: 'Intention acquired a bad name because it was often used in a strong sense, to refer to the biography or inner life of the artist, in ways that [. . .] are hard to prove [. . .]. However we do not need to throw out all notions of intention just because of such problems' (2007: 3).
19. According to Gledhill, who builds on Raymond Williams, film genres 'cannot be undone, for they are the sites in which [. . .] traditional, dominant and emerging ideas and feelings are called on as materials of dramatic conflict' (2018: xiv).

2. REPEAT TO REMAKE: DIABLO CODY AND KARYN KUSAMA'S *JENNIFER'S BODY*

> This is not an appropriation of dominant culture in order to remain subordinated by its terms, but an appropriation that seeks to make over the terms of domination, a making over which is itself a kind of agency, a power in and as discourse, in and as performance, which repeats in order to remake – and sometimes succeeds.
>
> (Butler 1993: 137)

Although there have been several notable exceptions (Halberstam 1995; Berenstein 1996; Pinedo 1997; Williams 2002; Cherry 2002), theoretical discourse centring on horror film tends to privilege the male gaze and, consequently, the male spectator. The pervasive assumption that women do not derive pleasure from horror films is confirmed in the popular press; despite the growing visibility of female horror fans, the narratives which circulate around them reproduce gender stereotypes, as can be observed in Michelle Orange's article for *The New York Times*:

> And yet recent box office receipts show that women have an even bigger appetite for these films than men. Theories straining to address this particular head scratcher have their work cut out for them: Are female fans of *Saw* ironists? Masochists? Or just *dying to get closer to their dates*? (2009 [emphasis added])

Given this critical landscape, it is perhaps not surprising that horror films authored by women have received so little scholarly attention.[1] If we take into account those directors who have made the most successful horror movies in film history, it may seem true that creativity within this particular genre is dominated almost exclusively by men. However, although historically there may have been few women directing horror films in Hollywood, there have been a considerable number of female screenwriters and other professionals working in this genre – for example, producer and screenwriter Debra Hill, known for *Halloween* (John Carpenter, 1978 and its sequel in 1981, directed by Rick Rosenthal) and *The Fog* (John Carpenter, 2005) – and who, not being considered authors of the films which they co-created, have gone unnoticed in horror film histories. In fact, as Alison Peirse has recently suggested in her call for contributions for a new edited collection *Women Make Horror*, there has been an invisible history of women working in the horror genre since the 1950s.[2] In American horror film, it is worth mentioning Mary Lambert, creator of the very successful *Pet Sematary* (1989) and other perhaps lesser known films such as *The Attic* (2007) or *Urban Legends: Bloody Mary* (2005); Kathryn Bigelow, who directed a horror-Western film about vampires, *Near Dark* (1987); Mary Harron, whose 2000 adaptation of Bret Easton Ellis's novel *American Psycho* has become an enduring cult classic; and Kimberly Peirce, who was in charge of shooting a remake of *Carrie* (2013), released by a major Hollywood studio, Metro-Goldwyn-Mayer. If we look beyond the American context briefly, we discover a number of female horror directors in France, within the so-called cinema of New French Extremity, which includes, among others, filmmakers such as Claire Denis (*Trouble Every Day*, 2001) and Marina de Van (*Dans ma peau*, 2002); in Japan we find, for example, Kei Fujiwara (*Organ*, 1996); and in Italy, Daria Nicolodi, co-writer of the famous *Suspiria* (1977). Specialised publications reveal an endless list of titles, such as *Dead Hooker in a Trunk* (2009) and *American Mary* (2012) by the Soska Sisters (or The Twisted Twins), the slasher film *Slumber Party Massacre* (1982) by Amy Holden Jones and Rita Mae Brown, *Freddy's Dead* (1991) and *Ghost in the Machine* (1993) by Rachel Talalay, *Blood Diner* (1987) by Jackie Kong and *The Office Killer* (1997) by Cindy Sherman, among many others. It is not my intention to offer a panoramic view of women filmmakers who work within horror film conventions. However, it is worth pointing to the current discursive visibility of, and an increasing critical and industrial recognition for, women's genre works; *Babadook* (Jennifer Kent, 2014) and *A Girl Walks Home Alone at Night* (Ana Lily Amirpour, 2014) are more recent examples of this recognition.

While, arguably, in the past few years there has been a significant breakthrough of women horror practitioners in film (and TV),[3] there is still a substantial gap in academic thinking about female filmmakers working in this genre, which urges us to rethink critical and methodological tools deployed by feminist film theory to address the complex relationship between women and horror. This chapter seeks to raise some questions about what is at stake when women directors make horror films in Hollywood, by offering an in-depth analysis of the much-maligned film *Jennifer's Body* (2009), written by Diablo Cody and directed by Karyn Kusama, which – just as its title unequivocally suggests – is thematically centred on the female body. The representation of Megan Fox, who plays the role of Jennifer Check – an eroticised and demonised object of the gaze, as made evident through the film's accompanying marketing material, including posters and trailers – seems to confirm the commonly accepted supposition that this genre acts as a vehicle for violently reinforcing patriarchy. What makes this film a compelling case study for feminist film criticism is the fact that, while the appeal to a male audience was foregrounded in both the marketing strategies and the critical discourses that circulated around the movie – for example, Robert Ebert defined the film as '*Twilight* for boys, with Megan Fox in the Robert Pattinson role'[4] – there has also been a substantial visibilisation of female horror viewing. These marketing strategies, which were very complex, since on the one hand they promoted the film as supposedly addressed to a male adolescent public and on the other as a 'feminist horror movie' for female fans, reveal a number of intriguing discourses on the gendered address of contemporary horror cinema. What is more, it is relevant that *Jennifer's Body* is a result of the collaboration between two women who drew on a genre traditionally codified as 'male', working within a predominantly male industry: the film, released in 2009, was produced by Fox Atomic, which at that time was a production label of the major film studio Twentieth Century Fox. The Cody-Kusama tandem opens up the possibility of inquiring into the problematic notion of collective authorship, as well as drawing attention to different professions in the film industry, given that, atypically, *Jennifer's Body* was marketed not through its director's authorial signature, but rather through its award-winning screenwriter's biographic legend, Diablo Cody. This particular characteristic of the advertising campaign, together with Cody's claims that *Jennifer's Body* is a feminist rewriting of horror cinema, generated a widespread discussion on the representation of violence and women's bodies in this genre and revealed certain assumptions concerning the male/female generic divisions, in particular in relation to women's participation in the mainstream Hollywood industry.

Trojan Horse: Diablo Cody's Commercial Auteurism

As with many other contemporary US filmmakers, Karyn Kusama entered Hollywood through the realm of independent filmmaking. Her breakthrough indie hit, *Girlfight* (2000), about a troubled teenage girl (Michelle Rodriguez) who becomes a boxer, despite the disapproval of both her father and competitors in this male-dominated sport, won her nationwide acclaim and opened up access to big budget productions. Her following project, *Æon Flux* (2005), released by MTV Films, is a science fiction film about a women warrior (Charlize Theron), expert in martial arts, whose mission is to destroy a surveillance station and kill the government's leader. These movies, together with *Jennifer's Body* – a horror flick with two strong female leads (Megan Fox and Amanda Seyfried) – consolidate Kusama's 'genre' pedigree,[5] as well as her interest in tough and resolute female protagonists. Nonetheless, it seems that her background and authorial image were not considered attractive enough for the marketing and promotion of the latter film, as the advertising campaign designed by the studio drew heavily on the public persona of the screenwriter, blogger and journalist Diablo Cody, leaving Kusama in the shadows.

Jennifer's Body was Cody's follow-up to *Juno* (2007), for which she was awarded a Best Original Screenplay Oscar in 2008. The insistent references to *Juno* in marketing for *Jennifer's Body*, underscored in film posters,[6] press kits, interviews and promotional articles – as an obvious attempt to repeat the box office success of Cody's previous film – highlighted her distinctive style traits and authorial signature: '[A]n offbeat writing voice marked by whip-smart dialogue and pop-culture savvy', according to the production notes. The comparison between *Jennifer's Body* and *Juno* – a coming-of-age drama-comedy about a teenager's unplanned pregnancy, which, again in the production notes for the former, was described as 'a warm, sweet, life-affirming movie' – is significant for another reason: the way in which these two pictures were set against each other seems to illustrate – and, at the same time, reproduce – traditional divisions between genres perceived as 'female' and 'male', which, in turn, accentuates the 'exceptional' nature of women working within the horror film conventions.

One of the marketing strategies was to frame *Jennifer's Body*, and the array of possible genre pleasures it offers, within the themes of revenge, empowerment and sexual liberation for girls. Film producer Jason Reitman said that right from the outset they wanted to hire a female director, so that the film would take horror in a 'new' direction, given that it would be 'told from a female point of view, starring women, and written and directed by women'. He explained what this female perspective might look like: 'The jock gets it. The sweet nerd gets it. The Goth kid gets it. This may just be Diablo's revenge on every type of boy she's ever met. If *Juno* is the film that speaks to her need for love, *Jennifer's Body* is the film that speaks to her need for revenge'.[7] Reitman's comments bring to mind the tradition of 'rape-revenge film' – a subgenre of exploitation cinema particularly popular in the 1970s, whose plot was based on the bloody revenge carried out by a female rape survivor.[8] This gesture, together with Cody's and Kusama's background as filmmakers interested in telling 'women's stories', apparently cements the 'feminist' status of *Jennifer's Body*.

Cody and Kusama themselves also repeatedly described their film as a feminist subversion of the horror genre, triggering an arduous debate on what it means for a film to be 'feminist', and also if mainstream horror cinema is the 'proper' space in which to undermine traditional gender roles. Diablo Cody, the more frequent spokesperson in the Cody-Kusama duo, emphasised that they had to struggle constantly with the studio producers, who, by means of test screenings, exercised considerable power over the film's content:

> Ordinarily, when you make a movie you have these test screenings, which are horrible. You go to some large shopping mall cinema in Huntington Beach, California, they bring in a bunch of kids, put them in the front [...] and at the end of the movie they fill out these little sheets. [...] I kept a lot of the score sheets because they had these incredibly articulate criticisms going on, like one said, 'Need more bewbs.' [...] The studio's looking at these going, 'We need more boobs, lady.' (in Guillen 2010)

The tensions between Cody and Kusama's creative vision and the commercial criteria of Hollywood film production are brought to light in their numerous statements in the popular press, in which the filmmakers highlight their attempts to rescue the 'subversive' content of the film. Cody confessed that 'they picked their battles', and despite admitting that they wish they had fought harder for certain scenes to be retained, 'just for fun', on the whole they were able to plead their case effectively and maintain a level of control over the content of the film (in Fine 2009). Another bone of contention was the issue of film promotion. Kusama complained on many occasions about the male-centred marketing strategies employed by Fox Atomic, saying: 'I don't know if selling the film as a straight horror film and selling it primarily to boys is really going to do any of us any favours, frankly' (in Miller 2009).[9] Cody, in turn, explained in another interview: 'We were trying to say stuff about body image and sexuality, about female friendships, about relationships. We tried to shove all our weird feminist ideals in there but package them in a glossy commercial way' (in Powers 2009).

The responses to these claims, which emanated mainly from online media, film critics, popular press and both professional and recreational blogs, were largely hostile, most of them contesting the feminist potential of the film. Notably, the issue of representation of the monstrous female body prevailed in almost all the negative reviews of the film. According to Heidi Martinuzzi – horror fan, writer and co-founder of *Pretty/Scary*, the website for women in horror – 'the main character is seducing men, and killing them. [...] It's a classic example of men not being able to trust women or the vagina. It's a modern adaptation of a succubus or a siren' (2009). Martinuzzi's reading of the film, which coincides with a great number of interpretations of *Jennifer's*

Body, presupposes that the protagonist's abjection and representation as monstrous can never be politically 'progressive', being necessarily a product, as well as a tool, of patriarchal misogynist discourse; codifying female sexuality as evil utterly erases Cody's and Kusama's 'feminist' intentions, which were supposed to distinguish their work, ideologically and probably commercially as well, from other similar productions. According to Martinuzzi:

> A film like *Jennifer's Body*, or *Tamara*, or *All the Boys Love Mandy Lane*, or *Teeth*, or *Species*, or *Ginger Snaps*, where women's sexuality is their only asset and usually represents EVIL, or at the least their only means of surviving in a male world, is a completely ANTI-feminist film. (2009)

Among the female fans of horror cinema (journalists, bloggers, non-professional viewers and so on), there were several voices which enthusiastically defended the film, interpreting Jennifer's monstrous behaviour as radically challenging the patriarchal order. Those viewers entered the debate regarding the 'feminist status' of *Jennifer's Body* resorting primarily to girl power slogans,[10] which – if we adopt Yvonne Tasker's and Diane Negra's (2007) definitions – would correspond to a 'postfeminist' sensibility, rather than a 'feminist' rewriting.[11] One of the film's fans, Ms Harker, contributed to this dispute as such:

> The use of sexuality by women should no longer be seen as a feminist failing but as a victory that women are comfortable within their skin. If they happen to chop a few heads of, eat some high school boys and kick alien arse then all the better! (in Colangelo 2009)[12]

The controversies around the feminist, anti-feminist or even postfeminist label of *Jennifer's Body* reveal complex processes of negotiation concerning horror film and its ability to address gender politics. Ben Kooyman (2012) observes in his article on the reception of *Hostel Part II* and *Jennifer's Body* that the negative responses to the latter – in most cases, openly aggressive and hostile – were partly influenced by the enduring prejudice against horror films, and by the fact that Diablo Cody, in speaking about feminism, was speaking 'on behalf of a generalized, unified and coherent entity that most feminists would argue does not actually exist' (2012: 181). There are multiple ways of understanding feminism, as well as infinite interpretations of it in the popular press, which additionally do not necessarily correspond to academic feminisms; as a result, it should not come as a surprise that Jennifer's monstrous femininity might be read in completely different ways, as fanfiction author Scarlet Scribe astutely puts it:

Feminist A might say, 'Jennifer has to rely on men for her continued well-being and becomes ugly when she doesn't. How can a woman relying upon a man be construed as feminist?' Feminist B might say, 'Jennifer eats boys to remain the woman she wants to be. It's about time a woman uses a man for *her* purposes. How can that not be feminist?' (2009 [emphasis in original])

Kooyman is right when he argues that the cliché that horror films are made purely for and by men in order to indulge sadistic, voyeuristic fantasies against women (and therefore have little social value) persists in debates regarding this genre, although some feminist critics – for example, Carol J. Clover (1992) and Barbara Creed (1993) – have questioned this assumption. This prejudice might be one of the main reasons why horror films authored by women create such a public disturbance, and at the same time why they have received so little theoretical attention from feminist film criticism.

The hostile, gendered responses to women directing horror films have a long history. The critical discourses that circulate around women who direct big budget horror films tend to emphasise the exceptional – and often 'morbid' – nature of both their tastes and their film practice. This was apparent, for instance, in the critical reception of Mary Harron's *American Psycho* (2000),[13] overlaid with moral panic about the literal representation of torture and death, or almost all of Jennifer Lynch's films. The latter was, as many press articles expressed it, 'lynched' for her film *Boxing Helena* (1993), due to the scenes involving its female protagonist's mutilation and torture. While her subsequent projects, like *Surveillance* (2008) and *Chained* (2012), won her critical recognition – she was the first woman filmmaker to win the Best Director Award at the New York City Horror Festival – at the same time, both attracted accusations of nepotism (it was claimed that she became famous thanks to her father, David Lynch) and even more sexist attacks rooted in the violence represented in her films (see Paszkiewicz 2018).

As I have argued elsewhere (2018: 50), in addressing women's film authorship in genre productions, it is necessary to take into consideration a number of factors: industrial pressure and institutional discrimination, the commerce of auteurism and the public profiles of women filmmakers, the collective nature of film production, film reception and the discursive circulation of women's cinema in a wider sense. In the case of contemporary horror cinema in particular, it might be useful to mention other contextual factors, such as those addressed by Pamela Craig and Martin Fradley (2010: 83): the perceived feminisation of contemporary horror cinema, the dismissal of youth-oriented films and 'their allegedly wholesale escapist allure' and the (gendered) allusion to the generic terrain of the soap opera contained in the recent manifestations of the horror genre, among others.

The public persona of screenwriter Diablo Cody, who in the critical discourses on *Jennifer's Body* was more frequently conceptualised as an auteur of the film than Kusama, is highly relevant to the discussion of the movie, as it profoundly affected its reception, generating widespread uproar when she claimed that the film was feminist. It is necessary to contextualise these claims within Diablo Cody's broader self-promotional activities, taking into account, for example, the recurrent backlash against her celebrity persona, especially in reference to her exotic-dancing past, as well as discourses surrounding her triumph at the Academy Award ceremony in 2008 when she won an Oscar for *Juno* (2007). Articles with titles such as 'From Stripper to Screenwriting Star' (Angelo 2011) and 'From Ex-Stripper to A-Lister' (Valby 2007) have been plentiful.[14] In her self-promotional activities and in the ways in which she attempted to frame audience reception of *Jennifer's Body* via publicity and interviews, she epitomises the commerce of auteurism, drawing on Timothy Corrigan's notion, who in his *Cinema Without Walls* showed how the auteur's 'promoted biography can pre-empt most textual receptions of a movie' (1991: 105).

Indeed, the construction of Diablo Cody's authorship is not limited to posters, production notes or other more conventional marketing practices carried out by film producers and distributors. The screenwriter embodies 'auteur as *commercial* strategy for organising audience reception' and clearly participates in 'a commercial performance of *the business of being an auteur*' (Corrigan 1991: 103, 104 [emphasis in original]). Cody, similarly to other contemporary women filmmakers, like Sofia Coppola or Lena Dunham, is well aware of the importance of creating her public image and has embraced the spotlight, actively cultivating her authorial figure through a variety of self-authorising strategies: interviews, promotional appearances, DVD audio commentaries, her Myspace and Twitter accounts and several blogs that she writes (and frequently abandons). Her memoir, *Candy Girl: A Year in the Life of an Unlikely Stripper* (2006), in which she chronicles her experience as an exotic dancer, has accrued her as many detractors as supporters, but has also undoubtedly helped her to launch a career in Hollywood. Drawing on Cody's growing popularity, her manager, Mason Novick, encouraged her to write her first screenplay, which resulted in the creation of *Juno*. After its success at the Oscars, Cody became one of the most renowned screenwriters in Hollywood; following *Juno*, she worked on *Jennifer's Body* (2009) and *Young Adult* (2011), directed *Paradise* (2013) and was also the creator, an executive producer and writer on the award-winning TV series *The United States of Tara* (2009–11). According to the journalist Erin Carlson, after *Juno* Cody started to dominate

> a tiny little niche of Hollywood stardom: the celebrity writer. Not even wordsmith heavies Paul Haggis, Wes Anderson or Charlie Kaufman have

stood in a spotlight so bright – but then, none of them had the allure of a pole-dancing past, punkish attitude or surprising smash-hit, Oscar-worthy pregnancy comedy. (2008)

It is noteworthy that in Diablo Cody's biographical legend, dominated by the 'Hollywood Cinderella' and 'ex-stripper' narratives, other traits of her professional life are considerably overshadowed: her ultimately critical attitude towards the sex trade, her position as an activist in the film industry (for example, as a co-founder of the feminist group Fempire, which supports women screenwriters) and her attempts to resist certain gender stereotypes, both in her films and in her personal life. In an interview published in *Bust Magazine* she asserted:

> I'm a 31-year-old feminist in Ugg boots and a T-shirt, so it's funny to me when anyone accuses me of trying to be sexy or cute. [. . .] I'm full-on rocking this post-feminist-academic-stripper attitude because I'm trying to confront, not titillate. (in Soloway 2009: 45)

Of course, these claims should not be isolated from their commercial and self-promotional context. As Kooyman suggests: '[G]iven the maligned status of the horror genre in many critical circles, it is important for film-makers to distinguish their products from others' (2012: 185).

Taking into account the industrial and economic dimension of filmmaking in Hollywood might help to steer the conversation away from a somewhat simplistic romanticising of Cody's biographical legend as a feminist auteur who is forced to wrestle with the cut-throat film industry. This critical repositioning is important for many reasons. First, because every reference to film authorship carries the weight of several centuries of literary and art historical criticism and yet, despite this fact, it has often been taken up too uncritically (Gaines 2012). Indeed, any account of film authorship must take into consideration the revisions of the *politique des auteurs* from structuralist and post-structuralist perspectives, as well as four decades of evolving feminist film criticism that seeks to rewrite existing models of auteurism, or even to call into question the very concept of the auteur, often considered highly restricting for women's film practice (Martin 2008). And second, because the notion of film auteurs who work within the Hollywood system and rebel against generic formats imposed by the industry presupposes that genres are fixed and static moulds, a supposition already questioned in Chapter 1. Therefore, rather than thinking about Diablo Cody as a subversive auteur, who 'transcends' the formal dictates of the industrial genre, I propose to look at how she activates its generative force in the service of women's stories, without diminishing the importance of her own agent-hood in response to the genre's historical developments.

Cody herself has often expressed her fascination with the generative force of horror film, recognising a 'subversive' potential already implicit in the work of genre, as, for example, in the figure of the Final Girl:

> I grew up on horror movies, especially those classic '80s horror movies with teenagers in peril, adults who don't listen, women who are either incredibly heroic or incredibly sexy or both. You'll notice that the last person standing in a horror movie is typically female, which is an interesting part of the genre. I didn't want to write a modern horror movie. I wanted to write a classic horror movie. I wanted the whole vibe to be 1983, and I think we pulled that off. (in Buhrmester 2009)

In many aspects, Cody's authorial intention is to actually *go with genre*, rather than *go against it*, to use the evocative terms of Jane Gaines (2012) in her reflection on genre and authorship in Alice Guy-Blaché's two-minute melodrama, *The New Love and The Old* (1912), in which Gaines argues against the notion of genre understood as a negative restriction on artists. Insisting on the productive dimension of generic repetition and on constant cultural reconfiguration, Gaines writes: 'I suggest – against genre as cramping authorial style – that we start with the social over the individual and conceive innovation as anticipated and "contained within" the generic, that is, in the sense of already there, already-in-form' (2012: 26). Thinking back to Alison Butler's notion of 'minor cinema', Cody's and Kusama's (collective) authorship is better understood as a continuous negotiation with inherently unstable and generative forms, rather than a romantic rebellion against industrially imposed conventions. Writing in a major language – for example, in the language of genre – may veer in unanticipated directions, providing new outcomes and new combinations. However, this task, as I will show later, can lead to a number of obstacles, which the screenwriter seems to be perfectly aware of:

> The tricky thing is if you're going to subvert those tropes [genre and gender], they have to be there [...]. We were constantly bobbing and weaving. Karyn and I talk about the film as a kind of Trojan horse. We wanted to package our beliefs in a way that's appealing to a mainstream audience. (in Orange 2009)

Cody recognises here that representing misogyny and objectification of the female body in order to critique them might not be enough and, if we look at the discursive circulation of the film, the good intentions were, indeed, inadequate for many viewers. As I will show in the following section, the representation of violence and the excessive display of Megan Fox's body, together with promotional strategies that proclaimed the film as 'feminist', were fiercely contested.

Whose Body?: Gendered Genre Address and Horror Cinema

The media fervour surrounding the representation of Jennifer in Cody and Kusama's film throws into relief the parallel between horror and pornographic cinema – two genres traditionally considered 'low' and which were baptised by Carol Clover (1992: 198) and Linda Williams (1991: 4) as body genres. These genres are characterised by an excessive exhibition of bodies on the screen, 'caught in the grip of intense sensation and emotion' (Williams 1991: 4), which produces powerful effects on the viewers' bodies. According to Williams, who in her influential essay 'Film Bodies: Gender, Genre, and Excess' also includes melodrama in this category,

> pornography is today more often deemed excessive for its violence than for its sex, while horror films are excessive in their displacement of sex onto violence. In contrast, melodramas are deemed excessive for their gender- and sex-linked pathos, for their naked displays of emotion. (1991: 2–3)

Nevertheless, it is not just *any* kind of body that is being exhibited. Body genres are based, according to Williams, on 'the spectacle of a "sexually saturated" *female* body and each offers what many feminist critics would agree to be spectacles of feminine victimization' (1991: 6 [emphasis added]). With this comment Williams underscores not only the centrality of the female body in body genres, but also the widespread assumption that women are necessary victims of pornographic, melodramatic or horror representations, since the image of the ecstatic or tortured woman is seen as a prelude to female victimisation in real life (1991: 6). The scholar problematises this approach by interrogating the status of such corporal excess: 'Are the orgasmic woman of pornography and the tortured woman of horror merely in the service of the sadistic male?' (1991: 5–6). The questions posed by Williams form part of a long-standing debate on the representation of female bodies in popular culture, and on the 'effects' of media images on audiences, which, as Joanne Hollows argues (2000: 21), tends to rely on the paradigm of 'images of women' and, in particular, on the underlying search for 'positive' female characterisation, which has been a constant in the feminist movement from its inception. I insist on the validity of these questions today because, more than twenty-five years after Williams's theorisations, the body which is represented, looked at and, as I have already begun to argue, fiercely debated – the body which, in Williams's terms, is *moved* and is the *moving* one – is still female.

The representation of Jennifer's body in Cody and Kusama's film as a site of negotiation between competing frames of reference – industrial, economical, authorial, spectatorial, among others – deserves closer attention. Perhaps one of the most interesting issues that emerge at the intersection of these frameworks is a tension built around the gendered address of the film, as it played out in the context of production, promotion and critical circulation. Despite the fact that the film was promoted by Cody and Kusama as a feminist revision of horror cinema for women, it is highly doubtful that the intention of the producers, who worked for one of the Hollywood majors, was to exclusively address the female audience. Notably, *Jennifer's Body* was received poorly by critics (at present, it stands at a forty-three per cent on *Rotten Tomatoes* and a forty-seven per cent on *Metacritic*), and it had a lukewarm box office take of $31.5 million worldwide. Writing for *io9* – a blog which focuses on science fiction, fantasy and other related areas – Annalee Newitz (2009) blamed the 'misguided, boy-targeted marketing' as responsible for 'its abysmal box office returns', observing that if the film producers had not failed to recognise the female address of the film, 'they might have had a cult hit on their hands'. In a similar manner, Brandon Gray (2009) from the *Box Office Mojo* – a website widely used within the film industry for tracking box office revenue – pointed out the centrality of Megan Fox in the advertising campaign, associating her with 'a fantasy for males', and expressed his view that the producers 'could have appealed more to females [. . .] through the picture's *Mean Girls* themes or the character played by Amanda Seyfried, who was minimized'. Indeed, a closer look at *Jennifer's Body*'s marketing strategies reveals that the film's advertising focused almost exclusively on Megan Fox's 'to-be-looked-at' celebrity image (and her high-profile *body* of the title), which undoubtedly eclipsed Amanda Seyfried in all of the film posters and other promotional materials, such as trailers, DVD covers and magazine profiles. After gaining a worldwide fame for her role in *Transformers* (Michael Bay, 2007), Fox appeared regularly on the covers of magazines such as *Maxim*, *FHM* (*For Him Magazine*), *GQ* (*Gentlemen's Quarterly*) and *Men's Health*, occupying a privileged position across several lists of the most 'sexy' women in the world. The synopsis of the film included on the back cover of the DVD undeniably plays on this celebrity image:

> Sexy temptress Megan Fox is hotter than hell as Jennifer, a gorgeous, seductive cheerleader who takes evil to a whole new level after she's possessed by a sinister demon. Steamy action and gore galore ensue as the male student body succumbs to Jennifer's insatiable appetite for human flesh.

In addition, as many film critics have remarked, the studio took advantage of the actress's 'confessions' regarding her bisexuality, and heavily marketed the lesbian kissing scene between Fox and Seyfried, together with Fox's line 'I go both ways', which was thought to entice and successfully attract male viewers (Murnane 2009). The analysis of marketing strategies for *Jennifer's Body* shows a set of suppositions in relation to the gender of the viewers and how these discourses imagine and produce the viewers in relation to these traits. The 'feminist/female' perspective of Diablo Cody, often associated with codifying the film as a teen movie about the process of maturation of two female protagonists and, further, with themes of revenge on boys as a source of female empowerment, was constructed as a female address. However, the overuse of the celebrity image of Megan Fox and, in particular, the exhibition of her body and focus on her kiss with Amanda Seyfried, together with genre conventions of horror film, were seen as a male address.

Indisputably, the two trailers for *Jennifer's Body*, as well as posters and DVD covers, were based on the excessive display of Fox's 'sexually saturated' body, which calls into question the 'feminist' label insistently accentuated in a number of interviews and press articles on the film. It may be argued that, against Cody's and Kusama's intentions, the marketing strategies were mainly focused on attracting young heterosexual male viewers as the primary consumers of the film, not on showcasing Jennifer as an agentic sexual being. From the very first images of the trailer, we are privy to Jennifer's naked body, as she swims nude in a lake. The fade shots and the slow pace editing emphasise her position as a desirable object. When she saunters through the school corridors, a series of shots place her in the centre of the frame and progressively fragment her body. The other students are blurred, while Jennifer stands out, due to her brightly coloured clothing and the lighting that illuminates her face. The slow-motion camera and the insistent focus on her body seem to disrupt the narrative flow. If we adopted Laura Mulvey's (1975) theory of visual pleasure, these images, together with the moment when Jennifer unzips her sweater, partially exposing her breast while her face remains out of frame, clearly correspond to fetishistic scopophilia: Jennifer's body is a spectacle, an object of desire that is isolated, displayed and made beautiful – in other words, a fetish offered to the (male) spectators' gaze.

Nevertheless, although Jennifer's body is clearly commodified by means of several filmic codes, a closer analysis of both trailers – the studio-made green band trailer, approved by the Motion Picture of America, and the restricted red band trailer – reveals that the structures of objectifying gaze may generate contradictory readings and address the viewers in multiple ways. One of the fundamental differences between the two videos is the text which appears on the screen. In the green band trailer we read: 'In every school // there's one girl // every girl wants to be friends with // and every guy // would die for'. This version, constructed around the relationship between the two female protagonists – highlighted by the inclusion of more dialogue back and forth between the young women and by editing, which associates Jennifer's monstrosity with her failure to be a loyal friend – clearly situates *Jennifer's Body* in the teen movies genre. Various shots and countershots between protagonists anticipate an obsessive relationship based on desire and hate, which prompts consideration of the film's potential female address.

While in the first trailer there is a greater emphasis on the leading actresses' names, well-known to the adolescent public, in the second one it is the name of the scriptwriter which occupies the privileged position and, moreover, this trailer clearly associates the film with the horror genre. We read: 'From the mind of Diablo Cody // comes a horror movie // like you've never heard before'. This sentence, along with the following lines which appear between the shots of Megan Fox – 'Behind her smile // under her skin // inside her body // lives a demon' – frame the images which display her figure as per horror film conventions, rather than those of the teen film. This version was considered a 'filmmaker's cut' by its creators. They explained: 'We think it captures the comedy and scares of the horror films we grew up on – a kind of nostalgia for when horror films were fun' (in Thompson 2009). Cody and Kusama point here to their intention to 'have fun' with the genre codes. Only this version of the trailer contains a humorous scene in which a mother foists pepper spray on her son, called Rose Panic, as protection against the town's boy-killer. In the background we hear the song 'I Know What Boys Like' by the eighties New Wave rock band The Waitresses, whose provocative lyrics, along with the image of the boy being dragged by a female monster mere moments after confidently assuring his mother of his safety and capability (notably, he claims, because he has started working out on a Bowflex), underlines the ironic distance from gender and horror film clichés. Cody and Kusama's trailer highlights the satiric traits of the movie, promising possible pleasures to the audience familiarised with horror film codes and ready to laugh at its conventions.

The two versions of the film trailer reveal several assumptions in relation to the gendered genre address at the same time as they show that it is necessary to maintain caution when considering marketing strategies as coherent or easily disposed of as tools of the dominant ideology, which reproduces traditional gender norms. Already in the mid-1990s Judith Mayne (1995: 171) warned against the tendency to glorify spectators' interpretative powers as completely free and autonomous agents and, simultaneously, to see films and marketing strategies as seamless narratives that produce a hegemonic, masculine, Oedipal, bourgeois spectator in some versions of reader-response theory and cultural studies. Drawing attention to paradoxes of spectatorship, which emerge from the tension between 'the competing claims of homogeneity (of cinematic apparatus) and heterogeneity (of spectator and therefore of different ways in which an apparatus can be understood)' (1995: 156), Mayne asserts that neither film texts nor promotion tactics can be considered monolithic. Although *Jennifer's Body*'s advertising campaign seems to be based on certain gender binary oppositions, the multiplicity of discourses circulating around the film should be understood as 'negotiation', rather than simply a set of 'hegemonic messages', if we adopt Stuart Hall's (1980) terminology.

As Rhona J. Berenstein (1996) demonstrated in her examination of Hollywood horror films produced in the early 1930s, gender traits are already performed on the level of marketing strategies, which inevitably provide, as well as condition, the possible interpretations of the film. Her study shows that 'male and female spectators were offered a range of publicity, exhibition, and critical discourses that invited them alternately to act in line with traditional gender mores and to act out unconventional gender roles' (1996: 85). Building on Berenstein's compelling work, it can be asserted that the viewers of *Jennifer's Body* were also offered a range of critical and promotional discourses that invited them to adopt or reject conventional gender roles. In this ongoing negotiation over the film's meanings, some spectators, perhaps inevitably, confirm traditional suppositions about the feminine/masculine pleasures division, participating thus in discourses on the gendered genre address. For instance, Jenni Miller, writing for *MTV Movies Blog*, defends the female address of *Jennifer's Body*:

> It's strong enough for a man, but made for a woman [. . .]. Sure, there's gore aplenty, and Megan flaunts her tight tummy in what seems like every scene, but the *real* story is about the dynamic between her character and Seyfried's character, Needy. The last snack on Jennifer's list is Needy's sweet boyfriend Chip, played by Johnny Simmons. So typical of high school girls, am I right? (2009 [emphasis added])

A clear demarcation between these two audiences and, implicitly, between these two genres (horror film and teen comedy-drama) is evident here: the *real* story, centred on the relationship between girls, is codified as female address. In the same vein, Scarlet Scribe explains why the detractors of the film did not actually understand it, substantiating the notion that women who enjoy horror are specifically (and only) drawn to particular thematic qualities: '*Jennifer's Body is about women* and *how they relate to each other*, the horror moments are there for style and allegory' (2009b [emphasis added]). Even though this interpretative strategy, employed by a variety of women spectators, is perfectly valid, I contend that it cannot account for the totality of their responses, viewing practices and personal experiences with the horror genre. Berenstein (1996) and Cherry (2002) offer evidence that women enjoy horror for multiple reasons, and, indeed, there were some female horror fans who demanded 'more blood' and 'more gore' in *Jennifer's Body*, thereby acting against traditional gender roles.

A completely different reading strategy was to consider *Jennifer's Body* as a cult film or a B-movie, a strategy which is probably closer to Cody and Kusama's authorial vision as expressed in the red band trailer. For instance, the influential *New York Times* film critic A. O. Scott (2009a) located the film within the ranks of some acclaimed horror directors, such as Dario Argento, Brian De Palma and Alfred Hitchcock, asserting that, despite its flaws, *Jennifer's Body* 'deserves – and is likely to win – a devoted cult following'. For Scott, formal perfection or narrative coherence have never been a significant criterion for horror movies and what distinguishes this particular picture is precisely its carnivalesque disarray: '*Jennifer's Body* [...] is an unholy mess. I mean that as a compliment' (2009a). A quick look at the popular review sites, with professional and non-professional critics, such as *Rotten Tomatoes*, *Metacritic* and *IMDb*, confirms that comments like 'it's not art', 'it's not *Citizen Kane*', 'guilty pleasure type of a movie', 'campy horror comedy', 'trash-horror classic', 'B-movie', 'great gory pulpy thriller', 'niche item' and 'kooky, kinky fun' generally correspond to good or very good evaluations of the film and imply the future possibility of its inclusion in the 'cult cinema' category. This category, as Joanne Hollows (2003) demonstrated, is unequivocally gendered as masculine, in opposition to mainstream culture, which is usually constructed as feminine.

These contesting discourses around the aesthetic and ideological status of *Jennifer's Body*, as well as its gendered genre address and spectatorial pleasures, reveal the multifaceted process of negotiation over horror film and women's participation in mainstream genre cinema, whether as filmmakers or as audiences. Without a doubt, the film draws out the tensions that arise from the conjunction of women's film practice, gender, horror cinema and feminism – issues dramatised in the production, promotion and reception of the film. Perhaps what is at stake in the case of *Jennifer's Body* is less the 'truth' about its claim to feminism – or even the feminism of the viewers or the filmmakers – and more the heightened awareness of 'feminism' as tool of significance in interpreting films in certain ways.[15] Understanding the ramifications of different conceptual frames within which women's work is located promises to replace demands for specific feminist outcomes by investigation of what is put into play in the multiple negotiations that take place around particular examples of women's work.

GIRLS GONE GORY

Dancing through the minefield of the contemporary horror film, with its bloody display of the all-too-often female body in bits and pieces, is fraught with danger for women.

But pleasure shares the field with danger.

(Pinedo 1997: 69)

While the prejudice against horror cinema as an inherently patriarchal and misogynistic genre produced for, and by, sadistic males has been challenged by many scholars, it is significant that neither women horror spectators nor women horror filmmakers have received considerable theoretical attention. Investigations into horror cinema tend to focus on films authored by men and on a filmic spectator usually identified as a young, heterosexual male. Significantly, two frequently cited academic works on gender representation in horror film, Carol J. Clover's *Men, Women, and Chain Saws* and Barbara Creed's *The Monstrous-Feminine*, do not focus on female spectators: Clover's conceptualisation of the Final Girl is mainly concerned with male identification with a female hero in slasher films (1992: 42–7), while one of Creed's central arguments is that the construction of the monstrous-feminine 'reveals a great deal about male desires and fears but tells us nothing about feminine desire in relation to the horrific' (1986: 70). Despite overtly feminist readings of the horror genre offered by Clover and Creed, their analyses are still based upon the assumption that heterosexual men are the primary consumers of horror films.

A close reading of *Jennifer's Body* offers an opportunity to consider women's skilled intervention in popular forms at the same time as it opens up a space for reflection on female spectatorial pleasures within horror cinema. The protagonists of the film, the demon-possessed Jennifer Check, who kills high-school boys by eating them alive, and her resourceful best friend Anita 'Needy' Lesnicki, who at the end of the narrative is forced to annihilate the monster, may be seen as embodiments of two of the most analysed representations of women in horror cinema: the monstrous-feminine (Creed 1993) and the Final Girl (Clover 1992), respectively. As I demonstrate in the following sections, it is both possible and productive to rethink these figures through textual analysis of the film that takes into account the metatextual play and ironic, intertextual rewriting of both classical horror and the slasher subgenre, as well as situating the film within the wider context of recent teen horror movies.

Monstrous-feminine and Intertextuality

In his influential book on gothic horror, *Skin Shows*, Judith Jack Halberstam argues that horror films are 'technologies that produce monsters as a remarkably mobile, permeable, and infinitely interpretable body' (1995: 21). He adds that monsters act as meaning machines that 'can represent gender, race, nationality, class, and sexuality in one body' (1995: 21–2). In recent decades, however, we have witnessed 'a switch in emphasis within the representation and interpretation of monstrous bodies [. . .] to a primary focus upon sexuality and gender' (1995: 24). This switch, clearly pronounced in the scholarly and critical writing on contemporary American horror film, is prominent in both marketing strategies and the critical reception of *Jennifer's Body*, since most of the writings about the film focused precisely on the representation of Megan Fox's body as a monstrous *female* body.[16]

At first sight, Jennifer might be considered a textbook example of the monstrous-feminine, if we follow Barbara Creed's psychoanalytic model for approaching monstrosity. Possessed by an evil demon after being a victim of a Satanic ritual (in a sequence that is as parodic as it is terrifying and which seems to build on the scenes of violation in the rape-revenge cycle), Jennifer uses her beauty to seduce adolescent boys, in order to feed on their flesh and blood. In this sense, she incarnates the *femme castratrice* – 'a modern-day version of the ancient Sirens, those mythological figures who used sailors to their doom through the beauty of their song' (Creed 1993: 128). The exploitation of her charms to lure the victims, as well as the representation of her monstrosity, which can be read through what Julia Kristeva theorised as abjection, since she is signified by her contaminated, animalistic and filthy body, covered with blood and bile, support Creed's argument that in horror cinema when a woman is monstrous it is almost always in relation to her procreative, sexual and maternal functions (1993: 7).

When Jennifer is not represented as monstrous, her body is depicted as an object of the gaze, by means of close-up and extreme close-up shots fragmenting her body and the use of high-key lighting and slow-motion camera, which exemplifies the mechanism of fetishistic scopophilia, according to the theory of Mulvey:

> The beauty of the woman as object and the screen space coalesce; she is no longer the bearer of guilt but a perfect product, whose body, stylised and fragmented by close-ups, is the content of the film and the direct recipient of the spectator's look. (1989b: 22)

In this sense, while the function of Jennifer as monstrous would be, borrowing from Creed, 'to bring about an encounter between the symbolic order and that which threatens its stability' (1993: 11), her quality of 'to-be-looked-at-ness' seems to reinstate her as a safe and pleasurable spectacle for the male audience. Following this line of interpretation, the monstrous-feminine in *Jennifer's Body* loses its subversive potential, not because it reaffirms the phallocentric notion of female sexuality as abject, but paradoxically because being a clearly glamourised monster it becomes 'not abject'.

Nevertheless, this interpretation, which emphasises the male psyche and male desire, does not reveal much about the female experience of watching horror films in the twenty-first century, nor does it account for the historic and cultural dimension of female monstrosity. According to Halberstam, although psychoanalytic tools are remarkably productive in approaching horror films, especially as far as notions of fear and desire are concerned, 'fear and monstrosity are historically specific forms rather than psychological universals' (1995: 24), hence the study of monstrosity should be historicised and addressed within particular cultural contexts. Following Halberstam, it is worth raising some questions here: can the construction of the monstrous-feminine in *Jennifer's Body* help to theorise female spectatorial pleasures in contemporary horror cinema? Or, conversely, can certain shifts in the gendered address of American horror cinema over the last two decades, both in relation to marketing strategies, as well as at the textual level, propel a reconceptualisation of the monstrous-feminine in *Jennifer's Body*? And, finally, what role do the intertextual layering and meta-filmic modality play in the rewriting of gender and genre in which Cody's and Kusama's film openly participates?

In reference to the latter, the employment of self-consciousness – as well as allusions to other horror films, which construct a dense maze of intertexts – is closely related to the configuration of the monstrous-feminine. It is noteworthy that the characterisation of Jennifer aligns her not with one, but with a considerable number of incarnations of the monstrous-feminine discussed by Creed. Apart from the previously mentioned *femme castratrice* – a typical protagonist of the rape-revenge film (although with certain differences, since the boys that she slaughters are not the ones that are responsible for her sacrifice/violation) – she embodies one of its most frightening variations, the *vagina dentata*. The image of her mouth evokes the vagina armed with teeth, which she uses to devour her victims, biting a bloody hole in their stomachs. In her analysis of *Teeth* (2007), directed by Mitchell Lichtenstein, another film which is built around this motif, Marta Segarra reminds us that 'the image of the *vagina dentata* presupposes an equivalence between mouth and vagina, between the action of eating and sexual relation' (2011: 174). Jennifer's terrifying jaw, which typifies this idea, as well as other allusions to *Teeth* in *Jennifer's Body*, do not seem to be coincidental. Cody and Kusama repeat a number of popular tropes from Lichtenstein's film, which at the same time is already a humorous revisitation of the *vagina dentata* motif – for example, by showing a waterfall where the water 'goes into this hole, and it doesn't come out', as the narrator of the story, Needy, tells us. The image of the waterfall is reminiscent of the lush lagoon situated just outside the small town in *Teeth*, which is where Dawn, the protagonist of the film, castrates Tobey after he rapes her. The visual metaphor of the *vagina dentata* – 'a bottomless abyss in which one can even disappear' (Segarra 2011: 173) – is pushed to a parodic extreme in *Jennifer's Body* when we are faced with a group of scientists dropping all kinds of objects down the hole – for example, floating balls – while Needy's voice warns us in an half-cryptic, half-ironic tone: 'Nothing ever surfaces. Maybe it's another dimension. Or, you know, just really deep'.

Cody and Kusama's humorous rewriting of the monstrous-feminine trope is not limited to only one of its facets – the *vagina dentata* – rather, it engages

Figure 2.1 Jennifer's jaw as *vagina dentata*.

with a number of recurring motifs found throughout the history of horror cinema. For example, Jennifer's character establishes a dialogue with the figure of the menstrual witch that boasts supernatural powers, who, just as with Carrie in Brian de Palma's film (1976) or the witches in *Suspiria* (Dario Argento, 1977), is capable of wreaking destruction on the community of a small American town.[17] Jennifer's power to control animals – a witch's typical gift – is usually brought out during scenes when a murder is taking place – for instance, in a sequence in the forest when the protagonist lures and attacks a school jock named Jonas. Rather than being scary, though, this sequence provokes laughter, because the mise-en-scène evokes the well-known images from the Walt Disney cartoon *Snow White* (David Hand et al., 1937), in which the protagonist, surrounded by her loyal animals from the forest, sinks into Prince Charming's arms. At the same time, Jennifer embodies a lesbian vampire with voracious sexual desire – in scenes when she licks her blood-coated lips, bites Needy on her neck, passing the 'virus' onto her, or when she eventually dies, from a stake to her heart. Being a lesbian vampire, she is doubly dangerous, since not only does she attack men, but she also seduces the 'daughters of patriarchy away from their proper gender roles' (Creed 1993: 61) – for example, when she tempts Needy to kiss her, disrupting her heterosexual relationship with Chip. In one scene Jennifer is transformed into a woman-snake, with slender, needle-sharp teeth and reptile eyes, who emits a hiss before attacking her victim. This woman-snake transformation, together with her compulsion to drink blood in the moonlight, evoke yet another variation of the narrative about female vampires, which is constructed around the moon, snakes and a woman's cycle, brilliantly analysed by Creed:

> All three [. . .] move through stages in which the old is shed and the new reborn: the moon moves through its cycle from the old to the new moon;

the snake sheds and renews its skin; woman sheds and renews her blood. (1993: 64)

In this codification of the monstrous-feminine through menstrual blood and the moon, *Jennifer's Body* engages with another contemporary film, *Ginger Snaps* (John Fawcett, 2000), with which it also shares plot similarities. In the latter film, a sisterly bond between two adolescent girls, Brigitte and Ginger Fitzgerald, is deeply affected by Ginger's transformation into an insatiable werewolf that must feed off human blood, after being attacked by a ferocious creature from the woods on precisely the same day as she experiences her first period. During their sexual encounters with schoolmates, both Ginger and Jennifer become aggressive, adopting a position which might be considered traditionally 'masculine'. In one scene, Ginger tries to hush a boy with whom she is about to have sex, telling him to 'just lie back and relax', to which he responds, offended, 'who's the guy here?' In a similar manner, Jennifer always plays the 'active' part when she seduces her victims – a role that is often treated humorously, for instance in the scene when Collin asks her, just before she pounces on him: 'Do you even know my last name?' The lycanthropic transformation of Ginger and the demoniac metamorphosis of Jennifer might both be seen as metaphors of their sexual aberration or as a transgressive rejection of the culturally prescribed gender roles,[18] since (as Creed eloquently demonstrates in her book), the abjection is always deeply ambiguous.

Last but not least, Jennifer embodies a possessed woman who vomits bile, self-mutilates and levitates in a way that is almost identical to Regan in *The Exorcist* (William Friedkin, 1973). In her analysis of *The Exorcist*, Creed writes that 'possession becomes the excuse of legitimising a display of aberrant feminine behaviour which is depicted as depraved, monstrous, abject' (1993: 31). Yet, Creed insists that despite the monstrous appearance of Regan, 'she remains a strongly ambiguous figure', because the

> carnivalesque display of her body reminds us quite clearly of the immense appeal of the abject. Horror emerges from the fact that woman has broken with her proper feminine role – she has 'made a spectacle of herself' – put her unsocialised body on display. (Creed 1993: 42)

Taking into consideration the parodic tone of *Jennifer's Body* and its insistent evocation of the most well-known horror movies in the history of cinema, it can be argued that the film is 'carnivalesque' not only in the abject exhibition of the feminine body, but also in its intertextual play with genre and gender conventions, since Jennifer performs several sorts of feminine monstrosity, while at the same time displaying her socialised – and not only unsocialised – body as I shall discuss in the next section.

The constant repetition of the monstrous tropes, notably intertwined in the horror genre with femininity, can entail – if we adopt Judith Butler's (1993) theorisations on gender – a rejection or a parodic subversion of the generic and gender laws. It is worth highlighting, though, that the knowing and reflexive commentary on the generic logic of horror film and the ironic use of gender stereotypes is not a new phenomenon in the genre,[19] nor does it necessarily lead to the critique of gender representation, as many feminist scholars have shown. Yvonne Tasker asserts that many contemporary films are 'both highly knowing about sex and gender (both cognizant of sexism and knowing with respect to sexual innuendo) and deeply invested in conventional modes of femininity' (2011: 68). Lisa Coulthard, in turn, observes in her analysis of *Kill Bill* (Quentin Tarantino, 2003) that the 'postmodern knowingness' of the film,

> which emphasizes its visceral and spectacular excesses of violent action and erotic feminine display, should not [. . .] be taken as an active critique or a transparent sign of shifts in societal and ideological constructions of gender and power. In framing themselves as self-referential and ironic play, many of these female-centered postmodern action films [. . .] appear to anticipate and deflect critical engagement by constantly reasserting the attention to surfaces, display, and viewing procedures shaped by consumption. (2007: 168–9)

Subversive or not, the carnivalesque play with monstrous tropes in *Jennifer's Body*, which relies on the aesthetics of artifice, excess and reduplication, does draw our attention to the generic conventions of horror film and to the constructedness of gender and, more particularly, monstrous femininity. According to film scholar Giulia Colaizzi:

> In the magnification of artifice, in duplication and in excess, an echo effect is generated which distorts and disfigures what supposedly should only be repeated, re-presented: the image reveals itself not as a mere copy or reflection, but as construction, as artefact [. . .]. The excess – understood as an excess of artifice, as the proliferation of gazes and readings [. . .] – makes visible the threads which weave together the representation. (2007: 125–6)

The excessive mutability of the monstrous-feminine embodied by Jennifer, which is produced by means of various allusions to filmic representations or even almost exact repetitions of scenes borrowed from different horror films – for example, the previously mentioned *Carrie* (1976), *The Exorcist* (1973), *The Evil Dead* (1981), *Ginger Snaps* (2000) and *Teeth* (2007) – distorts the image, uncovering the production process of monstrous-femininity on the screen. Rather than *being* a monster, Jennifer *becomes* a monster, whose body, in constant negotiation with the available generic conventions, is written and read through a densely intertextual process. Jennifer's monstrosity is, without doubt, a monstrosity of surfaces – a literal embodiment of what Tom Gunning refers to as the 'frenzy of the visible' (1994: 86) – which, being comprised of a number of monstrous-feminine facets, rips at the seams, disfiguring 'what supposedly should only be repeated, represented' (Colaizzi 2007: 125). In this sense, the film stages a *meta-representation* of monstrosity, which reveals itself as a device.

In line with these notions of artifice and excess in representing the female monster in *Jennifer's Body* is the commentary on the operations of suture in the horror genre made by Halberstam in his analysis of *The Texas Chainsaw Massacre 2*. Drawing on Kaja Silverman's work on suture – a notion which Silverman uses to identify the relationship between lack, or loss, and subjectivity within the activity of spectatorship – Halberstam argues that while in classical film the sutures should remain invisible, in the horror genre the suture appears 'as a surface effect':

> [T]he film constantly attempts to call our attention to cinematic production, its failures and its excesses. Horror film, in other words, is a critical genre and one that exposes the theatricality of identity because it makes specular precisely those images of loss, lack, penetration, violence that other films attempt to cover up. (1995: 152–3)

Making use of Halberstam's (1995) phrase, which makes reference to Judith Butler's famous *Bodies That Matter* (1993), the protagonist of *Jennifer's Body* embodies the *gender that splatters* (namely, which 'reaps at the seams') through the excessive repetition of generic horror tropes (see Halberstam 1995: 143). Jennifer, as the title of the film suggests, is all about the body, the surface material, brazenly artificial.

The self-conscious celebration of monstrosity offers a densely intertextual experience at the same time as it is potentially translated into a visceral impact on the audience. In this aspect, the film clearly participates in the body genres theorised by Williams, which are characterised by a (supposed) lack of proper aesthetic distance and an 'overinvolvement in sensation and emotion' (Williams 1991: 5). Instead of offering a cold Brechtian distance or destroying visual pleasure, as was postulated by Laura Mulvey in her model of counter-cinema, *Jennifer's Body* heightens spectatorial pleasures and disrupts the gender coding and power relations not by distracting us from, but rather by intensifying, our pleasures. In other words, if Cody and Kusama's film moves away from typical gender representations in horror cinema, it does so not by overtly criticising or opposing them, but rather by duplicating and exaggerating them.

Critical discussions of the spectatorial experience are incomplete without also addressing the question of female audiences and interrogating the extent to which they are able to enjoy horror cinema. How can we think about their possible spectatorial pleasures within or beyond the models of intertextual experience or visceral impact as conceived by Williams? In order to answer these questions, it is worth returning to Halberstam's idea that female monstrosity should be considered a historical and cultural construct. Indeed, the intersection between the female spectator and female monstrosity seen as a highly mutable concept is a fruitful place from which to address the film and the broader context of the production and promotion of horror cinema over the last two decades.

In his compelling analysis of contemporary American teen horror cinema Martin Fradley remarks that 'perhaps *the* key structuring element in the evolution of teen horror since the mid-1990s has been its overt address to a young female audience' (2013: 210 [emphasis in original]). Certainly, if we observe recent horror cinema marketing strategies, we quickly realise that it is not uncommon to find horror films advertised not only as 'female' (that is, addressed to women spectators), but also 'feminist'.[20] This shift towards a mode of direct female address is, according to Fradley, also indicative of 'shifts *within* the genre itself that render former models of genre criticism anachronistic when dealing with contemporary horror films that insistently foreground the female hero's expressionist transformation from an uncertain young woman to an adult' (2013: 210 [emphasis in original]). In this sense, the previously mentioned references to *Carrie* in *Jennifer's Body*, far from being a mere postmodern wink at the viewers, allow for a more contextualised interpretation of Jennifer's monstrosity, one which goes beyond the positive/negative images of women in horror cinema, as well as contributing to inscribing the film within certain tendencies which have emerged in this genre in recent decades. The paradigmatic traits of Brian de Palma's famous film, as listed by Pamela Craig and Martin Fradley, can be readily identified in *Jennifer's Body*: both films focus on the 'horrors of high-school socialization articulated in emotionally hyperbolic tones'; they present 'middle-class suburbia and [the] high school environment as an oppressively institutionalised gothic space'; and, as far as their generic status is concerned, they are both 'hybridised combination[s] of horror, comedy, soap opera melodramatics and exploitative teen drama' (2010: 89). *Jennifer's Body*, and other examples of teen horror films that hint at their predecessor *Carrie*, clearly taps into what can be considered 'a female experience' or, as Kathleen Rowe Karlyn calls it in her analysis of the *Scream* trilogy, 'issues of particular concern for teen girls: 1) sexuality and virginity; 2) adult femininity and its relation to agency and power; 3) identity as it is shaped by the narratives of popular culture' (2011: 101–2). While it is not my intention to examine all of the aspects mentioned by Rowe Karlyn, it is useful to underscore the role of *horror* cinema tropes in relation to these issues, in order to query their possible cultural significance in female spectatorial experience.

'Hell is a Teenage Girl': The Horrors of Socialisation

Peter Hutchings describes horror cinema as a male genre, 'produced largely by men for a predominantly male audience and addressing specifically male fears and anxieties' (1993: 84). According to Hutchings, in horror films we are usually faced with a male monster and a female victim, which idea led Linda Williams to consider this binary opposition in relation to Laura Mulvey's (1975) theory of visual pleasure. Just as the classical narrative cinema reproduces the structure of the active male gaze and the quality of 'to-be-looked-at-ness' of women, in horror film the male spectator identifies with the active subject of narration, exercising a punishing, controlling look, while women are denied this look or they are punished for exercising it (Williams 2002: 62).[21] When the woman looks, both as a character within the film and as a viewer in the audience, she is made to bear strong associations with the monster who (just like her) is codified by its difference from the masculine norm (2002: 62).

A closer analysis of *Jennifer's Body* shows that the monstrous protagonist is almost always seen from her best friend's perspective, Needy. The film opens with a tracking shot through someone's garden combined with slight and random camera movements that lead us to a house wrapped in darkness – a visual strategy that usually serves to codify the point of view of a malicious force or a stalker. The camera then shifts to focus on Jennifer's arm and dry lips as she chews her hair in a series of close-up shots, while we hear a voice blaring from a television, advertising sports equipment: 'I'm working the back of my calves, and I'm working my heart. We're talkin' about butt. We're talkin' about legs. [. . .] Whole body calorie burning. Whole body muscle toning'. The camera tilts up to reveal a long shot of Jennifer lying on her bed in her room. Suddenly, Needy's face emerges in the next shot, peeking unnoticed at Jennifer through the window. Jennifer turns to face it, but Needy is no longer there. We only hear her voice saying: 'Hell is a teenage girl'.

In contrast to Jennifer, whose character is represented from these very first shots through her (fragmented) body, Needy's subjectivity is constructed by means of her voice. The camera displacements approaching the house seem to act as a semi-subjective incorporeal eye, which – according to what horror conventions dictate – usually codifies a non-human perspective. In this case, however, it corresponds to Needy's point of view. The lack of synchronisation between her gaze, her voice and the image of her body, an operation which Kaja Silverman dubbed 'dis-embodying the female voice' – that is, 'the freeing-up of the female voice from its obsessive and indeed exclusive reference to the female body' (1990: 315) – is soon remedied, as Needy's voice coincides again with her corporeity. However, it is not insignificant that it is through her disembodied look and her disembodied voice that Jennifer's character is introduced.

After the second part of the prologue, in which Needy appears to be resident in a psychiatric hospital, the narrative jumps back in time to account for what happened, remarkably from Needy's perspective, as she is the narrator and – even if posters and trailers for *Jennifer's Body* might suggest the opposite – the main protagonist of the film. In the scene which follows the prologue, Needy reintroduces Jennifer with her gaze. This time, Jennifer is dressed in a cheerleader's costume, filmed with a slow camera and occupies the centre of the image, while by means of shot/countershot Needy's look is established. In this fragment, the use of voice-over, as well as of codes that construct Jennifer as a 'popular girl', unmistakably evokes the conventions of the teen film genre. The inscription of Jennifer in the school environment brings to mind a similar scene in *Mean Girls* (Mark Waters, 2004), in which the protagonist, Cady, looks for the first time at the most popular girl in school, who is surrounded by other teenagers, situated in the centre of the shot and filmed with a slow camera, in a manner similar to that employed with Jennifer. In *Mean Girls* Cady falls in love with Regina's ex-boyfriend, Aaron Samuels. Regina is a queen bee, the wealthiest and most attractive girl in school, who is leading the exclusive clique, called derogatorily 'The Plastics'. She and her friends try to make Cady's life impossible, so that the latter has no choice but to use the very same weapons in order to survive in the 'jungle': she becomes one of 'The Plastics'. Notably, the film, which turned out to be very successful at the box office,[22] was considered paradigmatic of the teen comedy genre, and the expression 'mean girl' spread throughout both mass media and academic discourse to talk about violence in schools carried out by young females.[23]

Figure 2.2   Jennifer as a popular girl.

Figure 2.3 Needy's gaze.

The reference to this film, highlighted in some of the reviews of *Jennifer's Body*, opens up a consideration of Jennifer as an incarnation of the 'mean girl': exuberant, aggressive and competitive. By means of the calculated, excessive characterisation, *Jennifer's Body* provides a witty critique on the ritualised construction of gender. Just as Regina and her friends discipline Cady's body in *Mean Girls* – for example, in the scene in which they explain the rules of the 'Girl World' ('You can't wear tank tops two days in a row, you can only wear your hair in a ponytail once a week. [. . .] And we only wear jeans and track pants on Fridays') – Jennifer also seeks to exercise power over Needy's physical appearance. For instance, when she is getting ready for a night out with her friend, Needy changes her outfit many times and comments sarcastically: '"Wear something cute" meant something very specific in Jennifer-speak. It meant I couldn't look like a total zero, but I couldn't upstage her either. I could expose my stomach, but never my cleavage. Tits were her trademark'.

Nonetheless, mostly because they are engaging with distinct genres, there is a significant difference between *Mean Girls* and *Jennifer's Body*. In the latter, we are not granted a typical happy ending sealed with heterosexual coupling, which tends to take place in the iconic 'prom scene' in teen films – just as *Mean Girls* and other narratives which follow this storyline show us – nor do we witness Needy's transformation into a popular girl, another teen movie trope (see, for instance, *She's All That* by Robert Iscove [1999] or *The Princess Diaries* by Garry Marshall [2001]). Interestingly, the actress who interpreted Needy's role, Amanda Seyfried, became famous precisely thanks to her performance in *Mean Girls*, in which she played one of 'The Plastics' – a popular and very attractive, but not particularly clever, adolescent. Her character in *Jennifer's Body* is quite the opposite: Needy is well-educated, perceptive and sensible and she takes a critical view of Jennifer and *her* ideals of beauty. Her gaze is mediated by the glasses she wears, which, according to Mary Ann

Doane, is one of the most remarkable visual clichés in the history of cinema, since the image of a woman with glasses 'is a heavily marked condensation of motifs concerned with repressed sexuality, knowledge, visibility and vision, intellectuality, and desire' (1990: 50). Even though this filmic strategy could serve simply to create an opposition between Jennifer – an attractive girl – and Needy – an ugly duckling – or, evoking well-known narratives addressed by feminist criticism, the binary opposition between the prostitute and the virgin,[24] at the same time, and drawing on Doane, this cliché

> has a binding power so strong that it indicates a precise moment of ideological danger or threat – in this case, the woman's appropriation of the gaze. Glasses worn by a woman in the cinema do not generally signify a deficiency in seeing but an active looking, or even simply the fact of seeing as opposed to being seen. The intellectual woman looks and analyses, and in usurping the gaze she poses a threat to an entire system of representation. (1990: 50)

The hegemonic system of representation is threatened not only by Needy's analytical capacities, as she usurps the critical gaze over her friend's body, but also by means of the strategic exaggeration which is employed to underscore the constructed nature of Jennifer's monstrous and non-monstrous representation. Remarkably, the magnification of artifice is equally expounded in the exhibition of Jennifer-the-demon and Jennifer-the-popular-girl, which traces many revealing similarities between these two figurations at the same time as it emphasises the production process of female monstrosity on screen. In such a way, the idea of media as social technology is foregrounded: rather than reflecting a prior reality, these figurations constitute a vehicle for the (re)production of meanings around gender, in line with Teresa de Lauretis's (1987b) theorisation of cinema. The fabricated nature of (monstrous) femininity seems to be confirmed by Jennifer herself when she articulates: 'PMS isn't real ... it was invented by the boy-run media to make us seem like we're crazy'. Media discourses around the figure of the mean girl act as yet another technology for creating the monstrous-feminine in contemporary Western culture. These constructions are, in keeping with sociologist Jessica Ringrose, regulatory strategies that maintain appropriate modes of repressive, white, middle-class femininity (2006: 405). Even if we agree that *Jennifer's Body* contributes to these discourses, it also exposes them by drawing our attention to the way in which the mass media participates in the very same process of fabrication of monstrous teenaged femininity.

Beyond simply unmasking the constructed nature of gender or self-consciously exposing the technologies of creating the monstrous-feminine (by exaggerating gender stereotypes in a satirical way, for instance), *Jennifer's*

Body also offers great potential for feminist appropriations of the horror genre, especially if we consider it in its specific historical and cultural moment. In his insightful study of the relationship between postfeminist discourse and horror cinema, Fradley explores 'the tension between the gendered (political) expression of recent teen horror and the increasingly widespread disillusionment with the limitations of postfeminist media culture' (2013: 207). For Fradley, teen horror cinema is symptomatic of, and possibly oppositional to, this hegemonic cultural shift (2013: 207), since in many contemporary films – Fradley mentions *Captivity* (Roland Joffé, 2007), *House of Wax* (Jaume Collet-Serra, 2005), *Ginger Snaps* (John Fawcett, 2000), *Teeth* (Mitchell Lichtenstein, 2007), *All the Boys Love Mandy Lane* (Johnathan Levine, 2006) and *Jennifer's Body* – a thematic preoccupation with neoliberal femininity and, at the same time, a critique of its individualistic and self-sufficient nature can be detected.

If we inscribe Cody and Kusama's work in this group, as Fradley suggests, Jennifer's monstrous figuration would stand for a hypersexualised and highly cartoonish image of neoliberal femininity: a pathological product of postfeminist media discourse, which, in line with Yvonne Tasker and Diane Negra's theorisation, celebrates white, middle-class, heterosexual femininity grounded in competitive individualism, with an emphasis on sexualised self-definition, personal development and empowerment through consumption (2007: 1–25). At one point, Jennifer urges her best friend to use her body to seduce and take advantage of boys in a nightclub. 'We have all the power. Don't you know that? These things? These are like smart bombs. You point them in the right direction, and shit gets real', exclaims Jennifer, grabbing Needy's breasts. When Needy wonders out loud how Jennifer plans on buying alcohol from the bar, she answers, 'I'll just play hello-titty with the bartender'.

Significantly, the self-conscious critique of neoliberal femininity is developed in *Jennifer's Body* by means of the productive use of generic conventions of horror cinema and, in particular, it connects with the figuration of the monstrous-feminine. After her demoniac transference, Jennifer is forced to consume human flesh and blood to keep the demon alive, but, actually, once transformed into a monster, her *modus operandi* and her motivations as a popular girl do not change significantly. If she does not get her dose of boys' flesh and blood each month, Jennifer's skin and hair lose their glow and she becomes unattractive or, as Needy astutely observes, 'ugly for her'. After feeding on adolescent boys, she enjoys great hair and a perfect complexion. In this sense, we could interpret Jennifer as a monstrous creation of hegemony, but not only in relation to her abjection – for example, as *femme castratrice*, who kills boys in revenge for being sacrificed/raped – but also in relation to her obsession with appearance and her absolute dependence on men. Following this line of interpretation, and going back to Creed's notes on

Regan in *The Exorcist*, who has broken with her proper feminine role, 'she has "made a spectacle of herself" – put her unsocialised body on display' (Creed 1993: 42), in the case of *Jennifer's Body* it is not only an unsocialised, abject and monstrous body, but also a socialised and glamorised one that is put on display.

Jennifer's status as an attractive girl, built on her self-awareness in terms of her physical beauty as a marketable good, her sexual availability and a somewhat grotesque version of the girl power maxims – which, as Kathleen Rowe Karlyn (2011) asserts, became popular in the 1990s – nonetheless has its fissures. 'I was the Snowflake Queen', proclaims Jennifer to Needy in the face of accusations of being insecure. 'Yeah. Two years ago, when you were socially relevant. [...] And when you didn't need laxatives to stay skinny', Needy responds poignantly, hinting at the short-lived nature of Jennifer's popularity and suggesting, perhaps, a possible decadence of postfeminist ideals. Needy's critical distance towards Jennifer's desperate attempts to conserve her image as an attractive girl, and her own resistance to being transformed into a 'hypersexualised monster' despite her best friend's insistence, points to the process of her personal growth, which might be considered a possible source of empowerment for female audiences.

Remarkably, in Needy's penetrating comments, intertextual mechanisms play an important role. One of the traits that she shares with other heroines – for example, with the Fitzgerald sisters in *Ginger Snaps* – is her great passion for horror cinema. That she is a fan is alluded to by her T-shirt and posters that cover the walls of her bedroom, which make reference to *The Evil Dead* (Sam Raimi, 1981), a B-movie horror flick with heavy doses of gore, humour and intertextual play. Needy's erudition stands in contrast to Jennifer's plain ignorance, who confuses *Rocky Horror Picture Show* (Jim Sharman, 1975) with a boxing film and whose filmic sensibility is expressed through films such as

Figure 2.4   Postfeminist regime exposed.

Aquamarine (Elizabeth Allen Rosenbaum, 2006) – a teen fantasy-comedy about a charming mermaid who asks two thirteen-year-old girls for help to seduce a handsome lifeguard named Raymond. Brigitte and Ginger, on the other hand, stand out among their peers because of their morbid obsession with murder and demise, revealed, for example, in their recreation of terrifying scenarios – presented as a school project – in which both sisters dramatise and photograph their fake deaths. In this sense, Needy, as well as Brigitte and Ginger, epitomise a new class of girl hero in horror cinema, who, according to Rowe Karlyn, 'knows her culture, from the legends underpinning its institutions to the popular culture and technology of her own generation, and uses the tools it offers as a means of rewriting old narratives that no longer serve her' (2011: 126). As I will show in the following section, it is also a girl who can protect herself through physical resources, and who can express rather than repress her rage.

The Final Girl and Female Spectatorial Pleasures

In this light, the violence that Needy resorts to as a Final Girl – who, according to Clover, is a female with traditional male qualities surviving to take revenge on the psycho killer – might acquire new dimensions. According to the slasher film conventions analysed by Clover, the scene when Needy kills the monster complies with these:

> If the early experience of the oedipal drama can be – is perhaps ideally – enacted in female form, the achievement of full adulthood requires the assumption and, apparently, brutal employment of the phallus. The helpless child is gendered feminine; the autonomous adult or subject is gendered masculine; the passage from childhood to adulthood entails a shift from feminine to masculine. (1992: 50)

By means of the appropriation of phallic symbols, Needy 'mans' herself and at the same time she 'unmans an oppressor whose masculinity was in question to begin with' (1992: 49). After Jennifer kills her best friend's boyfriend, Chip, Needy sheds her pink dress and puts on a sweatshirt, military pants and heavy boots. She then mobilises an 'active look' – in Clover's terms – to hunt the monster. The two girls fight, and before Needy *accidentally* stabs her best friend in the heart, Jennifer looks at the tiny blade of a Stanley knife in her hand and asks: 'Do you buy all your weapons at Home Depot? God, you're butch'. Needy responds with what can be read as a phallic fantasy of penetration: the weapon is for 'cutting boxes'. Taking into consideration its comical tone, the scene might be considered an ironic, self-conscious commentary on how the Final Girl has to be masculinised so that she can kill the monster, while Jennifer must be feminised (become a box) before she can play a victim.[25]

If we read this scene in consonance with Clover's conceptualisation, we must accept her argument that horror cinema is nothing more than 'the tale of maleness' (1992: 50–1), in which the surviving girl is a source of identification for the teenage male audience.

In the interpretative frame based on the critique of neoliberal femininity, however, these final scenes might generate further meanings and extend theoretical possibilities for considering Needy's violence. The annihilation of Jennifer, who, as I have previously argued, stands for a hypersexualised, aggressively competitive femininity, as well as the agent of postfeminist media culture and its violence inflicted upon Needy's body, might be considered a source of diverse pleasures for female spectators. By killing this character so decisively, the film eradicates a particular model of femininity, 'in order to replace it with another that is more knowing, less glamorous, and a lot more capable' (Rowe Karlyn 2011: 105). Keeping in line with this interpretative framework, instead of censuring Needy's violent behaviour or legitimising her actions by making use of girl power discourse, I am more inclined to reflect on what kind of violence is being enacted upon *her* body and other bodies in the film. There is a scene in *Jennifer's Body* which exemplifies my stance, as it highlights the violence of postfeminist culture, which – in the words of Fradley – seems 'a brutal Foucauldian nightmare' (2013: 211). Needy, similarly to Carrie in De Palma's movie, prepares herself – or, to be more accurate – is prepared for the high-school prom: she puts on a pink, ridiculously bouffant dress, while her mother almost burns her hair using a curling iron, so that her daughter can adhere to (her and society's) standards of traditional femininity. The result of these 'beauty treatments' is a somewhat grotesque incarnation of high-school prom queen/a caricaturesque Disney princess, whose apparently perfect appearance will soon be destroyed by dribbles of dirt and bile – the image which evokes both the prom scene in *Carrie* and the typical representations of the brutalised Final Girl in slasher films.

Figure 2.5   The brutalised Final Girl.

The image of Needy, who never expresses a wish to be a prom queen or a popular girl, covered with blood and dirt, allows for a reading of *Jennifer's Body* through an 'anti-makeover' scheme, which, as Fradley rightly notices, is typical of a number of recent teen horror films:

> The affective semiotics of teen horror's key visual trope – the exhausted female victim-hero, tearful, bloodied and psychologically traumatised – holds a dark social mirror to the consumerist pleasures valorised by post-feminist culture. Exemplified in popular films such as *The Devil Wears Prada* (Frankel, 2006) and *Sex and the City: The Movie* (King, 2008), the fantastical romantic comedy or 'rom-com' makeover celebrates traditional femininity and the transformative pleasures of self-actualization while systematically evading the social realities faced by young women today. (2013: 205)

In the scenes that follow the confrontation between the Final Girl and the monster in *Jennifer's Body*, the traditional slasher ending is displaced. According to Clover: 'The moment at which the Final Girl is effectively phallicised is the moment that the plot halts and horror ceases' (1992: 50). *Jennifer's Body*, in contrast, does not offer a return to the pre-existing order, seeing that Jennifer's demoniac powers, instead of being completely erased, are transferred to Needy. The ideological project that is central to popular horror film, understood as the 'purification of the abject' (Creed 1993: 14), is not completed on the narrative level since – borrowing from Creed – the abject is not ejected and nor are the boundaries between the human and non-human redrawn (1993: 46). We learn that Needy manages to escape from the psychiatric hospital – thanks to supernatural abilities she inherited from Jennifer – and the film concludes in a similar manner to *Teeth*: the protagonist gets a lift from an old man, who looks at her as if he is about to suggest a sexual favour in exchange for the assistance. Knowledge of what is about to take place causes the protagonist to smile – a gesture which suggests that Needy, just like Dawn in *Teeth*, is perfectly capable of defending herself against any possible assault or sexual blackmail.

Not until the final credits appear on the screen do we realise that Needy, transformed into *femme castratrice*, will take advantage of these new abilities to avenge Jennifer by killing the misogynist members of the band responsible for the sacrifice. The weapon she handles is the same knife used by the musicians to stab Jennifer, which, after having been thrown into the waterfall (acting as a sort of *vagina dentata*), is miraculously found by Needy in a small stream close to the highway. Nevertheless, the rape-revenge conventions to which the film clearly alludes, as well as the restorative character of this ending, are destabilised by the fact that we never actually see the murders take place. Instead, we are presented with snapshots of the victims, while a song with witty lyrics is heard in the background: 'Darlin' darlin' darlin', I can't wait to see you. Your picture ain't enough. I can't wait to touch you, in the flesh'. Finally, the snapshots that flick across the screen conclude with a black and white shot of the hotel where the murders took place (from the point of view of a security camera hung on the wall), which flashes with the blurred image of Needy, whose gendered body is similarly blurred under the hood she is wearing. Behind her we can see some groupies running towards the band's room, in the opposite direction from Needy, who is walking away from the room and who is certainly not 'needy' anymore. Interestingly, while Jennifer remained in her small hometown to eat local boys, Needy uses her power to seek revenge and escape her literal and metaphorical prisons.

Although this last figuration could be interpreted in terms of Clover's masculinised Final Girl, whose very *raison d'être* is to become a source of identification for teenage males, this conceptualisation, as Halberstam shows, 'remains caught in a gender lock' (1995: 143), since it does not address the potential for identification between female audiences and the aggressor, but instead re-establishes normative gender positions in relation to fear and violence. If we rethink the Final Girl figure in line with Halberstam's proposition, Needy might be read as a representation of the monstrous gender – or gender that splatters – which exceeds human categories, transforming into 'something messier than male or female' (1995: 143). Pointing to the queer tendency of horror film – that is, its capacity 'to reconfigure gender not simply through inversion, but by literally creating new categories' (1995: 139) – Halberstam

Figure 2.6   Becoming-monstrous: Needy at the hotel.

argues that the Final Girl's femininity is recycled and transformed in new gender regimes. In this sense, both Jennifer's excessive body, which represents various forms of monstrosity, and Needy's body, infiltrated by a demon and, ultimately, ambiguous in terms of gender and sexuality, destabilise the dominant regimes, even if the function of these new figurations is different. While Jennifer's principal role seems to be to reveal technologies and modes of producing the feminine monstrosity, Needy, by contrast, evokes the process of 'becoming-monstrous' defined by Halberstam as 'enabling and activating monstrosity as opposed to stamping it out' (1995: 143).

Much as it is potentially reductive to read Needy's transformation in terms of a phallic woman – a long-standing trope in visual culture – conceptualisations of the Final Girl as a utopic feminist subversion under the guise of liberatory fantasies of omnipotence à la postfeminist girl power is also problematic. An unconditional exaltation of the Final Girl in horror film as an agent of violence generates serious doubts about the extent to which these images can be considered empowering. Linking the proliferation of these representations with a postfeminist discourse centred on apolitical, individualistic and capitalist celebration of a violent woman, Lisa Coulthard demonstrates in her analysis of *Kill Bill* that rather than being phallicised or masculinised, the violent action heroine is 'postfeminised', since she embodies the ideologically and narratively unified fantasies of normative femininity (2007: 173): '[T]he film's depiction of female violence is entwined with discourses of idealised feminine whiteness, heterosexuality, victimhood, sacrificial purity, maternal devotion, and eroticised, exhibitionistic, sexual availability' (2007: 158). In the same fashion, it might be possible to consider Needy a postfeminised Final Girl – white, heterosexual and individualistic – who rejects any implication in feminism, collectivity or political action. Nevertheless, as I have attempted to demonstrate through the film's analysis, *Jennifer's Body* engages in a critical dialogue with this narrative, and is – and with this I return to Fradley's argument – both symptomatic of, and possibly oppositional to, this discourse. Significantly, the supernatural virus Needy inherits from Jennifer does not transform her into a hypersexualised demon, nor does it grant her the type of beauty Jennifer craved. On the other hand, the individualistic nature of her violence should be considered in relation to the popular genre script in which this violence is represented, since, as Rowe Karlyn reminds us: 'In Hollywood, collective histories are always retold as personal stories' (2011: 116). Therefore, when interrogating modes of femininity embodied by the contemporary Final Girl and the spectatorial pleasures that this figure generates, it might be fruitful to take into consideration the different ramifications and tonalities of the representational codes and modes of filmic violence, without losing sight of the generic traits in which these representations are inscribed.

Far from adopting a rather simplistic conviction that representations of women as agents of violence are immediately progressive, we should not dismiss images of violent females so easily. I agree with Fradley that it would be reductive to understand *Jennifer's Body* as legitimising Needy's violence against Jennifer's assailants, since the film functions metaphorically to reject the phallic logic underpinning sexual violence. What is more, it provides its protagonists (and viewers) an aesthetic access to violence and rage, released in a previously assumed male genre.

In Rowe Karlyn's words, the contemporary horror film provides 'an abundant storehouse of images and narratives valuable less as a means of representing reality than as motifs available for contesting, rewriting and recoding' (2011: 33–4). Perhaps more constructive is to think of the Final Girl not in relation to the notion of agency and empowerment, but rather through the complex relationship between representation and reality, along with the pitfalls of the often contested, but still predominant, paradigm of 'images of women'. 'Too often representations of the pernicious effects of homophobia, racism and sexism are collapsed by the viewer into homophobia, racism, and sexism themselves', rightly observes Halberstam in his article on imagined violence (1993: 196). In Halberstam's anti-essentialist theory of the representation of fear and violence, he proposes unhinging monstrosity from masculine power and fear from feminine victimhood, arguing that female violence is not a simple inversion, but it transforms the symbolic function of the feminine in popular narratives. Halberstam concludes that 'the power of fantasy is not to represent but to destabilise the real' (1993: 199).

What seems to trouble most critics who read *Jennifer's Body* as an anti-feminist, patriarchal product is that this process of 'destabilising the real' in the film does not rely on the creation of 'positive' representations of female protagonists, nor does it overtly criticise the ones which might be seen as 'negative'. What is more, the film's calculated excess, both in terms of gender and genre, does not offer a distanced contemplation or the pleasures of alienated spectatorship. In Dyer's words:

> This runs counter to the conventional wisdom regarding progressive art, beginning with the Enlightenment prizing of aesthetic contemplation and becoming politically hardened in the twentieth century, emblematically in Brecht's notion of Verfremdungseffekt, procedures of estrangement that supposedly force the audience to stand back from the work and consider it ideologically. (2007: 167–8)

The transformational powers of genre can render gender identities fluid, but this is not to suggest 'either an uncritical celebration of popular genres, or the inevitable subversion of gender, sexual or racial ideologies by genre's inherent self-reinventing reflexivity' (Gledhill 2018: xi). Rather, as Gledhill proposes, it is to recognise that as switching points between social activity and mainstream fiction, media genres, dependent as they are on commercial appeal to widespread audiences, must seek both referential and generic recognition, thus becoming sites in which social discourses and ideologies are put into the play of dramatic necessity. It is in popular film genres that the feminist critic can see what is thrown up as the stakes of gender, 'genrified' to dramatic ends. (2018: xi)

To what extent can a self-conscious attitude challenge gender stereotypes? Can the ironic combination of styles and representations question the norms? Is parodying the dominant norms enough to displace them or, on the contrary, is the denaturalisation the very vehicle for a reconsolidation of these norms, as Judith Butler proposes?

> Learning the rules that govern intelligible speech is an inculcation into normalised language, where the price of not conforming is the loss of intelligibility itself. [...] It would be a mistake to think that received grammar is the best vehicle for expressing radical views, given the constraints that grammar imposes upon thought, indeed, upon the thinkable itself. (1999: xviii–ix)

If we apply the notion of performativity to both gender norms and genre conventions, we could argue that although *Jennifer's Body* on no account presents a radical point of view, due to the limitations that the grammar of *mainstream* horror cinema imposes, the film bends the very same grammar and – paraphrasing Gilles Deleuze and Félix Guattari (1975) – it makes gender and genre stutter, without causing them to become unintelligible and rejecting spectatorial pleasures that emerge from the generic repetition. Rather than *being* a horror film, *Jennifer's Body participates in* horror film, inscribing itself in wider trends of its time and offering – and inflating to the fullest – certain clichés and representations that generate multiple possibilities of interpretation for its audiences.

Instead of viewing genre as a fixed mould that limits artistic creation, perhaps it might be better to consider it as a highly flexible and inherently generative format. Although, by definition, genre dictates determined aesthetic rules, it also implies its violation, as Jane Gaines reminds us: '[G]enre works are fascinatingly predictable as they are unpredictable, paradoxically, by virtue of their inevitable repetition in some innovative form of the form' (2012: 20). If innovation is already included in the generic, then rather than *undoing* genre, *Jennifer's Body* explores its productive potential, participating in its long-dated and continuous reinscription of the connection between women, horror and violence. In this sense, the film manifests the generative force of both gender and genre, going back to the 'same old story' and remaking it again and again.

Notes

1. For recent examples see E. Ann Kaplan (2012) on Nancy Meckler's *Sister My Sister*, a blend of the male-oriented horror genre with the woman's film; Karen Oughton (2014) on Mary Harron's *American Psycho* and the Soska Sisters' *American Mary*; and my book chapter on the remake of *Carrie* directed by Kimberly Peirce (Paszkiewicz 2018).
2. See: https://gothicfeminism.com/2017/10/11/exciting-new-cfp-women-make-horror/ (accessed 7 December 2017).
3. Peirse points to a new wave of women horror filmmakers who are garnering extensive and international critical interest. She specifically mentions *Prevenge* (Alice Lowe, 2016), *Raw* (Julia Ducournau, 2016), *XX* (Benjamin et al., 2017), *Egomaniac* (Kate Shenton, 2016), *The Bad Batch* (Ana Lily Amirpour, 2016) and *The Love Witch* (Anna Biller, 2016), the films which have been recently profiled in *Rolling Stone* (2016), *The Guardian* (2017) and *Sight and Sound* (2017). See: https://gothicfeminism.com/2017/10/11/exciting-new-cfp-women-make-horror/ (accessed 7 December 2017).
4. Ebert makes reference here to the successful *Twilight* (Catherine Hardwicke, 2008), which was codified in the critical reception of the film through its presumed 'female address': 'Just what we were waiting for, *Twilight* for boys, with Megan Fox in the Robert Pattinson role, except that I recall Pattinson was shirtless' (2012: 302). Ebert, just like some other spectators, seems disappointed by the lack of Fox's nudity in the film, contrary to what the film's trailer apparently promised.
5. After a seven-year break from filmmaking, Kusama directed *The Invitation* (2015), a critically acclaimed horror film about broken relationships. In 2017, she directed a short film for a horror anthology called *XX*, which boasts works from five female filmmakers. Kusama's short, *Her Only Living Son*, is a demonic possession story that reworks Roman Polański's *Rosemary's Baby* (1968). The director has recently divulged that she is surprised by her 'second act as a horror filmmaker', but she thinks that this genre really suits her and 'it is something that she wants to keep exploring' in her career (in Erbland 2017).
6. The posters read: 'From the Academy Award-Winning Writer of *Juno*'.
7. Production notes. Available at: https://robojapan.blogspot.com.es/2009/09/jennifers-body-200920th-century-fox.html (accessed 12 February 2017).
8. From the outset, the subgenre has attracted critical attention, especially from feminist perspectives – first, in relation to the male identification with the surviving female as a possible source of pleasure for young teenage boys (Clover 1992; Creed 1993); and later, regarding the spectatorial pleasures of female fans and possible empowerment through their identification with a violent protagonist who successfully carries out her revenge (Heller-Nicholas 2011). Jacinda Read counters the existing tendency to categorise rape-revenge as a subgenre of horror or exploitation cinema and posits that it is better understood as a narrative structure that has produced a generically diverse cycle of films. She also suggests that 'the rape-revenge cycle might be usefully read as one of the key ways in which Hollywood has attempted to make sense of feminism' (2000: 241).
9. In another interview, in which Kusama talked about her film *Invitation*, she mentioned some advantages of working on big budget productions: 'I made a couple of studio movies and really saw why people want to do it. You get incredible

resources, you work with some of the best crafts people in the world, and this was a different situation' (in Donato 2015).

10. Interpretations from this perspective abound on the Internet, especially those who reclaim images of violent women in popular genres, as this film review by heatheroffdead26, published on the *Internet Movie Database* (7/10/2009), shows: 'Can we just say – it's about darn time! And by that, I mean, finally! A "girl power let's kick some booty and make out with other demonic girls horror film"!! *Jennifer's Body* – and oh what a body it is – was a fantastic addition in to the snooze fest horror films that have been released as of late. The story (great dialog by Diablo, you go girl!!), the performances and the direction all rocked!'.

11. Broadly defined, 'postfeminism' encompasses, according to Tasker and Negra (2007), a set of assumptions that feminism has accomplished its goals, and is characterised by phenomena ranging from action films featuring violent heroines to the 'girling' of femininity.

12. This comment appeared under a post about the film, written by Brittney Jade Colangelo (2009), author of the blog *Day of the Woman: A Blog For the Feminine Side of Fear*, which stimulated an interesting debate between fans, revealing very complex negotiations about the representation of the female body in Cody's and Kusama's film.

13. According to an article for *The Guardian*, although many 'outstanding' directors were interested in adapting Ellis's novel, the producers opted for a female director, assuming that with a 'female perspective' they would be able to evade the protests over representations of violence against women (Bussmann 2009). Similar assumptions underpinned the hiring decisions in the case of Peirce's *Carrie* (Mischer in Chitwood 2013) and, as already mentioned, in the case of *Jennifer's Body*.

14. In this sense, it is interesting to mention that, unlike *Jennifer's Body*, Kimberly Peirce's *Carrie* did not provoke a public outcry over its 'feminist' label. Given Peirce's biographic legend as a queer filmmaker and her focus on marginal subjects in her films (she is best known for her successful independent production *Boys Don't Cry*, a dramatisation of the real-life story of Brandon Teena – a young woman who masqueraded as a boy and was raped and murdered in Nebraska), it is not at all surprising that her feminist credentials were not undermined in the critical discourses (see Paszkiewicz 2018).

15. See Ernest Mathijs and Jamie Sexton's (2012) analysis of the performance of gendered reception in the case of Catherine Hardwicke's *Twilight* (2008) and Rachel Talalay's *Tank Girl* (1995).

16. However, Anthony Hayt has recently argued that 'since 9/11, a common trend in horror film criticism has been to focus on the genre as a way of understanding and processing the trauma of the terrorist attacks that forever changed the cultural landscape of America, and of the world' (2017: 131). For Hayt, this approach that downplays gender is evidence of 'the misogyny of American culture at large, and of the "post-feminist" era specifically, by making moves to discount the importance of upholding the vigilance of gender-based political struggle in favour of more "important" political causes' (2017: 131–2). In this light, it is interesting to observe how the trauma motif is minimised and even ridiculed in *Jennifer's Body*: when the whole town is devastated by the deaths caused by the fire, the narrative focus remains on Jennifer and her transformation into a sexualised monster as a result of her sacrifice. It is not insignificant that the sacrifice scene plays out like a rape: Jennifer is bound and gagged as the lead singer of the band repeatedly penetrates her with a knife.

17. References to these and other films that portray menstrual monsters are manifested through a set of visual repetitions, as well as by means of allusions in the form of

posers in Needy's bedroom or even through dialogues – for example, in the scene in which Needy asks Jennifer: 'Is that my *Evil Dead* T-shirt?'

18. According to Craig and Fradley: '*Ginger Snaps*' vision of normative female heterosexuality as precisely a curse, a form of monstrous possession, offers an incisive critique of the limitations of gender roles and the (hetero)sexual double-standard' (2010: 90). For a more detailed account of *Ginger Snaps*, see also Nielsen (2004).
19. From the parodic *The Evil Dead I* and *The Evil Dead II* produced in the 1980s, through the profitable *Scream* saga in the 1990s and right up to *The Cabin in the Woods* in 2012 – which consolidates the satiric fusion of comedy and horror film – we are faced with an ironic distance to gender tropes.
20. For example, in the case of the previously mentioned *Ginger Snaps*. Paula Devonshire, producer of the critically acclaimed sequels of this film, has characterised all of the versions as feminist: 'I think it is definitely possible to make feminist horror movies and I think we have proven that with all three *Ginger Snaps* films' (in Barker et al. 2006: 68).
21. This deterministic and masculinised view of horror cinema has been questioned by many critics – for instance, Carol J. Clover (1992) and Rhona J. Berenstein (1996).
22. *Mean Girls* made almost 90 million US dollars at the box office, becoming one of the most profitable teen comedies of all times.
23. Water's picture is based on the book *Queen Bees and Wannabes*, written by the psychologist Rosalind Wiseman (2002). However, the representation of the 'mean girl' can be traced back even further – for instance, in the black comedy *Heathers* (Michael Lehmann, 1988), released fifteen years before Water's film.
24. It is worth mentioning that, contrary to the typical girl hero in slasher movies, Needy is not virginal nor sexually oppressed, thus the film breaks with the stereotypical binary we might expect: innocent woman versus monstrous woman. However, there is another interesting opposition between the two protagonists: Needy's nickname is a nod to her emotional over-dependency on Jennifer, while Jennifer's last name, Check, is a synonym for control.
25. The allusion to the butch figure might act as a mark of masculinisation, although it is also a clear reference to the homoerotic desire developed throughout the film between the protagonists.

3. HOLLYWOOD TRANSVESTITE: KATHRYN BIGELOW'S *THE HURT LOCKER*[1]

Presenting the 2010 Academy Award for Best Director, actress and filmmaker Barbra Streisand announced to the audience at the Kodak Theater: 'From among the five gifted nominees tonight, the winner could be, for the first time, a woman'. She checked the name in the envelope and, after a dramatic pause, she declared Kathryn Bigelow the winner. Although her gender was clearly underscored in this short but powerful statement, Bigelow herself made no reference to it in her acceptance speech. Instead, she praised her fellow nominees and emphasised the collaborative nature of her achievement, thanking the cast and crew who helped her make *The Hurt Locker* (2008). As she left the stage, the band, as though to highlight what Bigelow herself chose not to address, played Helen Reddy's 'I Am a Woman' – a song which became an enduring anthem for the women's liberation movement in the 1970s.

While many commentators in the mainstream press celebrated Bigelow's triumph as a female director in a predominantly male industry, the event also provoked a considerable number of negative responses. In her critical piece titled 'Kathryn Bigelow, the Absentee Feminist', Susan G. Cole accused the filmmaker of making no reference to the significance of her accomplishment for feminism and expressed her deepest regret that some 'feminist bashers [. . .] cheer her on for remaining resolutely gender neutral. They love the fact that she won her prize for a war movie that blows up, for being one of the boys, for telling feminists to get off her cloud' (2010). Bigelow's acceptance speech and critical responses to it should not surprise us if we consider Christina Lane's observation that 'her connections to feminism, as represented in public discourse, have always been ambiguous. She seems quite conscious of feminist politics and willing to engage with feminism, but she remains ambivalent about labelling her films in terms of gender politics' (2000: 101). As Shelley Cobb also argues, Bigelow (like Jane Campion – another successful filmmaker and the only woman to have won the Palme D'Or at Cannes)[2] often rejects the politicisation of her gender, while recognising the ongoing gender inequality of the film industry. Her position, according to Cobb, 'necessarily negotiates contemporary postfeminist culture that continues to claim that women can do whatever they want even as there has been growing acknowledgment in the media of the entertainment of inequality' (2015: 50). In the case of Bigelow, this negotiation is particularly fraught, not only because she rejects the 'feminist' tag, but also because she has consistently resisted any attempts to categorise her as a 'female' director – whether in relation to her films, her position in the industry or audiences. At the same time, the repeated insistence on Bigelow's seeming gender neutrality has been closely intertwined with critical discourses characterising her filmmaking as 'muscular', due to the fact that she usually works within presumed 'masculinist' genres (see Jermyn 2003).

It seems particularly revealing that, although Bigelow's status has been negotiated in various ways throughout her almost forty-year career, it is the 'tough guy in drag' tag (Nochimson 2010) that pervades in the responses to her winning the Oscar for Best Director. If, some decades ago, scholars tended to read Bigelow's penchant for directing men in (supposedly) male-orientated action genres as a way of destabilising gender stereotypes and positioned her as the 'Hollywood Transgressor' (Lane 2000; Jermyn 2003), after her subsequent success these traits were seen in a highly pejorative manner.[3] According to Rona Murray's study (2011), the reception of themes of gender transgression and masquerade, considered key artistic preoccupations of Bigelow's body of work in various critics' responses in the early 1990s, has changed drastically in the current context, 'from a perception of a positive political power in the transgressive representations of the earlier films to a more negative assessment of the transgressive nature of Bigelow herself as a successful women filmmaker in Hollywood' (2011: 2).

The lack of popularity and of international political approval regarding the war in Iraq, and the nation's subsequent occupation, is another crucial factor to consider here: making a film about a conflict that is still unfolding is a challenging task and one prone to elicit disparate opinions.[4] Indeed, many reviews of *The Hurt Locker* set out to demonstrate Bigelow's ideological alignment with American imperialism, stamping the director as a political conformist. These accusations resurfaced after the release of her following feature, *Zero Dark Thirty* (2012), which dramatises the international manhunt for al Qaeda leader Osama bin Laden. In contrast to *The Hurt Locker*, the latter movie features a female protagonist: Maya, the determined CIA agent whom the film depicts as highly capable and primarily responsible for finding bin Laden. In light of the current postfeminist context and its conservative backlash that reinstates models of individualist femininity (Faludi 2006; Negra 2009), as well as 'imperialist feminism's' role in the justification for the invasion of Afghanistan and Iraq,[5] Bigelow's approach to gender, both in her films and in the construction of her authorial persona, further complicates the reception of her triumph in the industry and the evaluation of the transgressive potential of her oeuvre.

Bigelow is, indeed, an uneasy figure for feminist film criticism. It is evident that she does not follow the model of counter-cinema and, according to what can be deduced from some of the critical responses to her films, she seems to be particularly enticed by its degraded 'other' – that is, popular, patriarchal, mainstream cinema.[6] This evaluation, however, does not do justice to the complexity of Bigelow's oeuvre; as some scholars have shown, most of her work has never sat comfortably in the presumed division between mainstream (commercial) and art-house (oppositional) cinema.[7] Although identified as 'mainstream', *The Hurt Locker* was made on a relatively low budget financed by non-Hollywood companies. After its first screenings at the Venice and Toronto film festivals, and its release in Italy in 2008, the film was practically ignored by distributors for several months, until it was picked up, in June 2009, for very limited distribution in the United States by Summit Entertainment, initially only in New York and Los Angeles. Even though it was purchased and distributed by a Hollywood conglomerate, the film earned fifty times less than *Avatar* (2009) – a sci-fi blockbuster directed by Bigelow's ex-husband, James Cameron, which competed with *The Hurt Locker* across several Oscar categories. Interestingly, despite these numbers,[8] *The Hurt Locker* was considered an abandonment of Bigelow's earlier experimental work for mainstream narrative fiction and, consequently, as an inevitable elision of feminist politics.[9]

In addition to reprimanding Bigelow for supposedly 'selling out' to join the Hollywood male elite, the reviews tended to criticise her for underrepresenting women in *The Hurt Locker*. Although it is true that Bigelow ignored the development of women characters in this film, emphatically decentring them in the narrative, this decision can be explained by the generic conventions of war films, which were overlooked in the rush to gendered judgment. Bigelow's interest in representing masculine subjects – a central tenet of her biographic legend repeatedly brought up in the context of the Academy Awards[10] – contributed to her positioning against James Cameron, who, as Christina Lane observes, has generally been interested in portraying female characters 'displaying muscular hard bodies, brandishing highly sophisticated weapons and devoting themselves to tough humanity-saving missions', and thus embodying 'an easily consumed feminism' (2003: 188).

The reviews which read *The Hurt Locker* as 'anti-feminist' or 'anti-women', in contrast to the apparently 'feminist' filmography of Cameron, reveal certain assumptions about women filmmakers and the types of films they make (or should make). For example, in condemning the Academy for overtly privileging 'the military landscape' and 'muscular filmmaking' over 'the domestic landscape' and 'the organic, life-affirming situations of romantic comedy',[11] film critic Martha Nochimson (2010) manifests a more conventional approach to genre and what appeals to women audiences. But, as Rona Murray rightly asks, 'if Bigelow chooses masculine subjects, doesn't that suggest that other women might want, at least, to watch the same?' (2011: 19).

The sort of comments that unequivocally place Bigelow's film practice within the supposedly 'masculine' realm of action and war genres, and often criticise her for it, seem to take for granted that genres employ a single gender address: a war film, which features central male protagonists and secondary female characters, is perceived thus in terms of the ubiquitous normative male spectator. This leads to the assertion, already questioned by a number of feminist film scholars,[12] that spectators necessarily align themselves according to the binary opposition of gender and that filmic pleasures are gender specific.[13] As Pam Cook has shown, 'the idea that certain genres are, or [. . .] have been, more "suitable" for women as either viewers or as filmmakers' relegates women to a separate space defined as 'women's culture' (2012: 38). This view can be traced in Bigelow's fear of being confined to the 'female/feminine' ghetto, as she confessed in a number of interviews. On the other hand, seeking to detect Bigelow's 'womanly gaze' by examining female characters in her films does not allow for the nuances in the director's film practice. As Deborah Jermyn observed in reference to *The Weight of Water* (2000), placing this type of expectation on women directors is not only reductive, since it risks underestimating various individual and institutional factors involved in the filmmaking process, and in Hollywood in particular, but it also presents theoretical difficulties, such as the subjective and highly mutable notions of femininity and masculinity (Jermyn 2003: 139).

Bigelow's triumph in the industry (if one judges triumph at least in part by the Oscar recognition, although not necessarily box office results) seems particularly problematic for feminist criticism, not only because of her apparent capitulation to the 'masculinist' mainstream action genre, but also because of her rejection of both feminist and gendered identities. Although she remained routinely silent on the issue of gender and was reluctant to talk about being a feminist touchstone – a gesture Manohla Dargis (2010a) considered a 'quiet yet profound form of rebellion' against 'nosy interviewers' who insist on designating her as a *female* director – her femininity is still a crucial trope, which has been central not only in the textual analyses of her films, but also in the popular and critical debates concerning her status as an auteur. It is significant that, following Bigelow's win, Sigourney Weaver – who starred in James Cameron's *Avatar* (2009) – allegedly attributed Cameron's 'defeat' in the Best Director category to the fact that he 'didn't have breasts', claiming that the Academy wanted to make history by naming its first ever female Best Director (Baldwin 2010). In the run-up to the Oscars, the opposition between Cameron and Bigelow was imbued with tabloid-style rivalry coverage. In *Forbes*, for instance, we could read: 'This time, it's personal. Why wouldn't Bigelow want to best her ex, especially when he reportedly left her for his lead actress in *The Terminator?*' (Blakeley 2010). As Yvonne Tasker and Eylem Atakav rightly notice, 'the melodramatic terms in which this run-off was covered was attributed by some media pundits to a desire to reinvigorate falling ratings for the once must-see ceremony' (2010: 66); however, the overtly sexist nature of some of these comments should not be ignored. Lane demonstrated in her earlier study on Bigelow's career that this association with Cameron, which is frequently entwined with allegations that their marriage benefited her career, has proven tricky for Bigelow's position as an auteur, as it reproduces the tenacious discourse of 'sexual favours' undermining women's hard work and professional authority (Lane 2000: 102).[14] According to Lane, their personal and professional relationship on a number of projects has raised uneasy questions for feminist criticism about how to write about women's work when those women actively seek production opportunities and commercial success by making use of their connections with men (2000: 102). The scholar posits that

> rather than attempt to gloss over these relationships, which are inevitable in a male-dominated industry, by positing a binary opposition in which a female author exists alone or not at all, we need to acknowledge this kind of partnership as a valuable and fruitful avenue for women's access into mainstream film and as a pragmatic necessity. (2000: 102)

Bigelow's status as an auteur is widely recognised, but at the same time subtly undermined. Despite her constant attempts to avoid becoming the story herself, discourses around Bigelow as a *female* filmmaker have accompanied her throughout her career. As is the case with other women filmmakers, the construction of her film authorship is closely related to the celebration of her appearance. In his *Variety* piece, titled 'Unlikely Rivals on the Oscar Circuit', Peter Bart traced a comparison between Jane Campion and Bigelow, but instead of focusing on their films or their careers, he dwelt on their appearance. The article, which disappeared from the official *Variety* website, was denounced by Melissa Silverstein (2009) in her blog *Women and Hollywood*.

In most profiles published in the mainstream media, Bigelow is depicted as a tough, cold and uncompromising woman who is completely focused on her career – an image which marries well with the supposedly conservative message of her last films. On the other hand, these same traits tend to be accompanied by attributes traditionally associated with femininity. In *The Guardian* article, which described Bigelow as the 'toughest director' in Hollywood, we can read:

> On paper, she sounds like the sort of woman who drinks men under the table having first beaten them at arm-wrestling and a Hummer rally. In person, though, she's tall and waif-like, gently spoken and regally handsome. She is 57, but looks a decade younger, and her hands make graceful movements in the air as she talks. (Rose 2009)

According to Jermyn (2003: 128), such detailed musings on Bigelow's body echo the discourses that circulated around another female 'pioneer' in Hollywood – Dorothy Arzner, whose films were similarly discussed in relation to her appearance. Drawing on Judith Mayne's account of the promotion of Arzner's films, Jermyn shows how these discourses sought to place her in relation to conventional standards of femininity, 'a struggle made all the more perplexing by Arzner's overtly "butch" persona' (2003: 129). Despite some differences (Bigelow adheres perhaps more readily to the standard norms of female beauty and heteronormative codes of gender performance than Arzner did), in both cases the discourses surrounding their star personas highlighted that these 'feminine' qualities coexist with their apparently 'masculine' traits, so that the latter are rendered less threatening (2003: 128). On the other hand, it is important to remember that this type of comment increases the discursive circulation of their biographic legends and notably influences their reputations as filmmakers and auteurs. Kathryn Bigelow, with her ability to handle big-budget films, can indeed be read as a commercial auteur in Corrigan's (1991) terms: she seems perfectly aware of the fact that her public appearances can determine if, and to what extent, she will be evaluated through the 'auteurist' criteria and, as a consequence, ensure her a variety of choices and available routes in her film career. In this sense, her resistance to conventional tropes of femininity and her embracing of a variety of masculine identities, both textually and extratextually, has undoubtedly contributed to an elevated degree of visibility and critical recognition.

On the whole, her authorial performance, incessantly mediated by a myriad of discursive forces, tends to produce opposing evaluations of her oeuvre: from an emphatic rejection stemming from some sectors of feminism that see her latest films as a sign of artistic bankruptcy to an unconditioned celebration of Bigelow as *the only* woman who has been granted exclusive membership to the male elite club of true auteurs. Paradoxically, both discourses, which seek to render Bigelow an exotic oddity, can be treated as two sides of the same coin: they are reactions to a woman director who refuses to make films according to gender expectations, who mobilises supposedly 'masculine' genres without openly attacking its conventions.

In the controversies surrounding *The Hurt Locker* – which arise from the various classifications of Kathryn Bigelow as anti-feminist, masculinist, mainstream – it is clear that Bigelow's status is under continuous negotiation. As Jermyn observed long before the filmmaker's triumph at the Oscars,

> as one of the few high-profile female directors in contemporary Hollywood cinema, and one who has distinguished herself in the action genre at that, she has become a curiosity, an oddity and object of fascination, whom critics and academics struggle to place. (2003: 127)

Bigelow's case seems particularly relevant to feminist film criticism, not only because of her growing media visibility, but also because it shows that the preoccupation with 'feminist aesthetics' or the 'woman's voice' in thinking about women's cinema may sometimes prove unproductive, especially if we approach a film such as *The Hurt Locker*, which raises considerable challenges to this paradigm. As Murray (2011) points out, *The Hurt Locker*'s critical reception has been dominated by discourses that obscured the wider repercussions and political implications suggested by her textual examination of masculinity, also present in Bigelow's previous films, such as *The Loveless* (1981), *Near Dark* (1987), *Point Break* (1991) and *K19: The Widowmaker* (2002). What is more, the predominance of these critical lines has seriously limited proper recognition of Bigelow in feminist criticism, which – by focusing on the issues of female representation – has often overlooked, for example, her skilful command of the genre. My aim here is not so much to champion Bigelow as a 'progressive', 'feminist auteur', but to present a framework that might prove useful for producing feminist readings of her films, throwing them into a 'feminist orbit', as invoked by Christine Gledhill (1994: 121). This is not, by any means, meant to imply that *The Hurt Locker* does not pose problems for such readings. With its focus on a delimited perspective of heterosexual male protagonists and engagement with US imperialist politics, it unquestionably poses many problems. In what follows, however, I wish to demonstrate how, while Bigelow's film can be readily available to conservative interpretations, it also opens up space and brings to the fore questions that disrupt such approaches. I believe that addressing a wider range of critical frameworks within which women's filmmaking can be discussed might help to redirect demands for a specifically feminist aesthetic or 'woman's voice' to an examination of the multiple factors that come into play in the struggle over making sense of particular examples of women's work.

If Bigelow's public figure has become a site of struggle over competing versions of her transgressive stance towards masculinity, so was the issue of the representation of war in *The Hurt Locker*. Some critics praised the filmmaker for her realistic aesthetics, foregrounding how the documentary-like style heightened the sensorial immersion of the audience and how the film succeeded in capturing the 'real' war (see, for example, Schwarzbaum 2009). Others, in turn, rejected Bigelow's cinematic vision for being 'too Hollywood' and conformist. A number of left-wing commentators, for example, blamed Bigelow for not providing a deep insight into the nature of the war in Iraq – in their opinion, *The Hurt Locker* avoided the wider political context, focusing solely on the celebration of individual heroism in Hollywood style. This was also the main concern of war photographer Michael Kamber (2010), writing for *The New York Times* photography blog. He perceived *The Hurt Locker* as not realistic enough, accusing Bigelow of glamorising the war and the protagonist, who 'appears to be fighting the war alone'.

The predominance of this interpretative framework is not surprising, since in the war film genre, correspondence with reality has always been an important criterion of validity. Instead of reading Bigelow's aesthetics as a documentary gesture that transmits an accurate description of warfare, in the following sections I will consider it – to quote Steven Shaviro – 'a delirious excess of postmodern vision' (1993: 9), which exemplifies, among other things, the director's meta-cinematic approach to filming. The concept is a good starting point for analysing, in the first instance, how the combination of the complex audio-visual grammar with the self-reflexive strategy of genre blending facilitates a sophisticated reflection on the generic process – in particular, in reference to how it engages with gender – and on the other hand, how the heterogeneous visual regimes that Bigelow orchestrates create fissures in the film's dominant frame and its basis in the narrative of Western heroic masculinity. Although Shaviro's term referred principally to overcoming the ocularcentric, representational paradigm, in favour of a paradigm of embodied perception, I find it highly useful to negotiate between these two approaches, in order to address the complexities in *The Hurt Locker* with regards to the spectatorial experience it offers.

Hypertrophy of the Visual

The ocularcentric paradigm, usually articulated through the metaphor of the eye, has long prevailed in feminist film studies, which drew a parallel between vision and specific patterns of control and mystification. This approach is often associated with the so-called 'apparatus theory', developed in analogy to both Plato's allegory of the cave and the Freudian unconscious. Following this line of research – inspired mostly by the work of Jean-Louis Baudry (1975) and Laura Mulvey (1975) – scholars paid special attention to a film's impression of reality and its power over the audience, derived from a series of factors: a passive immobility of the viewers, the darkness of the screening room, a clear separation from the outside world and so on. As feminist film theory has demonstrated, cinema grants viewers an illusion of control and power over what is being seen, reproducing a binary structure of looking and to-be-look-at-ness (Mulvey 1975). Needless to say, sexual difference is crucial here: the gaze is seen as 'an all-knowing entity, often assigned to the male patriarchal subject, comparable to the Cartesian eye/I' (Pisters 2003: 18). In her discussion of this paradigm, Patricia Pisters observes that the gaze can sometimes refer to 'a more abstract notion of the other as such' (2003: 18). This is made evident, for example, in 'The Oppositional Gaze' (1992), in which bell hooks famously drew on Frantz Fanon's work to pinpoint diverse factors of oppression that impregnate the Western gaze.

As Thomas Elsaesser and Malte Hagener (2010) observe in their evocative *Film Theory: An Introduction Through the Senses*, the eye, originally the organ of truth in a Cartesian sense, which 'stands for transparency and visibility', can also 'be the occasion for an unrelenting demand for self-examination to the point of self-incrimination' (2010: 84). Therefore, films that privilege sight in an ostentatious and excessive way, and thus clearly participate in ocularcentrism, can sometimes end up questioning it. *Peeping Tom* (Michael Powell, 1960), *Blade Runner* (Ridley Scott, 1982), *A Clockwork Orange* (Stanley Kubrick, 1971) and *Minority Report* (Steven Spielberg, 2002) all explicitly feature the eye as a *leitmotiv*, focusing our attention on, but also problematising, vision, control and mystification.

Vision and voyeurism are also at the core of Bigelow's recurrent obsessions: from her experimental short film *Set-Up* (1978), which features two men beating each other to a bloody pulp in a dark alley, accompanied by a voice-over of two professors, Marshall Blonsky and Sylvère Lotringer; her action thriller *Blue Steel* (1989), which enquires into the binaries of the gaze between a policewoman and a serial killer; to *Strange Days* (1995), a dystopian, science fiction neo-noir about SQUID technology, allowing a user to experience the memories and physical sensations recorded by others, in which Bigelow offers a self-conscious exploration of the gloomy implications of voyeurism.[15]

In her eighth feature, *The Hurt Locker*, Bigelow has also invested heavily in the gaze, as the numerous extreme close-ups of eyes and multiple perspectives offered in the film suggest. It is not a coincidence that in the film's opening sequence the images are technologically mediated – through a camera mounted on a remote-controlled robot sent in to investigate a suspected improvised explosive device (IED) – and that these first shots are clearly digitalised: it is only after a few seconds pass that the pixels begin to constitute a clear and precise image. As Robert Burgoyne observes in his reading of the movie, this

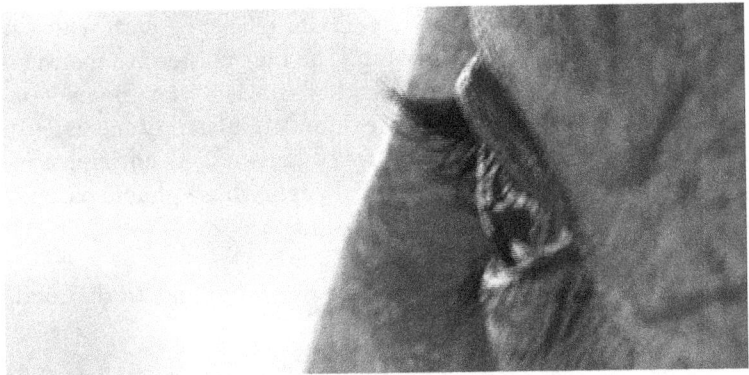

Figure 3.1 Eye and vision come under critical scrutiny in *The Hurt Locker*.

scene opens abruptly, *in medias res*, without preamble or narrative exposition, plunging us directly into a chaotic street scene in Iraq:

> In contrast to the traditional war film, where the cartography of the battlefield is defined from the outset with panoramic long shots and aerial overviews – a mapping operation that can be read as the cinematic analogue to the act of taking control of a geographic space (Conley 2007) – *The Hurt Locker* opens suddenly on an urban setting in which the streets have been turned into minefields and the markets into snipers' nests, visualising through a fast, fragmented montage an experience of war no longer defined by fronts or sectors, a war in which improvised bombs and irregular combatants are concealed in the folds and textures of urban life. (2012: 13)

The multiplicity of cameras, angles and points of view in *The Hurt Locker* do not imply, paradoxically, taking control of a geographic space – which, in the traditional war film, is achieved by means of panoramic and aerial shots, as Burgoyne rightly observes – but quite the opposite: it produces a sensation of panic and extreme fragmentation of the perceived reality. The spatial organisation, far from offering a Cartesian perspective, is fractured, confusing and disorienting, as Bigelow constantly alternates her angles and proximities between extreme close-ups and high-angle long shots, which are juxtaposed in the same sequence. Thus, we are confronted with the difficulty of making sense of the images and, as a consequence, the environment that is being depicted.[16]

The aesthetics of kinesthetic agitation, along with the cacophony of sounds (deep breathing, heartbeats, sirens and the shouts of the soldiers that dominate the soundtrack), create a claustrophobic atmosphere of anxiety and potential threat, contrasting with the cold and rational efficiency with which the protagonists are trying to dismantle a bomb. The men cluster around the monitor on which the robotic images are being broadcast. The moment is staged with obvious reference to sexual penetration, significantly mediated through the screen. The camera placed on the robot acts here as an inquisitive eye, a prolongation of the masculine, patriarchal gaze, whose phallic nature is made evident in the dialogue between the two soldiers:

> Sanborn [when the robot approaches a pile of sacks in the road]: Hello mama!
> Thompson: Now push it in.
> Sanborn: I can't get in.
> Thompson: What do you mean you can't get in? Pretend it's your dick, man.

The fantasies of penetration and risk control are, nonetheless, suddenly interrupted. The sequence culminates in the death of Staff Sergeant Thompson, who was in charge of the mission. As the bomb detonates, a slow-motion sequence plays out: the eruption of earth with Thompson's body flung towards the camera – and the spectator's space – his face, hidden under the visor, smeared and covered in blood.

Although undoubtedly focused on the gaze, rather than producing an illusion of control and omnipotence, the images that compose this initial sequence transmit the hypertrophy of the visual, borrowing another evocative term from Shaviro, who adopted it to analyse Bigelow's *Blue Steel*:

> Vision in *Blue Steel* is excruciatingly, preternaturally vivid; reality is heightened into feverish hallucination. Such a *hypertrophy of the visual* is Bigelow's way of undoing the security and possessiveness that have conventionally been associated with the 'male gaze.' Bigelow pushes fetishism and voyeuristic fascination to the point where they explode. (1993: 8 [emphasis added])

Similarly, the opening sequence in *The Hurt Locker* also suggests that Bigelow's central concern is not 'realist' transparency, but rather the critical examination of voyeurism and the fantasies of control, as well as the technologies of mediation. Arguably, the object of scrutiny and the focus of the film will be both the genre itself and the Western hero who emerges from this universe: Sergeant William James (Jeremy Renner), a new team leader of the US Army EOD team in Iraq, who replaces Thompson.

James is not well-received by his subordinates, mainly because of his maverick methods, seen by his teammates as imprudent and unnecessarily hazardous. He refuses to use remote-controlled robots to dismantle explosives, preferring to disarm them manually; he often removes his bomb protection suit, as it reduces his velocity and mobility, or disconnects his communication set when he is fed up with his teammates' warnings. Sergeant J. T. Sanborn (Anthony Mackie) and Specialist Owen Eldridge (Brian Geraghty), who are in the final thirty-eight days of their rotation, fear James will get them all killed by his reckless and unorthodox behaviour, and at some point seriously contemplate getting rid of him by 'accidentally' triggering an explosion. The only person with whom James seems to create an emotional bond during his stay in Baghdad is an Iraqi boy named 'Beckham' (Christopher Sayegh), who works at the military base selling DVDs to the soldiers. During one of the missions in an abandoned warehouse, James discovers the dead body of a young man, who has been surgically implanted with a bomb, and mistakes him for Beckham. At the end of the film, James returns home to his wife and their recently born son, but he struggles to adapt to the routine of civilian life, with its ordinary tasks such as shopping at the supermarket and participating in family dinners. Shortly thereafter, he voluntarily returns to Iraq to serve in another US Army EOD unit, with the subtitle on the screen informing the viewer that he is starting his 365-day rotation.

In many aspects, *The Hurt Locker* is a very conventional war movie, as it revolves around a series of easily recognisable clichés associated with the genre:[17] dead and wounded bodies, bonding through violence, fatherhood and representations of the cultural, national and religious other. War as a drug or intoxication – a perspective thrown into stark relief in the epigraph of the film[18] – was also one of the *leitmotiv* in *Apocalypse Now* (Francis Ford Coppola, 1979), in which Captain Benjamin L. Willard famously declared: 'When I was here, I wanted to be there; when I was there, all I could think of was getting back into the jungle'. This quote highlights another recurrent trope in war films, especially those depicting the conflict in Vietnam: the soldier's trauma when he returns home – a trope reproduced over and over in subsequent war films, including *The Hurt Locker*. This is probably because the representation of armed conflict in Vietnam War films has become one of the predominant modes of representing combat in US film culture. According to Bruce Bennett and Bülent Diken, its characteristics can be easily traced in *The Hurt Locker*:

> [T]he figure of the traumatized, institutionalised soldier unable to adjust to civilian life [...], the tenuous relationship formed between a soldier and a local boy, the invisibility or absence of an enemy, violent antagonism between fellow soldiers, the casual commission of war crimes by US troops, and the depiction of the subjective experience of war as cinematically hyperreal or hallucinatory. (2011: 171)

Other scholars, in turn, distinguish a subgenre of Iraq War films, typified by such movies as *The Situation* (Philip Haas, 2006), *In the Valley of Elah* (Paul Haggis, 2007) and *Redacted* (Brian De Palma, 2007). Robert Eberwein characterises the more recent Iraq War films in the following way:

> In contrast to films about the [first] Gulf War, which make extensive use of wide-angle shots conveying the bleak and endless desert landscape in which fighting occurs, these have a distinctive mise-en-scène that immerses us in cramped doorways and narrow, almost impassable streets. The soldiers either cannot tell whether they are seeing the enemy (the endless checkpoint confrontations) or are incapable of seeing them until it's too late (the suicide bombers' cars that explode, the gunfire that rains down from snipers above). [...] The general tone of the films is despairing, totally the reverse of the loyal and enthusiastic support we see in films made during and about World War II. (2010: 134)

Despite the contrast with the conventions used in epic films revisiting World War II or films about the first Gulf War – displaying massive aerial bombings and very low-level combat against insurgents – *The Hurt Locker* complies with many of the visual and narrative conventions of the Hollywood war movie in a wider sense. This conventionality – in particular, in reference to the film's plot – inevitably contributed to its conservative readings: an individual hero saves a community (both the Americans and the innocent Iraqis) and defeats his enemies, the Iraqi insurgents – a message that seems to support the so-called neoliberal warfare in the context of post-9/11 and its rhetoric of liberation.[19]

Nevertheless, Bigelow's film, in a similar manner to other recent instances of the Iraq War film, destabilises the heroic framework of the Hollywood war genre on a number of levels, beginning with the very mode of narrating. The structure in *The Hurt Locker* evokes a collection of 'serialised war correspondent dispatches', as Douglas A. Cunningham rightly observes in his article 'Explosive Structure: Fragmenting the New Modernist War Narrative in *The Hurt Locker*' (2010). The film's narrative is composed of seven episodes: the prologue, which depicts Thompson's death; several missions of the Company Bravo over the course of five disparate days; and, finally, an epilogue consisting of two parts, James's short stay with his family in the United States after his tour of duty in Iraq and his voluntary return to the combat zone. Throughout the film, the superimposed titles announce the Company Bravo's days remaining in Iraq (thirty-eight, thirty-seven, twenty-three, sixteen, two) and finally the cycle begins again with 365 days left. Interestingly, this countdown structure, which evokes the ticking of a bomb, does not offer a narrative causality; Bigelow is not interested in writing a faithful chronicle of events, but rather she focuses on singular episodes, apparently disconnected from one another (Cunningham 2010). The almost total absence of combat scenes and the evasion of classical Hollywood structure, based on narrative causality and the gradual increase of dramatic tension, are significant. The only episode which might be considered 'typical' of the classical war film is the duel between the snipers in the desert, which, in stark contrast to the other episodes, is practically deprived of dramatic tension. Its strategic placement, at precisely the mid-point of the narrative, suggests that the war represented in *The Hurt Locker* does not have a beginning or an end, but is comprised of a series of never-ending repetitions.

In addition to being episodic, then, the narrative can also be described as cyclic, as the film concludes with James's return to Iraq, and the final shot brings us back to the beginning of the story – different, but the same – as if it was a closed circuit. This ending, which depicts James walking alone along an empty desert road, echoes the typical closure of the Western, in which a solitary hero leaves the town and rides his horse into the setting sun.

The allusions to the Western genre play a vital role in *The Hurt Locker*, which is not surprising, considering the ideological centrality of the Far West myth, its values and iconography to American culture and the war film in particular. This genre is of great importance to Bigelow's film oeuvre in a wider sense, both in terms of her heroes and the settings in which their heroic actions take place; just to give a few examples, we could mention Caleb's confrontations with a group of vampires in *Near Dark*, a series of tense encounters between the protagonists in *Point Break*, which the director herself described as a sort of 'wet Western' (in Tasker 1993: 163) and the final shooting in *Blue Steel* between Megan and Eugene, all of which invoke the iconic Wild West duels.

In *The Hurt Locker*, most of the scenes take place in open spaces – paradigmatic of the representation of the frontier in Westerns – which are

Figure 3.2   James as the heroic figure in the untamed landscape who asserts mastery over the environment.

constructed around binary oppositions, as elucidated by Jim Kitses in his famous study *Horizons West* (1969): wilderness versus civilisation, West versus East, nature versus culture, individual versus community, good versus bad, strong versus weak, male versus female and so on. The Western thematic elements, delineated by Will Wright in the early 1980s, can be readily applied to *The Hurt Locker* and, consequently, they can contribute to our understanding of the film as a celebration of a timeless motif of heroism, built around 'the imagery of a wild, untamed, and dangerous landscape, but a landscape nonetheless in which a strong and resourceful (white, male) individual could assert his interests, fight his battles, and triumph over his adversaries' (1982: 122).

The allusions to the Western in *The Hurt Locker* are plentiful and easy to find: the music that evokes Ennio Morricone's soundtrack in spaghetti Westerns; a narrative conflict developed around some central iconographic elements that symbolise the civilised (soldiers) and non-civilised (Iraqi insurgents); Baghdad represented as a chaotic no man's land waiting to be 'ordered' by the hero (Bennett and Diken 2011: 168); and dialogues that regularly reference Westerns – for instance, when Sanborn wishes Thompson 'happy trails', or when James boldly exclaims: 'I'll tell you when I'm standing over [the bomb], cowboy'. In this sense, *The Hurt Locker* clearly draws on the masculine Wild West soldier bravado à la John Wayne. The adrenaline-addicted Sergeant James is, in a similar way, dangerously reckless, constantly putting his life and that of the members of his team at risk.[20]

In its apparently nostalgic exaltation of individual heroism – the protagonist, striving to be a cowboy, wandering the streets in a dead-end small town – the film moves through the territory of universal myths. 'War is a drug', we read in the film's epigraph, and this statement implies that Bigelow is interested in representing war as a generalised experience of addiction, rather than as an historically accurate account of a particular conflict, much as its 'documentary' aesthetics or the subtitle at the beginning of the film that informs us where the events take place (Baghdad) might suggest the opposite. Some reviewers considered this lack of specificity as an evasion of political baggage that 'ruined' other Iraq War films (Phillips 2009), while others read it as responsible for providing a timeless insight into the 'reality' of war and heroic action (Denny 2011).

However, I would like to suggest that Bigelow is not only concerned with the myth, but also with *how* the myth is constructed. Already in the first scene, when the assumed protagonist (Sergeant Thompson) is replaced so swiftly, the classical Hollywood identification patterns are called into question and the interchangeable status of the hero is foregrounded. This aspect points to Bigelow's interest in addressing an abstract masculinity, a cliché or an icon, rather than in focusing on psychological verisimilitude or character development. In fact, the aesthetics of generic cross-referencing, in particular in relation to the conventional tropes of masculinity – a traumatised soldier that cannot adjust to his new overwhelmingly domestic civilian life or a lone gunslinger in the Western – highlights Bigelow's meta-cinematic approach to depicting heroic masculinity. By means of dialogically interacting with conventions of several genres, she critically debates the nature of generic process and the production of meaning, at the same time pointing to the constructed nature of the familiar identities emerging from these filmic universes.

The narrative of an individualised heroism, thrown into relief by the meta-cinematic exposure, elicits both the almost erotic fascination with the figure of the hero and, at the same time, the awareness of its fabrication. The archetypal male hero is constantly being scrutinised under the inquisitive gaze of the camera. A combination of extreme close-ups, medium and wide shots from various angles, supported by swiping pans and tilts, nervous zooms in and out and a particular type of editing – dubbed by Manohla Dargis (2010b) as 'accordion-like', due to the constantly changing perspectives – dissect James's body with an almost surgeon-like precision. Although extremely active and positioned at the centre of the narrative, he possesses the quality of 'to-be-looked-at-ness', as theorised by Laura Mulvey; his 'body, stylised and fragmented by close-ups, is the content of the film and the direct recipient of the spectator's look' (1989b: 22).

It is clear that the protagonist is configured as an object of the gaze: in one scene we become aware of Iraqi citizens filming James, who is carefully positioned at the centre of the drama, defusing a car bomb. It is not a coincidence that so many scenes in *The Hurt Locker* evoke filmmaking itself. The presence of multiple cameras and multiple screens – a recurrent feature in contemporary war films (Pisters 2010: 232–52) – calls our attention to the mediated nature of these images, undermining their transparency and subjecting them to self-examination. In *The Hurt Locker*, the film itself becomes its main preoccupation: Bigelow creates a 'meta-war film' that interrogates its own processes of meaning production.

'We've got a lot of eyes on us', Sanborn states at one point – and this may refer not only to the number of onlookers observing the spectacle, but also to the sort of delirious vision this scene, and the film in general, orchestrates. An aesthetic strategy based on the jittery movement of the camera, fast editing, lenses that constantly focus and refocus, framing James from new angles, denies us spatial orientation, while at the same time conveys the sensation of visual vigilance which no longer belongs to the hero. As previously argued, the hypertrophy of the visual is Bigelow's way of undoing the mastery that has conventionally been associated with the 'male gaze' (Shaviro 1993: 8), inextricably intertwined with control and surveillance. The filmmaker multiplies vision, but at the same time refuses the visual plenitude of what is seen; neither James, nor the spectators, can visually take control of a space through the act

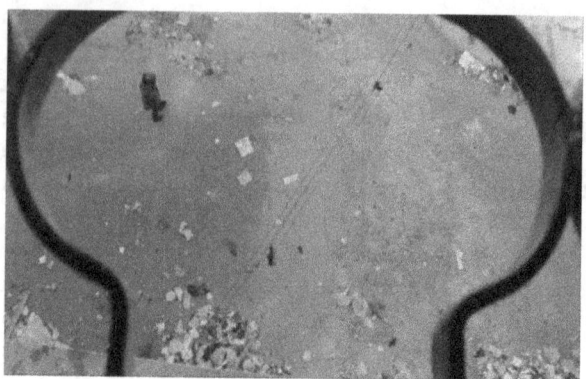

Figure 3.3 All eyes are on James.

of looking.[21] There are repeated camera shots of the local community as they observe the American soldiers taking charge of their country; likewise, there are numerous shots of the soldiers, in turn, looking back at the community in an agitated way. However, despite the act of looking back, the soldiers do not seem to 'see' or understand the reality of the situation in front of them. Both the looking and the looking back upset the corporeal steadiness of the Western hero and, at the same time, call into question the US mission in Iraq. This sensation of uncertainty and even failure of the American project – already anticipated at the level of narrative, when it is revealed that the base is not called 'Camp Liberty' anymore, but 'Camp Victory' – is transmitted visually in the powerful scene in which James, after successfully disarming a bomb, notices another wire and, after pulling on it, discovers more bombs hidden around him. In this, and many other scenes, James is viewed from high-angle, long-lens shots through windows and balconies, which render him the distant, vulnerable and exposed object of the gaze.

Ultimately, these scenes evidence that Bigelow does not simply present or celebrate the male icon, but rather she scratches the surface of this figure, exposing the discursive rhetoric of conventional masculinity and its founding in patriarchal and imperialist premises. In fact, James's addiction to the visceral excitement supplied by war – interpreted by some scholars as a nihilist attitude (Bennett and Diken 2011) – turns out to be particularly perturbing, as it questions the mythic evocation of men doing their duty and subtly subverts the tropes of paternity and legitimacy characteristic of Hollywood war films. Although combining conventional tropes of masculinity, Bigelow creates a surprisingly unsettling portrait of a hero. James's patriotism is deeply ambiguous. He is brave, not because he wishes to serve his country, but because he is addicted to the adrenaline resulting from the extreme danger of war. His motivations cannot be explained by fraternity or solidarity, since, as Bennett and Diken propose, the film eschews 'any romantic narrative trajectory in which fellow soldiers bond or commune through shared experience' (2011: 173). Finally, the familiar trope of fatherhood, deeply rooted in the ideology of the nation-state, is undermined in the troubling scene when James confesses to his baby son that there is probably only one thing that he loves: the thrill of combat.[22] In this sense, James constitutes a powerful contrast to Sanborn, who, undeterred by his own disappointment with war, deeply believes in his duty to serve his country and, over the course of the film, decides that he wants to be a father.

James's motivation effectively displaces him from the normative discourse of mythic atemporal heroism towards a desubjectivised frame, to use David Denny's (2011) term, founded on non-subjective sensorial affect. If we follow Brian Massumi's (2002) distinction between affect as the pre-personal, non-conscious experience of intensity, and culturally constructed and discursively based emotion, which is the social projection of a personal and biographical feeling, the intensity of affect in *The Hurt Locker* is something markedly different from well-defined emotion tied to nation, blood or nationalism.[23] Robert Burgoyne reaches a similar conclusion:

> Framing combat as an addictive pleasure, an ongoing, private and collective need, the film departs radically from genre convention, disdaining the formulas of older war films – the pathos formulas of sacrifice and loss – for a mode of address that emphasises the adrenalised experience of risk. Although traces of this theme can be found in films such as [. . .] *Apocalypse Now*, *The Hurt Locker* foregrounds the idea of private experience and pleasure in war, rendering war as a somatic engagement that takes place outside any larger meta-narrative of nation or history. (2012: 13)

Therefore, despite being obsessively focused on the spectacle of the male body, *The Hurt Locker* does not offer a nostalgic exhibition of the archetypical hero, since its images are too tense, too unstable and too agitated. Bigelow defamiliarises a series of generic clichés, often placing the spectator uncomfortably *inside* the events, rather than *outside* them, where they could be seen from a safe, unthreatening critical distance. In many of the scenes, we are visually, metaphorically and corporeally inside the protective bomb suit that the soldiers use to dismantle bombs: despite the armour, we feel the vulnerability of their bodies, their laboured breathing, the paralysing sensation of weight and the difficulty with which they advance towards the explosive artefacts. In these moments, vision is embodied and intimately connected with the corporeal ways of experiencing the world, as we are submerged in a frenetic world of images and sounds, where the border between the self and the other, the perceiver and the perceived is diluted, implicating us physically. It is here that the 'delirious excess of vision' – a central feature in Bigelow's aesthetics – exceeds the ocularcentric regime. As I will argue in the following section, the visceral aesthetics produce an affective immersion of the viewer, firmly placing *The Hurt Locker* in the paradigm of embodied perception, and highlighting an important, yet problematic, facet of Bigelow's film style.

War Genre as a Body Genre: Beyond the Gaze

In the Western epistemic tradition, the eye presupposes distance from the world, as Martin Jay demonstrates in *Downcast Eyes: The Denigration of Vision in Twentieth-Century French Thought* (1993). Similarly, in film theory the representational model of the voyeuristic eye implies distance between the film and its viewers, who maintain a transcendent position towards what is being seen: 'The lens of the camera, and therefore the eye of the spectator, remains at an imaginary viewing point, forever outside of the scene being viewed' (Shaviro 2003: 163). While remarkably fruitful, this paradigm cannot fully encompass the experience of viewing a film such as *The Hurt Locker*, which, in addition to the properly ocularcentric regime, mobilises other regimes – tactile, kinaesthetic and auditory – creating the sensation of an overwhelming emotional saturation. To think about these *other* ways of looking, much more affective than distanced, allows for the transcending of the apparatus theory, which gives the eye precedence over other organs of perception and disembodies the film experience by treating the eye as only a part of the brain, and not as a part of our body.

A number of scholars influenced by Deleuze's thinking have argued that psychoanalytic film theory, especially its Lacanian strand – revolving around such notions as specular and visual perception – systematically ignores the importance of the viewer's body as a continuous perceptive surface and as an organising principle for spatial and temporal orientation in the world and, more specifically, in films (Elsaesser and Hagener 2010: 100). Both Deleuzian and phenomenologically informed film theories[24] have widely questioned the psychoanalytic paradigm of lack, focusing on continuity and reversibility between the spectator and the film instead. As Shaviro understands it:

> Cinema's greatest power may be its ability to evacuate meanings and identities, to proliferate resemblances without sense or origin [. . .]. There is no structuring lack, no primordial division, but a continuity between the physiological and affective responses of my own body and the appearances and disappearances, the mutations and perdurances, of the bodies and images on screen. The important distinction is not the hierarchical, binary one between bodies and images, or between the real and its representations. It is rather the question of discerning multiple and continually

varying interactions among what can be defined indifferently as bodies and as images: degrees of stillness and motion, of action and passion, of clutter and emptiness, of light and dark. (1993: 255–66)[25]

Shaviro's evocative proposal proves highly useful in expanding our understanding of the war film. In fact, the so-called 'contact theories' in film studies have already been used productively in genre research, in particular in the discussion of three genres at the lower end of the cultural value hierarchy – horror, melodrama and pornography – all of which depend greatly on the viewer's corporeal reactions to the fictions represented on screen. These qualities can be easily extended to the war genre. In employing the aesthetics which intensify our affective engagement and dismantle our sense of separateness from the image, Bigelow's film does not distance itself, but rather participates in the contemporary war film format, conceptualised by Robert Burgoyne (2013) as a 'body genre' or 'a genre of embodiment', which, according to Linda Williams (1991) from whom Burgoyne borrows these terms, is a genre that revels in the showing of 'bodily excess'. Not only are the bodies on the screen caught 'in the grip of intense sensation or emotion', but there is also 'an almost involuntary mimicry of the emotion or sensation of the body on the screen' produced in the bodies of spectators (Williams 1991: 4–5).

This emphasis given to the corporeal and intense emotional saturation is potentially generative of the spectatorial mimicry postulated by Williams and is evident in several moments in the film: on the one hand, in the dramatisation of the failure of technology in the scene depicting Thompson's death in the film's opening scene; on the other, in James's disdain for war equipment and his voluntary exposure to the immediacy of risks, which might stand for an act of rebellion against the alienating machinery. James's relation to war is much more direct, physical and material than that of any other member of his team. Nowhere is it more evident than in the affectively intense sequence involving a 'body bomb' that James discovers during a raid in a warehouse. The reality of war and violence re-emerge in the most visceral way. Significantly, this sequence stands in stark contrast to the sequence in the desert, in which James's team is attacked by Iraqi snipers hidden in a distant building. These two crucial moments in the film, which will be discussed in detail in the following pages, underscore the complexity of Bigelow's project: the critical exploration of both the mode of 'war at a distance' or 'war without body', as well as of the technologies of mediation that are necessarily entangled in this mode.

Out of Joint: 'What are we shooting at?'

The desert sequence, in which American soldiers, concealed in a hideout, shoot at Iraqi snipers, while their adversaries return the fire sporadically, unfolds

Figure 3.4   The violence of the gaze.

in a practically blank landscape. Unlike the earlier scenes, which produced a sensation of disorientation and emotional overload, there is very little movement here. The sensations that predominate are tedium, apathy and physical exhaustion. We can almost feel the sweat and sand on the protagonists' bodies, the flies that stick to their humid faces, the chapped skin on their dried-out lips, their blurry vision and their heat as they aim at their targets through the telescopic visors in their guns. Bigelow's obsessive fascination with vision, which connotes surveillance and control, resurfaces.

Bruce Bennett and Bülent Diken (2011) discuss the sequence, and the film in general, in the context of what Deleuze conceptualised as time-images: purely optical or sound situations freed from the constraints of progressive narration, which produce what the authors dub 'dilated subjective temporality' (2011: 183). The protagonists transform into displaced spectators who no longer know how to (re)act. Their sensory-motor functions are distorted, and it is precisely this paralysis that opens them up to the virtual – a concept of time where the borders between the imaginary and the real, the virtual and the actual get blurred. In Deleuze's own words:

> The character has become a kind of viewer. He shifts, runs and becomes animated in vain, the situation he is in outstrips his motor capacities on all sides, and makes him see and hear what is no longer subject to the rules of a response or an action. He records rather than reacts. (2005: 3)

The particularity of the sequence is that, in contrast to other parts of the movie, arguably dominated by movement-images,[26] it is mostly composed of Deleuzian time-images. Such images, according to the philosopher, do not necessarily serve the purpose of carrying the narrative to an end, but rather 'as a stimuli for thought, because, by disrupting the chronological understanding of events, that is, by disrupting the perspective of the actual narrative by difference, their intervention enables the viewer to see time as a virtual whole' (in Bennett and Diken 2011: 183). Bennett and Diken contend, however, that the highly formalised time-images in *The Hurt Locker* do not become politicised: they 'do not stimulate thinking in the sense that its own narrative remains unaffected by its time-images' (2011: 185). In other words, they do not threaten movement-images that support the dominant level of the narrative and its rhetoric of nihilism – or, as other critics have argued, the heroic narrative of the US mission in Iraq. Nevertheless, in contrast to their findings, and following on from my previous readings of the importance of the gaze in Bigelow's oeuvre, I hold that these images open up other interpretative possibilities.

The sequence described above occurs right in the middle of the film – a fact that should not go unnoticed, considering Bigelow's rigorous structure. The soldiers stay in the shooting scene for hours – which occupies a mere five minutes of the projection time – until the sun sets over the horizon and James announces: 'Hey, Sanborn? I think we're done'. Deciding to represent the scene as such, Bigelow departed from the generic conventions of war film, where spectacular bombardments, palpitating battle scenes and choreographed individual combats constitute a crucial iconographic and narrative element. The sensation of tedium marks the cold, methodic process of killing. After Sanborn shoots the last adversary, James proclaims, as if he were playing a video game: 'He's down. Good night. Thanks for playing'. What follows is an extreme close-up of a bullet moving in slow motion, spinning towards the sand – an image which Bennett and Diken identified as a Deleuzian time-image: 'On such occasions, the images acquire an independent, material existence in themselves, while, at the same time, there emerges an ambivalent, indefinite and contingent quality related to the image' (2011: 183). The next shot depicts a building, seen from a great distance and through a blurry perspective, with the body of an Iraqi sniper hanging out of a window. Following this there is a shot of a whirlwind in the sand, an indicator of the passing time – notably, filmed using a zoomed-in shot, which creates a sense of estrangement. The whistling of the wind is intertwined with music that resembles the soundtrack composed by Morricone for spaghetti Westerns.

Not only the soundtrack, but also the mise-en-scène and several narrative elements take on certain attributives of the Western: an unexpected encounter with bounty hunters, the prolonged duel in the sun and the shot depicting a

Figure 3.5 Dilated temporality: the Western trope made eerie.

bullet hitting the sand. However, the combination of time-images together with the uncanny guitar accompaniment produces a disturbing effect which has little to do with the carnivalesque approach to representing violence in spaghetti Westerns. The ironic resonances of the Western seem to dramatise American failure in Iraq: the sequence development does not lead to a stable social order, and the climax – when the last Iraqi man dies – is deprived of any heroic or victorious tone. Significantly, the same guitar music is heard again at the end of the credits, just after 'Khyber Pass' – an anti-Bush anthem composed by the heavy metal band Ministry.

In light of this, the time-image of the spinning bullet appears to be more than a highly formalised and depoliticised shot, as Bennet and Diken view it; our identification with the camera is sinisterly divorced from identification with the protagonists. Although it highlights the gaze, the sequence transcends the model of an eye, in which the spectator constitutes herself/himself as a subject identifying with the character onscreen through the structure of looking. This device is also used at other moments in the film to represent death – for example, in the opening scene, in which, through close-up shots, rust and dust is shaken off the bodywork of an abandoned car in slow motion. The moment is a violent assault on the senses: the debris of the street is brought so close to us that we can almost touch it.

It is not insignificant that this enhancement of sensorial stimuli through the use of time-images that generate an alternative temporality happens precisely at moments when Bigelow decides to represent death or violence. In her study of the filmmaker's career, Caetlin Benson-Allott (2010) provides an extensive analysis of how Bigelow manipulates the typical rhythm of action cinema, frequently associating violence with boredom rather than righteousness. The filmmaker reworks action-hero masculinity by experimenting with genre conventions and, most notably, by slowing down cinematic violence. This

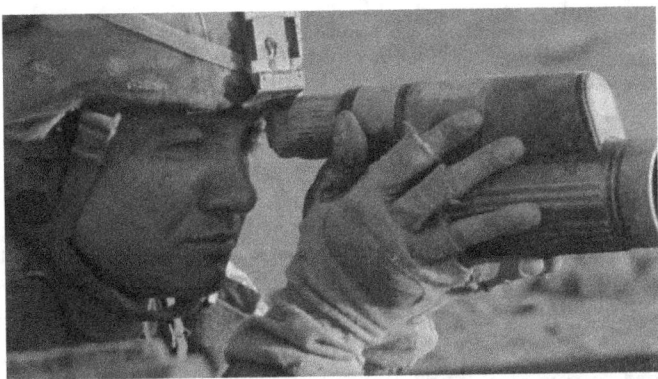

Figure 3.6 Guns as metaphor for cameras: meta-cinematic reflection on the war film.

is especially true in *The Loveless* (1982), *Point Break* (1991) and *The Hurt Locker* (2008). Even though she does not focus on time-images, Benson-Allott addresses the 'relentless duration' that characterises Bigelow's cinematography: 'For nothing much happens – but this nothing much nonetheless produces abrupt, brutal, and devastating violence' (2010: 34).

In my view, the scene in *The Hurt Locker* not only manipulates the pace to produce a particular affective experience and reflect on violence, but it also offers a meta-cinematic commentary on technologies of mediation. The time-image of the slow-motion falling bullet following the final sniper's death is preceded by a series of intense looking relations, mediated by the gun visors, which evoke both video games and the process of filming.

Patricia Pisters (2010) included *The Hurt Locker* within a group of film texts concerned with the meaning and effects of this mediation. The scholar draws on Jean Baudrillard and his essays 'The Gulf War Did Not Take Place' (2001), in which the philosopher famously argued that the Gulf War was distanced and cleansed through the technology of the image, to such an extent that it became a purely virtual war (Baudrillard in Pisters 2010: 235). However, contrary to Baudrillard's view, Pisters demonstrates how the relation between war and media is much more dynamic today. The scholar addresses the 'logistics of (war) perception 2.0', characterised, on the one hand, by the multiplicity of screens in combat scenes and, on the other, by the affective intensity of experiences generated by these profoundly subjective and chaotic images. The spectators are provided with a new film language that helps them to critically examine older representations of war. Therefore, and engaging with Baudrillard and his notes on the clean war, Pisters argues:

> We are not passive spectators captured by institutional or ideological power [. . .]. By being affected by these images, we can participate in

> bringing back reality to the heart of the vortex of our multiple screens. Paradoxically it is possible to conclude that in the face of the multiplication of ever increasing screens, reality does not disappear but returns with the affective vengeance. (2010: 250)

Bigelow's film, similarly to other examples of the Iraq War subgenre, such as *Redacted* (Brian de Palma, 2007) and *In the Valley of Elah* (Paul Haggis, 2007), raises a critique against war at a distance by drawing our attention to its mediated nature: not only are the American citizens detached from death, but the soldiers, who use remote-controlled robots and protective bomb suits to distance themselves from the materiality of war, are disconnected as well. As a response to this, *The Hurt Locker* affects with a vengeance at the same time as it participates in its own incrimination: after all, as in other war movies or video games that stem from them, *The Hurt Locker* is still a source of entertainment, which can, indeed, have a distancing effect. In fact, many of its scenes resemble first-person shooter games, beginning with the first sequence, when Thomson struggles to dismantle a bomb with a robot by manipulating it through a joystick of sorts. As Pisters reminds us, the use of video games for military training is well known – the American Army posted a free video game (*America's Army*) online, as a form of entertainment, education, propaganda and even a tool of recruitment. 'Video games look like war and war looks like a video game', concludes Pisters (2010: 243).[27]

Even though *The Hurt Locker* occasionally resembles a video game, its tedious, almost mechanical shooting, deprived of action and excitement, denaturalises the pleasure typically supplied by it. The boredom that saturates the desert sequence reinforces the idea expressed by Bennett and Diken: '*The Hurt Locker* is perhaps not so much a "war film" as an "asymmetric war film"' (2011: 176). One cannot ignore the fact that, at the same time as it produces a corporeal proximity to the American soldiers, the structure of looking marks a radical distance between subjects and objects of these gazes. The Iraqi snipers are under surveillance – accentuated by James's binoculars – transformed into objects (both military and of the gaze), distant, vulnerable and exposed to certain death. The Iraqi combatants exist almost off-screen, and are eliminated as if they were mere targets in a video game.

Such is the distance between the protagonists and the snipers that the latter, more than flesh-and-blood people, appear as ghost-like figures, completely deprived of their singularity. This mode of representing the Iraqis is employed at various moments in the film, and this is when, significantly, the methods of filming typical of horror movies are employed – for instance, handheld, point-of view camera shots peering around corners and looking through window openings. Lisa Purse's analysis of the scene in which James pulls a gun and points it at the taxi driver who suddenly appears in the deserted street during one of the missions is particularly illuminating here. Similar to the rest of the film, the sequence is shot from various angles and with a shaking handheld camera, 'but all of the shots of the Iraqi taxi driver are marked by the same characteristic, regardless of the camera angle or distance: each in some way obscures his face' (2011: 166). For example, the viewer sees James in the partially cracked rear-view mirror in the taxi cab, which distorts his face into a myriad of pieces, and some moments later this is followed by an extreme close-up of his eye. As Purse acutely observes, while we are granted access to James's words and thoughts in this scene,

> the extreme close-up of the Iraqi gives us no such access, and prevents us from reading his expression by limiting our visual access to only his eye. The side view is also more limiting than a frontal shot, picking up reflections on the eye's surface that obscure the delineation of the iris so that it is impossible to establish what direction he is looking in or what he is focusing on. (2011: 166)

According to Purse, Bigelow's filmmaking decisions reinforce negative conceptions of Iraqis and cause the spectators to forget about the wider context of the war, immersing them in the adrenaline-filled experiences of individual soldiers. This 'viscerally affective presentational style' dehumanises the Iraqis and risks perpetuating the long-established and racist cinematic stereotype of the Arab as unknowable, mysterious and potentially threatening (2011: 167).

Even though it could, indeed, be argued that these shots demonise Iraqi citizens, as many journalists lamented (Stobo 2010), in my view their main function appears to be constructing the US soldiers as alienated and transmitting their increasing paranoia. The Iraqis seem inscrutable and impersonal, but not necessarily dehumanised. They are observed through the camera, which, positioned on the same level as the guns, throws into relief the violence implicit in this act of visual appropriation. What is more, we cannot examine these scenes without taking into consideration the scenes that follow. In the first body-bomb sequence, as in the one towards the end of the film in which a man begs James to disarm the explosives adhered to his vest, the phantasmagoric figures of the Iraqis materialise as singular, flesh-and-blood bodies. Although in the first part of the film Bigelow seems to be far more interested in an abstract masculinity set in *any* war – as Bennett and Diken suggested – the second part brings us back to the singular: the materiality of *this* war.

The Body Bomb: The Horrors of Tactile Visuality

The sequence involving a body bomb commences when James, Sanborn and Eldridge enter an abandoned warehouse that has been repurposed as an explosives factory. The aesthetics of kinesthetic agitation and spatial disorientation permeates the mise-en-scène again. As previously argued, the excess of sensorial stimuli in the film destabilises the gaze, which traditionally connotes control and domination – over a territory or the observed bodies – and, consequently, frustrates the nostalgic representation of the Western hero. This questioning of heroic masculinity is, by no means, new in the war film, as Tasker and Atakav observe: 'The sort of "damaged" masculinity presented in *The Hurt Locker* is something of a cliché within the genre, one which the film relies upon rather than interrogates' (2010: 66). Nevertheless, Bigelow's film is not restricted to the exploration of the soldiers' masculinity. The excess of sensorial stimuli, which in the previous sequences acted principally as a way of frustrating the stability of the hero's gaze and transmitting his vulnerability, is drawn on another level here, since said vulnerability is addressed, significantly, in the second person.

According to Judith Butler, who explored the concept of vulnerability in her recent works, 'if I speak about "your vulnerability" then I am already in the position of one who is obligated to acknowledge what I name' (2014: 50). When Eldridge asks Sanborn whether he thinks that the body belonged to the 'little base rat' (referring to Beckham), the latter replies impatiently, 'I don't know, man. They all look the same, right?' James, confronted with the eviscerated indistinguishable body, is determined to recognise it as that of Beckham.[28] Following Butler, by asking 'who are you?', James 'seeks to establish a space of appearance for the Other' (Butler 2014: 49), who is now granted a singularity. The boy's painfully exposed corpse undermines James's sense of corporeal self-sufficiency, since, according to Butler, vulnerability and loss 'challenge the very notion of ourselves as autonomous and in control' (2004b: 23).

The grief and desolation suffused in the images suggest, at least, a profound ambivalence towards the American presence in Iraq. In his insightful analysis of the scene, Robert Burgoyne has pointed out its correlation with the horror genre: 'Arousing a sense of outrage and denunciation, the scene seems close to the emotional hyperbole of *grand guignol*, exploitative in its unrelenting depiction of body horror in the context of war' (2013). The exhibition of flesh and blood, as well as Sanborn's comment ('it's disgusting'), can be understood through Julia Kristeva's notion of abject as a 'place where meaning collapses', where 'I am not' (1982: 2). Abjection 'does not respect borders, positions, rules', disturbing 'identity, system, order', for which it must be expelled. It is not insignificant that James suddenly abandons his original intention to detonate the body, refraining from his first impulse to eject the abject, in order to re-establish the border between 'I' and 'I am not'. Instead, he buries his hands inside the boy's abdomen and works his way around organs, vessels and wires, in an attempt to defuse the device, which – as Burgoyne notices – brings together a bomb defusal and invasive surgery in a single frame of reference (2013). Instead of maintaining a visual distanciation from the corpse, which would hand control of the self and the Other over to him, James crosses the border which separates him from the boy's body. This scene, in contrast to that involving the desert combat, evokes permeability and contact. The viewers can almost feel James's fingers moving through the boy's flesh, they can hear it and they can even smell it – just as James smells the blood and flesh at one point and is forced to cover his face with a scarf, resembling a surgical mask.

To analyse the scene in light of Bigelow's manifest concern with distance and the medium of film opens up a potentiality to consider it through the famous analogy, posited by Walter Benjamin, between the cameramen and the surgeon. The philosopher compares this analogy to another one, the analogy between the painter and the magician, in order to reflect on the relationship of distance and proximity that they establish with matter – the body or the reality – and to think about how we relate to images in a wider sense. Benjamin elaborates on his argument regarding the tactile qualities of the cinema to trace changes in perception brought about by the advent of modernity and new technologies of reproduction – for example, film and photography:

> The surgeon constitutes one pole of an arrangement in which the other is occupied by the magician. The stance of the magician healing an invalid by laying-on of hands differs from that of the surgeon performing an operation on that invalid. The magician maintains the natural distance between himself and the patient [. . .]. The surgeon does the opposite: he reduces the distance to the patient a great deal (by actually going inside him) and increases it only a little (through the care with which his hand moves among the latter's organs) [. . .]. Magician and surgeon behave like painter and cameraman. The painter, while working, observes a natural distance from the subject; the cameraman, on the other hand, penetrates deep into the subject's tissue. The images they both come up with are enormously different. The painter's is an entity, the cameraman's chopped up into a large number of pieces, which find their way back together by following a new law. ([1936] 2008)

The Benjaminian analogy of surgeon-cameraman is highly productive, not only for thinking about what is represented onscreen – James's extreme care when his hands move among the organs – but also for thinking about the work of the filmmaker, who moves the camera in such a way as to penetrate the social reality and the body of the spectators. Just like a surgeon – who makes incisions, disconnects tissue, removes organs and recombines the materials – a filmmaker navigates his/her camera in the world, dissects its surfaces and chooses its dramas, recomposing them in a new sum by means of editing. Cinema makes evident this disposition of reality to be reordered and transformed, while at the same time it introduces us to new forms of visibility. The camera traverses the surface of the world, manoeuvring between 'its organs', making visible its structures – it not only illuminates, showing us what is hidden, but it also defamiliarises, reorganising and joining together the body in new forms. Bigelow, just like James when he opens the boy's corpse, reveals new views, transiting through the tri-dimensionality of the human body, inserting her scalpel. In this operation, she offers a new perception – the tactile comprehension of the flesh; the viewer feels (or understands) the film with his/her whole body, not only through the organs of sight or hearing.

Cinema is a technology which, according to Benjamin, incorporates and transforms not only social reality, but also the human body. In the scene discussed above, both the observed body and the observer's body come to the fore. The act of cutting – both onscreen and off-screen – produces a shock effect, similar to the one produced in horror cinema (the music in this scene also alludes to this genre), and it is closely related to the sense of touch. The shock effect is exactly what Benjamin considered a revolutionary factor of the mechanical reproduction of reality: although new technologies were born in the service of the phantasmagoria of capitalist culture, destined to distract and anaesthetise our senses, they could also raise awareness, bring the images closer to the masses and produce critical modes of relating to them.

Instead of offering a safe visual distanciation from the body, which in the Western tradition often results in objectification and grants a sense of control over self and others (Jay 1993), the camera brings the viewer as close as possible to the image, precisely at the moment when James permeates the border separating him from the boy's corpse with his fingers. The images are not marked, however, by the hygiene or cold-bloodedness with which surgeons proceed, and the war they evoke is removed from what Baudrillard described as 'war enclosed in a glass coffin [. . .] purged of any carnal contamination or warrior's passion' (2001: 243). In contrast to the earlier scenes – in which the Iraqi insurgents and civilians were observed at a distance in landscapes that evoked those of Westerns, and predominantly through gun visors, implying the structures of an imperialist gaze – here, the distance is painfully annihilated. In this sense, it could be argued that these images are open to haptic looking, borrowing the notion from Laura Marks (2000), developed from Deleuze and Alois Riegl's thought. In contrast to Benjamin, who saw tactile qualities across all cinematic technology, Marks attributes them mainly to experimental films – in particular, video production outside of the dominant Hollywood circuit. These qualities emerge mainly from the spectator's experience: her/his eyes 'move over the surface [. . .] rather than [. . .] plung[ing] into illusionistic depth' (Marks 2000: 162). Marks argues that while 'optical visuality depends on a separation between the viewing subject and the object', inviting 'a distant view that allows the viewer to organise him/herself as an all-perceiving subject' (2000: 162), haptic looking evades a distanced view, pulling the viewer closer, thus 'making oneself vulnerable to the image and reversing the relation of mastery that characterises optical viewing' (2000: 185). Therefore, whereas optical visuality privileges representational power over the image, haptic visuality underscores its material presence. Extending Marks's ideas on *The Hurt Locker*, the scene discussed above refuses the visual plentitude and mastery traditionally implicit in optical visuality, eschewing the controlling gaze over the boy's body. As Marks explains:

> Haptic visuality may 'fasten' on its object [...], but it cannot pretend fully to know the thing seen. [...] At the same time it acknowledges that it cannot know the other, haptic visuality attempts to bring it close, in a look that is so intensely involved with the presence of the other that it cannot take the step back to discern difference, say, to distinguish figure and ground. (2000: 191)

Marks's conceptualisation of haptic visuality has allowed for thinking about new articulations of the relationship between the viewer and the screen. Contrary to the earlier critical paradigm of eye/gaze theory, which associated the cinematic vision with the notions of control, objectification and the masculine (or colonial) looking, the paradigm of embodied perception encompasses positions that conceptualise film as a specific kind of contact: on the one hand, as an encounter with the racially or culturally coded Other – see, for example, Hamid Naficy's (2001) notion of accented cinema – and, on the other, as a haptic experience that helps question the very parameters of control (Marks 2000; Barker 2009; Beugnet 2007).

It could be argued, however, that the haptic imaginary can often cement, rather than challenge, conservative ideologies.[29] The body-bomb sequence, which culminates with an image of James holding the boy's body wrapped in a white cloth – evoking the biblical death of Christ – can be read as 'an ideologically loaded manipulation of audience emotion, depicting grotesque body trauma in order to make a flagrant political point about the villainy of the insurgency in Iraq' (Burgoyne 2012: 16). Yet, according to Burgoyne, while *The Hurt Locker* deploys 'the pathos formulas of sacrifice and loss', at the same time it defamiliarises them (2012: 13, 15). James's confusion over the boy's identity is also significant, as it demystifies the fantasy of bonding with the local population, as well as the idea of touch as contact which necessarily facilitates a meaningful encounter with the Other. Therefore, as Bigelow's film shows, this shift from look to touch does not necessarily imply a shift from a controlling, punishing eye to a caressing hand. Skin holds its own contradictions one should not ignore, as observed by Elsaesser and Hagener (2010:

115). In Mark's formulation, the skin – of the film and the human being – is conceived as an intact surface, whose extension is only grazed with our haptic caress. However, instead of leading to a carnal comprehension of alterity, or opening up a space of interpersonal and/or transcultural contact, touch can also point to violent collisions.

The body-bomb sequence illustrates how Bigelow creates tension between an abstract, mythical masculinity and the singular, material bodies at risk, negotiating between the optical representation and the materiality of haptic looking. This is where the representational power of the image intersects with its material presence, where archetypical Western hero, James, meets the Other in flesh and blood or, in Adriana Cavarero's words, where 'the embodied uniqueness [takes] the now famous name of "the face of the Other"' (2014: 27).

All in all, Bigelow challenges, but also simultaneously participates in, the visual and narrative conventions of the war film. In terms of iconography and structure, she evokes and rewrites a series of familiar representations in Hollywood movies, such as the Western hero, the Hard Body and the non-conformist in action cinema. Far from attempting to celebrate their mythical qualities or presenting nostalgic tableaux of the past, *The Hurt Locker* disrupts the timeless motifs of heroism and dramatises the failure of the American presence in Iraq. The constant cinematic exposure in *The Hurt Locker*, based on a complex web of looking relations, along with the process of genre blending, provides a reflection on the fabrication of the filmic hero, creating fissures in the dominant rhetoric, based on the narrative of Western heroic masculinity. But, as it furnishes a self-reflexive commentary on the mythic or technological mediation of war, denying the distinction between fiction and metafiction, the film does not offer a safe distance or the pleasures of alienated spectatorship. By highlighting the material, flesh-and-blood bodies at risk, defined by their potential for both affecting and being affected, the film questions the corporeal sufficiency and impenetrability of the hero, the display of which is a major convention in US war cinema.

What is more, Bigelow's contribution to the genre makes evident the ambiguous nature of the camera as a mediation between the body of reality, the body of film and the viewers' bodies. The images that she produces present themselves as an imitation or a construction of reality, questioning unmediated or referential notions of the real outside representation, but they also facilitate contact, a connection between the perceived and the perceivers as a part of the whole. *The Hurt Locker* places us inside and simultaneously outside events, intimately close and extremely far from what is represented onscreen. Bigelow's vision, excessive and delirious, is not based on a 'distanced, decorporealized, monocular eye mastering all it surveys' (Williams in Sobchack 2004: 59), but instead is highly heterogeneous, multiple and physically implicated in what it perceives. It is precisely due to this sensorial immersion and the visceral filming style that we cannot completely forget about the cruel reality of war that the film represents.

Notes

1. The seed of the present chapter can be found in my earlier pieces: 'Hollywood Transgressor or Hollywood Transvestite? The Reception of Kathryn Bigelow's *The Hurt Locker*', published in *Doing Women's Film History: Reframing Cinemas, Past and Future*, edited by Christine Gledhill and Julia Knight (Urbana: Illinois University Press, 2015) and 'Men of War: Affect, Embodiment, and Western Heroic Masculinity in *Dispatches* and *The Hurt Locker*', published in *Masculinities and Literary Studies: Intersections and New Directions*, edited by Josep M. Armengol, Marta Bosch Vilarrubias, Àngels Carabí and Teresa Requena (New York: Routledge, 2017). They both appear here with permission. Copyright © 2017 From *Masculinities and Literary Studies* (Josep M. Armengol, Marta Bosch Vilarrubias, Àngels Carabí, Teresa Requena eds.). Reproduced by permission of Taylor and Francis Group, LLC, a division of Informa plc.
2. At the time of finishing this book, Sofia Coppola became the second woman in the long history of the Cannes Film Festival to win Best Director.
3. The term 'Hollywood Transgressor' is derived from the subtitle of the monograph *The Cinema of Kathryn Bigelow*, edited by Deborah Jermyn and Sean Redmond (2003). When discussing these discrepancies regarding Bigelow's oeuvre and its significance for feminism, it is worth distinguishing between feminist academics and professional critics influenced by feminism.
4. This aspect distinguishes *The Hurt Locker* – and other films that depict American conflicts at the beginning of the twenty-first century – from Hollywood films about Vietnam. As Tasker and Atakav observe: '[T]he time lag between the Vietnam War and the emergence of Hollywood movies dealing with it is an obvious indicator of the difficulty of this unpopular and ultimately unsuccessful US endeavour' (2010: 59).
5. See Gayatri Spivak (1988) on the mission of rescuing brown women from 'savage' brown men; more recently, see Lila Abu-Lughod (2013).
6. See Joanne Hollows (2000).
7. See Jermyn (2003).
8. The production budget of *The Hurt Locker* was around US$15 million, while *Avatar* was filmed with a budget of approximately US$237 million (*Box Office Mojo*). *Avatar* earned US$2.7 billion dollars worldwide, becoming the highest-grossing film ever, while *The Hurt Locker* made almost US$50 million, making it the least popular Best Picture winner in Oscar history. It is worth noting that a film's financing arrangements do not necessarily correlate exactly to its aesthetics. However, it is interesting to observe that the discursive contraposition of Cameron's and Bigelow's respective films has sometimes placed them at opposite ends of a high culture versus low culture spectrum. A number of major media critics produced a clear dichotomy: a Hollywood 3D mega-budget sci-fi flick versus a presumed smaller-scale art-house war film. This was not the case with most feminist critics, though, who saw Bigelow's *The Hurt Locker* as 'mainstream'.
9. Bigelow's first feature films, *The Loveless* and *Near Dark*, were filmed on low budgets and have gained cult status. *Point Break*, with a budget of US$24 million and an US$83.5 million gross, was Bigelow's first box office success. This is the point at which the filmmaker had to deal with accusations of 'selling out' for the first time. The film was rejected from Bigelow's 'canon' and its reception was

dominated by conservative readings that set out to demonstrate its status as low-quality cinema. As Tasker shows, it was not considered feminist enough in comparison to *Near Dark* and *Blue Steel* (1999: 15).

10. This statement is not entirely true if we look at other films directed by Bigelow and their heroines: Megan, the protagonist in *Blue Steel*, Jean in *The Weight of Water*, Maya in *Zero Dark Thirty*, and various secondary characters, such as Mace in *Strange Days*, Tyler in *Point Break* and Mae in *Near Dark*, who were often read from a feminist perspective.
11. The complex questions about gender that these comments raise cannot be addressed in detail here (see Paszkiewicz 2015).
12. See, for example, Clover (1992) and her discussion of cross-identification in horror cinema.
13. For Dargis, the success of *The Hurt Locker* helped to dismantle a significant number of stereotypes about what kind of films are viewed or enjoyed by women: 'It was historic, exhilarating, especially for women who make movies and women who watch movies, two groups that have been routinely ignored and underserved by an industry in which most films star men and are made for and by men. It's too early to know if this moment will be transformative – but damn, it feels so good' (2010a).
14. This is not the first time that press coverage privileged Cameron's career and his personal relation with Bigelow over her success, interweaving this discourse with insinuations that she owes everything to their marriage (see Lane 2003: 187).
15. At the time of completing this book, Bigelow's latest film, *Detroit* (2017), has been released. Written by Mark Boal, the film is based on the so-called 'Algiers Motel incident', a police raid during the city's historic 1967 riots. As in all Bigelow's films, the subject of the movie is violence – in particular, the disturbing police brutality of white police officers against black residents of Detroit. The film has sparked intense debate over cultural appropriation – raising questions as to whether white artists can appropriately depict black pain and oppression – and has been rejected by some journalists as distastefully voyeuristic and even immoral. Critics have traced similarities to *Zero Dark Thirty* and its depiction of torture, as well as a voyeuristic scene of rape and murder in *Strange Days*. In the latter film, inspired by the 1992 Los Angeles riots that followed the Rodney King verdict, Bigelow also explores themes such as racism, abuse of power and police brutality.
16. Films that deploy rapid editing, mobile framing and shaky camera movements to produce a sensory overload and 'overpower' audiences are easy to find in Hollywood: we could mention, for example, high-speed action movies such as *Transformers* (Michael Bay, 2007), *The Dark Knight* (Christopher Nolan, 2008) and the *Bourne* franchise. In this sense, *The Hurt Locker* clearly participates in the acceleration of mainstream American cinema in general. It could be argued that all of these films dissect space and destabilise spatial integrity, thus producing the sensation of disorientation (see Purse 2016).
17. Although there is no definite definition of the war film, I assume in this volume that a war movie is a film that places soldiers in front of their enemies, depicts combat scenes and/or the soldiers' return home. For a discussion of the possible problems that emerge from this definition, see Neale (2000: 117–19).
18. *The Hurt Locker* opens with the reporter Chris Hedges's (2002) remark that: 'The rush of battle is a potent and often lethal addiction, for war is a drug'.
19. See, for example, Holloway's (2008) study of 9/11 and the War on Terror, which he reads not as a rupture in American history, but as events which had deep roots in Western cultural and intellectual tradition.
20. James, who has apparently deactivated 873 bombs, saving many lives, embodies

a typical Western hero: his style of acting is easily comparable to Alan Ladd's in *Shane* (George Stevens, 1953) or John Wayne's in *The Searchers* (John Ford, 1953).

21. The excess of sensorial stimuli might also be considered a strategy to frustrate the archetypical display of the Hard Body, characteristic of the action-adventure films of the 1980s – the figure to which James clearly alludes – and which, as Susan Jeffords (1993) famously argued, promoted a concept of the nation as gendered: strong, tough and assertive.
22. 'As you get older, some of the things you love might not seem so special anymore', he explains. 'By the time you get to my age maybe it's only one or two things [. . .] with me I think it's one'. The immediate cut to a shot of helicopters leaves us without a doubt about what James refers to.
23. Here Massumi follows French theorists Deleuze and Guattari, who famously describe affects in French as 'asubjectifs' (1987: 183), as beyond subjectivity.
24. It should be underlined that, although authors such as Vivian Sobchack or Laura Marks occasionally refer to Gilles Deleuze in their approach to film image, their theories of embodied perception rely on the phenomenological notion of the subject that *perceives*. Deleuze, in turn, privileges the notion of cinema beyond any conception of subject or object. The philosopher sees images on an immanent plane, without taking into account a perceiving subject or intentionality, both of which are central to phenomenology. See Claire Perkins's (2004) illuminating observations on this distinction.
25. In a follow-up article, Shaviro (2008) offers a revision of his earlier stance on psychoanalysis.
26. Most of the episodes in *The Hurt Locker* have a rational chain of causes and effects, operate according to chronological time, narrative progression and depict at least one character who reacts to situations according to a 'sensory-motor' scheme – that is, a logic of linear interactions based on causality (see Deleuze 1985: 155).
27. We could also mention the co-implication between war and TV. In October 2011 the US channel G4 released a documentary series *Bomb Patrol: Afghanistan*, which follows members of an EOD in Afghanistan. Promoted as a real-life version of *The Hurt Locker*, the project was extensively criticised for selling war as entertainment (Duboff 2010). This mutual relationship between war and TV is not new, and can be traced, for example, to the night videos of massive aerial bombardment during the Gulf War or even simply news programmes, which increasingly rely on suspense to hook the audience.
28. In fact, we never get to know Beckham's real name, which adds an ironic tone to James's desperation to recognise the singularity of the boy.
29. See Rushing's (2016) analysis of what he calls 'skin flicks': *300* (Zack Snyder, 2006), *The Legend of Hercules* (Renny Harlin, 2014) and *Pompeii* (Paul W. S. Anderson, 2014).

4. GENRE IN THE MARGINS: KELLY REICHARDT'S *MEEK'S CUTOFF*

One of the most recognisable women filmmakers in contemporary American independent cinema, Kelly Reichardt, might not initially appear to be a particularly obvious candidate for this volume, as she does not tend to be associated with popular genre film. Her artisanal, small-scale mode of production and relatively low budgets[1] have possibly granted her greater autonomy than that enjoyed by the filmmakers working within the major studios (for example, Cody and Kusama, discussed in Chapter 2); however, at the same time this production mode has represented a serious resource restriction, which, as I will argue later, is conceptually and materially inseparable from Reichardt's austere aesthetics. The director's film style is commonly read in connection with international art cinema, both historical and contemporary: on the one hand, critics have drawn a number of comparisons between her work and that of Italian neorealists, and on the other, they have inscribed it in the recent phenomenon of 'slow' or 'contemplative cinema'.[2] Nevertheless, as Elena Gorfinkel aptly suggests, Reichardt's oeuvre 'sits at the cusp of experimental and classical film traditions' (2016: 123), and it departs in many respects from her more 'radical' contemporaries – for example, in terms of shot structure and slow style, which is, in fact, not so slow if measured against other films created by prominent figures of contemplative cinema, such as Béla Tarr or Tsai Ming-liang.[3] More importantly, Reichardt clearly works with 'the tropes of a specifically American idiom' (2016: 123) – namely, the generic conventions of the road movie. In fact, all of her features to date notably draw on this genre, employing what Gorfinkel describes as 'the beckoning horizon of wide-open [...] landscapes and their tarnished promises of freedom, autonomy, and self-reliance' (2016: 123): her debut, *River of Grass* (1994), described by the filmmaker as 'a road movie without a road' (Skinner 2016); her 'Oregon trilogy', comprised of *Old Joy* (2006), *Wendy and Lucy* (2008) and *Meek's Cutoff* (2010); the subsequent *Night Moves* (2013) and the more recent *Certain Women* (2016) which feature a car as a central trope. However, while road movies are, by definition, focused on mobility and independence, Reichardt's films trace different trajectories by positioning lost, socially displaced and marginalised wanderers at the heart of her narratives, and emphasising the arrested nature of their journeys: '[T]he affective slackness of their suspended agency, their "stuckness," non-productivity, and inability to progress within the harsh demands of an exhausting, social, material world' (Gorfinkel 2016: 123).

If Reichardt's cinematic endeavour is to unmask the American myth of mobility, then this demystification cannot be more evident than in her Western *Meek's Cutoff*. As has been widely demonstrated, both the road movie and the Western stage national discourses of 'progressing' masculinity, based on the ethos of freedom, velocity and speed. According to Yvonne Tasker: 'In the broadest terms the Western deals with the formation of America, its articulation of masculine identity bound up with the establishment of white male authority over territory and peoples that seemingly require subjection' (2017: 112). As I will show in this chapter, Reichardt's film sets out to question the faulty leadership and racial and gender prejudices that emerge from this drive for colonisation and settlement by reconfiguring time and space not as vehicles of progress or heroic action, but as paralysis, blockage and restraint. In contrast to previous readings that considered Reichardt's work through her 'slow style' or, at best, 'anti-Western' aesthetics, I seek to underscore the filmmaker's generative use of the Western's conventions. Although Reichardt's contribution to the 'slow' tendency emergent in contemporary cinema is indisputable – and I will, indeed, address some of this tendency's characteristics, such as temporal dilation, the use of the long take and a focus on phenomenological realism (Flanagan 2008) – I believe one should not underestimate the generic logic of the Western that makes such rewriting possible.

While building on the existing critical writing on the filmmaker, in this chapter I interrogate how the prevalence of the interpretive framework in the reception of *Meek's Cutoff* which incorporates it into the individualist models of auteurist discourse of resistance towards genre and exceptional individual achievement has somewhat delimited the ways in which to conceptualise Reichardt's work and, in particular, her skilful command of the Western. Drawing on the burgeoning scholarship on independent cinema (Tzioumakis 2006; Newman 2011; White 2015, among others), I will first delineate the ways in which Reichardt's authorship and biographical legend are constructed in close relation to processes by which independent cinema is legitimised and conceptualised discursively in opposition to Hollywood and, indeed, more often than not, genre. Going back to the premise of this book, instead of promoting the discourse of exceptionality (typical of women filmmakers working in forms conventionally perceived as 'male', such as Kathryn Bigelow studied in the previous chapter), my aim is to articulate a more dialogical understanding of women's relationship to genre cinema and, in this case, independent film, as well as to question the binary oppositions that underpin the model of counter-cinema, such as popular/elitist, politically conservative/engaged, generic/auteurist.

Genre, Women Filmmakers and Independent Cinema

In general terms, there seem to be two different (but complementary) understandings of popular cinema in scholarly writing: the notion can refer either to films that are *enjoyed* or *consumed* by large numbers of people or to films that are *aimed at* a large mainstream audience. In their edited collection on the topic, Richard Dyer and Ginette Vincendeau point to a distinction between 'audience preferences' and 'box office receipts' – that is, between films that express thoughts and feelings of the 'people' – in other words, 'what people like' – and films that are commercially successful. Dyer and Vincendeau additionally observe that the term 'popular cinema' entails a 'productive messiness', which emerges from its use as synonymous with 'commercial', 'entertainment', 'mainstream', 'genre' and 'Hollywood' (Dyer and Vincendeau 1992: 2). Yet, Victor Perkins's contribution to the volume adds another interesting aspect to this debate that is particularly relevant to my discussion: he argues that 'popular cinema' is very often a category of access – for example, a French film can be accessible to mass audiences in France, but its subtitled version will be considered art cinema aimed at a niche market in Great Britain (1992: 196).

If we choose to adopt the 'market approach', then Reichardt hardly qualifies as 'popular', as she does not work within the paradigms of commercial genre cinema in the same way as Kathryn Bigelow or Nancy Meyers, who succeed according to the terms set by the dominant US film industry. Perkins's criteria of 'access', however, helps to redirect this debate and consider the ways in which Reichardt's work is, in fact, visible and 'popular' within certain contexts of production, exhibition and discursive circulation – in particular, in the context of American independent cinema. Reichardt's films are distributed globally, through a number of art cinema and independent cinema networks, such as, for instance, the international festivals circuit.[4] The latter has been crucial in establishing her directorial reputation and her status as an auteur; Reichardt's participation in the Cannes Film Festival with *Wendy and Lucy* in 2008 represented a major boost to her career in the United States and has undoubtedly granted her an elevated degree of visibility, both in the popular press and in film studies.

The question of access is significant because independent cinema, now operating as a marketable label comparable to 'genre' or 'auteur', has infiltrated popular culture, through film magazines, blogs and, most notably, distribution channels, such as Netflix, Amazon, Vimeo and iTunes, accessible to mass audiences worldwide (Newman 2011). Academically speaking, American independent film has also become 'popular' in recent years; since 2000, more than thirty monographs have been published on the topic. These publications, alongside a large number of academic essays and non-scholarly, more commercially focused publications, have helped establish independent cinema as a specific category in the US film industry, beyond the typically negative definitions that characterised it 'on the basis of existing outside the "mainstream" represented by the output of the major studios' (King et al. 2013: 1). The term 'independent', which previously denoted any film production placed outside the ambit, reach and influence of Hollywood, currently encompasses different movements, forms and expressions, such as black independent film, exploitation filmmaking, new queer cinema or smart cinema, among many others. Bearing in mind this diversification, as well as the circulation of several terms used to refer to this film sector, such as 'indie' or 'Indiewood', the problem of definition is pressing.

Janet Staiger, in her essay 'Independent of What?' (2013), eloquently addresses perhaps the most polemic issue in this debate – that is, to what extent we should define independent cinema on purely industrial or economic bases. Staiger posits that while 'independent' principally refers to the mode of financing and/or distributing films, 'indie' should refer to a particular mode of film practice with its own specific historical context, distinct conventions and set of implicit viewing procedures. Yannis Tzioumakis (2013), in turn, offers a useful periodisation of American independent cinema, identifying three distinctive periods: 'the independent years' (from the late 1970s to the end of the 1980s – in particular, until the release of *sex, lies, and videotape* in 1989), 'the indie years' (from 1989 to 1996/1998)[5] and 'Indiewood' (from 1998 until the 2010s). *Meek's Cutoff* was released in 2010, a period of transition in the independent sector, marked by important closures and the sales of the major film studios' specialty divisions (most significantly, the sale of Miramax in the same year), as well as the introduction of new Internet-based initiatives, such as online crowdfunding, alternative distribution and exhibition channels – for example, YouTube (King et al. 2013: 4). However, Reichardt's film can still be framed within the Indiewood era, given the commercial and cultural significance of this label in American culture – although, certainly, the film was produced not at its centre, but rather at its margins.

The traditional divide between Hollywood and Indiewood – in particular, with reference to industrial, economic and even stylistic parameters – is not easy to trace today. Without denying some conspicuous differences between films produced in major studios and films at the lower financial end of the spectrum – and, therefore, arguably involving less pressure from producers and increased control for creators – perhaps it would be more fruitful to focus on critical discourses that accompany these films and which, undeniably, require different interpretive perspectives. Instead of considering independence in terms of finance or distribution – criteria which have been extensively debated in recent years – it is more illuminating to underscore how independence connotes a series of values that are supposedly absent from Hollywood productions, which are usually associated with highly conservative, conventional and schematic entertainment forms. In Tzioumakis's words: '[I]ndependence in American cinema had become associated with intelligent, meaningful, often challenging but always full of spirit filmmaking, while production by the majors was associated with conservative, conventional, formulaic and spiritually empty efforts at entertaining an increasingly young audience' (2006: 13). While borders between independent cinema and Hollywood have become increasingly blurred in terms of financing and style,[6] the former is still constructed through a marked opposition to the Hollywood system: 'The value of indie cinema is generally located in difference, resistance, opposition – in the virtue of alternative representations, audiovisual and storytelling styles, and systems of cultural circulation' (Newman 2011: 2). Independent cinema, therefore, is not simply a combination of industrial or economic conditions that determine film production, circulation and reception, but rather 'a taste culture to distinguish non-mainstream movies as more artistically serious and legitimate than mainstream films but also as mature in comparison with multiplex fare and audiences' (Newman 2011: 48) or a Foucauldian discourse that creates objects of knowledge and 'expands and contracts when socially authorised institutions (filmmakers, industry practitioners, trade publications, academics, film critics, and so on) contribute towards its definition at different periods in the history of American cinema' (Tzioumakis 2006: 11). These practices, following Foucault, 'realise and set the conditions for discourse, while discourse, reciprocally, feeds back utterances which facilitate practice' (Foucault in Tzioumakis 2006: 11).[7] The discourse of independence, associated with values such as authenticity,[8] self-expression and freedom from industrial constraints, constructs identities towards which filmmakers and communities of viewers aspire, along with univocal moral valences: 'Independence is a virtue, and the mainstream is commercialized, overhyped, sensational, and associated with undesirable conceptions of the cinema audience as an undifferentiated mass, or as an exploitable niche with inferior taste (e.g., children, girls and women)' (Newman 2011: 223).

According to Sherry B. Ortner, independent cinema sees itself as 'telling the truth' or 'show[ing] the reality', in contrast to the 'lies and falseness' of Hollywood movies (2013: 3). This rhetoric of opposition, implicit in independent cinema, is also crucial to certain models of women's cinema – in particular, the model of counter-cinema as antithetical to commercial films.[9] Hence, independent cinema seems to be ideally suited for counter-cinema female practitioners; in fact, statistics confirm that the number of women in this sector is proportionally higher than those who work in the film industry in Hollywood. The reports prepared by Martha Lauzen (2016; 2017) for the years 2015 to 2016 show that nineteen per cent of the filmmakers who directed narrative features screening at the festivals were women (by genre, women are much more likely to direct documentaries than narrative features, as in the former they accounted for thirty-five per cent), while in the case of the top grossing films in 2016, women accounted for seven per cent of directors, down two percentage points from nine per cent in 2015 and 1998. These numbers translate into a greater critical recognition: if, in the mainstream cinema we had to wait for more than eighty years to witness a woman filmmaker win an Oscar in the Best Director category, by contrast, in the independent sector women directors have been winning prestigious prizes for some decades now.[10]

Nevertheless, this apparently more equitable environment is not without discrimination. According to a study published by the Sundance Institute and carried out by the University of Southern California (Smith et al. 2013), women face considerably more difficulties than men when completing their films and developing sustainable careers in the independent sector. All this adds up to diverse strategies of de-authentication: women do not have the same relationship to the discursive formation of independent cinema as men have, for example, in regard to the construction of film authorship or the ways in which the generic classifications are produced. Although there are many women practitioners who work within the indie sector, rarely are they considered auteurs, nor are the same parameters of evaluation applied to them as to their male counterparts.

Drawing on Geoff King, Michele Schreiber argues that 'the independent sphere was, and still is, far from the idyllic equal opportunity democratic collective that one would hope it would be' (Schreiber 2014: 168). She adds that the leading books on the topic of independent cinema 'place women, people of color, and gay and lesbian filmmakers in their own chapter(s) with the discussion of the broader tendencies within the contemporary independent sphere largely dominated by the stories of Caucasian, heterosexual, middle-class men' (2014: 168). The *ethos* of the independent (male) artist is materialised and cultivated in film pantheons erected by the popular press and by academia, which include star auteurs such as Quentin Tarantino, Wes Anderson, Charlie Kaufman, Neil LaBute, Hal Hartley and Todd Solondz.[11] As Claire Perkins convincingly argues in her discussion of the marginalisation of female directors in and through the industrial and critical discourse of indie cinema:

> In a manner that explicitly recalls the 'gender-bound enthusiasm' of the original *politique des auteurs*, these male directors are the 'rebels on the backlot' who 'take back Hollywood.' They are credited with the transformation of commercial filmmaking into a better, more artistic type of popular fare. (2014: 140)

These 'wonder boys' are rebellious in as much as they revisit the traditions of classical genre filmmaking by crossing them with the stylistic innovations of art cinema, as well as an intense self-consciousness and the use of allusion and quotation. The genre labelling (or, frequently, lack of such labelling) of the work of male indie directors is inextricably intertwined with the process of canonisation. Female-directed films, like those of Nicole Holofcener for instance, are frequently characterised (and thus often diminished) by the popular press as *chick flicks* – a phenomenon that does not occur to other indie directors who make films with comparable aesthetics. Schreiber raises an important question in reference to this process of absorption into mainstream, formula-ready categories: 'Why is it easy for viewers to identify differences between independent and Hollywood "men's" films, but not independent and Hollywood women's films?' (2011: 180).

The relationship between film genres and independent cinema is complex, because the discourse of independence seeks to place itself in opposition to Hollywood output, perceived as having low standing regarding cultural hierarchies of taste and, further, associated discursively with femininity (Newman 2011). While a number of filmmakers return on a regular basis to these formulas – for example, Jim Jarmush's road movies, Tarantino's and the Coen brothers' generic amalgams, Courtney Hunt's *Frozen River* (2008) and Debra Granik's *Winter's Bone* (2010), which dexterously combine the Western, melodrama and film noir – there is a generalised perception that indie films do not adhere to the category of genre films or, at least, they are not read as such in the critical discourses. When genre appears in these discourses, this happens almost exclusively along the lines of a constructed divide between feminine and masculine culture: male filmmakers succeed in inserting art in mass culture, codified as feminine, but if a woman filmmaker does genre, especially those genres traditionally considered 'for women', she is no more than a mere manufacturer of standardised goods (see also Chapter 6 on Nancy Meyers in the context of Hollywood).

The gender-based divide also manifests itself – although in different ways – in Newman's book, in which the scholar distinguishes two main categories of American indie cinema (which act, above all, as modes of reception): character-centred narrative films and films that display formal play with conventions. In the first category the scholar includes female- and male-authored works that are characterised by 'indie realism' and social engagement, providing studies of Nicole Holofcener's *Walking and Talking* (1996), Sofia Coppola's *Lost in Translation* (2003), Todd Solondz's *Welcome to the Dollhouse* (1995) and John Sayles's *Passion Fish* (1992), whereas in the second he offers a close analysis of films by the Coen brothers and Quentin Tarantino through the notion of pastiche and narrative games.[12] Returning to Roberta Garrett's (2007) argument about the 'masculine' dimension of postmodern cinema in general, it is not surprising that these formal games are not traditionally attributed to female filmmakers, who are much more readily associated with realist aesthetics and social engagement.

A filmmaker such as Kelly Reichardt – and, in particular, her film *Meek's Cutoff* – does not fit comfortably in either of these two categories. Reichardt's Western – a historically codified male form – could be seen as an anomaly within women's cinema, while, precisely due to its generic adhesion to a more 'legitimate' genre, it could also be easily inserted in the *ethos* of independent artist. At the same time, and taking into consideration its association with independent cinema as a discursive formation opposed to the dominant film industry, *Meek's Cutoff* perhaps comes closest to the model of counter-cinema, politically oriented to subvert Hollywood moulds and ideologies. It is against this conceptual background that Christina Lane's observation is particularly apt:

> [T]he director is generally assumed to be less 'mediated' within the context of low-budget, counter-cinema. We need to recognise the ways in which avant-garde and oppositional cinemas are no less discursive than Hollywood productions – there is no such thing as 'pure' art form. (2000: 47)

Therefore, Reichardt, who undoubtedly works outside the mainstream, is no more immediately accessible or 'real' than Hollywood directors, such as Nancy Meyers or Kathryn Bigelow; she has not perhaps mastered the commercial performance of the self (Corrigan 1991) in a comparable measure, but she still navigates the economy of the independent film industry, demonstrating her economic resourcefulness and participating in press publicity, which shapes the reception of her persona and her films.

The counter-cinema approach – an outlet for articulating resistance and struggle – might lead to the romanticising of Reichardt via auteurism's 'cult of the artist', while it also risks overlooking the conventions of the Western – in particular, the dynamics of fulfilling or thwarting viewers' expectations inscribed in all generic processes. However, I argue that Reichardt's critical project is possible not only by virtue of the 'oppositional' aesthetics of art film, which the filmmaker undoubtedly employs, but also, and perhaps most of all, by virtue of the genre she chose to work with. The critique of sexism and racism she executed in her revision of the Western is possible not in spite of, but precisely due to the conventional and stereotypical nature of the iconography she mobilises, which – thinking back to Johnston's evocative postulation – is far more easily detachable from the myth in popular forms than in art-house film: 'Myth uses icons, but the icon is its weakest point' (Johnston [1973] 2000a: 23).

The Frontier Myth

The wide, magnificent landscape stretches to a far horizon. A group of pioneers, driven by the idea of an epic destiny, wander with their precarious wagon trains across vast desert, participating in a utopian project of constructing a new civilisation 'from scratch'. In *Meek's Cutoff* Kelly Reichardt mobilises a dense semantic domain, constructed and reconstructed by thousands of films, beginning in 1898 with Thomas Edison's one-minute Westerns. Reichardt's fourth feature[13] is based on a real story about the Oregon Trail, also known as the 'Terrible Trail' – one of the main wagon routes and emigrant trails that connected the Missouri River to valleys in the West. It was used by pioneers, who, driven by the Manifest Destiny Doctrine,[14] were traversing more than 3,000 km, mostly on foot, leading their horses and wagons to save energy and water. Reichardt, alongside her screenwriter and frequent collaborator, Jonathan Raymond, draws on a historical figure, frontiersman Stephen Meek – who was hired in 1845 to guide the first wagon train along the route and 'lost' a caravan of 200 wagons in the Oregon desert – as well as on diaries of this expedition, most of which were written by women. When referring to *Meek's Cutoff*, the filmmaker insisted that she never used the word 'Western' while on set and in the presence of the film's actors (Gross 2011). In the DVD description, the film was described as 'a stark and poetic drama set in 1845', with the term 'Western' noticeably missing. Despite avoiding this generic label, it is evident that Reichardt inevitably positioned her work in a particular way in relation to this iconography.[15] While the makers of *The Great Train Robbery* (Edwin S. Porter, 1903), in spite of its reputation as the first Western, probably did not know they were making a Western (Dyer 2007: 92), *Meek's Cutoff* is an extremely self-aware meditation on the genre. This is because, as Richard Dyer observes,

> the Western is instantly recognisable, in its look (cowboys and Indians, homesteaders, prairies and deserts, townships, ranches and saloons, sometimes wagon trains, sometimes cavalry, playbill lettering, certain

stars) and its sound (gunshots, horses' hooves, the link of spurs, laconic male speech, distinctive musical scoring) [...] You won't get all of these in any one film but you will get enough to evoke a world and with that other expectations: narrative situations (e.g. chases, shoot-outs, barroom brawls) and thematic structures (e.g. the confrontation of wilderness and civilization). (2007: 93)

It is all these features, not only present in the films, but also depicted on posters, trailers and reviews, that make the Western particularly 'amenable to self-awareness'; 'its very distinctiveness is liable to make people especially aware that they are making or choosing to go to see this kind of thing' (2007: 93).

As many critics have demonstrated (Kitses 1969; Slotkin 1992), the Western, representing the colonisation of the West, is at the heart of white America's narrativisation of its history and the construction of its national identity. Peter Flynn argues:

Manifest destiny; rugged individualism; a pre-modern Eden of moral simplicity; a future built on the harmonious union of man and nature – all four cornerstones of the American psyche, each with their locus on the single moment of expansion and creation. No other period in American history has so frequently been called upon to define and solidify national identity. (1998)

The history, culture and geography of the West have been frequently represented as the America of an imagined golden age, nostalgically recalled again and again in the cinematic tradition. For instance, in one of his Westerns of the classical period, *Wagon Master* (1950), John Ford clearly participates in this narrative on the origin of the nation, offering an idealised view of Mormon pioneers' journey to the San Juan River. 'A hundred years have come and gone since 1849, but the ghostly wagons rollin' West are ever brought to mind', sing Sons of Pioneers – one of US earliest Western singing groups – in the film's soundtrack.

In contrast, Reichardt's depiction of the same period does not attempt to endow it with historical or mythic qualities, nor does it offer a nostalgic revitalisation of the Western genre. Rather, as several critics have noted, the film condemns the racism and sexism that undergird the conquest of the West, providing a powerful critique of Manifest Destiny and the foundational myth of a pre-modern Eden, while at the same time dramatising the failure of the American project in the twenty-first century conflicts in Iraq and Afghanistan. One of the central motifs in *Meek's Cutoff* is the so-called frontier myth. According to Richard Slotkin, this myth, expressed in American literature, historiography and cinema, is based on the supposition that the conquest of the wilderness and the subjugation or displacement of the Native Americans who originally inhabited it have been the means to our achievement of a national identity, a democratic polity, and ever-expanding economy, and a phenomenally dynamic and 'progressive' civilization. (1992: 10)

The figure of the hero is essential in this mythology, for 'when history is translated into myth, the complexities of social and historical experiences are simplified and compressed into the action of representative individuals or "heroes"' (1992: 14). The myth of the Western hero distinctively involves, as Tasker writes, 'a *white* American masculinity which is deemed necessary for the formation of a lawful community, and thus the definition of the nation' (2017: 112 [emphasis added]).

In *Meek's Cutoff*, the filmmaker scrutinises the frontier myth under a magnifying glass, throwing into relief how it is placed in a symbolic framework built around a series of conceptual binaries: wilderness/civilisation, nature/culture, Indian/white, weak/strong, female/male (see also Kitses 1969; Wright 1975). The myth's gendered nature is made evident by Meek himself when he proclaims: 'Women are different from men. [...] Women are created on the principle of chaos. The chaos of creation, disorder, bringing new things into the world. Men are created on the principle of destruction. It's like cleansing, ordering, destruction'. In addition to dramatising these oppositions, Reichardt dissects the figure of the frontier hero, who 'stands between the two opposed worlds of savagery and civilization, acting as a mediator or interpreter between races and cultures but more often as civilization's most effective instrument against savagery' (Slotkin 1992: 16). He is a white man 'who knows Indians', including how to think and fight like an Indian, turning their own methods against them (1992: 16). In *Meek's Cutoff*, however, the hero's competence and knowledge are severely questioned: he is an arrogant, reckless and racist guide – who insists that he knows a shortcut and is responsible for getting the group lost – and therefore embodies the failure of the patriarchal authority that has long been so central to the mythology of the Old West.

The context in which the film was made is vital to apprehending the depths of this demystification: much as with Ronald Reagan in 1980s, the president George W. Bush was also frequently depicted as a *cowboy* of international affairs, especially after his 'preventative' attack on Iraq. Bush constructed himself as a president-hero and a solitary warrior, aligning the war in Iraq with inherently American values. Reviewers and press notes for *Meek's Cutoff* charted multiple analogies between Bush and Meek, the latter of whom repeatedly asserts throughout the film: we are 'not lost, [we] are just finding our way'. Both the screenwriter and the filmmaker have stated on several occasions that the film could be read as a comment on the racial oppression that characterised the Bush administration's second term, but also the repetitiveness of American history in general, marked by 'issues of conquest and whose life has more value – which comes down to racism' (Reichardt in Fuller 2011: 42).

Certainly, Reichardt is not the first to mobilise and revise the conventions of the Western to explore present-day ideological tensions. The Western, but also genre in a wider sense, has always been sensitive to the social and cultural environment. As John H. Lenihan (1980) has demonstrated, Westerns produced in the 1950s dramatised a series of preoccupations linked to the Cold War that pervaded American society at the time. Westerns in the 1960s and 1970s, in turn, unmasked the increasing cynicism and violence of several wars waged by the United States in that period. Subsequent films substantially revise the history of the West, reclaiming presence and the voices of those previously excluded: Native Americans, Latinos, Afro-Americans, Asians and women (see Limerick 1987; 2000). Perhaps the most prominent, or at least the most frequently quoted, example of these revisions from a gender perspective is *The Ballad of Little Jo* (1993), directed by Maggie Greenwald. This film, inspired by the true story of a woman who struggles to escape the stigma of having a child out of wedlock by living disguised as a man, was critically consecrated as a feminist subversion of the Western (Modleski 1998). *Meek's Cutoff* can be inscribed in this broader process of rewriting women's position in mythologies of the West, but as I will argue over the following pages, it does so in a different manner to *The Ballad of Little Jo* and other films in which women come to occupy the main role in the story, becoming adventurous cowgirls or undertaking heroic action traditionally reserved for male protagonists.[16] Films that strategically position women in the traditionally male Western roles – such as *Annie Get the Gun* (George Sidney, 1946), *Calamity Jane* (David Butler, 1953), *Cat Ballou* (Elliot Silverstein, 1965), *Cattle Queen of Montana* (Allan Dwan, 1954) and *Johnny Guitar* (Nicholas Ray, 1954) – tend to

> push the genre flavour towards acceptable feminine spheres of melodrama and the musical, often getting a laugh out of the cowgirl protagonist and insisting on the need for her to learn femininity in order to get the thing she obviously most wants, a man. (Dyer 2007: 113)

Instead of inserting women protagonists in the privileged centre of the narrative action, *Meek's Cutoff* displaces the sense of action altogether.

Despite the fact that Reichardt's film operates within a recognisable generic framework, it retains a critical distance from familiar Western aesthetics and their ideological formations. This happens, in the first place, on the visual level. In the classical Western the majestic locations, represented through Technicolor panoramas of wilderness and unreachable horizons, connote the promise of great discoveries and new beginnings.[17] The wide-screen Panavision format is ideally suited to 'the sagas of migration, heroic action and expansive gestures of freedom', as Sara Gwenllian Jones observes (2003: 59). Reichardt revisits these widescreen vistas, enclosing the far-reaching landscapes in narrow, claustrophobic frames.

Much has been written about the fact that the film was shot in the Academy ratio of 1.33:1 – the near-square rather than rectangular frames (1.85:1) – which not only concentrates our attention on the daily tasks performed by the women, but also powerfully transmits the limited vision of the protagonists and spectators. The bonnets the women wear restrict their range of vision just as Reichardt formally restricts ours through her choice of ratio; similar to the square frame that delimits the visual field, the headwear eliminates the protagonists' peripheral vision. This unique framing technique – Reichardt's attested aesthetic decision – was discussed in an interview with Terry Gross on her National Public Radio show, *Fresh Air*. Gross started her interview claiming that she 'thought something was wrong with the film and kept wanting to pull back the curtain on either side of the theatre', and Reichardt responded that 'the square was typical for the early Westerns. [. . .] But for my purposes, I felt like the square gave you a sort of idea of [. . .] the closed view that the women have' (in Fuller 2011: 42).

The bonnets, which serve as a protection from the harsh sun by effectively covering the women's faces, render them anonymous, as well as highlighting their exclusion from decisions about their own fate. Throughout the film, the three women are often framed together, and away from the men. While the men draw apart to debate their course, the camera constantly keeps the women at a distance – a device that underscores the spatial organisation of knowledge.

Figure 4.1 The gendered organisation of space: men withdraw to deliberate the course, while women look on from a distance.

The aural perspective also places us in their frustrating position. The women are forced to spy on the men from a distance, straining to eavesdrop on their low, barely audible dialogue; silences and elliptical speech prevail throughout the film.

The events seem to be communicated, thus, from the perspective of the women: in one of the first images, the film shows one of the wives, Millie, wading through the water, waist deep, cautiously transporting a caged canary on her head, which might be taken to symbolise the position of the protagonists; the film culminates with Emily's (another protagonist's) face, framed by the tree branches – a shot that undermines the importance of her gaze. Not only do these images bring to light the prescribed power relations in the group of migrants (women's suspended agency and muted observation, as they are literally deprived of face and voice), but they also signify the female contingent's inquisitive and incriminating gaze, which calls into question some of the most enduring Wild West mythologies. Very often we are offered shots of Emily observing the men: they seem pompously secretive, which only intensifies her scepticism. The pioneers are lost from the outset, a fact made clear with the first distinguishable word to emerge at the beginning of the film, carved on the dried carcass of a fallen tree. Their guide seems increasingly incompetent. 'I don't blame him for not knowing. I blame him for saying he did', Emily clarifies at one point. The focus of her probing look is the self-appointed Western hero, in particular his boastfulness and racism – for example, when he brags about his courage, telling stories of the Indians' savagery in order to convince his followers that they are surrounded by cruel enemies from whom only *he* can protect them. Meek epitomises the sort of masculinity that Hollywood movies have long celebrated: a male identity premised on violence which protects a community.

The hero's doubtful status – in particular, in relation to violence – is not new in the genre: 'The Westerner at his best exhibits a moral ambiguity which darkens his image [...]; this ambiguity arises from the fact that, whatever his justifications, he is a killer of men' (Warshow 1964: 95). However, what Reichardt also exposes here is the Western's co-implication with particular concepts of racial identity and the fear of racial miscegenation that underscores the typical representations of Indians in many Westerns – for example, in John Ford's much discussed *The Searchers* (1956). The latter centres upon the white settler's family, which is shattered by the intrusion of a hostile Other when the protagonist Ethan's young nieces are taken by a Comanche war band. The protagonist's acid towards, and deep hatred of, Indians – he swears that he would kill his niece if it turned out that she had been 'defiled' by the savages – evokes the racist hatred that Meek displays on many occasions. This attitude is, nevertheless, openly defied: 'Is he ignorant or is he just plain evil? That's my quandary. It's impossible to know', Emily tells her husband, angrily challenging Meek's authority and racial hatred in ways that none of the men are willing to do.

Emily soon becomes attached to another guide: a lone Cayuse Indian (Rod Rondeaux), who is captured and threatened with death by Meek, but finally protected by Emily, who hopes he will lead them to water. The protagonist initiates a perturbing alliance with the prisoner: she gives him food and repairs his shoe, because she 'wants him to owe her something', as she rationalises to Millie. She stands for the most progressive character in the film, since – in stark contrast to Meek's racist remarks – she seems to show empathy for the captive. However, as Gorfinkel rightly observes in her analysis of the film, her feelings towards the Cayuse are deeply ambivalent, for she establishes 'a capitalist logic of debt as the essential social bond or condition of their relationality',[18] while 'reinscribing her racial and economic privilege and patrimony, her sense of white Eurocentric pride' (2016: 133). Emily, of all the characters, is the one who will try to teach the Cayuse a 'civilising' lesson: 'you can't even imagine what we've done, the cities we've built', she tells him.

Therefore, in addition to the myth of the frontier hero who 'knows Indians', the film revisits the iconic figure of 'the homesteading white woman common to fictions of empire and the US Old West alike', whose ideological function has been, indeed, a 'civilising' one (White 2017: 219). As Patricia White comments in her insightful reading of the film: 'Historically and hegemonically, the colonial mistress is portrayed as the tamer of both Western masculinity and the childlike natives, imperial patriarchy's moral compass' (White 2017: 219). In revisionist variants of the colonial fictions, the presence of a white woman may itself call into question these fictions: '[W]hen doubt and uncertainty [about the imperial project] creep in, women begin to take centre stage. The white male spirit achieves and maintains empire; the white female soul is associated with its demise' (Dyer 1997: 184). *Meek's Cutoff*, similarly to *White Material* (Claire Denis, 2009), a contemporary film about the legacy of colonialism also analysed by White, acknowledges this symbolic function of white settler women, implicated in imperial and expansionist projects: 'The limitation of – and to – the white women's point of view is the ethical challenge' posed in both films (2017: 221).

In light of this, it is significant that, with the arrival of the tribesman, yet another structure of the gaze is established: the colonial looking between the pioneers (Emily included) and the Native American captive, unable to communicate with them. Paranoia, hostility and fear of the Other, transmitted visually by a series of shots/reverse shots, become predominant in the second half of the film. In Gorfinkel's words, the newcomer becomes 'a pure site of difference, an empty sign of unfathomable alterity' (2016: 126); there are no subtitles provided to communicate his speech, and thus his language is as incomprehensible to the settlers as it is to the majority of the film's viewers. Emily, just like other

Figure 4.2 The duel of the gazes.

characters in the film, is terrified, and in her first encounter with the Cayuse she deploys a gun. The figure of the protagonist armed with a rifle, reproduced in the film's poster, traces a correspondence between female empowerment and white vigilantism. If, according to Robert Warshow, the values of the Western are expressed 'in the image of a single man who wears a gun on his tight' (1964: 105), then Emily effectively reinstates this image, without necessarily questioning its values.

Although her temporary alliance with the Cayuse seems to undermine patriarchal white power – Emily symbolically takes control of the trek when, eventually, she points her rifle at Meek – the last shots of her doubt-filled gaze at the film's conclusion, framed and in part obscured by the branches of a lone tree, half dead and half alive, invites mistrust of her choices and fear regarding the future fate of the settlers. The Cayuse may lead them to water or directly into the hands of his fellow tribesmen. In this sense, while the protagonist's look, visually contoured throughout the movie by the bonnet or the branches that conceal her face, could connote an incriminatory challenge, it could also evoke her partial view, limited knowledge and inability to make the right decisions. Reichardt manages to displace the Western male hero from a traditionally male-dominated genre, as she did in her previous film, *Wendy and Lucy* – in this example, positioning a woman at the heart of a road movie – but at the same time she underscores the heroine's precarious relation to power, raising serious doubts about her 'civilising' mission.[19]

The Everyday as an Affective Temporality

The decision to employ the square, instead of the rectangular, format has multiple implications throughout the film: on the one hand, it limits our vision, while condensing and intensifying the structures of the gaze; on the other, it focuses our attention on small details represented onscreen. In contrast to the classical Western, in *Meek's Cutoff* the scenes depict the everyday, the quotidian: the filmmaker is particularly attentive to small gestures, usually marginalised, discarded or imperceptible in Hollywood fictions.[20] In several interviews, Reichardt repeatedly stated that if her film can be classified as a Western, it is one told from the point of view of the woman who pours John Wayne's coffee (in Morrison 2010: 41). By employing stationary and relatively long shots, the filmmaker frequently depicts the three women going about their daily tasks: grinding coffee, knitting, washing the dishes, drying out wet clothing, looking after the cattle, setting up the camp and preparing food. Detail is omnipresent and, sometimes, ominous – for example, in the shot of a lost scarf dragged by the wind on the cracked salt flats, desperately pursued by Glory.

This focus on visual, but also sonorous, detail[21] has prompted readings of the film from a 'neo-neorealist' perspective. *The New York Times* film critic A. O. Scott draws a comparison between Reichardt's cinematic oeuvre and that of Ramin Bahrani to trace emerging aesthetics in recent American independent films that engage with contemporary social realities and 'counter the tyranny of fantasy entrenched on Wall Street and in Washington as well as in Hollywood'. Just as neorealism set out to represent the impoverished Italy of the 1940s and 1950s, reflecting the climate of fatalism during the post-war period, neo-neorealism also grapples with the 'dismaying and confusing real world' (2009b), plunged into a financial and social crisis and in the swirl of post-9/11 anxiety. 'Their local, intimate narratives remind you that, in spite of the abundance of American movies, there is an awful lot of American life that remains off screen' (2009b).

Meek's Cutoff shares many resemblances, in ethical and aesthetic terms, with the foundational texts of neorealism – in particular, Vittorio De Sica's *Ladri di biciclette* (1948) and *Umberto D.* (1952). The first is a drama in which the lack and subsequent pursuit of a simple object, such as a bicycle – similarly to *Meek's Cutoff*, where this object is water – constitutes the narrative drive of the whole film. The oft-commented scene in *Umberto D* (Bazin [1958–62] 2008: 265–369), in which the maid Maria closes the kitchen door with her foot while grinding coffee, a small action with which she expresses her fatigue, is evoked by a number of similar moments in Reichardt's film, which also focuses on the quotidian, minor gestures of the women.

Cinema, according to André Bazin – one of the key theorists that addressed Italian neorealism – has the potential to capture an image of the external world, which is formed automatically without any creative human intervention ([1958–62] 2008: 28). After the disaster of the Second World War, Bazin favoured realism – a supposedly more democratic and egalitarian aesthetic, which was seen to contribute to cinema's objectivity. The 'realist' directors, in contrast to German expressionists or the Soviet filmmakers who underscored the importance of the montage, employed relatively static and long shots and episodic structure – that is, stories lacking in major dramatic events. The quality of slowness was valued particularly highly by Bazin, who saw it as the most suitable tool for expressing quotidian rhythms with the greatest precision possible.

Reichardt's style epitomises, at first glance, Bazin's 'episodic mode', as it employs 'real time' to create 'a cinema of duration', granting each mundane event the same narrative weight. *Meek's Cutoff* 'evacuates eventfulness, in the pursuit of dedramatised scenarios in which incident replaces event' (Gorfinkel 2016: 124) – for example, in a much-analysed scene wherein Emily loads and fires a gun in her first encounter with the Cayuse (Hall 2014: 136). As James Lattimer (2011: 38) observes in his attentive analysis of the film, details which seem innocuous at the beginning of *Meek's Cutoff* start to gain in significance (for example, in one of the first shots someone is gathering water from the river), while episodes which initially appear to be significant as regards narrative development do not lead anywhere (such as the discovery of the gold in the desert). However, while Reichardt's work seems to echo the social realist film tradition, I coincide with Lattimer's observation that the filmmaker complicates Bazin's requirements, as she 'aims to accentuate the narrative's dramatic construction rather than allowing it to disappear into realist transparency' (2011: 40). In other words, she keeps her audience aware of the generic conventions, instead of creating an illusion of reality – for instance, by drawing our attention to the usual 'ellipsis' in classical Hollywood. Many everyday actions that are not shown in Westerns were, in fact, typical actions for the pioneers settling in the American West. These quotidian tasks are made, nonetheless, strange and almost eerie when they occupy the foreground of the Western. According to Lattimer:

> The critical distance created here does not, therefore, lead the viewer to reflect upon the (neorealist) portrayal of social reality, but rather upon

the standard portrayal of reality in the Western, exposing the mechanics of genre convention before addressing any social considerations. At the same time, however, the intrinsic physicality of these activities does create a link between the viewer and the historical social reality being portrayed, a corporeal identification with the sheer physical harshness of a settler's life that remains undisturbed by any genre confusions. (2011: 40)

This quotation throws into relief the seemingly paradoxical duality of Reichardt's endeavour: the filmmaker offers self-conscious, nearly metageneric-like, rewriting of the Western, while managing to transmit the inherently fleshly quality of pioneers' experience, which arguably produces corporeal identification with what is represented onscreen. To quote Mary Harrod's insightful observation on Amy Heckerling's heightened genericity, Reichardt's Western 'evokes the simultaneity of discourse's status as highly fake yet our experience of it as "real" and/or affectively meaningful' (2016: 63).

This convergence of fakery and feeling, or hyper-aestheticisation and the phenomenal 'real', is written in the language of the everyday, which is not only a thematic concern, but also a device to make us aware of the artificiality of the Western conventions and, at the same time, the structuring principle of an alternative temporality. In the aforementioned interview on National Public Radio, Gross comments that the bonnets and the boxier frame contributed to her 'claustrophobia in a wide open space', to which Reichardt responded that the square was a tool for manipulating the landscape and narrative time: 'The square [. . .] keeps you in the present, where the characters are. I had a rule that there would be no vistas, because I didn't want to be romanticising the West at this point in the journey' (in Fuller 2011: 42). In another interview she mentioned that due to this particular framing, 'you wouldn't see tomorrow or yesterday in the shot' (in Longworth 2011).

The diluted temporality in *Meek's Cutoff* produces a profoundly affective experience, which underscores the gruelling sensation of time passing. This can be observed from the opening sequence, which portrays the migrants traversing a rushing river. The segment lasts more than three and a half minutes. There is no dialogue; the only thing we hear is the sound of water as the camera shows, from a detached observational distance and in long takes, the pioneers methodically carrying their belongings across the deepening river. In the next scene, we see several shots of the caravan, followed by a shot of clouds at dusk moving in real time. One distant landscape transforms into another through extremely slow fades and we often see the silhouettes of the wagons and the pioneers appearing simultaneously at the top and the bottom of the shot. Nobody speaks until the seventh minute of the film. The journey has only just started, but it already seems interminable.

In her evocative analysis of this opening sequence Gorfinkel argues that it

Figure 4.3 Sheer duration: superimposed images in *Meek's Cutoff*.

'speaks to the contradictory and distinct nature of Reichardt's formal manipulation of time and her use of slowness as an allegorical material, as much as, or in excess of, sheer durational material' (2016: 132). While the filmmaker clearly conjures up the iconicity of the Western, emphasising the strangeness of the settlers' presence in this landscape in an almost hallucinatory way, she uses this iconicity to transmit, in the phenomenological sense, the monotony of a day, the sensation of circularity, the futility of progress and the state of waiting (Gorfinkel 2016: 131).[22]

Many of these shots, which use the fixed frame, as well as the long take, evoke immobility that is akin to the long exposure photograph. In his reflection on this photographic method, which required the person who was being photographed to stay immobile for quite some time, Walter Benjamin famously argues that this duration not only teaches the subject 'to live inside rather than outside the moment', but also compels them to 'grow into the photograph' ([1931] 1972: 17). For the subject to 'grow into the photograph', he or she must inhabit the time it takes for the light sensitive plates to register his or her presence in an arrested manner. Immobility and suspension – both of which Benjamin refers to – resonate with the aesthetics deployed in Reichardt's film. Press materials for *Meek's Cutoff* quote 'Stillness', an essay written by Charles Baxter (1997), in which he argues, drawing on Marilynne Robinson, that Wild West mythologies 'are warped in the direction of gunplay, warfare and conquest, John Wayne, open spaces, and slaughter'. Later he asks:

> What if, [Marilynne Robinson] suggests, alongside that noisy male-dominated set of myths, there is another one more commonly perceived by women, a West dominated by space and silence? A West of silences, in which the openness is an invitation not to action, but to what I have been calling here a trance condition. (in Fuller 2011: 42)

Devoid of the epic tone characteristic of traditional Westerns, the story in *Meek's Cutoff* is earthly and inhabited by duration, rather than heroic action. Silence and the languorous pace, punctuated by the pioneers' squeaky wagon wheel, which together generate the sort of 'trance condition' mentioned in the quote above, challenge the viewers' expectations regarding the Western. It is these features that contributed to the classification of the film as a prime example of 'slow cinema', a label which has been widely employed to describe current trends in international art film – in particular, its move towards realist, contemplative or simply 'slow' aesthetics. Jonathan Romney sees this type of cinema as inherently political, by the virtue of its capacity 'to suspend our impulses and reactions' and help us 'to engage more reflexively with the world' (2010: 44). He writes:

> The current Slow Cinema might be seen as a response to a bruisingly pragmatic decade in which, post-9/11, the oppressive everyday awareness of life as overwhelmingly political, economic and ecological would seem to preclude (in the West, at least) any spiritual dimension in art. (2010: 44)

Matthew Flanagan, in turn, bemoans the fact that Hollywood's intensified continuity 'has transformed a cinema of efficacy into a cinema of acceleration, giving way to a dominant practice' that creates 'perpetual, perspectiveless flux, a flux which defers judgement to a later, saner time, which never comes' (2008). The aesthetics of slow cinema, as 'a form of cultural resistance' against both the Hollywood-style fast editing and particular ways of living in general,[23] seems to be diametrically opposed to genre:

> [The filmmakers] opt for ambient noises or field recordings rather than bombastic sound design, embrace subdued visual schemes that require the viewer's eye to do more work, and evoke a sense of mystery that springs from the landscapes and local customs they depict more than it does from generic convention. (Sandhu 2012)

This, of course, brings us back to the 'civilising' mission of art films, as well as the long-standing discourses on taste and culture in a broader sense, which operate to distinguish 'fast, aggressive cinema for the mass market and slow, more austere cinema for festivals and arthouses' (Bordwell and Thompson 2011).[24]

Most critics and scholars read *Meek's Cutoff* as one of the prominent examples of these tendencies, considering Reichardt's resistance towards narrative progression as a definite deconstruction of the classical Hollywood Western and praising it for its political and social implications. Despite its wide critical acclaim, *Meek's Cutoff* also met with negative responses to its slow cinematic pace, especially from a number of Western fans – as the reviews of the film found on *Metacritic, Rotten Tomatoes* and *IMDb* testify. Indeed, one viewer raged on *Metacritic*: 'Please somebody shoot me for watching this movie! My God this is the worst Western I have ever seen. I think 60% of the movie was watching scenery and not attractive scenery' (RayKinsella, 11/01/2011). In a similar vein, although in a different register, *The New York Times* critic Dan Kois compared watching *Meek's Cutoff* to eating unpalatable 'cultural vegetables' and polemically confessed that he is 'suffering from a kind of culture fatigue' from having to watch slow art films, 'no matter how good they may be' for him.[25] Kois depicted the film as 'a quiet, arduous chronicle of a long journey [. . .] seemingly portrayed in real time'. By the end of the film, he felt as if he 'had been through a similarly gruelling experience' (Kois 2011).

Film scholar Steven Shaviro has famously challenged some of the tenets that sustain the slow cinema aesthetic: 'There's an oppressive sense in which the long-take, long-shot, slow-camera-movement, sparse-dialogue style has become entirely routinized; it's become a sort of default international style that signifies "serious art cinema" without having to display any sort of originality or insight' (2010). He considers some recent examples of 'contemplative cinema' a cliché, and he also questions the basic assumptions underlying the current film criticism:

> It's very consoling and self-congratulatory for old-line cinephiles (a group in which I fully include myself) to tell ourselves the story that the current cultural landscape's insistence on rapidity and speed and instantaneous gratification is a monstrous aberration, and that we are maintaining truer values when we strive to slow everything down. (2010)

While I agree with Shaviro's critique of the cultural legitimation of the 'slow' as inherently subversive and his defence of the political potentialities of the 'cinema of acceleration', as epitomised by Kathryn Bigelow and discussed in Chapter 3, I also believe that in the case of *Meek's Cutoff* slowness is relevant and political, as it opens up space for more textured commentary at work in her oeuvre. Slow cinema's preoccupation with corporeal realism and 'the physicality of animate and inanimate matter, bodies and landscapes', as well as its eschewal of narrative progression through which 'the perceptual and material qualities of the image are enhanced' (de Luca in Gorfinkel 2016: 124), is extremely useful for thinking about *Meek's Cutoff*. It is interesting to notice how slow cinema's theorists recuperate, in fact, some of the ideas expressed by Deleuze on post-war European cinema (1985), also archiving 'both profilmic weariness in performing bodies and in producing extrafilmic fatigue in the spectator' (Gorfinkel 2016: 126). One cannot ignore a number of similarities between some recent examples of 'slow cinema' and the already discussed Italian neorealist aesthetics, or works by Jean-Luc Godard, Jacques Rivette, John Cassavetes and Chantal Akerman. All of these filmmakers draw on the aesthetics of slowness, pay attention to the domestic, material everyday and foster a corporeal immersion in alternative temporalities through the use of long takes and static framings.

In its mode of observing the minor gestures of women through such devices as long and almost immobile shots, *Meek's Cutoff* is particularly resonant with Chantal Akerman's *Jeanne Dielman, 23 Quai du Commerce, 1080 Bruxelles* (1975), the main premise of which is also an observation of the quotidian and gendered labour processes. Akerman's way of charging the protagonist's everyday with temporal weight triggered a rethinking of critical tools deployed by feminist film theory and criticism at that time (Bergstrom 1977). Much has been written about how, by means of 'real time' employed to represent the daily domestic routine of the protagonist, and without omitting any aspect of cooking and cleaning, Akerman destroys visual pleasure, replacing Woman as myth, as reinforced by Hollywood cinema, with a demystified female character, historically situated in all her prosaicness.

However, instead of considering the everyday in *Meek's Cutoff* through this category of 'real time', I find it much more illuminating to explore the affective experiences that are generated at the intersection of specific articulations of filmic temporality and the daily routine of its protagonists, which many of the reviewers compared with fatigue or exhaustion. As Effie Rassos demonstrates in her study of Akerman, both Bazin's and Deleuze's ideas are particularly revealing in this respect, as they significantly move beyond the concept of 'real time' – that is, when the duration of the plot seems to be equivalent to the duration of the projection time. This line of scholarly enquiry, which has long predominated the analysis of the quotidian and its connection to cinematic realism, overlooks the affective and sensorial dimension of viewing time, often neglecting the relationship between spectator and screen, or the time of the viewer, which does not have to be necessarily equivalent to the characters' time (Rassos 2005: 11–12). For Bazin and Deleuze, as well as phenomenologically informed theories that followed their postulates, the idea of cinematic time constitutes the basis of cinematographic realism, which invariably implicates the viewer and the viewing body. Nevertheless, while Bazin ([1958–62] 2008) employs this conception of filmic time to further his ontological arguments regarding cinema, Deleuze (1985) is more interested in the ways in which the affective temporality produced by the cinema brings the body of the character/actor closer to that of the viewer. The Deleuzian concept of the time-image is profoundly linked with that of affect: through the time-image (a particular construction of filmic time, which evades the sensory-motor schema and is based on purely optical or sonorous situations), the corporeal connection with what is represented onscreen is greatly intensified.

As with the example of *Jeanne Dielman*, rather than reflecting 'real time', *Meek's Cutoff* generates an excessive experience of time for the viewer: the viewing time is not 'real'; rather, it becomes exorbitant. Even though, as already hinted, Reichardt's long takes are not really long in comparison to her slow cinema contemporaries, they transmit a profound sensory impression of slowness as sheer duration. The minor gestures and details of the women's daily routine do not constitute merely a narrative level in the film; they construct hyperreal temporal structures that are physically felt on the viewers' bodies. This filmic temporality in *Meek's Cutoff*, similar to the one produced in *Jeanne Dielman*, could be conceptualised as the quality of 'nothing happens', in Maurice Blanchot's terms (1987: 15). 'Too much celluloid, too many words, too much time, is devoted to "nothing of interest"', writes Ivone Margulies in her monograph *Nothing Happens: Chantal Akerman's Hyperrealist Everyday* to describe moments 'in which the representation's substratum of contents seems at variance with the duration accorded to it' (1996: 21). In contrast to Italian neorealists such as Vittorio De Sica, Roberto Rossellini and Cesare Zavattini, Akerman self-consciously destabilises the principles of realism, pushing the idea of static display to its extreme:

> In *Jeanne Dielman*, Akerman disables romantic connotations by giving to the mundane its proper, and heavy, weight and by channelling the disturbing effect of a minimal-hyperrealist style into a narrative with definite political resonances. Her attention to a subject matter of social interest is literal – fixed frame, extended take – and so stylised as almost to be stilted. In this way, she denotes the idea of display itself; her cinema focuses hyperbolically on what Cesare Zavattini claimed as the main requirement of neorealist cinema – 'social attention'. (Margulies 1996: 23)

Meek's Cutoff similarly questions the traditional mode of viewing, which is based on temporal elision and compression, causing us to see (and feel) the quotidian gestures by representing them in a highly aestheticised and hyperbolic way. This aesthetic (excess of time, excess of detail, excess of gesture) produces a sensation of passing time, but also a profound sense of estrangement.

There is a moment in *Meek's Cutoff* that reverberates deeply with *Jeanne Dielman*. This particular scene, which follows the morning tasks and domestic responsibilities of the women, opens with a shot of the sky at dawn, which cuts to focus on Emily lighting a lantern to comb her hair. What follows is a forty-three second wide-angle shot that shows women lighting campfires; further, we see Emily grinding coffee beans at a painstakingly slow pace. The scene brings into being the excess mentioned by Margulies: there is too much celluloid and too much time devoted to 'nothing of interest'. The scene encompasses the span of four minutes, which seems an unjustifiably long time to focus on an event apparently devoid of narrative significance; time and silence are so immense that the scene feels much longer than the four minutes.

The inspiration for this, and other similar moments, came from women's diaries, which according to Reichardt 'begin with big ideas and grand dreams when they start out, but as they go on, the trip turns into a stripped-down, bare-bones list of chores' (in Quart 2011: 41). We could interpret these scenes in a realist fashion, as an attempt to 'uncover or "rediscover" female pioneers' struggle' (Hall 2018: 144). As Dawn Hall argues:

> Since Reichardt shows action in real time, she creates empathy that, it could be argued, is hard to achieve with intensified continuity editing. Slow cinema may be helping audiences to find and solidify otherwise fleeting empathic threads, so they experience greater understanding, which may in turn act as a means of reflection. (2018: 142)

While I agree that the scene submerges audiences 'in a female experience of settling the west – a story rarely articulated' (2018: 144), it is important not to overlook how overtly stylised and 'excessive' time-wise it is, despite its ostensibly minimalistic and austere aesthetics.[26]

On the other hand, I would like to suggest that rather than empathy, the scene facilitates a sensuous, bodily connection with what is perceived onscreen. As already mentioned, fatigue and weariness are central affects generated by the film. Gorfinkel offers an extremely illuminating mapping of the most prominent mobilisations of fatigue and tiredness as figures inherent in art-house cinema, addressing both their theoretical and philosophical manifestations, as well as their historical and socio-economic contexts.[27] After the Second World War, she argues, cinema has generated images of exhausted bodies, characterised by 'weariness and waiting', which produced an archive of gestures linked to tiredness (2012: 313). It is in this tradition of tired bodies that Gorfinkel inscribes two contemporary films, *Rosetta* (1999), directed by Jean-Pierre and Luc Dardenne, and Reichardt's *Wendy and Lucy* (2008), both of which focus on exhausted female bodies, constituted by drift, dispossession and 'endurance'[28] – a term that blends endurance and duration:

> The endurance of fatigue assigns a corporeal persistence, a certain resilience through and toward, a physical withstanding, a bearing of pressure, and a relation to something that passes through the flesh as well as a capacity to withstand the abrasion, the distress of the temporally

and physically wearying. Endurance thus can operate as a concept that has valence for understanding the temporality of cinema's corporeal aesthetics (and its attendant modes of spectatorship); it can be a means of accounting for the processes of remaining, enduring, and persisting through forms of duress and despite them. (2012: 318)

Gorfinkel's analysis is particularly useful for tracing a number of possible intertextual echoes between *Wendy and Lucy* and *Meek's Cutoff*, as well as for rethinking the political potential of the alternative temporalities that they generate. *Wendy and Lucy*, filmed in the wake of economic crisis and Hurricane Katrina, tells the story of a young woman travelling to Alaska with her dog Lucy, where she hopes to find work. Much like *Meek's Cutoff*, *Wendy and Lucy* rewrites a cultural form codified as male, a road film – 'a genre of mythic, masculinist American mobility and individualist adventure' (Gorfinkel 2012: 334).[29] Reichardt demystifies this genre, infusing it with a perturbing immobility and precariousness (Wendy never manages to leave the unnamed town) – features that characterise the film's aesthetics as well: its stripped-down, modest narrative comprised of minor events, static shots and grey and desolated mise-en-scène (see Gorfinkel 2012). This aesthetic corresponds to the economic limitations under which the film was made, as Reichardt has affirmed on many occasions ('Wendy and Lucy: Press Notes', 2008).

Meek's Cutoff, similarly to *Wendy and Lucy*, was filmed in the affective climate of the present economic impasse that Lauren Berlant (2007; 2011) has described as a state of 'crisis ordinariness'. In her study of several films by the Dardenne brothers, Berlant points to how their protagonists are 'stuck in what we might call survival time, the time of struggling, drowning, holding on to the ledge, treading water, *notstopping*' (2007: 279 [emphasis in original]). In a similar manner to these films, Reichardt's work also offers a figuration of fatigue and exhaustion of the bodies on the margins, which fail to be recognised or find viable living conditions. The promise of happiness – their goal to find a place to settle – is eventually reduced to basic survival, as they struggle to progress in the right direction on the waterless wastes of the desert, in the very limited time they have.

In her piece on *Meek's Cutoff*, Gorfinkel examines the political and theoretical implications of the aesthetics of austerity, demonstrating that, while long takes and a durational style form part of global slow cinema tendencies, Reichardt's main intervention is foregrounding 'the linkage of quotidian activity and forms of arduous, painful labour with temporalities of exhaustion and dispossession for subjects on the margins of American life' (2016: 124–5). *Meek's Cutoff* contemplates minor gestures, rather than focusing on the narrative drive, placing an emphasis on fatigue as a fundamental symptom of survival, which, according to Gorfinkel, is 'the constitutive condition of early twenty-first-century modernity' (2012: 342). But to return to the question of genre, Reichardt also significantly engages with the quality of autonomy and individuation in a wider sense, which has always been the basis for a road film's quest structure and the conquest narratives that underwrite the Western. Reichardt refuses to offer wide picturesque views of majestic landscapes that emphasise ease of movement and reinscribe a nationalist ideology of progress, effectively displacing 'the representation of westward expansion as a magisterial exercise in a mastery of, and a triumphalist claim to, space' (Gorfinkel 2016: 128). In her reading of the film, Gorfinkel shows how Reichardt notably challenges not only the ethos of velocity embedded within these genres, but also 'the luxury of meandering drift or time luxuriated usually associated with modernist *flânerie* and its senses of drift' (2016: 130).[30] In contrast to many of the contemporary examples of slow cinema, here walking is 'stripped of [the] capacity for virtuosity in the mirroring of camera movement or individuation with the walkers' (2016: 131). There are no extended following shots that move with the characters' meandering. The protagonists' walking highlights instead 'struggle, difficulty, blockage, impediment and endurance rather than freedom' (2016: 130).

The shots of Emily and Millie crossing the desert transmit precisely this 'exhaustion of the drift': they remain 'in the same place within the composition for the duration of the take, their faces worn, their features slackened' (2016: 131). They are also, notably, depersonalised. The garments that they are wearing, the colourful dresses and bonnets that shroud their faces, unify and deindividualise them, in the same way that the style of performance does. This style of acting, deprived of any melodramatic tone or affective intensity, could be read through the notion of *flat affect*, as theorised by Berlant (2015). Berlant draws on Raymond William's 'structures of feeling' to think about

> a cultural style that appears as reticent action, a spatialized suspension of relational clarity that signifies a subtracted response to the urgencies of the moment (the historical moment, the sexual moment, the intimate moment, the moment where survival time is being apprehended, absorbed, and encountered). (2015: 191)

Flat affect remains diametrically opposed to melodramatic emotional intensity, as it moves in different registers: monotony, distraction, dispersion, absence, contention, indifference and dissociation.[31]

Michelle Williams, the actress that plays Emily,[32] arguably generates her onscreen presence through flat affect. Emily – in contrast to other women in the Western genre, such as Judy Garland in *The Harvey Girls* (George Sidney, 1946), Doris Day in *Calamity Jane* (David Butler, 1952) and, more recently, the protagonists of *Bad Girls* (Jonathan Kaplan, 1994) – epitomises

GENRE IN THE MARGINS: KELLY REICHARDT

Figure 4.4 Flat affect and underperformed emotions.

containment, enigma, coldness, monotony and absence, which challenges the more traditional representations of 'female' emotions in film history. Already in Reichardt's previous film, *Wendy and Lucy*, Williams communicated this affective neutrality: her expressions are reduced to a minimum. Reichardt emphasised: 'I knew I needed someone who could be very still without coming across as emotionally dead' ('Wendy and Lucy: Press Notes', 2008). Williams seems to suppress emotions and exteriorise the apparent emptiness that surrounds her; this inexpression or even resistance to represent legible emotions can be interpreted as an attempt to avoid drawing attention to herself or as a rebellion against the demands to give a settled response to a situation – a response that would box her into the melodramatic registers traditionally embodied by female characters in the Western.

LAND, NOT LANDSCAPE

Even though it seems that Emily and the other women are *Meek's Cutoff*'s main protagonists, one cannot overlook another 'protagonist' in Reichardt's film. Frequently, the filmmaker places the camera on the ground, limiting the expansiveness of the shot and filming the characters from below, as if her aim was to align our gaze with the dusty dry earth. In these moments, landscape – an inspiration and the 'material' out of which the Western genre is created – is made visible and palpably material by foregrounding the rough-textured topographies of the terrain. We do not necessarily identify or empathise with the characters, but we register the abyss of the landscape, the anguish of the absence and the incapacity to progress.

In her study of imperial fantasies of nineteenth-century novelists and poets, who in their portraits of Africa and India charted a link between landscape and the female body, Anne McClintock comments: 'Symbolically reduced, in male eyes, to the space on which male contests are waged, women experience particular difficulties laying claim to alternative genealogies' (1995: 31). Film scholar Sue Thornham (2016) revisits this concept of 'alternative genealogies', taking into consideration some of the cinematic landscapes in films directed by women: '[N]ot a country at all, but the material out of which countries are made' (Moers in Thornham 2016: 214).[33] While pointing to some of the challenges that emerged from gynocriticism, marked by the much-disputed concepts of female writing, women's culture and continuity in women's tradition, Thornham addresses the concept of legacy in women's cultural creation, setting out to explore 'genealogical intertexts' in Andrea Arnold's *Wuthering Heights* (2011), Emily Brontë's writing, Jane Campion's films and Fay Godwin's photography. Godwin significantly rejected the title 'Landscapes' for her compilation of works, published in 1985, replacing it with the word 'Land', in order to transmit its material qualities. According to Thornham, her photography, as with *Wuthering Heights* and other female-authored contemporary films, such as those by Claire Denis or Lynne Ramsay, focuses on textures and evokes the sense of touch, and in this respect it constitutes an alternative landscape, 'the material out of which countries are made', in Moers's words. The scholar observes that 'in these photographs we are addressed tactually, through texture, touch and a form of intimate witnessing, rather than through the formal framings of landscape' (Thornham 2016: 221).

The Western landscape, in spite of being frequently admired for its beauty and majesty, tends to operate as a mere background to the heroic action of (male) protagonists. Marked by colonisation – by those masculine crusades over a territory – it has, indeed, been associated with the female body or with the body of the cultural Other. Alternative landscapes, Thornham (2016) argues, drawing on Rosi Braidotti, correlate to *other* topographies, which, rather than adhering to the narrative of conquest, transmit the indeterminacy of a female nomadic subject. In *Meek's Cutoff* landscape is likewise characterised by displacement of this nomadic subject, but at the same time it is overwhelmed by containment, austerity and claustrophobia, evoked not only at the film's representational level, but also, as already argued, in a shared phenomenological presence.

Building on Thornham's idea of 'genealogical intertexts', but without limiting the scope of analysis to female-authored texts, it could be argued that the way of representing landscape in *Meek's Cutoff* resonates deeply with Robert Adams's work, who in his photographic representation of the American West also encloses his compositions in square, and not rectangular, frames, or with that of Edward Weston, who underscores textures of American deserts – for example, in *Cracked Earth* (1938), portraying Borrego Desert. On the other hand, in its affective treatment of the landscape, *Meek's Cutoff* evokes other films directed by women, analysed by Thornham – for example, the often discussed *The Piano* (1993), in which the land, not simply landscape, is the main protagonist. Jane Campion brings the bush to centre stage, along with its attendant cultural and political connotations in New Zealand, where it tends to be associated with the penetration of Anglo-Saxon colonisation. According to Harry Orsman, the New Zealand usage of 'bush' probably comes from the word 'bosch', used by Dutch settlers in South Africa to designate uncultivated country. The term was subsequently brought to New Zealand and Australia, where it acquired the meaning of 'lands yet to be colonised' (1997: 108).

Campion represents the bush not as a land to be subjugated or colonised, but as a limitless, fluid and constantly changing space, emphasising its textures, which provide a tactile viewing experience. For Sue Gillett (1999), Campion's 'attention to surfaces' resists and arrests the 'forward and through movement' of the film's narrative impulse. Likewise, in Arnold's *Wuthering Heights*, the sensations 'of a space without boundaries and of objects and non-human lives [are] so intensely realised that they arrest narrative and produce a gaze that is so close that it seems like touch' (Thornham 2016: 222). In a similar fashion, images in *Meek's Cutoff* open up to affective viewing and tactile visuality, generating a sensory and corporeal experience of the cinema as a material world: the richly textured ground and the emphasis on material culture and the materiality of the bodies stimulate a sensual, bodily response, which surpasses the comprehension of film in purely visual terms. It is this type of viewing experience which is attested to by one of the reviewers, when he writes about 'the intensity of light on sunbaked earth and the dust that billows up with each turn of the wagon wheels, but seems to bake that heat right through your pores and into your bones' (Alleva 2011: 20).

A number of scholars have turned to a phenomenological comprehension of the body to argue that film theory and criticism have addressed, almost exclusively, visual and intelligible qualities of cinema (that is, what the narrative or the images signify/represent) and less the sensorial impact (how films make us feel).[34] The centrality of the perceiver's body is fundamental to Vivian Sobchack (1992), who, drawing on Merleau-Ponty's phenomenology, mobilises the concept of embodiment to think about the eye and vision in tactile terms. This conception of affective viewing experience through corporeal and sensual responses to film can be traced to Benjamin ([1936] 2008) – in particular, his notion of 'a tactile eye' – or Siegfried Kracauer's phenomenological approach to the medium, according to whom, 'the material elements that present themselves in film directly stimulate the *material layers* of the human being: his nerves, his senses, his entire *physiological substance*' (in Sobchack 2004: 55 [emphasis in original]).

This approach positions the viewer as a feeling, living body who responds to the material body constituted by the cinema, understood as 'life expressing life, as experience expressing experience' (Sobchack 1992: 5). We do not watch movies only with our eyes, but we assimilate them somatically, with all our body, being affected by the images even before the cognitive information can be processed or before our unconscious identification with the characters onscreen occurs:

> Even at the movies our vision and hearing are informed and given meaning by our other modes of sensory access to the world: our capacity not only to see and hear but also to proprioceptively feel our weight, dimension, gravity, and movement in the world. In sum, the film experience is meaningful *not to the side of our bodies but because of our bodie*s. (Sobchack 2004: 59–60 [emphasis in original])

Sobchack examines the first shots in *The Piano*, arguing that her fingers 'knew' what was onscreen, even before conscious recognition took over:

> As I watched *The Piano's* opening moments [. . .] something seemingly extraordinary happened. Despite my 'almost blindness,' the 'unrecognizable blur,' and resistance of the image to my eyes, *my fingers knew what I was looking at* – and this *before* the objective reverse shot that followed to put those fingers in their proper place [. . .]. My fingers *comprehended* that image, *grasped* it with a nearly imperceptible tingle of attention and anticipation and, offscreen, 'felt themselves' as potentiality in the subjective and fleshy situation figured onscreen. And this *before* I refigured my carnal comprehension into the conscious thought: 'Ah, those are fingers I am looking at.' Indeed, at first, prior to this conscious recognition, I did not understand those fingers as 'those' fingers – that is, at a distance from my own fingers and objective in their 'thereness.' (2004: 63 [emphasis in original])

Other scholars similarly engage with the sense of touch as a starting point to think about the reversibility inherent in any viewing experience: the spectator *touches* and at the same time *is touched* by the film. Laura Marks employs the Deleuzian term of 'haptic visuality' to describe a mode of viewing sensitive to the textures of the images, which happens when 'the eyes themselves function like organs of touch' (2000: 2). Haptic images bring the viewer closer to the surface of the image, collapsing the distance between the two, creating a form of mutual contact: 'The viewer relinquishes her own sense of separateness from the image' (Marks 2000: 124); film, therefore, 'transfers the presence of that object to viewers' (Marks 2000: xvii). For Martine Beugnet (2007: 3), to be affected physically by a work of art means surrendering the will to achieve absolute control over the image. This haptic visuality is implicitly read here as a mode of relationality which a film can open us to, as it does not consist of identifying or dominating the image, but creating a tactile space of intersubjectivity between the viewer and the screen. Such a position is clearly opposed to the theory of subjectivity and identification found in Lacanian psychoanalysis, which localises the relationship between the film and the viewer on a more abstract mental plane. Rather than focusing on lack, the phenomenological paradigm underscores the intersubjective space of spectatorial experience, based on the notion of a subject who perceives: he or she does not control nor necessarily understand what is presented onscreen, but rather engages in a relationship of tactility with the image.

While there is always a risk of associating the haptic with a naturalised femininity – an identification that Marks clearly rejects – I agree with Thornham's suggestion that 'for women, who have been reduced to space, there is something crucial at stake in using it differently, in deploying its opacity and "physical intensity" as a way of "ripping open" the smooth fabric of narrative' (2016: 218). Interestingly enough, *Meek's Cutoff* highlights textures and materiality – cracked earth, rocky hills, monochromatic tones of dryness – but the film's aesthetics are, perhaps somewhat paradoxically, 'unsensual' (Denby 2011). Despite the desert's very tactile qualities, the film provides a 'haptic inhospitability and a sense of alien threat' (Gorfinkel 2016: 129). Such images of barrenness, Gorfinkel argues, 'gain an apocalyptic charge, summoning an ecological imaginary of blight and ruin, a time outside time' (2016: 129). The previously discussed affective immobility of the protagonists is framed in constrained, empty spaces with opaque and flattened surfaces. This way of representing the landscape, which, in contrast to classical Westerns, is anything but nostalgic, worries one of the myths central to the Wild West, reproduced by Frederick Jackson Turner in his portrait of the frontier: '[F]ree land as rebirth, a regeneration, a rejuvenation of man and society constantly recurring where civilization came into contact with the wilderness along the frontier' (Smith 1950: 253). The classical Western's palette of sepia and burned yellow and orange ochres is diluted with the white and grey tones. The wide sky, variously arching blue or ash-white, extends above bleak desert and merciless alkaline lakes. The desert seems stripped, evacuated and lifeless – a powerful contrast to the long light-hued dresses of the protagonists. The paradise is lost: at some point we see the canary's cage dangling empty from the frame of the wagon, 'a small death elided' (Gorfinkel 2016: 130).

The symbolic weight of these scenes is affectively meaningful: the discursively coded tropes are closely intertwined with the indexical 'real', making the limits between the two modes of perception blurry.[35] *Meek's Cutoff* employs the conventions to acknowledge their role in mediating the mythic – American freedom, space and mobility – yet, it also pushes these conventions further, making the film 'not just something cerebrally observed but felt' (Dyer 2007: 133).

Figure 4.5   Haptic inhospitability of the land(scape).

Thus, the affective qualities the film generates through its representation of the desert are not necessarily detached from the more conscious cognitive perception. As Mary Harrod argues in her article on the aesthetics of pastiche:

> For while the way in which we experience the phenomenal world can be reduced to physical responses to external stimuli, such interactions are, simultaneously, always mediated by human perception. This is coloured – whether unconsciously or at the level of cognition – by previous experiences; and these include experiences of mediation itself, as in watching a film. In other words, all experience is always both immediate and, to varying degrees, mediated. (2010: 26)

Building on Harrod's call to 'question the very status of the category of epistemology – as divorced from embodied, affective sentiment: a realm which has traditionally been gendered feminine' (2016: 58), I would like to conclude that the landscape in *Meek's Cutoff* constitutes the film's visual, phenomenological *and* conceptual centre, bringing us back to the problem of genre. Reichardt's obsession with stripped, evacuated landscapes – 'a Beckett-inflected scenario of absurdity, bound by waiting, opacity and non-knowledge' (Gorfinkel 2016: 126) – clearly position her within a set of tendencies seen in global art cinema. Yet, it is also clear that the filmmaker mobilises our shared knowledge of the iconicity embedded in the traditional Western – in particular, its usual figuration of landscape: a territory upon which the sagas of conquest are waged, a background of heroic action and expansive gestures of the (male) hero. If, as Teresa de Lauretis claims, 'the image of landscape as a perspectival space centred on the hero [. . .] is a necessary part of the grandeur and authority of masculinity' (1984: 107), then *Meek's Cutoff* displaces this imaginary altogether. Reichardt's contribution is not only to produce an alternative landscape, marked by textures and materiality, as well as troubling arrest, but also to underscore generic conventions and standard representations of the desert in Hollywood films. Just as the material fabric of the Western – the images of cracked earth parched dry by the scorching sun – rises to the surface, the materiality of the film medium is also underscored: the reduction of the usual widescreen image leaves part of the screen blank, interrogating the viewers and drawing their attention to what has been intentionally removed. *Meek's Cutoff* is all about these blanks, silences, omissions, restrictions, margins, voids, doubts and absences: it makes us see the imperceptible (the smallest quotidian gestures of women, usually excluded from the Western genre narrative), hear the inaudible (the whine of wheels, the creak of wagon frames, the clang of bowls) and, finally, graze the untouchable.

In his analysis of the Western genre and its particular forms of self-awareness – spaghetti Westerns and Westerns centred on women – Richard Dyer argues that 'by virtue of, respectively, geographic distance and a major change in generic gender organization', both groups of films 'tend to be especially aware of the Western as a distinct choice with distinct expectations, an awareness liable to result in pastiche' (2007: 94). In reference to the latter, he observes: 'A genre so overdetermined in terms of gender as the Western is liable to be thrown out of gear when there are sex role changes: a change in gender role is a change in the generic convention' (2007: 113). Dyer analyses *Bad Girls* (1994) and *The Quick and the Dead* (Sam Raimi, 1995), which apparently have nothing in common with *Meek's Cutoff* in terms of dramatic action and female characterisation; yet they do share at least one feature: all three films highlight conventions as such by offering gender dislocations and including elements 'that prompt reflection on what they are doing' (Dyer 2007: 95). Reichardt's inconclusive ending in *Meek's Cutoff* offers precisely such reflection. Meeks's power is eventually revoked: after his threats and promises, the leader finally admits his failure, ceding his authority to those who have been kept voiceless: the woman and the Native American. As already mentioned, the caravan happens upon a tree, which discovery could imply the presence of water. However, even though there is some greenness on the tree, the upper branches are dead. The next shot shows Emily's face as she turns to look after the Cayuse. In a reverse shot we see him stopping to look back, after which he turns and walks away across the desert plain towards the distant horizon. This ending emblematises the film's emphasis on movement without advancement, as well as its performative nature, as epitomised by Meek's enigmatic, self-conscious statement: 'We are all just playing our parts now. This was written long before we got here'. The film's ambiguous ending can be extended to the logics of the genre and authorial discourse of originality and exception: mirroring Emily and the Cayuse challenging Meek's individualist status as a begetter of truth and knowledge, Reichardt seems to question whether she is the centre and author of discourse, accepting her position as ingrained in 'the realm of the already said' (Dyer 2007: 180).

In an interview with Karina Longworth for *The Village Voice*, Reichardt shared how, on the final day of filming, the production budget finally ran out and she was faced with the reality that they could not film the ending included in the script: 'The sun went down, everyone was leaving the next day, and we couldn't afford the animals another day. So a new ending had to be constructed. Michelle, Rod, and I went back with a five-person crew and shot it' (in Longworth 2011). This anecdote puts into relief the sense of 'incompleteness' that informs the sequence and, in fact, the movie as a whole,[36] which, after all, depicts a journey that never ends. In addition, it points to the economic precariousness that affected the filming. Gorfinkel's framing of aesthetic possibilities of the film in terms of a discourse of austerity is particularly apt here:

> Austerity, a loaded term, resonates with a twenty-first century economy order and the neoliberal imperatives and policies of the George W. Bush and post-Bush era that insist that citizens do less with less, policies of recourse attrition that have led to the dispossession of the already marginalized. (2016: 124)

Taking into consideration the context described by Gorfinkel, *Meek's Cutoff* fits in well in the category of 'minor cinema', not only due to scarce means of production, but also for its use of the 'minor' format: the choice of everyday language over the epic one and the reduction of the scale of the actual expedition by employing a small group of actors to depict the journey of a thousand settlers that followed Stephen Meek through the Oregon desert. Reichardt is not necessarily a 'minor' artist in terms of critical appreciation – her work has been showcased at a number of festivals, and she is a recognised figure in the American film industry – but her films can be viewed as such, if one understands the concept of 'minor cinema' as a type of practice which makes political use of very limited resources. In the words of Mette Hjort: 'The term minor points, then, to the existence of regimes of cultural power and to the need for strategic resourcefulness on the part of those who are unfavourably situated within the cultural landscape in question' (2005: ix).

The optics of minor cinema, which allows for a rethinking of women's cinema beyond the romantic conceptualisations of the author based on values naturalised in the discourse of independence – such as rebellion, authenticity, absolute control over creation – seems highly relevant here, because minor cinema, as already hinted, may be produced 'within the major languages, not only of genre [...] or national cinemas but also of such supposedly alternative formations as New Wave or independent cinemas' (White 2008: 413). Reichardt creates in a major language (that of the Western genre and international slow cinema), but she employs this language in particular ways. Her work, as an example of minor cinema, is 'not "at home" in any of the host cinematic or national discourses it inhabits, but [. . .] is always an inflected mode, incorporating, reworking and [sometimes] contesting the conventions of established traditions' (Butler 2002: 22).

But, thinking back to Deleuze and Guattari, the 'minor' refers, above all, to 'the revolutionary conditions for every literature within the heart of what is called great (or established) literature' (1975: 33). A 'minor' writer deterritorialises the major language through a process that Deleuze and Guattari compare to stuttering and stammering, sobriety, silence and interruption. The regimes of signification become strange, and the major language is subject to continuous variation. This definition of the 'minor' resonates with *Meek's Cutoff*, which instead of directly opposing the major language of film genres, conjugates it to deterritorialise some of its aspects. Reichardt seems to take this movement of deterritorialisation further than any of the filmmakers addressed in this volume, pushing the generic tropes to its limits and disturbing its common usage. This deterritorialisation is produced in *Meek's Cutoff* in both the film's theme (in its displacement of the male hero in favour of a female protagonist) and the film's visual aesthetics, by way of static framings, lethargic rhythm and emphasis on the materiality of the landscape, which departs from the dominant modes of representation in Hollywood and facilitates a deep sensorial immersion with what is represented onscreen. Reichardt summons the Western's past to imagine alternative landscapes and new itineraries, without delimiting the beginning or the end of this journey.

Notes

1. *Meek's Cutoff* was Reichardt's first film made with a seven-figure budget: US$2 million dollars. It earned US$1.2 million dollars worldwide.
2. See, for example, Hall (forthcoming).
3. See Gorfinkel (2016: 125).
4. According to Patricia White, film festivals are particularly relevant to the study of women's cinema, as they 'provide sound evidence of the ongoing relevance of the concept of women's cinema – characterised by women's access to the means of production, the commitment to telling women's stories, and an address to viewers' diverse gendered experience within a dynamic public sphere' (2009: 155).
5. These dates refer to Miramax big budget productions, such as *The English Patient* (Anthony Minghella, 1996) and *Shakespeare in Love* (John Madden, 1998), as well as the so-called 'third wave' of production and distribution companies, such as Artisan (1997), USA Films (1998) and Lions Gate Films (1999). Tzioumakis's periodisation criteria are linked with the evolution of different generations of specialty divisions in big corporations and the subsequent destabilisation of differences between the Hollywood products and a large part of the independent sector.

6. According to Newman (2011), independence has been co-opted by the studios when they created or acquired 'mini-majors', such as Miramax (Disney), Focus Features (Universal), Fox Searchlight (Fox) and Sony Classics (Sony).
7. While I am aware that the existence of different terms to describe independent cinema involves a wider debate (and is a source of much confusion), in this chapter I will use the terms 'indie' and 'independent' interchangeably to refer to the discourse of independence, in Tzioumakis's terms.
8. The notion of authenticity is, above all, a cultural artefact devised to be sold on the market (see Newman 2011). On the other hand, the filmmakers' autonomy is often a matter of interpretation and discursive positioning, as well as an outcome of the process of authentication. See, for example, Peter Krämer's (2013) analysis of Stanley Kubrick, in which the scholar points to a set of factors that restricted Kubrick's autonomy in his first film productions in the independent sector (potential distributors, reports of organisations that financed the films and so on). This explains why Kubrick returned to the Hollywood studios, where he was able to retain greater control over his films, partly due to his aggressive self-promotion as an auteur.
9. It is worth clarifying here that terms such as 'counter-cinema', 'independent cinema', 'experimental cinema' and 'art-house cinema' are not synonymous, and each of them has a long and complex history. See Christina Lane's (2000: 21) discussion of the difference between 'counter-cinema' and 'independent cinema'.
10. For example, *Working Girls* (1987), directed by Lizzie Borden, which won the Special Jury Prize at the Sundance Film Festival.
11. See Biskind (2004), King (2005; 2009), Waxman (2006) and Mottram (2006). As Belinda Smaill observes (2013), today 'independent' is mainly understood as a marketing label, associated with the 'cool' outsider image of Quentin Tarantino. A number of critics have pointed to the elitist and masculinist nature of this maverick sensibility, which permeated the indie sector, while excluding women from this increasingly commercialised auteurist identity (see, for example, Lane 2000: 201).
12. Interestingly, in his 2005 book *American Independent Cinema*, Geoff King points to the connections between the independent mode of filmmaking – viewed as resistant to the standard Hollywood narrative conventions – and women's film practice: 'To eschew plot-centric forms in the cinema is, in many cases, to choose or suffer operation on the limited resources available in the independent sphere, to be relegated to what some would consider a secondary position akin to that generally offered to women in society. The corollary should be that women are more likely to be at home in the indie sector, which may be true in some respects as far as sensibility is concerned but is clearly not the case in terms of equal availability of opportunities or resources' (2005: 227). While King rightly points to gender inequalities in Hollywood *and* in the independent sphere, his conflation of independent filmmakers' deviation from traditional plot-centric (and we could add 'genre') conventions, women filmmakers and their (supposed) sensibility is rather problematic (see also Schreiber 2014: 156). Many women have no other choice but to work in films that engage with character development and relationships as their core focus because of a lack of resources. They are less likely to obtain financing for genre films, such as the Western and horror cinema, forms traditionally codified as 'male' (see Lane 2005).
13. The film was shown in competition at the sixty-seventh Venice International Film Festival in September 2010. Before that, it appeared at festivals in Toronto, New York, as well as at the Sundance Film Festival.
14. Needless to say, the reasons for emigrating from the East cannot be reduced to this ideological impulse to expand the settled area of the continent. One could mention

indentured service, starvation, poverty, jail and a stagnant economy, among many other factors.
15. In this sense, it is interesting to compare Reichardt's statements with those of John Ford, who, as Richard Dyer writes, identified himself at a meeting of the Hollywood Directors' Guild in 1950 in the following way: 'My name's John Ford. I make Westerns' (in Dyer 2007: 92). Both Ford and Reichardt inevitably display, if with varying degrees, reflexivity towards the genre.
16. In general terms, when women are disguised as men in Westerns, this 'transvestism' is only provisional. For example, in *Westward the Women* (William A. Wellman, 1951), a film about an experienced wagon master, Buck (Robert Taylor), who is hired to bring marriageable women west to California to join the lonely men who live there, women are brave and don men's clothes during the journey, but when they are about to reach their destination, they return to their dresses and 'feminine' role. They epitomise, just like women in Ford's Westerns, 'domestic' values: they embark on a journey into the wild frontier zone to impose order and convert it into their new homes. Therefore, this role reversal only reaffirms the Western's traditional gender binaries.
17. For example, Andrew V. McLaglen's *The Oregon Trail* (1967), which *Meek's Cutoff* seems to evoke, depicts a wagon train journey from Missouri to the promised land of Willamette Valley. In contrast to *Meek's Cutoff*, McLaglen's Western was filmed in Panavision, contains plenty of action, drama and romance, as well as a clear beginning and end. The guide, Dick Summers, in contrast to Meek, is competent, he knows how to communicate with Indians and he eventually leads the protagonists to water (see Morrison 2010: 40–4).
18. According to Gorfinkel, *Meek's Cutoff*'s 'larger narrative arc destabilises the notion of property which underwrites the logics of self-possession that motivates Manifest Destiny, conceived as central to the American "character"' (2016: 134). The Tetherows lose their wagon and their remaining water, a scene in which all the property and capital is destroyed and made cruelly irrelevant. Earlier in the film they dispose of several of their possessions to lighten the load of their wagon – for example, a rocking chair, 'another palliative bourgeois object to soothe the passing rhythms of time' (2016: 134).
19. In her tremendously illuminating analysis of the film, Patricia White extends this aspect to a feminist critique of the category of the auteur within world cinema circuits, reading Reichardt's film as 'not only a displacement of Hollywood's cultural imperialism but also an ethical challenge to US independent cinema's understanding of its place in the world' (2017: 221). Reichardt displays an awareness of the limitation of her own perspective and 'civilising mission' as a white filmmaker.
20. In *The Oregon Trail* we are also provided with scenes of women's everyday actions, but – according to Susan Morrison – these actions are intertwined with much more dramatic moments (2010: 42).
21. We hear a lot of ambient noises in the film: the creaking wagon wheel, the sound of animal hooves, the jostling of objects in wagons and so on.
22. 'In multiple registers, of narrative, theme, and form, goal orientation and telos are confounded and derided, and the expedition's transit seems like a maddening loop, without a capacity to progress' (Gorfinkel 2016: 126).
23. Film critic Sukhdev Sandhu (2012) suggests that slow cinema is like the slow food movement. See also Flanagan (2008), Schoonover (2012) and de Luca (2011).
24. Patricia White (2017) focuses on the gendered dimension of this discourse, observing that a 'woman director' can add cultural value and contribute to this divide: she functions like a white woman coloniser, promising 'civilisation' and refinement.
25. Film critics Manohla Dargis and A. O. Scott also contributed to this debate,

publishing 'In Defense of the Slow and the Boring' (2011) in the pages of the same newspaper.
26. Gorfinkel comments on the gendered division of this labour, showing how 'gender, exhaustion and labour systematically adjoin questions of race, a relationship complexly negotiated within the film' (2016: 133). In the scene discussed, Emily states begrudgingly that they are 'working like niggers once again', which points to the association of their work with 'a racial horizon of a pre-civil war slavery economy' (2016: 133).
27. Gorfinkel demonstrates that within the discourses of twentieth-century aesthetic theory, the condition of exhaustion is eclipsed by more privileged states of consciousness, such as boredom, ennui, distraction and shock.
28. Gorfinkel (2012: 345) explains the word 'endurance', employing the term 'induration', used in medical contexts to describe hardness or a loss of elasticity, and also referring to the French word *endurer* (to endure, to resist). In addition, the notion of enduration makes reference to Bergsonian *durée*.
29. One could also chart other intertextual relations. Recent female-authored genre films about women who live in extreme poverty, such as *Frozen River* (Courtney Hunt, 2008) and *Winter's Bone* (Debra Granik, 2010), display many similarities to *Meek's Cutoff*, which represents the pioneer women working hard, while men 'decide the course'. All of these films (about white women with scarce resources, struggling to survive) combine a neo-neorealist aesthetic with mainstream 'male' genre tropes and might be read as artistic responses to detrimental effects of the contemporary neoliberal economy on working-class women's lives. See Ortner (2013) and, more recently, Badley (2016).
30. As Gorfinkel reminds us (2016: 130), wandering is a primary feature of modern art cinema, both the post-war and contemporary slow cinema (the latter is, in fact, often called a 'cinema of walking').
31. See also Jackie Stacey's (2015) illuminating article on Tilda Swinton's styles of 'flat affect' as an aesthetic relationality.
32. This also applies to other characters in the film, apart from Meek.
33. The gendering of space/place as feminine and time/narrative as masculine is discussed in detail by Thornham in her book *What If I Had Been the Hero?* (2012: 126–30).
34. For example, publications by Vivian Sobchack (1992; 2004), Laura Marks (2000), Jennifer Barker (2009) and Martine Beugnet (2007).
35. Mary Harrod (2016) reaches a similar conclusion in her analysis of Amy Heckerling's films. See also Harrod's forthcoming book on the heightened genericity and pastiche in contemporary women's filmmaking in Hollywood.
36. In contrast to the cathartic ending in *Wagon Master*, in which the pioneers manage to reach the river. Similarly, *The Oregon Trail* also provides us with a complete story of migration, from the beginning to the end.

5. GENRE ON THE SURFACE: SOFIA COPPOLA'S *MARIE ANTOINETTE*

When commenting on her third feature, *Marie Antoinette*, screenwriter and director Sofia Coppola claimed that she 'wanted to avoid doing a biopic because [she] hate[d] that kind of *typical structure*'. She wanted it to be 'more impressionistic' instead, 'more a portrait of what it might have been like from [the Queen's] point of view' (quoted in Freer 2006: 150 [emphasis added]). Her statement is emblematic of the tensions that have long existed between genre and authorship, especially as they play out in the so-called indie or Indiewood landscape. Usually associated with independent features[1] and a consistent impressionist, directorial signature, Coppola clearly adopts an authorial stance here in an attempt to distance her work from the 'typical' genre structure of a biopic. This strategy of denial recurs in the discourse of independence, which tends to posit its cultural artefacts against the mass-produced and formula-based Hollywood genre films. As Michael Newman puts it:

> In independent cinema, a process of authentication (or de-authentication) functions within sites of both production and consumption, as a way of guaranteeing the authenticity of texts through positioning in the market of culture. This occurs on multiple levels: textual (forms and meanings of films) and paratextual (promotional discourses such as trailers and ads, as well as critical discourse) and contextual (institutions of cinema and culture). (2011: 226)

The process of authentication in independent cinema, which relies largely on authorship as an important category of validity, might be seen as one of the main reasons why many filmmakers would want to dissociate themselves from 'the mainstream' and 'the generic'. This is evidenced by Kelly Reichardt, when she adamantly claimed that *Meek's Cutoff* was not a Western, emphasising her (authorial) rewriting of a historical event instead (see Chapter 4). Coppola's film practice has been likewise defined through a focus on creative autonomy and the personal nature of her films, rather than complying with the 'simply' generic. However, even though it might, initially, seem that her films present a radical departure from genre – to the point that it is doubtful whether they can be analysed through this framework – there seems to be a conscious positioning which depends greatly on generic devices. This is particularly evident in the case of *Marie Antoinette*.[2] Critical discourses have predominantly read it through an authorial lens, but, in fact, the film draws heavily on familiar generic tropes, and it can be easily inscribed within the recent resurgence of the biopic.[3]

Loosely based on Lady Antonia Fraser's revisionist biography *Marie Antoinette: The Journey* (2001), Coppola's film covers the period in the Queen's life from 1768, when the fourteen-year-old Austrian Archduchess arrived at the French court in Versailles to marry the Dauphin, to her escape at the height of the French Revolution, just before the palace was raided by a rioting mob (and, significantly, before her execution in 1792 at the age of thirty-seven). If we follow Belén Vidal's definition of the biopic as a classical genre – 'a fiction film that deals with a figure whose existence is documented in history, and whose claims to fame or notoriety warrant the uniqueness of his or her story' (2014: 3) – then *Marie Antoinette* certainly fits into this category, as much as Coppola denies its adherence to this genre.[4] Coppola's resistance has a lot to do with her authorial branding and practice as an independent director, which seems to be at odds with the genre so strongly associated with Hollywood studio filmmaking (Custen 1992);[5] but in fact, as Dennis Bingham astutely observes, referring to a wide range of contemporary directors, 'nobody wants to be caught making a biopic' (2013: 237). Bingham, much like several other scholars who undertook a critical reassessment of this genre during the last decade, points to its prolific but also maligned nature, calling it 'A Respectable Genre of Very Low Repute' (2010: 3): 'middlebrow', 'tedious, pedestrian, and fraudulent' (2010: 11), and disparaged in a similar way as the 'woman's picture'. In the same vein, Vidal also argues that the biopic constitutes 'a sort of a heavy armor that constrains filmmakers' creative movements', and this explains why many directors – the scholar mentions Todd Haynes, Jane Campion and Steven Spielberg – have expressed disdain for its 'cradle-to-grave' formula (2014: 2). In referring to *Lincoln* (Steven Spielberg, 2012), Spielberg noted that he 'never saw it as a biopic', but rather 'a Lincoln portrait, meaning it was one painting out of many that could have been drawn over the years of the president's life' (in Vidal 2014: 2) – and these comments resonate with Coppola's own statements on *Marie Antoinette*.

The notion of the portrait is crucial to understanding Coppola's positioning on the high art versus mass culture spectrum, as well as her attitude towards the process of adaptation, both Fraser's book and the history of this period and figure in a wider sense. The filmmaker asserted in many interviews that she took artistic liberties with the source material, insisting that the film was not intended as a history lesson. The loose portrayal of historical events in eighteenth-century France met with mixed responses, from appreciation of its satiric tone and visual style to harsh criticism aimed mainly at factual inaccuracies and the contemporary soundtrack. Directly following its premiere at the 2006 Cannes Film Festival, the film was famously dismissed by some critics for its lack of historical integrity. As Manohla Dargis recounts in her piece covering the event:

> Though no one called for the filmmaker's head, *Marie Antoinette*, Sofia Coppola's sympathetic account of the life and hard-partying times of the ill-fated queen, filled the theater with lusty boos and smatterings of applause after its first press screening on Wednesday. (2006)[6]

Writing for the magazine *L'Internaute*, Évelyne Lever described the film as 'far from historical reality', contrasting *Marie Antoinette* with 'better historical films', including Kubrick's *Barry Lyndon* (1975) and Hytner's *The Madness of King George* (1994), which succeeded because their directors were 'steeped in the culture of the time they evoked' (Lever 2006).

These kinds of responses are, of course, not surprising, because in the case of biopics – as with other genres placed at the intersection of fiction and history, such as the historical film, the epic, the costume drama and the docudrama – historical accuracy has always been an important factor of critical assessment. It is, as Vidal puts it, 'the fundamental link to historical fact that seals the generic contract between producers and audiences of biographical film fictions, with the attendant pleasures of recognition' (2014: 3).[7] And, even though historical genres are invariably underpinned by 'the act of *imaginative* recreation' (Burgoyne 2008: 7 [emphasis added]), this reinvention of the past does occasionally meet with fierce resistance. In Bingham's broad discussion of 'the rocky' reception the biopic has generally received, he reaches the conclusion that it is precisely 'the collision of actualities and dramatic fiction' which causes such criticism (2010: 14).

All in all, the debates about authenticity, historical accuracy and the issues of representation or misrepresentation have always accompanied the historical biopic.[8] In this regard, *Marie Antoinette* is not an exception. However, what is markedly different here is the gendered discourse that surrounded the film, in which the authorial persona of Sofia Coppola – in particular, her status as a *female* director – has had a considerable influence on how her work has been read and evaluated. Coppola, one of the most discussed female directors in the last two decades, is clearly embedded in the 'commerce of auteurism' (Corrigan 1991: 101–36); she actively participates in constructing her public image and branding her films by providing them with a recognisable niche identity, 'as an indie-boutique "arthouse" director who has a solid grasp of mainstream popular culture from within a changing studio system that relies increasingly on mega-blockbusters and remains overwhelmingly male-dominated' (Lane and Richter 2011: 189). As with Kathryn Bigelow or Diablo Cody, she is aware of the importance of promoting her directorial identity, and she has been likewise granted an elevated degree of visibility and critical, as well as industrial, recognition: with *Lost in Translation* (2003) she won an Academy Award for Best Original Screenplay and became the third woman, and the first American woman, ever to be nominated for an Oscar for Best Director.[9]

Her authorial status and unique position as a successful woman working within the masculinised realm of Indiewood – a status which is at the same time acknowledged and denied – makes her a compelling case study for feminist criticism. As Belinda Smaill (2013) notes in her comprehensive overview of the filmmaker's career, Coppola defies easy labelling, mainly because her filmmaking practice diverges from the models established by previous generations of female directors, especially those working in Anglophone cinemas. At the same time as she shies away from the social realism favoured by many of these female filmmakers, she also does not fit well within the paradigms of the Hollywood commercial cinema, as do Kathryn Bigelow or Nora Ephron, and in this respect 'her brand, as a female director, is unique and without clear precedent' (2013: 153).

While during the first decade of her career Coppola seemed to constitute an uneasy fit for collections dedicated to women's cinema, more recently her status and career trajectory have been attracting more and more critical attention. Perhaps owing to this renewed interest in the filmmaker, *Marie Antoinette* has also undergone a process of academic revaluation. A number of scholars have acknowledged the significance of Coppola's personal style as well as her gender politics, seeking to rescue the film from its status as an underrated work (Lane and Richter 2011; Cook 2006; 2014; Matin 2012; Smaill 2013; Handyside 2015; 2017).[10] In looking at Coppola's brand authorship in relation to contemporary media industries, these scholars consider it within a web of texts – including fashion magazines, promotional materials and director's profiles – and in this sense their analyses are illustrative of the new critical paradigm in studies of women's film authorship, as elucidated by Catherine Grant:

> A reasonably confident return to considering various aspects of directorial 'authors' as agents: female subjects who have direct and reflexive, if

obviously not completely 'intentional' or determining, relationships to the cultural products they help to produce, as well as to their reception. (2001: 124)

The existing scholarship on Coppola shows that the close, 'interactional' examination of promotional and critical discourses surrounding her films can be extremely useful to uncover a series of underlying assumptions and narratives that circulate around her celebrity persona and her performance as an auteur.[11] The significant prevailing discourse in the construction of her brand authorship is possibly the one that focuses on her family connections and her privileged position in the American film industry. As Smaill (2013) demonstrates in her in-depth analysis of this discourse, Coppola's career has been more often than not attributed to her *special* status as the daughter of Hollywood royalty: as the offspring of Francis Ford Coppola, she was accorded both wealth and exposure to the dominant film industry, which contributed to her perceived lack of skill or 'true' talent as a director. The fact that she 'did not enter Hollywood from a position wholly outside the industry, as is almost always the case with female directors' (Smaill 2013: 153), has certainly complicated her identity as an auteur and contributed, perhaps, to her earlier exclusion from the feminist canons of women filmmakers.

This dominant narrative defining Coppola's public image has been made particularly evident in *Marie Antoinette*'s discursive circulation. In *The Guardian* article published on the occasion of the film's release, the director is introduced in the following way: 'Sofia Coppola could easily be a character in one of her own films, a day-dreamy, slightly disconnected but immaculately stylish waif who seems all at sea in a world of extraordinary privilege' (O'Hagan 2006). This portrayal, which encompasses various narratives that circulate around Coppola,[12] collapses her authorial persona with the way she represents her female characters – a common reading strategy applied to women filmmakers in general (for instance, Nancy Meyers, as discussed in the next chapter). Her family's name is emphasised on three occasions in the article, not only to trace her upbringing in a high-status environment ('she was born Sofia Carmine Coppola on 14 May 1971, into a Hollywood dynasty where her father, Francis Ford Coppola, reigned supreme'), but also her uniqueness in the industry as a whole ('no other young female film director possesses her kind of clout in Hollywood, and this is not just to do with her dynastic name'). Coppola's relationships with other famous men are also accentuated in the profile, which relates that while *Lost in Translation* was said 'to have echoed the fracturing of her marriage to the hipper-than-thou director Spike Jonze', Coppola was later linked to Quentin Tarantino, who included her name in the credits for *Kill Bill Vol. 2* in 2004 (O'Hagan 2006). The association with Tarantino has later proven particularly tricky for Coppola's status as auteur; when her next feature, *Somewhere* (2010), won the Golden Lion at the Venice Film Festival (where it was in competition against Darren Aronofsky's *Black Swan* and Kelly Reichardt's *Meek's Cutoff*, among others), the press criticised the fact that the jury for the prize was presided over by Tarantino, whom Coppola dated briefly after divorcing Jonze.

These types of comments reinforce the prevailing ideology of family connections and sexual favours, echoing similar accusations faced by Kathryn Bigelow during her career, mainly due to her personal and professional relations with James Cameron (see Chapter 3). But if Bigelow managed to enter Hollywood's 'big boys' club' (Muir 2010), Coppola belongs, in turn, to a 'cool kids' club' (Rozen 2006), with a different sort of sensibility and brand image, clearly marked in terms of social class and taste determinants.[13] Drawing on Diane Negra, Smaill (2013: 152) suggests that Coppola embodies the difficult balance between bourgeois and bohemian taste formations that is so central to the marketability of American independent cinema. However, the case of Coppola is particularly revealing, as her attunement to a culture of affluence is frequently linked to a lack of merit. The industrial and cultural context of independent cinema structures the reception of many contemporary filmmakers, such as Tarantino, Jonze and Wes Anderson; however, none of them have suffered from the crisis of credibility that has haunted Coppola throughout her career. Smaill convincingly argues that:

> In part, it is the affluence of her narratives, their languid meditation on the lives of those who seem to take for granted their advantage, that evokes questions around the relevance of Coppola's work. This questionability is doubled (and personalized) when coupled with Coppola's own femininity and privilege. The ostensible problem or difficulty here is not with gender *per se*, but with high bourgeois femininity. Her cinema and her brand is deemed, by some, to be unworthy because it is too whimsical, too effortless, too much the product of an un-validated access to power. (2013: 159)

Smaill is right in observing that, although associated with independent taste formations in general, Coppola's films are perceived in strictly gendered terms, because of their association with *bourgeois* femininity and their unashamed celebration of material culture and consumerism. This interpretative framework, which loomed particularly large after *Marie Antoinette*, was later reinforced with the release of both *Somewhere* (2010), a drama about a renowned actor and his eleven-year-old daughter,[14] and *The Bling Ring* (2013), a satirical crime film about a real-life group of teenage thieves who burgled the homes of several celebrities. All three films, which deal heavily with the famous, were read as an extension of Coppola's public identity and were criticised as excessively concerned with frivolity and superficiality. For example, Agnès Poirier, *Libération*'s film critic, who dubbed *Marie Antoinette* 'a scandal', chastised Coppola for making what she perceived as an 'empty' film devoid of any political content: 'History is merely décor and Versailles a boutique hotel for the jet set, past and present [. . .]. All we learn about Marie Antoinette is her love for Ladurée macaroons and Manolo Blahnik shoes' (Poirier 2006). Similar comments appeared after the release of *The Bling Ring*, Coppola's second-lowest rated movie after *Marie Antoinette* according to *Rotten Tomatoes*, which includes mostly North American reviews. The site's consensus reads: 'While it's certainly timely and beautifully filmed, *The Bling Ring* suffers from director Sofia Coppola's failure to delve beneath the surface of its shallow protagonists' real-life crimes'.[15]

Needless to say, this sort of criticism feeds not only on Coppola's films themselves, but also on her brand image in a wider sense, deeply embedded with an ostentatious exhibition of commodity cultures. As Fiona Handyside (2015; 2017) observes, Coppola's 'writing of the self', both in terms of her media image and film publicity, is moulded by notions of chic, girlish femininity (which continues to be the case at the time of writing, when the filmmaker has just turned forty-six). During her career, she has undertaken a wide range of activities that associate her with the world of fashion: the director has worked with the designers Louis Vuitton and Marc Jacobs (the latter named a bag after her; she was also the face of his perfume), and in August 2013 she appeared on the cover of Australia *Vogue*. She cofounded a clothing label called Milk Fed with her friend Stephanie Hayman, which still exists as a lucrative Japanese franchise. Apart from working on several music videos for groups such as The White Stripes and Air, she has also directed a number of commercials for Dior, Gap and H&M, among others. Her enduring fascination with fashion is nowhere better manifested in *Marie Antoinette* than in an iconic scene in which the Queen and her friends enjoy a shopping spree and feast on luxurious goods. The sequence, which as many critics have observed produces a sensation of sensory overload, is edited rhythmically to 'I Want Candy' by the 1980s British new wave band, The Bow Wow Wow, and is composed of various shots of sumptuous fabrics, luscious cupcakes, champagne glasses filled with strawberries and pastel-coloured shoes, with a controversial brief glimpse of a blue Converse sneaker among traditional period footwear. The montage culminates with Marie's stylist arranging a ridiculously voluminous wig, while the Queen asks: 'It's not too much, is it?'

This method of filming, which clearly evokes the vivid MTV style of video editing, is later echoed in similar scenes in *The Bling Ring* – in particular, those that depict the teenagers marvelling at the abundance of shoes, bags, dresses and jewellery. The fetishistic focus on the feminised world of objects is evident here and was widely dismissed in the discursive circulation of the film. Calling

Figure 5.1 Luxurious footwear in *Marie Antoinette*.

Figure 5.2 The abundance of shoes and accessories in *The Bling Ring*.

The Bling Ring 'narratively static and morally banal', Joe Neumaier from *New York Daily News* (2013) complains that 'half the movie is spent watching shallow kids try on other people's clothes'.

The complex grid of references between *Marie Antoinette* and *The Bling Ring* is particularly ripe with significance with regards to Coppola's take on the world of fame and privilege.[16] In fact, both films can be read as a self-reflexive comment on American celebrity youth culture. Coppola received criticism that her *Marie Antoinette* cast seemed like 'spoilt 5th Avenue New Yorkers', to which the filmmaker responded by saying that she wanted 'to emphasise that they are teenagers and to mark the difference between their world and the stuffy court world' (in Cheshire 2015: 119). It is not a coincidence that Coppola's version of the Queen was routinely referred to as an eighteenth century Paris Hilton (see Cheshire 2015: 119). The infamous socialite, who was, in fact, one of the victims of the actual Bling Ring robberies, made a cameo in the latter film, appearing as herself, and some scenes were shot in her own home in Los Angeles – and these decisions suggest Coppola's playful appropriation of contemporary celebrity culture, in which she also actively participates.

While several journalists were thoroughly annoyed by Coppola's overt concern with fashion and youth sensibilities, considered as responsible for the films' supposed shallowness, others read her oeuvre as a subtle attack on twenty-first century Hollywood. The dominant film industry was compared to the self-absorbed obscene luxury of Versailles and Hilton's excessive lifestyle: 'The clothes, the parties, the flatterers, the entourage, the sham marriages and passionate adulteries: it's American celebrity culture but with better manners and (slightly) more ridiculous clothes. Affairs of state are conducted almost as it they were movie deals', we read in A. O. Scott's (2006) review of *Marie Antoinette* significantly entitled 'Holding a Mirror Up to Hollywood'. Nevertheless, as Nathan Heller observes in his *Slate* review of *Somewhere*, Coppola's attack on Hollywood is necessarily problematic due to her privileged upbringing, as it places her in a position of unusual cultural tension:

> Coppola's insider criticism of Hollywood, her disdain for the industry that her own career relies on, leads her into a strange territory between hypocrisy and candor, privileged lament and fearless protest. This indeterminacy gives her work the back-and-forth flicker – and intrigue – of a lure in water. (2010)

Coppola's 'back-and-forth flicker', as she seeks to illuminate the bubble of fame from the inside, evokes Diablo Cody and Karyn Kusama's 'bobbing and weaving' in their own critique of the dominant film culture from within the system, while remaining commercially successful (see Chapter 2).[17] As previously argued, their assumed access to Hollywood power (and patriarchy) makes the scholarly assessment of their film similarly problematic.

Bringing together *The Bling Ring* and *Marie Antoinette* in a discussion of Coppola's interest in celebrity culture sheds light not only on the filmmaker's uneasy position within the elite world of the American film industry, but also on women's relationship to mass culture in general. The representation of affluence in Coppola's films is often perceived as 'too unself-conscious and lacking in an ironising critique' (Smaill 2013: 152). This supposed lack of critical distance, inextricably tied to the film's deficit of quality, could be inscribed within the wider conceptualisation of mass culture as clearly gendered. As Andreas Huyssen (1986) argued in his study of High Modernism, which defined itself in opposition to mass culture, discursively aligned with the female, a woman is perceived as too approximate to her body and to the world of material objects to gain broader perspective and, thus, to engender proper critique. Coppola's association with the feminised mass consumption profoundly affects her status as an auteur, which is widely acknowledged but at the same time (not so subtly) invalidated. As many scholars have shown, the mechanisms of devaluation of women's participation in popular culture, both as producers and consumers, are frequently developed through culinary metaphors (see also Chapter 6). Critics have likened *Marie Antoinette* to 'licorice' (Stevens 2006), 'eye candy [. . .] no more nourishing than a bonbon' (McCarthy 2006) and a 'sugarcoated romp' that doesn't take itself 'particularly seriously' (Morris 2006). In the newspaper *Le Figaro*, historian Jean Tulard called *Marie Antoinette* 'Versailles in Hollywood sauce', saying that it 'dazzles' with a 'deployment of wigs, fans and pastries, a symphony of colors', which 'all [mask] some gross errors and voluntary anachronisms' (2010). Writing for the *Philadelphia Inquirer* Steven Rea downplays *Marie Antoinette* as 'a gorgeous confection, packed with gargantuan gowns and pornographic displays of pastry-stuffs' (2006), while Sean O'Hagan observes in his positive review of the film: 'It is a gorgeous-looking soufflé of a film whose perceived lack of a political subtext or even point of view has [. . .] caused an unholy row in France' (2006).

Ultimately, Coppola's gender does matter when it comes to the critical evaluation of her films, dismissed consistently as decorative, frivolous, superficial and not *distanced* enough. The common perception that her work is unworthy, because it lacks depth or substance, remains closely intertwined with her (authorial) performance of bourgeois femininity and relies upon a series of discourses around women and commodity cultures that are highly problematic. And, although the critical reception of *Marie Antoinette* reveals different discourses about Coppola's directorial signature, the foregrounding of the 'surface' seems to be a recurring, common conceit. The perceived focus on this key element – which overlaps with other features, such as a narrative emphasis on girlhood and 'the feminine', lack of emotional intensity and excesses of consumption – generates divergent assessments of Coppola's films, from marvelling at their carefully composed imageries to considering them as somewhat inferior in comparison to a more 'solid' historical cinema.[18] As a matter of fact, it is common practice to describe Coppola as a filmmaker 'of the image' – that is, a filmmaker devoted to visual beauty, rather than a plot. Even the positive reviews, which praise the director's style, are dominated by this discourse – for example, when they emphasise that what *really* matters in the film is its style, not the story. Indeed, *Rotten Tomatoes*' consensus states: 'Lavish imagery and a daring soundtrack set this film apart from most period dramas; in fact, style completely takes precedence over plot and character development in Coppola's vision of the doomed queen'.[19]

Perhaps somewhat paradoxically, the foregrounding of the surface goes hand in hand with authorial depth, since, to quote Pam Cook, 'in Coppola's film, style is substance' (2006: 40). Nevertheless, as I seek to demonstrate in the following section, Coppola's attention to different surfaces speaks volumes not only about her authorial stance, seemingly oppositional to generic identities, but also about the very *substance* of the genre. In my exploration of the multiple and interrelated facets of *Marie Antoinette* I contend that Coppola's engagement with familiar conventions is far more complex than current analysis of her work has acknowledged. By way of contrast with the majority of critical readings of the film in the vein of 'visual beauty' and scholarship that have characterised it almost exclusively in terms of authorship, I argue, drawing predominantly on genre theory, that Coppola's fascination with surfaces and materiality – made evident by her shots of food, fabrics and furnishings throughout the film – is not something exclusive to her authorial style.

In her article on *Marie Antoinette* Anna Backman Rogers rejects the idea that the film is all 'style' with little 'substance', arguing that its 'surfaces contain depths that cannot be conveyed through the more traditional format associated with the historical costume drama' (2012: 81). While I agree with Backman Rogers on her first point, the relationship between surface and genre in *Marie Antoinette* seems more intricate to me. In fact, as Saige Walton suggests, 'the extravagant and surface-led history of *Marie Antoinette* is well suited to the conventions of the costume drama or bio-picture, where a sumptuous focus upon clothing, texture, and setting are abiding concerns' (Walton 2016: 148). Coppola's attention to surface is manifested, therefore, not against, but through the fabric of the costume biopic.

In what follows I consider surface as a key term not so much to frame Coppola's directorial signature, but rather to inscribe *Marie Antoinette* within the gendered history of the two genres mentioned by Walton: costume drama and biopic. I am particularly interested in investigating the gender anxieties that underlay the labelling of these genres by film criticism and also tracing the manifold ways in which *Marie Antoinette* complicates the relationship between genre and authorship in a wider sense. Following Kathleen McHugh's (2009) call to consider women's cinema beyond paradigms that marginalise it as 'exceptional anomaly' (a product of the *female* auteur), my aim is to articulate a more historical sense of women's contribution to mainstream genre production. In order to do this, I will establish intertextual relations with other female- and male-authored costume dramas, in particular, Sally Potter's *Orlando* (1992) and Saul Dibb's *The Duchess* (2008). The web of possible intexts between these films points more broadly to the complex network of possibilities and constraints for female authorship within this genre, as well as suggesting a critical shift towards a postfeminist moment, informed by changing discourses on consumption and feminine agency.

Costume Drama and its Gendered Past

In his review of *Marie Antoinette* for the *Independent on Sunday*, Jonathan Romney notes how many critics conflated Marie Antoinette and Sofia Coppola, dismissing the film as 'a rich girl's fantasy about a rich girl' (2006). He continues: 'Some detractors complained the film wasn't a serious historical drama; others were disappointed it was a more traditional heritage outing than anticipated, rather than the radical genre-busting promised by the chic cast' (2006). His comments encapsulate a number of overlapping discourses that circulate around Coppola, which, as previously argued, contribute to the construction of her authorial identity: on the one hand, they are indicative of Coppola's biographic legend, which remains intimately intertwined with the reception of her films, and how this legend is often used in ways that belittle her credibility as a director; on the other, they evidence the dynamic of 'going-with'/'going-against' genre, and, in particular, the expected generic subversion ('genre-busting') implicit in the discourse of independent cinema. Perhaps most notably, Romney's observations bring to the fore the issue of generic labelling, as he clearly distinguishes 'a serious historical drama' from 'a more traditional heritage outing'.

This labelling is by no means neutral, and it deserves closer critical attention. The distinction Romney touches on points to the complex process of the gendering of genres and echoes what Chris Robé (2009) analyses as the long-standing dichotomy between the legitimate, politically progressive historical film and the costume drama's supposedly reactionary tendencies. In his essay, Robé investigates how the (predominantly male-produced) body of US criticism reinforced traditional gender hierarchies, consistently celebrating Hollywood's male-centred genres, such as historical biopic, over female-centred ones, like costume drama. The directors of the former, according to Robé, have been seen to employ mainstream cinematic conventions to produce politically engaged films that address 'complex historical and contemporary issues from a predominantly working-class perspective' (2009: 71), while female-centred, 'feminine' costume dramas have been thought to privilege bourgeois spectacle, which presumably dissuades spectators from paying attention to more serious themes.

This ideological critique of the costume film is immediately apparent in the case of Sofia Coppola, who, as previously seen, was criticised for producing a 'pretty-looking'[20] film with no political resonance that, to quote Wesley

Morris, 'skims with style', even if it is 'mostly surface' (2006). If we compare these comments with the 1929 review of *The Passion of Jeanne d'Arc*, in which the author reasons that the film 'is an historical film, but not a costume film', as it possesses 'no specious prettiness, but hardness' (Potamkin in Robé 2009: 71), the ideological operation inherent to the gendering of genres becomes even more evident. It is in this early review, according to Robé, that Potamkin establishes a clear-cut dichotomy that will determine all of the later US left-wing film criticism's demarcations between the costume drama and supposedly more legitimate historical films: 'spectacle versus theme' (2009: 72).[21]

Needless to say, this desire to establish a precise genre demarcation is underpinned by a particular understanding of the author-genre dyad. While the male-centred historical films stand out for their deliberate and 'sophisticated' use of the mainstream cinematic conventions to produce radical or progressive meanings, the costume drama – associated with women, spectacle and consumer cultures – can only operate as an expression of the dominant ideology that governs the bourgeois film in general, as it distracts spectators from a film's themes 'by engrossing them with the empty affect of the mise-en-scène's surface details' (Robé 2009: 72). In light of these comments, it is interesting to note how such visually stunning period dramas as Miloš Forman's *Amadeus* (1984) or Stanley Kubrick's *Barry Lyndon* (1975), both of which Coppola's film was often compared to, won universal praise and critical acclaim, while *Marie Antoinette* was often dismissed as being too centred on the bourgeois spectacle of decorative objects.[22] As it turns out, male authors with strong personalities can engage in the 'contemptible' realm of the costume drama, and do well out of it, as long as they maintain sufficient distance from its generic conventions. In contrast, the critical reception of Coppola's concern with the feminised space of the costume drama (and, significantly, with the adolescent female protagonists) throws into stark relief the enduring belief that a woman is generally too close to material culture to instigate a legitimate critique.

These highly problematic gender assumptions in US film criticism are mirrored in 1990s British film studies' reflections on heritage cinema, which were also guided by the critique of spectacle found in the costume drama. In particular, they addressed the historical spectacle's supposedly reactionary idealisation of the past, which diverted attention away from the complex socio-historical contexts. Just like the so-called 'postmodern nostalgia film', derided by Fredric Jameson for failing to engage with broader historical force, the costume drama has often been accused of 'privileging style over substance and historical authenticity' (Garrett 2007: 129) – and, in case of the latter, this contempt was closely bound up with the 'feminine' preoccupation with clothing and interiors. In his 1993 article 'Re-presenting the National Past: Nostalgia and Pastiche in the Heritage Film', film historian Andrew Higson associated slow-paced narratives and exuberant, static mise-en-scènes, showcasing sumptuous period costumes and lavish décor of palaces and mansions, with innately conservative, bourgeois and imperial values, conforming to, as it does, an iconography of upper-middle class or aristocratic privilege. The visual splendour of architectural sites, interior designs, furnishings and period artefacts, usually at the expense of the plot, was thus seen as responsible for undercutting any serious themes – for example, the historical experience of the impoverished masses: '[T]he past is displayed as visually spectacular pastiche, inviting a nostalgic gaze that resists the ironies of social critiques' (Higson 1993: 109). As Garrett observes in reference to Higson's analysis, the heritage film seems to pursue 'surface authenticity (of costume and décor) at the price of a deeper authenticity', and this critique intersects with Jameson's view of the nostalgia film as 'all style and no substance', which fails to reflect critically on the past cultural forms it evokes (2007: 130, 128).

It is in a context shaped by these discussions on the aesthetics of the heritage film that feminist film criticism set out to focus on its gender politics.[23] In parallel with other strands of feminist criticism, which reclaimed the pleasures of spectacle, emotion, exuberant mise-en-scène (first in melodrama and later in the chick flick), scholars such as Claire Monk and Belén Vidal put gender on the agenda of the heritage film debate. They insightfully point to how the ideological critique of nostalgia overlooked many aspects in heritage cinema – for example, its consistent emphasis on female viewers and their pleasures. In the midst of the self-reflexive turn in period films of the 1990s and 2000s, and the subsequent emergence of a post-heritage paradigm in academia – which suggests more broadly 'a celebratory turn to postmodern cultural recycling and the aesthetic possibilities offered by pastiche'– other pleasures of heritage cinema were also emphasised: the performative, self-referentiality and irony (Vidal 2012: 100). According to Claire Monk, the period films that feature post-heritage aesthetics – that is, that display 'a deep self-consciousness about how the past is represented' – often also exhibit 'an overt concern with sexuality and gender, particularly non-dominant gender and sexual identities' (1995: 33). Rather than a rupture, however, she considers these films as a development of the potential already discernible in earlier examples of the heritage film – in particular, in Merchant Ivory productions of the 1980s.

With its focus on the pleasures of the heritage spectacle, such as 'female' looking, self-referentiality and a playful view of history, as well as its interest, as I demonstrate later, in gender performativity, *Marie Antoinette* could, indeed, be placed within this tradition of the (post-)heritage film. And if post-heritage aesthetics have been widely understood as 'a move away from the fetishisation of authenticity towards a hybrid aesthetics and the mixture of genre conventions, anachronisms and high/low cultural references' (Gibson in Vidal 2012: 100), then Coppola's film – which merges historical material indiscriminately with pop music, Converse All Stars sneakers and actors speaking with American accents – clearly participates in this shift.

There are, of course, some important differences between costume dramas and heritage films that complicate *Marie Antoinette*'s generic pedigree. As Vidal clarifies:

> The term 'heritage film' co-exists with the more strongly generic 'period film' and 'costume film' (or 'costume drama'). All terms convey a type of film that places its characters in a recognizable moment of the past, enhanced by the mise-en-scène of historical reconstruction. (2012: 1)

Nevertheless, 'heritage cinema', because of the wider connotations it usually carries in British film studies, might be seen to engage more directly with nation, and, in particular, 'the ways in which national cinemas turn to the past at different moments of their histories in search of their own foundational myths' (2012: 3).[24] And despite the fact that *Marie Antoinette* undoubtedly deals with the iconography of Frenchness, Coppola's is an external, not an inside view of history. This further highlights the film's status as 'non-authentic', as a product for global consumption, which – as was also the case with her previous film, *Lost in Translation*, and its creative reimagining of Tokyo[25] – renders it especially susceptible to accusations of frivolity and superficiality.

Bearing these differences in mind, *Marie Antoinette* shares many features with its more 'properly' heritage counterparts. The most frequently discussed female-authored period dramas, *Orlando* (Sally Potter, 1992) and *The Piano* (Jane Campion, 1993), can be readily comparable to *Marie Antoinette*. Although all three films draw on the conventions of period drama in distinctive ways, their deep interest in mise-en-scène's surface details clearly intersects with gender critique. Not only do they offer various modes of dismantling 'patriarchal constructions of culture and nation to reflect on an alternative heritage' (Vidal 2012: 92), but they also display particular modes of affect and embodied memory (see, for example, Wortel and Smelik 2013). 'It's kind of like a history of feelings rather than a history of facts', Kirsten Dunst said in reference to *Marie Antoinette* (in O'Hagan 2006), and this comment can be applied to all of these films. By intensifying the sense of affective closeness, rather than cold distance, they 'work hard at stressing the *presentness* of the adaptation rather than its *pastness*' (Vidal 2012: 103 [emphasis in original]), and, in this sense, they question the perspective of heritage cinema as inherently static.

This affective intensity is particularly evident in *Marie Antoinette* when the film switches, briefly, from the excessive and artificial routine of Versailles to a more 'natural' form of life in Le Petit Trianon, where the protagonist spends her days reading, listening to music and playing with her daughter in the garden, significantly dressed in less restrictive clothing.[26] Various shots show her lying on the ground, on a bed of flowers and/or touching different surfaces (the grass fronds, water in a pond and even air – for example, during her return from a masked ball, when we are presented with close-up images of her hands extended outside the carriage taking in the breeze) which produce sensuous imagery and material presence similar to that invoked in *The Piano*.[27]

The web of potential intertextual relations between *Marie Antoinette* and other costume dramas is particularly rich if we consider their constant fluctuation between physical (and social) mobility and gendered constraints.[28] Julianne Pidduck's analysis of the deliberately slow pacing in *Orlando* – 'dilatory, languorous pattern of sequential segments of (in)action' (1997: 180) – is especially revealing. Potter's lethargic hero 'becomes, almost in spite of her/himself, *mobile*, as she/he moves through different historical circumstances. But hers/his is a fickle quality of agency, reliant on the whims of chance' (1997: 181 [emphasis in original]). *Marie Antoinette* can be similarly characterised by an extended aesthetic 'being', rather than a narrative progression or heroic 'doing', and, in this sense, it can also be read as a metafictional gendering of representations of history.[29] This attenuated narrative movement is developed in both films in intensely claustrophobic domestic spaces. In *Marie Antoinette*, the composition of the shots often stresses rigidity and entrapment. When the Queen is represented in outside locations, the framing and camera pullbacks highlight Versailles completely overwhelming the protagonist in terms of scale, sinisterly detaching her from the public realm (see also Lane and Richter 2011).

The limits on physical mobility are visually materialised in *Orlando* and *Marie Antoinette* not only through spaces, but also through the suffocating laced corsets and voluminous dresses, which make it hard to breathe and move. As Pidduck observes in reference to *Orlando*:

> The awkwardness of these overblown costumes is reinforced through a consistent use of perfectly orchestrated balanced visual compositions and long static shots which create a luscious stage on which to observe the actors going through their painstakingly choreographed, if meaningless, paces. (1997: 176)

Not only this, but there is also a visual blending between the newly corseted Orlando and the world of material objects – for example, when she dodges, awkwardly and with considerable difficulty, items of furniture laden with white sheets along the long gallery. Significantly, in Potter's and Coppola's films, the costumes chromatically rhyme, echo or blend into the mise-en-scène – for example, the blue-on-blue tones that predominate just after Orlando's transition to a woman and following Marie's transition to become the Dauphine of France during her journey from Austria to Versailles. In the

Figure 5.3   Orlando as a frosted blue cake.

'Society' parlour scene, 'Orlando is immobilised like one elaborate, frosted blue cake on a love seat' (Pidduck 1997: 176). Marie is likewise paralleled with the lavish pastries, abundantly displayed throughout the film; as the Duchesse de Polignac remarks at one point, 'she looks like a little piece of cake'.

It is evident that both films foreground a fascination with commodity cultures, although Coppola seems to be far more engaged with surfaces and the materiality of what is represented onscreen. The visual alliance of decorative objects with the female body recurs throughout. This is immediately clear when Coppola exploits the texture of the image, dissolving the Queen's figure and rendering it almost indistinguishable from the material objects in the palace, which are constantly brought into focus. This happens, for instance, when Marie Antoinette receives a scolding letter from her mother, reiterating to the young woman that she has a true purpose beyond the superficial play in which she indulges – namely, to produce an heir to the throne:

> Dearest Antoinette, I'm pleased to tell you how wonderful your brothers and sisters are doing in their marriages [. . .]. All this news which should fill me with contentment is diminished by reflections on your dangerous situation. Everything depends on the wife.

Maria Theresa's voice-over fills the room, while her daughter, dressed in a floral gown, practically blends in and disappears into the ornate floral-patterned wallpaper. The letter falls out of her hands, she sinks slowly to the floor, pressed against the wall and almost becoming one with it. The movement

Figure 5.4 Marie Antoinette blends and disappears into the ornate floral-patterned wallpaper.

of the camera matches the pace of her movements and draws us tentatively closer to Marie Antoinette. This scene, which culminates in a close-up on her tearful face, is highly emblematic of how the protagonist's pain is visualised and played out through the sensuously textured details of the mise-en-scène.

In her thought-provoking analysis of the phenomenology of cinema's baroque flesh, Saige Walton dwells on how 'movement, materiality, decorative décor, surfaces, and textures function as highly charged repositories of meaning' (2016: 153). In her analysis of *Marie Antoinette* Walton argues that the protagonist's sense of self is often fused with the furnishings, as can be observed in another scene, in which we see her crying in a corner of the room, filmed using a medium shot and portrayed as a wrinkled pool of silk on the floor. As Walton observes in reference to this moment, the protagonist 'is strikingly and texturally analogised to the gathered [. . .] fabrics of the curtains that she sits beside [. . .]. Here, the film once again expresses materially resonant parallels between her dress, her flailing political position, and the décor of the mise-en-scène' (2016: 154). The excess that frames Marie Antoinette makes her practically disappear in the decadent materiality of Versailles, similarly to Orlando, who blends with the chaise longue in the previously mentioned parlour scene.

While both Orlando and Marie Antoinette seem to be firmly anchored in space and their bodies – which is emphasised visually by their exuberant dresses, the mimesis with the textured world of material objects and their frequent immobilisation in the frame – they also are, perhaps paradoxically, caught in transition. The films toy incessantly with gender performativity, and they both stage 'makeover' moments: when Orlando changes sex from man to woman and when the fourteen-year-old Marie Antoinette is stripped naked and dressed in the image of a French Dauphine during the 'handover' ceremony.[30] The excess of the costumes and ridiculousness of the rituals that Orlando and Marie Antoinette undergo highlight the artificiality of these transformations.

It is not coincidental that both films display a visual tension between seeing and being seen: Orlando and Marie Antoinette appear to be not only participants in, but also spectators of, their respective stories. They are clearly aware of their objectification, but, despite this, they knowingly co-create themselves as images and material objects to be looked at. 'Marie looks *like* cake while she looks *at* the camera', observe Christina Lane and Nicole Richter (2011: 193 [emphasis in original]) in reference to the film's opening sequence.[31] In this much discussed scene, the title character reclines on a luxurious settee against a pastel blue background, while a maid pampers her extended leg. Framed in long shot, she dips her finger into the top of an exquisite pink pastry, licks it and suddenly turns her head towards the camera and stares directly back at the viewer with a knowing smile, as if to say 'What?'

The Queen's direct look at the camera echoes Orlando's similarly enigmatic mode of address in Potter's adaptation of Virginia Woolf's novel, which – as many scholars have claimed – offers a humorous commentary at key moments during the film. This address has sometimes been interpreted as a self-conscious rejection of the conventional notions of authenticity in favour of a dialogic retelling of the past, as well as foregrounding authorship in terms of revision

Figure 5.5 Marie Antoinette's direct mode of address.

and collaboration, instead of the more traditional, gender-based rhetoric of production and paternity, in which the (male) author seeks to establish his authority over the text and reinforce his authorial originality (Vidal 2005; Cobb 2015).[32] It can also be read more broadly as one of the key features of post-heritage aesthetics, increasingly 'meta-aware' about gender, the power of representation and image-making.

The combination of the highly stylised objectification of the female protagonist and a direct mode of address evokes a similar moment in Dorothy Arzner's *Dance, Girl, Dance* (1940), in which the dancer, Judy, interrupts the spectacle, turns towards the audience and tells them how she sees them. According to Claire Johnston:

> This return of scrutiny in what within the film is assumed as a one-way process constitutes a direct assault on the audience within the film and the audience of the film, and has the effect of directly challenging the entire notion of woman as spectacle. ([1973] 2000a: 31)

The return of the gaze is made evident in several scenes throughout *Marie Antoinette* – for example, with the protagonist's arrival to Versailles. 'The court of France is not like Vienna [...] all eyes will be on you', warns Marie's mother, when her daughter is leaving Austria for France and, indeed, when she finally arrives at the court, all eyes *are* on her. However, although she is on display, the protagonist is also allowed to look at her audience. As Marie Antoinette exits her carriage, she walks between the people who silently stare at her. For most of the scene we are granted her point of view, which emphasises their off-putting gaze (see also Kennedy 2010).[33]

Ultimately, Marie Antoinette, perhaps more than Orlando, is defined by her status as an object to be looked at. Interestingly, the two films create friction between images and sound, albeit in a different way. Orlando is a bearer of the look and a bearer of the voice. In the opening scene we see the protagonist, reading literature. He walks from right to left, while the camera moves from left to right. When he changes direction and walks from left to right, the camera moves from right to left. Cristina Degli-Esposti argues that from its very beginning the film implies that 'the camera will not follow the character', but 'it will be there for the character to find, to address' (1996: 84). The initial words of the novel ('There can be no doubt about his sex ...') enunciated by the biographer, in Tilda Swinton's voice-over, are interrupted by the character onscreen. The close-up shows him leaning against an oak, his face framed in profile, but he turns to the camera and proudly states 'That is, I', as soon as the voice-over refers to him as 'he'. Hence, the cinematic Orlando establishes ownership of his/her story and forcefully appropriates the identification of the self, disrupting the textual and visual objectification.

Marie Antoinette's strategic stillness at the beginning of the film reveals that, in comparison to Orlando, she has little mobility and almost no voice. As Lane and Richter argue: '[T]he only character-voice that the audience is given the privilege to hear is Marie's mother, who repeatedly interrupts the life Marie pursues to remind her of her duty to bear children' (2011: 195). In this sense, even though the two films clearly address a series of gendered power structures, with a particular emphasis on the constraints on white bourgeois femininity, *Marie Antoinette* seems to be less radical in terms of representing gender and sexuality. Coppola's protagonist appears to be entrapped in her femininity; Orlando, in turn, is allowed to adopt a myriad of gender identities, even though, in the end, as Roberta Garrett has shown, the protagonist fully embraces strategic female subjectivity.[34] The deliberately feminist mode in which Potter's film engages is perhaps less evident in Coppola's work, whose heroine is not explicitly feminist, or at least has not been viewed as such, if we examine the critical responses.

The same might be said if we compare *Marie Antoinette* with *The Piano*. Both films engage with scenarios of sexual objectification, and they might be accused not only of exposing, but also of participation in, the mechanisms of patriarchal oppression (Vidal 2012). Nevertheless, *The Piano* seems to be more readily available to feminist readings, mainly due to its focus on a robust female character, 'victimised by cultural expectation and yet resisting the roles mapped out for [her] in patriarchal society' (Smaill 2013: 153). Smaill suggests that, in comparison to Campion's typical female characterisation, Coppola's protagonists 'embody "coolness" [...] and youth allure' (2013: 156), which tend to be associated with a postfeminist rejection of second-wave feminism. Indeed, as many critics have argued, with its distinct engagement with visual pleasure, Coppola's *Marie Antoinette* seems to be more easily aligned with the pleasures of postfeminist consumerism than with explicit feminist politics.[35]

In this sense, *Marie Antoinette* resembles another contemporary film, *The Duchess* (Saul Dibb, 2008), analysed by Vidal in reference to this shift in feminist politics: 'Whereas *The Piano* and *Orlando* arguably open spaces for feminist reflection in a postfeminist moment, the links between feminine identity, romance and consumption come to the fore in later post-heritage films informed by changing discourses on feminine agency' (2012: 105). Based on Amanda Foreman's biography of the eighteenth-century English aristocrat Georgiana Cavendish, well known for her beauty and fashion sense, the film emphasises a feminine construction of self through consumption, and maps a series of anxieties about the postfeminist present. *The Duchess*'s young heroine is, just like Marie Antoinette, imprisoned in a marriage that has been arranged solely in order for her to produce a male heir and, similarly to the French Queen, she becomes a fashion icon, famous for her extravagance and spending habits. The foregrounding of the costumes is nothing new in the genre, but its relation to the issues of self-representation, consumption and celebrity cultures, as dramatised in the film, can be inscribed within the wider trends in postfeminism, invested in traditional forms of women's culture, such as fashion, make-up and beauty treatments. As Vidal mentions in her insightful analysis of *The Duchess*, the film constructs 'a double edged discourse on clothes that highlights the function of costume as an outlet for sensual pleasure, a means for empowerment and self-expression, as well as a tool for the control of women' (2012: 106). The discourse on femininity and power is highly ambiguous in many of the contemporary costume dramas: 'These stories stress the fairytale motif of the princess in a golden cage, but the consciousness of her emotional isolation is tempered by the unlimited possibilities of consumption and self-display afforded by her royal status' (2012: 109–10).

If we extend these observations to Coppola's biographic legend, it is easy to understand why a significant majority of critical readings of her films have characterised them almost exclusively in terms of postfeminist concerns about 'female' consumption and leisure. These interpretations dwell on Coppola's underscoring of 'girlness' and 'girl culture', which, after all, epitomise postfeminist values (Projansky 2007: 45).[36] Indeed, it may be argued that in foregrounding the lifestyle of an affluent *young* woman – which, as previously mentioned, is frequently intertwined with the reception of Coppola as a female auteur, operating in a bubble of fame and privilege disconnected from harsh reality – *Marie Antoinette* rejoices in versions of femininity empowered by consumer and celebrity cultures. In reference to this aspect, Fiona Handyside (2015) comments that Coppola's view of girlhood is, nonetheless, removed from the celebratory rhetoric of 'girl power', as her films stage contradictions and paradoxes of women's position in popular culture without necessarily seeking to resolve them. In a similar vein, Backman Rogers convincingly argues that, although scholars 'are not mistaken in identifying a post-feminist strain in the film's mise-en-scène, [. . .] the film enacts a critique rather than an outright endorsement of such a de-politicisation' (2016).[37]

Depoliticised or not, both *The Duchess* and *Marie Antoinette* participate in the contemporary climate of postfeminist cultural norms and, in this sense, as Vidal concludes, they are 'symptomatic of a shift from the retrieval of women's histories and aesthetic experimentation of the 1990s post-heritage film to the commodification of feminism' (2012: 110). Taking these transformations into consideration, both within the genre itself and also in the critical reception, it can be stated that, instead of rebelling against its generic past, *Marie Antoinette* clearly belongs to it, participating in the genre's continuous rewriting of the discourses on femininity, power and consumption. And if the exploration of female experience through markedly feminised space – by means of an emphasis on exuberant mise-en-scène, affect and commodity cultures, all historically gendered as feminine – is already present, and extensively exploited, in the genre, then it is possible to attribute Coppola's aesthetics not so much to her quintessentially 'female' identity or authorial subversion, but to the historical processes of the recombination already included in the generic.[38]

The Great Man's Genre? On Authorial Depth and Generic Surfaces

It seems likely that, while the analysis of *Marie Antoinette* through the rubrics of the costume drama places it within a markedly feminine sphere, considering it a historical biopic might help to redirect our attention to other interpretative paths. Despite its occasional dismissal (as several scholars contend) in film studies and authorial canons, biopics have, in fact, always ranked higher on the cultural hierarchy scale than the costume drama (Robé 2009).[39] However, as I will discuss in the following pages, ascribing Coppola's film to this slightly more 'reputable' genre hardly erases the gendered power structures that permeate this cultural form.

Dennis Bingham's scholarly monograph on biopics, *Whose Lives Are They Anyway?*, proves this point. After defining biopic as a dynamic genre, which 'narrates, exhibits, and celebrates the life of a subject in order to demonstrate, investigate, or question his or her importance in the world', Bingham sets out to address the male biopic and the female biopic as 'essentially different' genres, the former generally dealing with great accomplishments, the latter with female victimisation (2010: 10).[40] The dual structure of his book, which is divided into two parts, the first of which is titled 'The Great (White) Man Biopic and its Discontents' and the second 'A Woman's Life is Never Done: Female Biopics', further emphasises this view. While the 'Great Man' variant of the biopic usually deals with 'a visionary with a pure, one of a kind talent or idea who must overcome opposition to his idea or even just to himself' (2010: 7), biopics of women, in contrast, 'are weighted down by myths of suffering, victimization, and failure perpetuated by a culture whose films reveal an acute fear of women in the public realm' (2010: 10).

Bingham's methodology also mirrors this gender-based differentiation. Adopting the notion of genre as a cycle, he argues that the biopic has undergone different historical stages of development, disintegration, investigation, parody and revival (2010: 11). However, this seems to be true only for the male variant: 'Films about men have gone from celebratory to warts-and-all to investigatory to postmodern and parodic'; biographies of women, in turn, have their own 'patterns of development, ideologies, conventions' and 'their own distinct alternatives to the classical paradigm of the biography' (2010: 22). From the stars of the studio era who played queens, such as Greta Garbo as *Queen Christina* (Rouben Mamoulian, 1933) and Katherine Hepburn as *Mary of Scotland* (John Ford and Leslie Goodwins, 1936),[41] to the 1950s biopics which focused on entertainers, and the 1980s cycle exemplified by *Gorillas in the Mist* (Michael Apted, 1988), women have remained trapped in 'a cycle of failure, victimization and the downward trajectory' (Bingham 2010: 23–4). Ultimately, the woman is degraded, and the drama is perceived as possible only *in* degradation (2010: 221).

Arguably, Coppola's *Marie Antoinette* complies with the 'downward spiral' convention discussed by Bingham. In fact, as Bingham himself observes:

> Marie Antoinette is a subject who seems camera-ready for all the conventions of the female biopic, from the apolitical, clueless woman who heedlessly spends the royalty into the ground, to the victim of [. . .] national politics who helplessly finds herself in that always-irreversible downward spiral. (2010: 363–4)

While the film clearly dramatises the opposition between private and public persona – a common trope in both male- and female-oriented royal biopics – it (over)emphasises women's traditional orientation to home, marriage and motherhood, displacing public ambition and achievement onto male characters. In the cultural framework of eighteenth-century France, marriage and motherhood, and not public accomplishments, are Marie Antoinette's ultimate task and fulfilment: her body is not her own; it belongs to the world of politics. She is only useful for bearing children, which event will cement the friendship of Austria and France. And if women represented in biopics are 'more famous for suffering and victimization than for anything they accomplished or produced' (2010: 214), as Bingham suggests, then Coppola pushes this idea to its extreme: not only does Marie Antoinette fail (initially) to produce an heir, but she also engages in rabid consumption; this gives her temporary relief in her suffering, while at the same time perpetuates the power structures.

However, this interpretative framework might be destabilised in various ways. It is significant that the film does not offer images of the Queen's death (her neck on the guillotine), but only subtly anticipates it by depicting Marie Antoinette bow to the waist before the mob gathered in front of her palace window. Her trajectory is not genuinely downward, as at the end of the film we are not presented with scenes of imprisonment or executions. The last look at Versailles – a static shot of her bedchamber, pillaged by the angry mob (a scene which, significantly, occurred off-screen) – is the only allusion to punishment in the film.[42]

As Bingham argues in his insightful reading of this scene, the entire film is condensed in the last shot:

> [T]he morning dressing rituals, the early sexual failures with Louis, a metaphor for a woman's femininity played out in public and the symbol of it destroyed. It's also a symbolic imprisonment and execution, as every

Figure 5.6 The palace is destroyed, but Marie Antoinette (temporarily) escapes punishment.

means by which Marie was defined by court and public is summed up in that bedchamber, and now it has been killed. (2010: 376)

But there is also a sense of escape communicated in this shot: '[T]he woman herself finally eludes those who think they have defined her. The Revolution thinks it has killed the scapegoat Marie Antoinette, but all it has guillotined is the female role, the foreign femme fatale, the free-spender' (2010: 376).

Marie Antoinette both fits and fails to fit within the generic mould of 'female biopic', which tends to drag the spectator through the process of dehumanisation. In this sense, Bingham's comparison between the 1938 MGM *Marie Antoinette* (W. S. Van Dyke) and Coppola's version is particularly revealing. The former presents the protagonist as a tragic figure, 'with 158 minutes' worth of opportunities to suffer radiantly' (2010: 363). It does not explore the failure of the royal couple to consummate their marriage for the first seven years (due to the Motion Picture Production Code restrictions) and downplays the Queen's relationship with Count Fersen of Sweden. By contrast, Coppola offers a more nuanced view of the marriage: the film depicts Marie and Count Fersen's affair beginning years after Marie and Louis finally overcome their sexual problems; Coppola avoids suggesting, thus, that the affair with Fersen grows directly out of Marie and Louis' failed marriage, as is emphasised in the MGM version (2010: 375). What is more, her liaison with Count Fersen is very brief and by no means justifies her actions in the film; in fact, he very quickly disappears from the film altogether.

The characterisation of Marie Antoinette in Coppola's adaptation is complex: she is not the merciless Queen who said to the starving crowd 'let them eat cake' (in the film, the iconic phrase is dismissed straightforwardly as gossip, as the protagonist herself laughs it off),[43] but she is not a victim either, at least not in traditional ways. On the other hand, in terms of affective register and the dramatic action, she is very different from the paradigmatic biopic heroines who refuse to be victimised – for example, the oft-quoted case of Erin Brockovich, an ambitious young woman who was instrumental in building a successful legal case against a patriarchal institution, as depicted in Steven Soderbergh's (2000) eponymous box office hit. In this respect, *Marie Antoinette* might be compared to Mary Harron's *The Notorious Bettie Page* (2005), discussed in Bingham's study, which also takes as its subject an infamous woman, a bondage model who gained a significant profile in the 1950s for her pin-up photos:[44]

> Each of the films posits an iconic female exhibitionist inside a very patriarchal order. These are women under glass, objects of a patriarchal gaze that variously ogles them and indicts them [. . .]. They explore what it feels like to be looked at, as an object, as a public fixture, and as a significant image. (2010: 349–50)

Coppola and Harron, two filmmakers interested in exploring the nature of female celebrity in the early twenty-first century, seem highly self-conscious of the biopic genre – for example, in the ways in which they avoid the melodramatic plot structure, the downward trajectory and the conventional aesthetic of victimisation.[45] Both films have been frequently dismissed by critics as 'flat' or lacking emotional or psychological depth, and for sending ambiguous messages about their protagonists. As films about women whose behaviour has been deemed 'inappropriate', they might be considered 'anti-biopics': a subversion of the 'Great Man' genre norm that mocks the very notions of heroes and fame, both of which are ingrained in traditional biopics.

Bingham's extensive analysis of *Marie Antoinette* and *The Notorious Bettie Page*, although most illuminating, does not exhaust the possible interpretative frameworks, nor does it avoid the gender lock implied in his differentiation between the male and female biopics. Interestingly, although he praises both films for avoiding the spiral of victimhood, at the same time he considers that they lack a 'positive tone': 'A problem with both films is that they might seem works of negative virtues, notable for what they do not do' (2010: 376). It is my contention that, even though Bingham addresses to some extent the postmodern 'knowingness' of both works, he perhaps somewhat overemphasises the issue of female representation at the expense of wider resonances of their investigatory, self-referential features. This is probably due to the paradigm of subversion that guides his analysis: female biopics as created by men versus feminist revisions of them. 'Female biopics can be made empowering only by a conscious and deliberate application of a feminist point of view' (2010: 10), Bingham states in his book. By underscoring the oppositional dimension of this rewriting, he contributes to an understanding of feminist film practice as necessarily antithetical to the mainstream generic conventions.

In contrast to this reading, I would like to give prominence to what Coppola *does* with the genre, addressing the multifarious ways in which she engages with the historical subject matter, both in terms of narrative and style. My intention is not to distance the effects of the supposedly feminising aspects of the costume drama (such as a focus on a young female protagonist, private life, costumes and interiors) or to masculinise them by framing the film as a 'meta-aware' authorial biopic tending toward political topics, but rather to emphasise the complexity of the biographic project that Coppola undertakes and the implications of reading it through these variable generic lenses.

Just like Woolf's and Potter's *Orlando*, *Marie Antoinette* brings to the fore its own artificial form, which manages to question the master narrative of History.[46] Coppola employs what Pam Cook defines as 'travesty' – a common device in literature and theatre which 'irreverently wrests its source material from its historical context, producing blatantly fake fabrications that challenge accepted notions of authenticity and value. It brazenly mixes high and low culture, and does not disguise its impulse to sweep away tradition' (2006: 38). Paul Byrnes once shrewdly observed that 'the biopic is a discredited and disreputable genre, because so many bio-pics tell lies about their subjects' (in Cheshire 2015: 12), but Coppola is even more radical than this: not simply because she is not particularly interested in securing an 'accurate' depiction of Marie Antoinette as the historical figure, but also because she never attempts to look past her iconicity, being more concerned with how she was portrayed for centuries.[47]

To return, momentarily, to the opening shot in *Marie Antoinette*, it is significant that the first image of the protagonist is accompanied by the British post-punk group Gang of Four's song, entitled 'Natural Is Not In It', which constitutes a fitting *leitmotiv* in a film that questions the stability of the narratives of the self and fetishistically exhibits a world of pure and extravagant artifice. It is also, quite aptly, a film about images: both historically and culturally engraved images of women, closely intertwined with a broad range of commodity cultures. Coppola's focus on the image, and not on the identification of a unified self, might be seen as a continuation of Woolf's and Potter's intricate biographic endeavours, also deeply self-conscious about women's image-making. Woolf's famous selection of tampered photographs and historical paintings – inserted into *Orlando* in the service of the fake biography she was writing – mirrors the protagonist's chameleon-like personality and questions the veracity of the narrative. The use of paintings is also important in

Marie Antoinette: towards the end of the film, we learn of the birth and death of Marie's third child through a series of portraits shown in a still frame. In the same sequence, we see different portraits of the Queen with text imposed on her figure – 'beware of deficit', 'Queen of debt!' and 'spending France into ruin!' – all which point to her lack of popularity due to her spending habits. Here, and in other moments throughout the film, we are not privy to the 'real' Marie, but instead we are confronted with the myriad identities imposed on her, both by French society and the film itself. And Coppola is determined to make the audience aware of this; the protagonist is all image, simultaneously defined and constrained by it.

This is where the idea of the film's surface as substance comes to the fore again. Instead of exploring the historical depth of Marie Antoinette, the filmmaker pays attention to the outward details, which underscore the artifice of her biographic project. In this manner, she subtly undermines the iconography associated with the genre, which tends to 'foreground its production values via sustained focus on objects that have been painstakingly re-created for the sake of authenticity' (Backman Rogers 2012: 94), and she does this by engaging with contemporary commodity cultures. For instance, she avoids the typical colours used in portraits of the French court in favour of pastels inspired by the fashionable macarons of the Parisian pastry house Ladurée. Her revamping of the genre is not distanced, however, but filled with affective potentialities of the image. In this sense, as Walton's analysis shows from a phenomenological perspective, the film's attention to surfaces – costumed, human, decorative and architectural – is rich in meaning. Particularly fascinating is Walton's reflection on clothes. Drawing on Stella Bruzzi and her affirmation that the costume drama can 'look through or look at clothes' (in Walton 2016: 148–9) – that is, highlight the accuracy of costuming, maintaining claims to historic authenticity or 'enact a textural eroticism' – she observes in regard to *Marie Antoinette*:

> [. . .] while the film makes use of typical costume drama conventions such as clothing, setting, décor, and so on to capture its era of French absolutism (looking 'through' clothes), it uses textural expressivity to generate affective shifts in mood, tone, and atmosphere and project emotion on the sensuous surface of the film's body (looking 'at' clothes). The film's textural displays do not foster eroticism but other feelings such as insecurity, boredom, luxurious indulgence, surfeit, and foreboding. *Marie Antoinette* looks through clothing to capture the theatricality of the absolutist baroque and how power was bound up with appearances. At the same time, it looks at clothing and at the expressivity of texture to deploy its materialist aesthetic. (Walton 2016: 149)

In reference to this recurrent duality, looking through and looking at surfaces, Walton addresses several moments in which the 'film's vision drifts between the inside and the outside' (2016: 149) – for example, during the protagonist's journey to the handover ceremony, when we watch her through the gilt-edged windows of a carriage, drawing childish patterns on the glass. Framings of Marie Antoinette either within or through reflective surfaces are a constant in the film (Walton 2016: 149).

For Lane and Richter, these ongoing tensions between interior and exterior spaces speak to the difficulties of Coppola's own position within the American and global film industries, 'as a filmmaker who is both on the inside looking out and on the outside looking in' (2011: 189).[48] In their comprehensive analysis of Coppola's brand image, Lane and Richter demonstrate how her films simultaneously mobilise and resist the mystique surrounding the romantic cult of the (male) director, and how the filmmaker herself struggles to assert her creative, professional and authorial agency in the contemporary cinematic field.[49] Coppola dwells on the effort and cost involved in the attainment of such a position, but she also self-consciously performs cinematic authorship through a markedly feminised space; just like Marie Antoinette empowers herself through a logic of consumerism, Coppola's authorial persona also achieves 'modes of self-representation within the realm of material objects and spectacle' (2011: 193). Lane and Richter's discussion of production through consumption is particularly useful to question traditional paradigms of authorship in a wider sense, which rest firmly on such cultural binaries as production-interiority-masculinity versus reproduction-corporeality-femininity:

> It is certainly true that the filmmaker's perspective is rooted in 'production' in the sense that she is committed to creativity and artistry. But just like Marie, Coppola exploits elements of consumption in her efforts to say something productive about her creative position within the world of commerce. (2011: 200)

Lane and Richter's thought-provoking take on Coppola's expression of her authorship through spectacle, surface and repetition, which questions the originality and the genius of the Great Man that permeates the conventional conceptualisation of film auteur, can be extended to our understanding of genre. If, as they consider, 'Marie's consumption can be understood as a radical act' (2011: 198), then Coppola's engagement with the feminised sphere of costume drama can also be understood as such. The filmmaker destabilises the oppositions between art and commodity culture, creative and passive, originality and reproduction, mobilising the powers of repetition and ritual. Anna Rogers (2007) analyses the pointlessness of the rites of the dining ceremonies, which are consistently repeated to maintain the tradition of the court. Significantly, Coppola 'chooses to focus on items of food as artefacts rather than nourishment; these platters of food become abstract works of art, sometimes even grotesque spectacles (a large jelly containing strips of meat that wobbles when poked with a fork)' (Rogers 2007). This observation can also apply to the logics of the genre and the seemingly 'redundant' nature of its repetition, 'making the need for change and insurgence all the more vital' (Rogers 2007). Instead of rebelling against the (generic) rituals, however, the filmmaker offers a remaking through the very repetition of these rites, often privileging surface over depth, artefacts over nourishment, pointless consumption over production. Marie Antoinette finally comes to terms with Versailles's rituals, using them productively and to her own benefit, and Coppola similarly embraces the laws of generic repetition. Keeping our attention trained on the generic rituals and the textural expressivity of the mise-en-scène – the very fabric of costume biopics – the film looks not only *through*, but also *at* genre. Therefore, it is possible to contend that *Marie Antoinette* becomes a metaphor not only for Coppola's auteur status within the larger industrial system, but also of her attitude towards the dynamics of repetition, as it problematises the opposition between (authorial) depth and (generic) surface.

Luke Collins offers a provocative reflection on this issue in his discussion of Kathryn Bigelow's *Point Break*: instead of envisioning genre as a 'vessel' to be filled with authorial substance, the genre itself can be seen as a surface, as 'a series of recognizable signs made available for consumption by the audience' (2012: 55). If we follow this line of reasoning, *Marie Antoinette* repeats its generic form, and we experience this form as generic surface: 'Surface donates here the pleasure of experiencing (consuming) a known product. It is the pleasure of the return, the consistency and, at its extreme, the invariable' (2012: 63). Coppola's *Marie Antoinette* is self-referential to the extent that it exhibits an awareness of the limits and, above all, potentialities of the genre, by fleshing out its usual attention to surfaces and the fetishisation of commodity cultures. Or, adopting Collin's vocabulary, instead of filling in, it fills out. 'The fullness that this produces is a flatness: a surface', which constitutes not a negative construction, but 'a challenge for theory and criticism that traditionally rely on paradigms of cultural depth' (2012: 54). If, as Lane and Richter observe, 'by becoming more and more of an image, [Marie Antoinette] reveals the emptiness at the center of the "illusion of fullness" that the Versailles community strives to create' (2011: 201), the same could be said for the 'illusion' of authorial depth that the critical discourse around Coppola strives to detect. While reclaiming women filmmakers is important for feminist film criticism, reading *Marie Antoinette* through the notion of generic repetition has crucial implications for considering the category of female authorship itself. This exploration of the generic surface as 'a negotiated repetitious space' (Collins 2012: 55) challenges both the view of genre as static and the binary trap of reading films as either 'personal' or 'generic'.

Collins's preoccupation with surfaces in his discussion of *Point Break* leads him to conclude that Bigelow's work does not interrupt cultural or political discourse. Similarly, in the case of *Marie Antoinette*, the focusing on the 'surface' and 'consumption' at the expense of the 'deeper' meanings is also sometimes taken to connote superficiality in terms of (feminist) politics – qualities that have been paralleled, as we have seen, with Coppola's bourgeois lifestyle. Her films, described at times as 'pretty', 'decorative' and 'delectable', tend to be perceived as lacking critical engagement and dismissed as too concerned with privilege and frivolity. Not only in critical circulation, but also in scholarly writings about the film, discussions of Coppola's celebration of 'girl culture' and neoliberal discourse on empowerment through consumption are abundant and easy to find. I want to conclude, however, that surface cannot be separated from the content, and it is, in fact, possible to reconcile image and complexity, production and reproduction, creation and consumption. Indeed, even though *Marie Antoinette* is mainly concerned with surface and appearances, it is not superficial in its politics.

In her discussions of gender and decorative image, Rosalind Galt questions the assumption that 'prettiness' supersedes content and that it possesses no thematic or political bearing, arguing:

> *Marie Antoinette* stages the fetishistic status of the royal body as a question of production design. The film connects a feminised world of objects (for instance, a deliberately anachronistic discourse on the shoe as commodity fetish) with the class and gender politics within which Marie's body can be owned first by the state and then violently by the people. [. . .] this discourse on the historical objecthood of the female body strikingly refuses to blame the woman for her out-of-control consumption. (2011: 22)[50]

The 'out-of-control consumption' depicted in the film reveals women's discursive association with, and creative reappropriation of, a feminised world of objects, but it also constitutes a key feature in Coppola's negotiation with genre: the film's reinvigoration of the conventions of the costume biopic – including engagement with surface and a critical alignment of 'decorative' objects with the female body – might be considered a form of (gendered) politics. To paraphrase Robert Hahn's writings about *Lost in Translation*, the film accepts the limits and artifices of these conventions, but it finds ways of getting under its own skin (2006: 154–5).

Notes

1. As hinted in the previous chapter, the term 'independent cinema' is notoriously difficult to define. In reference to Coppola's film, it has been argued that *Marie Antoinette* 'uses an independent cinema aesthetic in a Hollywood biopic with a 40 million dollar budget' (Kennedy 2010). The film was financed by a major Hollywood studio, Columbia Pictures, although with co-distribution deals with French Pathé and Japanese Tohokushinsha Film. Drawing on Michael Newman, 'independence' does not necessarily imply being autonomous of the dominant Hollywood industry – in fact, Coppola's films are implicated in funding structures that are not separate from the mainstream – but rather refers to a detectable group of filmmakers that are seen to go beyond the formal and ideological conservatism of the Hollywood system (see Smaill 2013: 155).
2. It could be argued that Coppola's films are not easily recognisable as genre films, but they do play on audience knowledge of Hollywood genres – notably, those codified as female genres, such as the romantic comedy (*Lost in Translation*) and costume drama (*Marie Antoinette*). Coppola's latest film to date, *The Beguiled* (2017), promoted by the press as belonging to the 'Southern gothic genre' and, occasionally, 'gore' promises to direct the filmmaker's career in new directions. In reference to this movie, Coppola admitted: 'I had never done anything like a genre film, so I had to do that but still keep it in my style and world that I like to work in. And maybe having a plot. That was kind of new for me. (Laughs)' (in Ford 2017).
3. See, for example, Vidal (2014), Cook (2014) and Cheshire (2015).
4. Defining a biopic is difficult, since unlike most other genres, there is no specific set of codes or conventions (see, for example, Cheshire 2015: 4–5). For the purposes of this chapter, I assume the common definition of the genre offered by Vidal (2014).
5. According to Bingham, in the 1980s the biopic shifted from a producer's genre to an auteurist director's genre, with prominent examples from Martin Scorsese, Spike Lee, Oliver Stone, Mary Harron and Julian Schnabel (Bingham 2010: 17–18).
6. The oft-quoted anecdote marked the early reception of the film, even if, as Robert Ebert later clarified in reference to the Cannes screening, only a couple of journalists had disliked the film and the media had sensationalised the event (2007: 885).
7. As Vidal clarifies, what distinguishes the biopic from other genres which feature historical characters and biographical tropes is the fact that 'in the biopic an individual's story comes to the fore' (2014: 3).
8. See, for example, Bingham (2010: 14).
9. She also became the first ever American female director to win the Golden Lion at the Venice Film Festival for *Somewhere* (2010) and, at the time of writing, she has made Cannes Film Festival history by becoming the second woman in the event's seventy-year history to win Best Director for her film *The Beguiled*. Prior to this, Yuliva Solntseva won Best Director for her 1961 war drama *Chronicle of Flaming Years* about the Russian resistance to the Nazi occupation during the Second World War.
10. Pam Cook and Samiha Matin specifically address the issues of genre: Cook's contribution discusses the film in relation to the recent revival of the biopic, with a primary focus on Coppola's authorial signature; Matin, in turn, explores *Marie Antoinette* from the perspective of a costume drama and its traditional emphasis on the position of women at the juncture of public and private.
11. As Fiona Handyside has convincingly argued in her recent monograph on the filmmaker, Coppola's authorship oscillates between two models, both of which are inseparable from the question of gender: an institutional authorship – predicated on production values, and inviting readings in terms of a unified, coherent body

of work – and a twenty-first century celebrity brand version of authorship (2017: 18). While the first, traditional approach towards agency, understood as talent or genius, focuses on the production of films, the latter is constructed extratextually: '[T]he unity comes not from the films themselves but from the power and significance of the Coppola name as marketing and branding device' (2017: 16).

12. These narratives include, among others: mood and style as focal points in her films, her concern with fashion and youth culture and, above all, her advantageous position in the industry.
13. Almost no critic could resist the temptation to emphasise that her father has executive-produced this and, in fact, all of her features – 'a luxury, it is fair to say, that many aspiring writers and directors would trade their proprietary screenwriting software for' (Heller 2010). It is often stressed how she is a beneficiary of creative privilege, with conditions that any other director could only dream of. 'Versailles administrators granted Ms. Coppola, the 35-year-old writer-director, unprecedented access to the chateau and its grounds', stated the *New York Times* article, 'French Royalty as seen by Hollywood Royalty' (Hohenadel 2006). As Dana Stevens wrote in *Slate*: '[Coppola] is the privileged little girl in Charlie and the Chocolate Factory whose father, a nut tycoon, makes sure his daughter wins a golden ticket' (2006).
14. Coppola's sympathetic portrait of her heroine in *Somewhere* as a 'poor little rich girl' has been interpreted as a representation of her own experience as a child of Hollywood and privilege (Hohenadel 2006).
15. Available at: https://www.rottentomatoes.com/m/the_bling_ring_2013/ (accessed 20 May 2017).
16. On Coppola's self-conscious engagement with fashion and celebrity culture in these films, see also Handyside (2017: 136–59) and Paszkiewicz (forthcoming).
17. Even if only in relative terms. *Marie Antoinette* was considered a moderate financial success; it took in more than US$60 million with a budget of US$40 million.
18. It is worth mentioning here that, in fact, the notions of 'style' and 'look' have always informed the basis of the 'masculine' auteur theory and its focus on mise-en-scène – for example, as manifested in Éric Rohmer's belief in the 'profundity of the superficial' (in Handyside 2017: 139). According to Handyside: 'Coppola retools the idea(l)s of image dominating script and flourishes of personal style that dominate classical film theory, giving them a feminine makeover' (2017: 138).
19. The devotion to visual beauty rather than plot or narrative progression is perceived to be responsible for creating a specific atmosphere, foregrounded in many of the reviews: 'Marie Antoinette is all atmosphere', 'it is an oddly empty film', we read in the *Rotten Tomatoes* reviews. Available at https://www.rottentomatoes.com/m/1158195_marie_antoinette (accessed 20 May 2017).
20. See, for example: http://www.listal.com/viewentry/81376 (accessed 20 May 2017).
21. See, for example, Robé's (2009) discussion of *La Marseillaise* (Jean Renoir, 1938) and *Marie Antoinette* (W. S. Van Dyke and Julien Duvivier, 1938). The latter was accused of reifying the people into an undifferentiated crowd. The former was referred to, in turn, 'as a corrective to the Hollywood costume drama's use of spectacle, which focuses on personal, "depoliticised" issues' (2009: 77).
22. As Roberta Garrett observes, drawing on Pidduck: 'It is not uncommon for critics to draw a distinction between a conservative, traditional "bad" costume drama (Merchant Ivory productions, Austen adaptations) and the innovative use of costume and interior in the films of "auteurs" such as Peter Greenaway and Derek Jarman' (2007: 132).
23. For example, the influential studies of the British costume film in the 1930s and 1940s by Sue Harper (1994) and Pam Cook (1996) addressed the hyper-feminised

costumes and elaborate set designs, and initiated debate regarding femininity, spectacle and lack of authenticity in the genre.
24. According to Vidal, heritage cinema is not exactly a genre in the industrial sense of the term, but rather a concept that has its roots in British film studies, 'where it has become associated with a powerful undercurrent of nostalgia for the past conveyed by historical dramas, romantic costume films and literary adaptations' (2012: 1).
25. *Lost in Translation* received huge backlash from several critics who decried Coppola for relegating the Japanese culture to, in Peter Brunette's words, 'Kodak moments'. Racist charges culminated just before the Academy Awards ceremony, when the members were encouraged to vote against the film in all categories in which it was nominated for an Oscar (see Kennedy 2010).
26. This association between women's freedom and nature is ridiculed in *Marie Antoinette* – for example, in the opera scene, in which the protagonist performs a (pastoral) fantasy of a country girl.
27. The haptic quality of these images is bolstered through the specific treatment of time, which some scholars compared to Deleuzian time-images. See Rogers (2007); see also Wortel and Smelik (2013) about 'textures of time' in *Marie Antoinette* and Handyside (2017: 15) about how Coppola's haptic approach to filming undermines a purely visual approach to femininity.
28. In her analysis of aesthetics and politics of contemporary costume films, Julianne Pidduck addresses these films as a 'quintessentially "feminine" genre characterised by limited character mobility or physical, social and corporeal constraint' (2004: 16). Rather than an inherent quality determined by the gender of their authors, I understand these features, alongside Matin, as 'tactical aesthetics': deployment of a certain style 'to access power which makes use of gendered acts, expressions, dress, and etiquette to design new advantages' (2012: 97). See also Paszkiewicz (forthcoming).
29. As Pidduck clarifies, *Orlando* combines, in fact, two opposing narrative forms: the 'female' costume drama with its 'detail-rich meandering, languorous quality' and the more dynamic 'masculine' genres of the biographical quest and journey (1997: 172).
30. *Marie Antoinette* is full of these rites of passage; after the first morning ritual, in which the highest-ranking female present in the Queen's bedroom has the honour of dressing the Queen (Marie had to wait, naked and freezing, until the women finally decide who should clothe her), she reasonably observes: 'This is ridiculous'. Comtesse de Noailles (Judy Davis) poignantly responds, 'This, madam, is Versailles'.
31. The scholars argue that not only do these shots acknowledge our awareness of the camera, but they also display a preoccupation with the woman's ability to look, as a primary female pleasure.
32. Shelley Cobb, who focuses specifically on the intersection of female authorship, the practice of adaptation and self-authorising strategies for the woman filmmaker, argues that in many contemporary films made by women 'the female author on screen represents both the woman writer of the novel and the woman filmmaker of the adaptation' (2015: 20). See also Paszkiewicz (forthcoming).
33. Todd Kennedy (2010) makes a compelling point that the reason for the film's relatively poor box office was its insistence on making us identify with Marie Antoinette's abjection – forcing the audience to experience both empathy and disaffection with Coppola's flawed heroine.
34. In contrast to Woolf's 'original' gender indeterminacy, according to Garrett (1995: 94).
35. Coppola's use of visual pleasure, in Mulvey's terms, has often been the spark of critical backlash, particularly in the case of *Marie Antoinette* (see Kennedy 2010).

36. See also the recent book by Handyside (2017), *Sofia Coppola: A Cinema of Girlhood*.
37. Other scholars also read Coppola's films through the feminist lens. See, for example, Smaill (2013) and her discussion of Coppola's work in comparison to Chantal Akerman's *Jeanne Dielman, 23, Quai du Commerce, 1080 Bruxelles*. The quality of repetition in the morning wake-up routine in reference to Akerman is also discussed by Bingham (2010: 371).
38. As Roberta Garrett observes in reference to *The Piano* and *Orlando*, these films 'are not alternative or "counter"-period dramas (although they may present a counter-history), rather they illustrate the genre's radical potential to readdress historical gender inequalities with a contemporary eye, a tendency which is present, to a lesser extent, in most examples of the ongoing cycle' (2007: 153).
39. Coppola figures in what Bingham describes as the emergence of the biopic as an auteurist genre in the 1980s (in contrast to its former incarnation as the producer's genre), which granted it a certain level of prestige (2010: 19–20).
40. There is an interesting parallelism with Robé's investigation on the historical film/costume drama demarcation: US critics were 'unaware of how traditional gender hierarchies structured [their] own celebration of films and genres that often punished strong women in the name of more important causes [historical film] while condemning the films that failed to do so [costume drama]' (2009: 72).
41. In the 1930s, the female biopic mainly represented queens. As Bingham observes, 'their power of command' is usually in conflict with 'women's emotional, romantic, dependent natures' (2010: 217). Overall, in contrast to Great Man films, female biopics found conflict and tragedy in a woman's success: 'Early deaths were preferable to long lives. Female biopics frequently depicted their subjects as certainly or possibly insane, made so by the cruelties of a victimising world' (2010: 217). This trend is still valid in the post-war female biography, according to Bingham.
42. It could be argued that even though the film does not depict the punishment, most (Western) viewers know how the 'real' story ends. The Queen's death is precisely why she became famous. In this regard, the downward trajectory is not completely subverted, as Coppola does not, in fact, rewrite the (unhappy) ending. However, it is significant that the filmmaker eschews the dramatic events and avoids images of female victimisation in a traditional sense, in stark contrast to other royal biopics. I would like to thank Andrea Ruthven for this insight.
43. The iconic 'let them eat cake' appears in the film non-diegetically and is followed by Marie Antoinette responding that she 'would never say that'.
44. On Harron's biographies of disreputable women, see Badley (2018).
45. They do not display pathos associated with femininity, in contrast to 'the social and moral elevation of the tragic hero' (Doane in Bingham 2010: 218).
46. See Garrett's (2007) broader discussion of the fictionalising process underlying Western grand narratives and her analysis of *Orlando* and *The Piano* as examples of both self-consciously politicised feminist film practice and cinematic versions of historiographic metafiction.
47. In this respect, it is interesting to observe how Coppola purposely avoids key 'historical' moments traditionally conceived as essential to the myth of the Queen, such as The Affair of the Diamond Necklace; but at the same time she does depict the offending piece of jewellery resting between Marie Antoinette's cleavage when the protagonist is relaxing in her luxurious bathtub. This is one of the many examples of how we are encouraged to read (and consume) Marie Antoinette as an icon, rather than a real historical figure.
48. Similarly, Handyside also analyses the issue of space in relation to 'the complex network of possibility and constraint for female authorship in the contemporary cinematic field' (2015).

49. Lane and Richter (2011) convincingly argue that Coppola's complex strategies of financing and distribution enabled her to actively participate in the fashioning of herself as a filmmaker.
50. See also Backman Rogers (2012).

6. WHAT A *WOMAN* WANTS? NANCY MEYERS'S *THE INTERN*

Nancy Meyers is probably the most successful woman filmmaker of all time, at least if gauged in relation to the terms determined by the Hollywood mainstream. While most of the filmmakers examined in this volume have not enjoyed sustained employment in the dominant or even independent sector, Meyers has managed to consistently produce films at the forefront of the US film industry for almost forty years now, obtaining sizeable budgets and directing box office hits such as *What Women Want* (2000), *Something's Gotta Give* (2003), *The Holiday* (2006), *It's Complicated* (2009) and, more recently, *The Intern* (2015). *What Women Want*, which she both produced and directed (and for which she also acted as an unacknowledged co-writer), went on to become both the highest-grossing romantic comedy ever, earning US$374,111,707 worldwide, as well as the most commercially successful film ever to be directed by a woman at that time.[1]

Meyers's long career and directorial brand are unique in contemporary Hollywood – an industry that has routinely marginalised or excluded women filmmakers. Hilary Radner has argued that Meyers is one of the very few female auteurs of what she calls 'neo-feminist' cinema,[2] which 'facilitates the marketing of her films within Conglomerate Hollywood' (2011: 172). In her ability to make her films marketable and to create a recognisable auteur identity, she constitutes yet another example of authorship as a commercial performance in Corrigan's (1991: 104) terms. Her visibility and success are significant, since, as Michele Schreiber observes, 'while female directors have always been a rarity in Hollywood, those with name and "brand" recognition are even rarer' (2014: 143).

In her valuable overview of Meyers's career thus far, Deborah Jermyn aptly observes that 'if Meyers is recognised for anything among those familiar with her name, it is for being Hollywood's reigning "romcom queen"' (2018: 57). The filmmaker is promoted, and actively promotes herself, in association with female-centred and female-oriented romance genre films, focusing on what she describes as 'telling women's stories' (in Freeman 2015). In this sense, she is positioned at the opposite end of the spectrum from Hollywood directors such as Kathryn Bigelow, 'whose "brand" revolves around the fact that she is a woman who makes "men's" films, much to the ongoing fascination of critics' (Schreiber 2014: 144). However, as Jermyn rightly observes, the moniker 'romcom queen' obliterates, perhaps somewhat paradoxically, the significance of a range of unique and valuable insights she brings to the genre, as well as downplaying a distinctive style she has developed and which her fans clearly identify and anticipate: 'Hers is a mode in which lovingly drawn interiors and mise-en-scène combine with an affection for the golden age of Hollywood elegance and classical style, contemplative dialogue and story turns' (Jermyn 2018: 62).

Meyers's creative engagement with the genre of the romcom and her ability to secure significant financing for her films – especially at a time when Hollywood is increasingly interested in what she calls 'the Superman, Batman, Anythingman' films (in Freeman 2015) – grants her an indisputable place in Hollywood's history and in the history of films made by women.[3] This is a huge achievement, considering that even within the 'feminised' sphere of the romcom, men have directed the majority of the films (Garrett 2007). Yet, despite her commercial success in Hollywood, her multifaceted career as a writer/producer/director, the consistency of style and themes across her films and, above all, her huge popularity across a wide range of audiences – much as the critical discourses insist on labelling her movies as 'only for women' – Meyers's work has been largely ignored in film literature in general, and feminist film studies in particular. Although there are some notable exceptions[4] – most significantly, Deborah Jermyn's monograph, recently published in the Bloomsbury Companions to Contemporary Filmmakers series, which promises to rectify this omission – Meyers's status, and career trajectory as a female filmmaker, has gained surprisingly little scholarly attention.

In this chapter I seek to contribute to the incipient scholarly re-evaluation of the filmmaker's work by offering a close examination of how she can be conceptualised as a skilled and experienced director within the much-derided genre of romantic comedy. My aim is not only to grant her the recognition she deserves, but also to reconfigure the debates about women's cinema, women's film authorship and genre, which have severely delimited the significance of women's contribution to mainstream production in a wider sense.[5] Recognising the relevance of Meyers's success for feminist histories is urgent, but perhaps even more urgent is addressing the critical discourses that frequently dismiss her work as trivial and too concerned with privilege – which reveal striking commonalities with the ways in which Sofia Coppola's work has also been derided. Over the course of her career, reviews of Meyers's films have referred to her visual emphasis on interior design and on ageing protagonists as a way to frame her directorial signature, and at the same time they have often disavowed her status as an auteur in highly disparaging, or even vitriolic, terms. Jermyn's feminist reading of *the-figure-of Meyers* and the continued critical deprecation of the director is extremely useful in underscoring 'how much of the invective regularly directed at Meyers herself has [. . .] been acutely gendered in nature' (2018: 58). By drawing on a range of US and UK reviews of her films, Jermyn charts different narratives that construct the filmmaker's public image, unravelling that Meyers's distinctive mixture of biographical details, privileged status within the masculinised Hollywood industrial context, and her film style characterised by a central focus on domestic mise-en-scène has led to significant success and also to derision and heavy criticism. Particularly interesting is Jermyn's analysis of the constant invocation of Meyers's work as a form of 'softcore designer porno' – a term that crops up repeatedly in reviews of her films. Jermyn argues that this terminology 'operates as an insidious reminder that the person behind these films, this too fancy mise-en-scène, these lowbrow preoccupations, *is a woman*', and 'that the "proper" territory for women in film is not behind the camera but within the realm of sexual spectacle, inhabiting a space in which they should expect to remain outside authority, agency and production' (2018: 64 [emphasis in original]). Jermyn's contribution is important, because she points not only to the usual scorn for the 'women's genre' of the romcom and for the female audiences that enjoy it – issues to which I shall return later – but also 'for [Meyers] as a woman director – in a manner which film scholarship, and feminist film criticism particularly, to date has neglected to sufficiently scrutinise and rebuke' (2018: 59). As she astutely sums up after bringing to light a perturbingly substantial volume of personal, misogynist attacks on the filmmaker, deriving mostly from the mainstream media, these sorts of comments suggest that 'there is a reason why the contemporary rom-com gets a bad rap, there is someone we can blame for all this scorn for the genre – and that someone is Nancy Meyers' (2018: 64).

Similarly to Jermyn, Hilary Radner (2011) and Michele Schreiber (2014) have also paid attention to Meyers's preoccupation with domestic mise-en-scène, closely intertwined with discourses on women, consumption and commodity cultures. Radner discusses how the 2006 *Architectural Digest* article that featured Diane Keaton's Hamptons house in *Something's Gotta Give* is an example of the 'film's dependence upon an aesthetic defined by the visual vernacular of tasteful (and expensive) consumerism' (2011: 179). In her fascinating analysis of the film she argues that the press coverage of the set design serves to emphasise the role of popular cinema as 'a literal shop window' (2011: 179). Schreiber detects a similar mode in *It's Complicated*, which was accompanied by articles that appeared in the pages of *Elle Décor* and *Traditional Home*. This tendency continues with the *Intern*: in 2015, at the time of the film's release, *Jezebel* included a 'Which Nancy Meyers Kitchen Are You?' quiz, *Vogue* invited readers to 'Shop Nancy Meyers's Most Enviable Interiors', while *Architectural Digest* offered 'a tour of the stylish sets of *The Intern*'.[6]

While Schreiber addresses these types of intertexts to claim that the romcom (female) viewer's pleasures are intimately bound up with excessive spending and consumption – an issue examined in detail in the next couple of sections of this chapter – she also makes an interesting observation about how the opulence of mise-en-scène in romcoms is almost never acknowledged by anyone within the world of the film and 'is merely passed off as normal' (2014: 147). She argues that, in discussing big budget films and their mise-en-scène, 'male-driven' genres like science fiction and action films, or directors like George Lucas and James Cameron, specialists in flashy special effects, are usually at the heart of the conversation.

> But just as economics play a big part in how these fictional worlds are built, made more mesmerising, and consequently more memorable, they are also a fundamental component of women's genre filmmaking. And, no one is better than Meyers at building memorable and awe-inspiring visual environments. (2014: 146)[7]

Undoubtedly, while it is important to acknowledge the filmmaker's skilful construction of lavish sets as a key feature in 'Meyers's style', it is also interesting to see how this element is not foregrounded in male-produced contemporary romantic comedies (for example, Judd Apatow's films), and how often this critical framework parallels the question of surface with superficiality, reducing her films to home décor catalogues, and in this way belittling both her authorship and her audiences. Not unlike Coppola's films, Meyers's work has been repeatedly referred to as focused on the *look* – praised by interior design professionals, but 'regularly maligned by film critics who see her devotion to intricate colour and style coordination as a kind of empty and shallow distraction' (Jermyn 2018: 63). All filmmakers are attentive to creating the appropriate settings in their films, but it seems that in the case of *women* directors this aspect might prove detrimental to their critical reputations.[8] As Jermyn rightly observes in reference to Meyers:

> [H]er *skill* in this realm, that distinctive quality which one can well imagine would be remarked on as a laudable 'eye for detail' in a male

director (cf. Douglas Sirk's acclaimed reputation for adopting sumptuous colour), is used in Meyers's case to imply she can't really 'do' more substantial work like original character or plot. (2018: 63 [emphasis in original])

These comments resonate with the critical circulation of Coppola's work, as discussed in the previous chapter. However, while the latter's authorial focus on mise-en-scène has been as often praised as derided, probably given the cultural value granted to independent cinema and its strategic positioning against mainstream genre production, Meyers's concern with 'houses' is seen as 'predictable, repetitive, superficial, rather than, much more positively and as (masculine) auteur theory would have it, an individuated signatory flourish' (Jermyn 2018: 63).

This depreciation has also permeated feminist responses to her films, which tend to intertwine the lifestyle fetishism displayed by Meyers's protagonists with her own privilege, as she can certainly afford such a lifestyle; indeed, it is not a coincidence that one reviewer called Meyers a 'writer-director-personal-shopper' (Henderson 2015). Manohla Dargis's review of *The Intern* argues:

> The director Nancy Meyers doesn't just make movies, she makes the kind of lifestyle fantasies you sink into like eiderdown. Her movies are frothy, playful, homogeneous, routinely maddening and generally pretty irresistible even when they're not all that good. Her most notable visual signature is the immaculate, luxuriously appointed interiors she's known to fuss over personally — they inevitably feature throw pillows that look as if they've been arranged with a measuring tape. These interiors are fetishised by moviegoers and *Architectural Digest* alike, ready-made for Pinterest and comment threads peppered with questions like, 'Where do I get that hat?' (Dargis 2015)

The carefully composed imagery and the life of privileged women protagonists, present throughout Meyers's films, contribute to a critical alignment between the filmmaker and her work, and at the same time lead to the perceived lack of credibility as a director. Meyers's own advantageous position as a filmmaker – a white upper-class woman who has achieved commercial success in the Hollywood film industry, traditionally dominated by men – has, indeed, made her an uneasy subject for feminist analysis.

Perhaps it is not *despite* the commercial nature of Meyers's success, but precisely *because* of it, that she has attracted so little academic attention within feminist film studies.[9] Meyers's films appear to embody, both textually and extratextually, what Tasker and Negra consider images of a postfeminist culture, which, they argue, 'works to commodify feminism via the figure of woman as empowered consumer' (2007: 2). Her protagonists – the independent, white, upper-middle class women with successful professional careers – empower themselves by buying and putting on clothes and taking care of their home interiors. If we add to the equation the ambiguous status of the romantic comedy genre in general, historically seen as inherently conservative and increasingly invested in 'the contemptible realms of cliché and consumerism' (Jermyn 2018: 58), then Meyers's exclusion from feminist canons seems far less surprising.

In contrast to these readings, however, I want to look at the complex ways in which the narratives around Meyers, both in and outside of her work, open up space for disruptions and incongruities that undermine such readings. Meyers's case is particularly interesting for feminist criticism, as it allows for a broader discussion on women's film authorship as a commercial brand or, in Corrigan's terms, 'the commercial dramatization of self' (1991: 108), which reveals a series of discourses on creation, authority and artistic legitimacy at a particular socio-historical moment. How can we think about women's mediated authorships, without falling into a fallacy of acritical celebration of the filmmakers as postfeminist icons and without underestimating their position in the contemporary film industry? What advantages, conditions and limitations do this legitimacy and authority entail? What does it mean to be a (commercial) auteur specialising in the romcom genre and what are the political implications of this conceptual framework? As I will show in the following pages, the ways of constructing women filmmakers' visibility and commercial appeal can become highly problematic, as they frequently confirm the link between femininity, women and mass culture, de-authorising these authors and belittling their status as cultural producers with an immense impact on the contemporary film industry.

'Cookie-cutter' Authorship

The critical reception of Meyers's oeuvre forms part of a much longer history of taste formation, in which, as many feminist critics have demonstrated, hierarchies of 'quality' are based on the binaries of gender. Most male-written reviews that accompany the release of each of her films incessantly return to culinary metaphors and the category of the 'chick flick', used sometimes in a derogatory way in reference to films that have an 'innate' appeal to women and which are perceived as intensely emotional and relationship-based.[10] In his review of *The Intern* Peter Bradshaw (2015) dubs the film 'a too-sucrose Ephron-lite cringe-fest', adding: 'I sometimes have a bit of a sweet tooth for Nancy Meyers's Ephron-lite diversions, but this, frankly … eww. The cutesiness factor and ickiness quotient are just too high'. Writing for *Slant Magazine* Eric Henderson (2015), in turn, professes:

Meyers isn't a gifted director, and her meandering scripts mark her as an even less talented writer, but she's unquestionably committed to her auteurist signature of giving her female protagonists their cake and letting them eat it too, even if she fails to give moviegoers what *they* want.

The process of devaluation of the film – and its presumably female viewers – revolves around language based on ingestion, incorporation and absorption, which reduces women's cultural practice of viewing to mechanical satisfaction of their 'instinctive' appetite. In Meyers's case it becomes transparent how the grouping of these metaphors interweaves with the reading patterns of her oeuvre, profoundly affecting her credibility as an auteur or, rather, de-authorising her as such. As discussed in Chapter 1, women exist in popular culture as insatiable, passive consumers with no restraint or emotional distance, but almost never as auteurs.

Similar discourses have accompanied Meyers throughout her whole career.[11] The aforementioned comments about *The Intern* resonate with Owen Gleiberman's (2006) review of *The Holiday* for *Entertainment Weekly*: 'I'm sad to report that it's just a cookie-cutter chick flick, albeit one made with some fancy butter and powdered frosting [. . .]. So eat up, chick-flickaholics! Even if you know it's not good for you'. The cookie-cutter metaphor is particularly striking, as it throws into stark relief how the negotiation (or, to be exact, the cultural battle) over Meyers's status as an auteur cannot be separated from other phenomena that mould women's authorship: the cultural, critical and industrial gendering of genres and, in particular, the critical scorn towards the chick flick; the problematic relationship between popular genres, authorship and subversion; and, finally, the so-called feminisation of mass culture in a wider sense (Huyssen 1986; Hollows 2000).

Romantic comedy – not unlike other female-orientated genres, such as romance, soap opera and melodrama – has often been perceived as trivial and crassly commercial, as well as intrinsically toxic for its (supposedly female) audiences. As Jermyn observes: 'Meyers holds the dubious distinction of being seen as the sovereign of a genre which, in the hierarchies of critical esteem and academic gravitas, is the cinematic bottom-feeder that lurks somewhere beneath the action movie' (2018: 57). In Jermyn's 2009 book *Falling in Love Again*, co-edited with Stacey Abbott, the authors aptly sum up a number of possible reasons for the low critical regard that typically meets the contemporary romcom:

> First, its audience is enduringly presumed to be predominantly female and 'chick flicks' in all their incarnations are frequently critically constructed as inherently trite or lightweight. Second, romantic fiction generally is thought to be essentially calculating in its execution, cynically

> manipulating an emotional and sentimental response from the viewer [. . .]. Furthermore, the genre is widely depicted as slavishly formulaic, adhering to well-worn and obvious conventions (boy meets girl; boy and girl face obstacles to their romantic union; boy and girl conquer obstacles to find true love). Finally, the perception of comedy per se as inherently frivolous and anti-intellectual has resulted in its critical and cultural marginalisation, where it is presumed that eliciting laughs from the audience is antithetical to 'serious' reflection. (Abbott and Jermyn 2009: 2)

Most relevant to my argument here is Abbott and Jermyn's reference to formulaic consistency as one of the negative features of the romcom genre, which contributes to its perceived superficiality and conservative perspectives. Of all genres, perhaps romcom has suffered most from this 'aesthetic determinism', as Mary Harrod, drawing on Celestino Deleyto, calls it, which is reproduced by much genre criticism and which reinforces the still powerful negative association between genre and popular culture. She writes: '[R]om-com is the victim of a circular argument whereby it is seen to be typified only by those highly conventional films including the most conservative perspectives and therefore it is designated the most conventional and conservative genre' (2015: 20).

This brings us back to the question of authorship within popular forms. As previously noted, female-oriented genres are rarely associated with auteurs, in contrast to the traditionally conceived 'male' genres, such as the Western or horror cinema. There are, of course, some exceptions, notably including male filmmakers: the already discussed Douglas Sirk (in the realm of melodrama) and Woody Allen (in romantic comedy). As Abbott and Jermyn show, Allen's 'nervous' romantic comedies succeeded in attracting both scholarly and critical attention because they were seen at the time as '*reinventing* a tired and predictable genre' (2009: 2 [emphasis in original]). Allen's *Manhattan*, like its predecessor *Annie Hall* (1977),

> placed an unlikely neurotic and narcissistic male in the lead (anti-)hero role, a figure far removed from the dashing romantic norm; and it dared to end equivocally, without a happy ending or a romantic future evidently in place. To win critical approbation within the broad arena of the rom-com by the late 1970s, it seemed, one had to *undo* the popular image of it. (2009: 2 [emphasis in original])

In such instances, the very act of creation presupposes a relationship of 'authority' (control and property) between the author and film genres, understood here as formulas that need to be transcended. 'True' auteurs work *against* generic conventions; if the director is 'strong' enough, he can even transform the 'prohibited' genres, such as melodrama or romcom, into something more than flicks for 'crying' or 'easily impressionable' women. This was precisely the case with Douglas Sirk, who, as already mentioned in Chapter 1, attained the status of 'progressive auteur' because he was perceived as rewriting melodrama's generic conventions to challenge the values of the consumerist society in which his films are set, managing to insert 'art' into a feminised mass culture (Klinger 1994: 1–35). In contrast, if a woman creates within genres considered 'feminine', she can be no more than a reproducer of standardised formulas. Robert Ebert's review of Meyers's *It's Complicated* proves precisely this point:

> *It's Complicated* is a rearrangement of the goods in Nancy Meyers's bakery, and some of them belong on the day-old shelf. Oh, how I hate food analogies in reviews. In a season of blessings, there are several better choices than this one. Truth in criticism: I must report that I expect *It's Complicated* will be terrifically popular with its target demographic, which includes gal pals taking a movie break after returning Christmas presents. Not everybody is in a mood for *Avatar*. (2009b)

Thinking back to Huyssen's (1986) argument, *It's Complicated* could never be considered an 'auteur film', as it does not maintain 'autonomy' in relation to the realm of the 'everyday' and it is not experimental or radical enough; instead of rejecting, it assimilates classical cinematic codes and traditional forms of representation. Conceiving of female film practice as reproduction, a mere 'rearrangement of the goods', raises important questions about the subversion and authorship of the women who choose to work within popular genres. If we temporarily suspend this imaginary and define genre not as a formula, but rather as a process or shared space of continuous change and negotiation, what figurations of authorship could we begin to theorise? How can we think about the relationship between popular cinema and women's film authorship? If we understand film genre as a process, in what ways can women filmmakers subvert it?

Again, Abbott and Jermyn's discussion of the romcom, which questions the common perception of genre as a formula, proves extremely useful for moving beyond the subversion fallacy and considering authorship in different ways. As the scholars astutely observe: '[The] popular account of the romcom, which, like the critique it formulates, might itself be described as "well-worn", fails to recognise adequately a number of significant qualities within and issues raised by the genre': the powerful emotional and personal investment of the viewers; the genre's continuous inflections, rather than clearly delineated boundaries; and its status as 'a *living* genre', even though it frequently relies on older traditions and conventions (2009: 2–3 [emphasis in original]). Furthermore,

Abbott and Jermyn make an important point about the social relevance of the romcom:

> While many other genres, such as the Western and horror, have been widely explored with a recognition of their capacity to evolve, the contemporary rom-com has less often been understood as one that continues to negotiate and respond dynamically to the issues and preoccupations of its time. (2009: 3)

Drawing on these insightful remarks, in the remainder of the chapter I analyse how Meyers uses the romcom to offer incisive social commentary on contemporary gender roles and sexism, despite the genre's reputation for inherent unprogressiveness.

Non-romantic Comedy?

Meyers's latest film to date, *The Intern* (2015), has been dubbed in its critical reception as 'a romantic comedy without the romance' (Berardinelli 2015). The filmmaker herself has emphatically rejected this generic label, explaining in publicity for the film:

> I didn't want to write another romance. I never wanted to write another scene in a restaurant between a man and a woman [. . .]. I just didn't have it in me to write one more of those things. And I felt sort of done with the romantic story. (in Larocca 2015)

However, given Meyers's authorial brand and the fact that her wider oeuvre is unequivocally inscribed in the terrain of the romcom, it is fair to say that *The Intern* is positioned, at least to a certain extent, in relation to this genre; by discussing the film in the context of the romcom's development, I will show how Meyers, indeed, draws heavily on this tradition.

Romantic comedy has long been a solid pillar of Hollywood production, from the early comedies of remarriage produced in the 1920s and 1930s, the classic screwballs in the 1930s, through to the sex comedies in the 1950s and 1960s and Woody Allen's 'nervous comedies' of the 1970s, to the massive revival of chick flicks since the 1990s;[12] yet, as I argued in the previous section, despite its constant presence in popular cinema, the romcom has often struggled to be taken seriously. In comparison to other genres, it has been frequently written off as irrelevant and/or pernicious for its audiences, and this prejudice is inseparable from the ideological operation of dismissing popular forms perceived as 'female' in a wider sense.

However, more recently, the increased popularity of contemporary female-orientated film cycles, as defended by Roberta Garrett (2007), has been followed by the burgeoning of new critical work in the field. In contrast to the previous denigration and neglect that pervaded film scholarship in this area,[13] the current publications on romantic comedy by scholars such as Jeffers McDonald (2007), Abbott and Jermyn (2009), Deleyto (2009), Schreiber (2014) and Harrod (2015), among many others, take the genre seriously and, in doing so, they question the prior assumptions about its low cultural place as regards hierarchies of taste. In general terms, all of these studies show how, on the one hand, romantic comedies have been accused of reinforcing women's traditional gender roles and, on the other, how they have been championed as pleasurable and potentially empowering manifestations of popular culture.

As Mary Harrod (2015) aptly observes, the romantic comedy's status as an object of cultural suspicion and scorn has been closely bound up with the issue of the 'happy ending' (endorsing heterosexual coupling), viewed as responsible for forcing conservative ideologies upon its viewers. Although this supposition, especially popular in the wake of 1970s post-structuralist film theory, has been 'seriously challenged through the expansion of cultural studies in the 1990s and the move to return agency, historical contingency and social identity to the film viewer' (2015: 19), it has far from disappeared from film studies' debates on the contemporary romcom. The subsequent chick flick's co-implication with postfeminist concerns (Radner 2011; Schreiber 2014) – and the presumed conflict between feminism and postfeminism – has further complicated this debate and paved the way for the persistence of sceptical attitudes. For instance, scholars such as Tasker and Negra (2007), who offer a powerful feminist critique of contemporary postfeminist media culture, tend to attribute an implicitly reactionary ideology to these genres. Yet, in parallel with earlier feminist studies' interrogation of romance for the pleasure it can offer female audiences (Modleski 1982; Radway 1984; Stacey 1994; Rowe 1995), which rehabilitated romance as a space to explore women's life experiences,[14] recent commentators on 'chick culture' have placed more emphasis on female viewers' pleasures as potentially empowering and on how these films raise questions about 'women's place – their prescribed social and sexual roles, the role of female friendship and camaraderie – and play out the difficulties of negotiating expectations and achieving independence' (Ferriss and Young 2008: 4).

Regardless of this struggle over the progressive or conservative nature of female-orientated romance narratives, these publications illustrate, above all, the astonishing heterogeneity of the genre. The rich diversification of interests that has marked this cinematic form in recent years is reflected, for example, in Abbott's and Jermyn's collection of essays, *Falling in Love Again* (2009), which covers, among other topics, the queer pleasures of *Miss Congeniality* (Donald Petrie, 2000), the romcom personas of J. Lo and Bill Murray, high school prom-coms, male-centred romances like *Wedding Crashers* (David Dobkin, 2005) and romance beyond Hollywood: American independent romantic comedies and the Bollywood romance film.

Taking into consideration this breathtaking diversity, the problem of definition is inevitable. Celestino Deleyto's broad characterisation of the genre, which goes beyond rigid classification, is particularly relevant to this study, as it helps detect romcom conventions in films which are not necessarily identified as such:

> The genre of rom-com can [. . .] be seen as the intersection of three, closely interrelated elements: a narrative that articulates historically and culturally specific views of love, desire, sexuality and gender relationships; a space of transformation and fantasy which influences the narrative articulation of those discourses; and humour as the specific perspective from which the fictional characters, their relationships and the spectator's response to them are constructed as embodiments of those discourses. (Deleyto in Harrod 2015: 20)

This critical framework constitutes a useful point of reference for analysing *The Intern* as a (non-)romantic comedy – a film which, as I will argue, draws nonetheless on several of its generic conventions. Even though, untypically for Meyers, *The Intern* does not involve a budding romance between the main protagonists, it is built around a process of bringing them together, which is, after all, one of the defining features of romantic comedy. Jules Ostin (Anne Hathaway), the founder of a start-up company in Brooklyn, an immensely successful online clothing store called About the Fit, is assigned seventy-year-old Ben Whittaker (Robert De Niro) as part of a senior internship programme. Despite the fact that Jules previously agreed to the placement, she is somewhat sceptical about the prospect of working with Ben – but 'she has to set the tone', as she is chastised by her personal assistant, Cameron, who pushes for the idea. The collaboration with the new intern does not work for Jules – or, at least, this is what she initially believes – and thus she decides to transfer Ben to another department. She almost immediately changes her mind, however, as Ben quickly manages to get into her good graces.

Their working relationship, which soon turns into a close friendship, seems to follow the romance's conventional narrative pattern: the initial incompatibility and antipathy (on Jules's part, since she does not want to engage with Ben and keeps their interactions to an absolute minimum);[15] the subsequent bonding (for example, their trip to San Francisco); the presence of the 'wrong partner' to whom the protagonist is erroneously committed (Jules's cheating husband, Matt, played by Anders Holm); the misunderstanding that temporarily disturbs or threatens to put an end to their relationship (essentially, in two specific instances: first, when she makes a hasty decision to transfer Ben and second, when Ben keeps the truth from her regarding her husband's affair); and, eventually, the re-establishment of the relationship between the pair. Despite the fact that Jules eventually works things out with Matt, deciding to give their marriage another chance, the narrative does not conclude with the focus centred on this particular coupling. In the final sequence, Jules goes out looking for Ben to tell him the good news and finds him enjoying his t'ai chi exercise group in a park. She decides to join him, finally letting herself relax. The sense of 'belonging together' clearly marks *this* reunion and not the prior reconciliation with Matt.

This sense of 'belonging together' – and, at the same time, the separation of others from the central couple – is produced in *The Intern* through a number of typical generic devices associated with romantic comedy. One of the usual ways of setting the protagonists apart in romcoms is staging their escape or shared fun and freedom from socially constrained behaviour. The scenes of bonding that draw on this convention fixate on Ben and Jules, leaving Matt firmly outside the narrative focus. In one particular sequence, they stay late at the office – Jules, because she is behind with her work; Ben, because he insists that he 'can't leave before the boss leaves' – and what was initially supposed to be two people working overtime becomes a late night Facebook lesson, in which Jules teaches Ben how to create a profile, over pizza and beers, as they enjoy their time together. Significantly, this is when Ben reveals to Jules both that he is a widower and that he used to work in the very same building that now serves as Jules's offices; it also marks the moment when Jules finally warms to Ben's companionship: she 'friends' him via the social network, but she also, significantly, befriends him in real life. Later in the film, the couple travels to San Francisco on a business trip, and they decide to 'have a little fun' on the plane. The conventions of a romcom are mobilised again: while they enjoy their food and drink wine, we are privy to Jules telling Ben a story and laughing so hard that she cannot get the story out. Various romcoms feature the aeroplane trope or make substantial use of airports. As Mary Harrod has argued in her analysis of this setting, the plane scenes 'represent a postmodern twist on the emblem of traditional community coupling, the girl next door, who becomes either figuratively or literally the girl in the next door seat' (forthcoming 2017). Drawing on Marc Augé's description of the 'non-place', she states that 'staging encounters in liminal spaces endows them with a sense of heightened possibility for extraordinary intersubjective fusion' (forthcoming 2017).

This close, emotionally intense and non-sexual bond between a young woman and a significantly older man – 'an unlikely millennial-boomer friendship', as a reviewer of the film aptly observes (Macon 2015) – might not seem that common in the romantic comedy genre; perhaps Sofia Coppola's *Lost in*

Figure 6.1 *The Intern*'s central couple: Jules and Ben.

Translation is Meyers's most direct referent. The dramatisation of intimacy between friends in a wider sense can be, nonetheless, inscribed within the development of the genre, since, according to Celestino Deleyto, heterosexual love has been increasingly challenged in many romantic comedies and occasionally replaced by friendship (2003: 168). In this respect, it is interesting to observe how *The Intern* draws on a contemporary offshoot of the genre – the 'bromantic comedy', which usually adheres to the formula of the romcom, but gives more narrative space to the close male friendships. Tamar Jeffers McDonald (2009) designates this category of films 'homme-coms' and includes titles such as *40 Days and 40 Nights* (Michael Lehmann, 2002), *Along Came Polly* (John Hamburg, 2004), *The 40-Year-Old Virgin* (Judd Apatow, 2005), *Hitch* (Andy Tennant, 2005) and *Wedding Crashers* (David Dobkin, 2005). In her study Jeffers offers a fascinating take on bromance as the male answer to the female-centred chick flick, which in its use of sexual humour undercuts some of the sentimentalism associated with what she considers the 'Ephronesque' romcom. Interestingly, this relatively new development in the genre challenges the idea that romcoms necessarily 'start, and end, with a woman, with her desires and dreams, her temporary frustrations and eventual fulfilment' (2009: 146), even if, as Jeffers clarifies, the post-classical romantic comedy is still associated predominantly with women.[16] The scholar writes in reference to the bromance variant:

> These texts set out to explore and test the contours of the genre by repositioning the centre, rehearsing all the generic basics – dating rituals,

feigned indifference, heartfelt passion – but making them new by considering them from a male point of view. (2009: 147)

With this in mind, it is significant that *The Intern* starts with the male protagonist's perspective: Ben is battling boredom and wants to change his life. And, although Meyers's film is not strictly speaking a 'bromantic comedy' – it finds its narrative, and emotional, centre in Ben's relationship with Jules – its well-used tropes are easy to find, perhaps most notably in the interaction between Ben and his much younger colleagues that work in Jules's office. They hang out together at, and after, work and, similarly to other brom-com characters, they 'worry about relationships, dating rules, makeout conventions, what to say and wear, just as women have been doing in rom-coms for so long'; in this regard, they parallel the trope of 'the supportive group of friends [. . .] found so often in the Ephronesque rom-com' (Jeffers McDonald 2009: 152). Nevertheless, Meyers's take on bromance is particularly revealing, as it displays a self-conscious attitude towards these conventions – in particular, in relation to gender and age representation. Meyers finds humour in Ben adjusting to his new workplace, as well as his co-workers adjusting to his unique presence (for example, during a highly amusing interview sequence and on his first day of work when he removes his antiquated accessories from an old leather briefcase). Ben's quiet confidence is contrasted with the immature young men's inability to deal with most 'adult' situations, such as renting a flat, apologising to women and choosing the right outfit for the office. He becomes something of a father figure to them – for example, when he offers Lewis tips on what to wear when making a delivery to Beyoncé and Jay-Z ('put on a proper shirt with a collar' and 'try to bring the hair down'), provides Davis with a place to stay at his house after he is evicted by his parents (and wakes him up in the morning in case he oversleeps) and helps clueless Jason out after he cheats on Jules's secretary, Becky. The latter scene illustrates how Meyers's creatively merges the bromantic tropes with the theme of the generational gap as a locus of humour:

> Jason [after confessing that he slept with Becky's roommate]: Ben, you have a lot of experience, how long will she be mad at me for?
> Davis: Jay, I have zero experience and I can tell you there's no coming back from this one.
> Ben: I assume you've talked to her, apologised, told her what she means to you . . . You didn't talk to her? What did you do? Send her a tweet?
> Jason: No. Of course not. I texted her, like a billion times, she didn't answer, then I e-mailed her, but you know, like a nice e-mail, a long one. [. . .] With the sad emoticon. Crying . . . [Ben looks at Jason over his eyeglasses]. I should probably just actually speak to her. Obviously.
> Ben: Can't imagine it would hurt.

Figure 6.2 What men want: bromantic protagonists in *The Intern*.

In her use of bromantic elements, Meyers is knowingly referencing Judd Apatow's popular homme-coms. As Manohla Dargis observes in her review of *The Intern*, the three protagonists, Lewis, Davis and Jason, serve as Seth Rogen, Jonah Hill and Michael Cera from *Superbad* (Greg Mottola, 2007), 'whose sloppy clothes and facial hair emblematise not only their arrested development but also a crisis in masculinity' (Dargis 2015). This crisis in masculinity is closely related to the protagonists' 'messy' physical appearance, ridiculed in *The Intern* as childish and silly.

As Jeffers argues, one of the most distinctive features of the male-centred homme-com is its bold prioritising of the bodily – and particularly the sexual – aspects of romance, 'in all its messiness', which often take the form of scatological and carnal motifs (2009: 148).[17] Excrement, urine and ejaculate are recurring tropes in these films. The homme-com's usual insistence on the comedy derived from orgasm and ejaculation is epitomised in *The Intern* in Ben's interaction with the in-house massage therapist, Fiona (Rene Russo), significantly witnessed and commented on by his younger colleagues. In one scene, Ben is sitting at his desk when Fiona begins massaging his shoulders, as a 'gift for a job well done'. She slides her hands down his back, Ben inhales deeply and his eyes go wide, while Lewis and Davis smile at one another and look at Ben's crotch. Davis tosses a newspaper on Ben's lap to cover up his erection. When Fiona leaves, Ben puts a fist out on either side and both boys cheerfully pound him. Another similarly 'raunchy' scene occurs when Davis mistakenly thinks he has walked in on Fiona and Ben having sex – a recurring trope in bromantic comedies. However, it is worth mentioning that *The Intern* turns out to be fairly naïve in its 'carnal' moments if we compare these two scenes to, for example, the explosive diarrhoea featured in *Wedding Crashers* or several gags revolving around erection, urination and masturbation in *The 40-Year-Old Virgin*. While in these comedies the 'gross-out' scenes are equally intertwined with the more staid, quiet romantic moments (Jeffers 2009: 154), it is the tender and emotional scenes that predominate in *The Intern*.

Although the bromance moments in *The Intern*, presumably conceived to enhance the film's potential appeal for male audiences, might seem secondary at first glance, they speak volumes about the development of the genre and the process of the gendering of genres in a wider sense. According to Jeffers, the 'gross-out' moments, which have been identified as 'male-orientated', might be seen as a conscious rejection of the standard conventions of the contemporary romcom, which has tended to downplay the importance of sex, especially since the 1990s (2009: 148).[18] Despite its disruptive potential, however, 'narrative closure within this new grouping of films is only achieved by a capitulation to monogamy' (Jeffers 2009: 158). Detecting the same conservative tendencies in the homme-com that she sees in *When Harry Met Sally* (Rob Reiner, 1989) and its successors, such as Nora Ephron's paradigmatic *Sleepless in Seattle* (1993), Jeffers contends that, in fact, both forms of the genre are based on the assumption that 'men want sex, and women withhold it from them, urging them to grow up and settle down' (2009: 159). Jeffers denounces these contrasting principles, which are frequently exercised to legitimise men's desire for premarital sex, while refusing to grant the same privilege to women. She concludes:

> Although the reintroduction of sexual topics to the rom-com is, arguably, necessary for its continued survival as a genre, it seems to me dangerous to allow the double standard to creep back into popular assumption, after the feminist movement and other political and cultural manifestations of the 1970s, including the radical rom-com, all did their best to banish it. This is what will happen, however, if we assign interest in sexual topics solely to men and thus exile the body and its urges and emissions to a sub-genre 'meant for' male audiences. (2009: 159)

In light of this, it is interesting to notice how Meyers, who in contrast to Nora Ephron does not generally downplay sex in her movies,[19] emphasises both characters' sexual life in *The Intern*. However, while Ben's sexuality is represented mainly through bromantic conventions, Jules's is depicted with a more serious tone: after initially experiencing problems in this sphere, Matt and Jules finally engage in sex – a scene with no homme-com elements in sight.[20] It seems as if Meyers intended to provide 'sexual topics' for both male and female audiences, albeit according to their 'own' generic conventions.

Without referring to audience research, one could speculate that – similarly to *What Women Want*, as analysed by Jermyn – 'it was the promise of a "man's view" on women's [. . .] lives' (2018: 66), the positioning of De Niro as the star and the cross-gendered appeal of the homme-com that account for the box office performance *The Intern* garnered.[21] In this sense, it could be argued that, similarly to Jules's successful brand, Meyers's film is also 'about the fit' – serving the demanding and apparently more diversified customer needs in the contemporary romcom. The filmmaker has mastered the ability to brand herself in association with female-oriented romance genre films, while arguably attracting a wider variety of audiences and therefore remaining commercially successful. She provides mainstream, (presumably heterosexual) male and female audiences with 'what they want', and it is precisely this approach that has made her the single most profitable female filmmaker. Even though one should not cast aside the problematic aspect of the assumptions that underpin the film's gendered address, it could be argued that, while it clearly serves the capitalist ends of product selling, *The Intern* also wittingly comments on the process of the gendering of genres – a point to which I return in the following sections.

For now, though, it is important to look in greater depth at Meyers's narrative focus. What becomes evident is that, even though *The Intern* opens with Ben's perspective and incorporates some bromantic features, the film is as much about Jules as it is about Ben, or, to be more accurate, about the relationship between them. The latter was subject to intense debate in the critical reception of the film. While some reviewers praised Meyers, saying that 'it is a pleasure to see a movie in which a woman is not punished for being professionally ambitious' (Freeman 2015), others complained about its conservative, and even paternalistic, stance. As Guy Lodge wrote in *Variety*, *The Intern* suggests that 'behind at least one successful woman stands an older, wiser man' (2015). A number of critics lamented that Meyers's film promotes a discourse about emotionally unstable women over which a male protagonist must keep constant vigilance. Jules seems to have 'a host of neuroses that are frequently assigned to harried working women', until Ben, a retired company man from 'a simpler time', intervenes, building up her confidence again and showing her how to move forwards (Macon 2015).[22] The seventy-year-old gentleman acts as a sort of 'Mr Fix It': with paternal confidence he helps Jules get on track, both at the office *and* at home. He tidies up a cluttered table – that, for some reason, she refuses to tell someone to clean – he chauffeurs her around town and provides her with emotional support, both when her husband is unfaithful to her and when she is pushed by her board of directors to interview potential CEOs, who are supposed to help ease her workload. 'You started this business a year and a half ago by yourself and now you have a staff of 250 people. Remember who did that', Ben says reassuringly to a distraught Jules, who desperately attempts to balance her professional and personal life; indeed, at one point, she seriously considers hiring someone simply to buy herself the time to repair her marriage. Throughout the film, Ben encourages Jules to think about how much this decision would impact upon her authority and the possible knock-on effects regarding her creative freedom. Interestingly, *The Intern* could be treated as a mirror reversal of the gendered office politics in *What Women Want*, in which the misogynist hero, Nick (Mel Gibson), is unable to accept a female manager and constantly undermines her professionally. In *The Intern*, Ben is the only one who *really* supports her while she is constantly told by her investors that she needs to bring in a (male) executive. He also stands against the discourse that confines women to a domestic space – personified by other mothers represented in the film, who not so subtly undermine Jules's capacity to take care of her daughter, Paige.

However, Kathleen Rowe Karlyn urges us to reconsider these new romcom heroes, who are willing to listen to and help women.[23] Even though they initially appear to be liberated from 'a repressive masculinity classical romantic comedy valued' (1995: 196), they, in fact, very often represent an appropriation of 'femininity, feminised genres, and feminism', which is used to prop up their own authority, invoked 'to "instruct" women about relationships, romance, and femininity itself' (1995: 196–7). In Jules's case, there is certainly 'something wounded or undeveloped in *her* – qualities which allow the hero to demonstrate his greater wisdom, charm and sensitivity' (1995: 197 [emphasis in original]). If we add to this the fact that Matt, Jules's husband and stay-at-home dad, engages in a clichéd romance with another mom because Jules did not have time for him, then *The Intern* might, indeed, be read as perturbingly conservative: 'If you're a working mom who's killing it at a job you love, don't be surprised when Daddy is called in to help run the numbers and hubby starts playing around', Alexandra Macon (2015) bitterly commented in her review of the film.

Nevertheless, in what follows, I suggest that *The Intern*'s self-aware representation of the romance and the characters themselves, as well as the very logics of the genre of the romantic comedy, which continues to negotiate and respond dynamically to social realities, might help destabilise the potentially patronising tone of the film. Meyers's view is arguably a nostalgic one, as she repeats the form and affect associated with the classical romantic comedy. But, as I argue later, she does it in a performative manner, which points to the constructed nature of this (re)imagining.

Roberta Garrett's (2007) account of the proliferation of self-reflexive practices across female-oriented chick flicks since the 1990s, both male- and female-authored, is a useful starting point for thinking about how Meyers's aesthetics could be inscribed within wider trends present in both Hollywood and independent filmmaking. As already mentioned (see Introduction), Garrett observes that the self-conscious devices increasingly incorporated in the new female-orientated cycles 'are often used [. . .] to ameliorate the sentimentalism, and feminine naivety associated with older, pre-feminist female-identified forms' (2007: 7). In the following pages I consider how *The Intern* interweaves older forms of romantic comedy with its current preoccupations, typifying the trends delineated by Garrett. Meyers's reflexivity and generic self-consciousness, associated with the more 'cerebral' pleasures of male viewing, is intimately bound to the more affective comprehension that the film facilitates. The detailed analysis of the film's unremitting allusionism, both at textual and extratextual levels, will reveal that Meyers's self-reflexive strategies invoke two issues of central importance to this book: the question of female authorship in a male-dominated film industry and the genre's development in the Hollywood context. As previously noted, much criticism conflated Meyers's film with her biographical legend, in ways that often disparaged her credibility as a director. I will revisit these references to show how *The Intern* comments on the filmmaker's position within the Hollywood conglomerate, her attitude towards the feminised genre of the romcom and the fantasy-making through the language of love and commodity consumption.

Alongside Meyers's authorial persona, the stardom of Robert De Niro and Anne Hathaway will also be discussed, as they were an important ingredient in the marketing campaign, figuring centrally in promotional devices, such as the official trailer and the main poster. The latter, which features the tagline '*Experience* never goes out of *fashion*' (emphasis added), arguably combines two key terms that encapsulate their respective biographic legends. The primary undertone generated by Hathaway's presence comes from her performances in *The Princess Diaries* (Garry Marshall, 2001) and *The Devil Wears Prada* (David Frankel, 2006), which play a significant role in establishing a metatextual dialogue with the postfeminist romantic comedy and its contradictions for both the protagonist and Meyers as a director in a man's world. De Niro's presence also played a big part in the shaping of frameworks of expectation around the film. As I argue later, the film draws on two major trends in his career: an earlier association with more 'serious' dramatic performances and a later move towards comedies, specifically those which mobilise the mid-life crisis as a frame of reference, also typical of Meyers's oeuvre. The filmmaker capitalises on these two rather different associations, which constitute a significant part of the 'ongoing whirl of intertextual reference' (Stam 2000b: 66) within which the film is situated.

Anne Hathaway: Hollywood's Makeover Queen

Within a cinematic arena, Anne Hathaway's career illustrates the different permutations of girlishness in the twenty-first century. Perhaps the primary association brought by the actress is from the Disney comedy film *The Princess Diaries* (2001), for which she won the Teen Choice Award for Choice Movie Actress – Comedy. Her role as Mia Thermopolis, a teenager who discovers that she is heir to the throne of the fictional kingdom of Genovia, and thus has to undergo a complete transformation accordingly, was symptomatic of the widespread popularity of the chick postfeminist aesthetics – 'girlpower, a focus on female pleasure and pleasures, and the value of consumer culture and girlie goods, including designer clothes, expensive and impractical footwear, and trendy accessories' (Ferriss and Young 2008: 4) – which, significantly, is also at the core of *The Devil Wears Prada* (2006), another key film in Hathaway's professional trajectory. In the latter, she starred as Andy, a journalist who takes a job as a junior assistant to a powerful fashion magazine editor (Meryl Streep). Comparing these two films is illuminating for multiple reasons. They not only display a special interest in clothes – *The Devil Wears Prada* was, for this reason, dubbed a 'fashion flick'[24] – but also they stage the process of the makeover, both of which are recognisable tropes in postfeminist media culture (Schreiber 2014: 142), emphasised in films such as *Pretty Woman* (Garry Marshall, 1990) and *Romy and Michele's High School Reunion* (David Mirkin, 1997), among many others.[25] Suzanne Ferriss points to a long tradition of chick flicks that depict a transformation from a seemingly unattractive girl to an attractive woman:

> From *Now, Voyager* (1942) to *Funny Face* (1957) to *Moonstruck* (1987) to *She's All That* (1999) to *My Big Fat Greek Wedding* (2002), the so-called 'unattractive' girl sports a frumpish wardrobe and bookish glasses that signal her intelligence and independence, but lead men to shun her. (2008: 41)

In *The Princess Diaries* the similarly 'frumpy' protagonist undergoes a glamorous transformation. Her glasses are removed and broken in half, her eyebrows plucked, her hair groomed and straightened. Once she has been put through a number of beauty treatments, she is dressed in expensive clothes. Clothes also play an important role in *The Devil Wears Prada*, within which the makeover significantly starts with a change of wardrobe. However, just like in Marshall's film, it involves other changes as well, such as make-up, a new haircut and, most importantly, the newly gained sense of self-realisation and confidence.[26] As Ferriss argues: 'Despite its apparent superficiality, the makeover does have high stakes: the woman's life itself is transformed' (2008: 41). In case of *The Devil Wears Prada*, the makeover leads to professional achievement, which is significantly privileged over romance, as Hilary Radner observes in her analysis of the film:

> Though, in spite of her sexual infidelity, [the protagonist] repairs her relationship, agreeing to a commuter partnership, the real satisfaction in the ending derives from Andy's success in the workplace, and perhaps from the fact that though no fashion victim, she is no longer the awkward frumpy recent college graduate of the film's beginning, but a trendy, stylish career woman. (2011: 145)

Even if, in the end, Andy's ambitions are not in the area of fashion, empowerment and professional success come not in spite of, but through consumption and image transformation.[27]

If we extend Hathaway's reputation as 'Hollywood's Makeover Queen' (Devin 2001) to *The Intern*, we can trace an evolution of her character from the unruly, big-hearted and somewhat awkward and unpopular girl, who grudgingly follows the 'princess rules', into a determined businesswoman, a founder of a successful e-commerce company, as well as a mother and a wife. The protagonist in *The Intern* is a high-powered career woman clearly based on Hathaway's actual public figure: a young mother, born in Brooklyn, with a demanding job, who has become a postfeminist icon herself.[28] Jules's independence is represented in *The Intern* by the bike she likes riding through her office – an old warehouse significantly also located in Brooklyn.[29]

Michele Schreiber argues in reference to this trope of an independent woman: 'Meyers's films are distinctive in that they gesture towards a realisation and embodiment of second-wave feminist ideals in which a woman can unapologetically value her career and successfully balance this with other aspects of her life' (2014: 145), but they blend these ideals with the postfeminist language of empowerment through consumption. However, it is worth noting that this image of a glamorous, empowered and independent woman, who can combine a professional career and healthy love life with ease – celebrated by postfeminist media culture – is undermined in various ways in *The Intern*. To quote Meyers's earlier picture, 'something's gotta give'. Jules is a caring mother and is passionate about her career, but she is also sleep deprived, chronically late to meetings and possibly an obsessive-compulsive (she constantly cleans her hands with sanitiser). She also disrupts the work-life balance of others: her overworking filters through to the lives of her employees, especially her secretary Becky.[30] Jules's husband seems, initially, to be the perfect partner for her, but, as it turns out, he blames her for depriving him of 'me time'. The film is about 'the plagues of career women who want it all, [but] apparently can't have it all', bemoans Manohla Dargis (2015) in her review of the film. What Dargis reads as an unequivocal regression in feminist politics might also be considered a profound disillusionment with postfeminist chick flicks, epitomised perhaps most prominently by the television series *Sex and the City*: its embrace of consumerism, which does not provide true freedom, but rather the freedom to shop (Holmlund 2005). *The Intern* seems to scratch the surface of this postfeminist discourse, opening up spaces that are potentially oppositional to it.

Meyers's take on independent women is, of course, not without its problems, not only because of the issues brought up in the aforementioned review, but also due to its unrelenting focus on heterosexual, white, upper-middle class femininity. Jules seems to be the prototype for what has been dubbed 'white feminism': young, independent, tough, yet severely limited in scope. One cannot overlook the opposition between the overwhelmingly white employees in Jules's office and the mostly Latina female workers folding the clothes and placing them in the bags in a factory. In this respect, I agree with Schreiber's contention that in Meyers's films 'the language of this independence is spoken with a vocabulary of desire made possible by the commodities that an upper-middleclass status makes available' (2014: 145).

Even though Meyers is not conscious enough about intersectionality, she does offer some interesting insights on the postfeminist model of the contemporary romcom, perhaps expressing the bitterness of the twenty-first century feminist towards some of its values. Assuming that Jules stands for *The Devil Wear Prada*'s Andy post-makeover, then *The Intern* seems to ask what happens after young women succeed and gain power. Jules does not go through a makeover in the traditional sense, but she clearly undergoes a transformation. At the beginning of the film, she is visibly stressed, overburdened with tasks, staying late in the office and eating alone (an image which exposes the contradictions inherent in the neoliberal, individualistic society: the wall-bound offices are eschewed in a bid to promote collaboration between the employees, but they end up alienated at their desks and not interacting with each other when they are not under supervision).[31] At the end of the film, we see her more relaxed, integrated, connected to nature and to others. She makes an effort to remember her employees' names and to attend office birthday parties. If, as Schreiber argues, Meyers tends 'to camouflage the contradictions that underlie her films – between her representations of strong, seemingly independent women and their reliance on the language of love and commodity consumption to speak this independence' (2014: 148)[32] – in *The Intern* this language changes over the course of the film, making room for an ethical being-with, notably beyond the heterosexual romance.

Another interesting aspect is Meyers's interrogation of the relations between age and gender. The filmmaker departed from her usual interest in the older, very successful woman, who typically stars in her films, turning instead to the 'adolescent girl-woman archetype' forged by Nora Ephron (see Schreiber 2014: 145). Embracing girlishness and the pleasures provided by 'girly' popular culture is one of the distinctive features in postfeminist media culture, and has been sometimes read as a repudiation of feminism (Negra 2009;

McRobbie 2004). However, I would suggest that, perhaps contradictorily, even though Jules is young, she has grown out of the postfeminist girlishness featured in *The Devil Wears Prada*. She has taken on adult responsibilities (imposed on her, some might say, by the patriarchy): marrying, having children, making a home *and* having a professional life, all of which with almost no 'girly' pleasures in sight. While it might be argued that a clothing business is itself the epitome of girlishness turned womanhood – Jules gets to *clothe* the girlish pleasure of buying, wearing and shopping for clothes into an appropriate 'grown-up' career[33] – at the same time this shift is not represented as cheerful or unproblematic, as it goes beyond the mere pleasures of empowerment through consumption. To reference 'What a Girl Wants' – a famous Christina Aguilera song, which also serves as the title of Diane Negra's book (2009) on the topic of consumerism and postfeminism – Meyers's film is more about 'what a *woman* wants', swinging the pendulum back as a response to the combined pull of postfeminist and feminist forces. What she wants is not a glamorous makeover, but to continue to do what she loves, without being dismissed and/or punished for being successful.

Meyers's constant use of direct or indirect cinematic allusions to *The Devil Wears Prada* is significant here. The humorous referencing is usually mobilised to reverse power relations from the earlier film, as Meyers flips the premise of *The Devil Wears Prada* by making Hathaway the creator of a successful fashion business. In *The Devil Wears Prada* Andy, just like Ben, attended Northwestern University, and neither of them are particularly interested in the clothing industry. They both have demanding bosses: Miranda, the chilly editor of *Runway*, and the certainly less ruthless but similarly reserved Jules. As their interns, they spend increasing amounts of time at their superiors' beck and call. This happens, for instance, when Andy is given instructions to bring the 'Book' to Miranda's home, along with her dry cleaning: under no circumstances should she speak with anyone in the house. Falsely led by Miranda's twins, she ends up interrupting Miranda and her husband having an argument. This scene is echoed in *The Intern* when Ben is instructed to pick up Jules ('be there at 7:45, ring the bell and walk away') and he unintentionally enters the house, intruding on Jules's domestic sphere. Later in the film, Jules spills soy sauce on her Stella McCartney jacket and Ben is told to take care of it. The film finds humour in making Ben, played by De Niro – usually associated with 'tough' masculinity – take part in 'girly' tasks. Leaving aside the potentially problematic aspect of this reversal, it could be argued that Meyers picks up *The Devil Wears Prada*'s reflection on women and power, already explored in other successful chick flicks – in particular, *Legally Blonde* (Robert Luketic, 2001) and *Working Girl* (Mike Nichols, 1988).[34] As such, *The Intern* could hardly be viewed as a 'break out' in terms of the type of material that Hollywood has been producing over the last three decades. Kathrina Glitre comments in reference to what she considers Meyers's 'popular feminism': '[T]he figure of the independent woman sells because she provides a pleasurable fantasy of power and success' (2011: 18). In this sense, instead of opposing, *The Intern* fleshes out some of the genre characteristics. Ultimately, the film is as much about Meyers's conflicted ideas about powerful women as it is about the generic development of the romcom. If postfeminist values marked the decades of the 1990s and 2000s, Meyers seems to ask: what is next?

Nancy Meyers in Dream/Factory

Meyers's work has regularly been read as obliquely autobiographical, and the filmmaker herself has not discouraged these interpretations: 'I'm writing a lot from my own experience, obviously I write a lot about women and when I got divorced I wrote about divorced women'.[35] In reference to Meyers's own career and personal life (in 1999 she divorced the director Charles Shyer; she has two daughters with him), it is interesting to underscore how *The Intern*'s bold defence of working mothers might be read as the filmmaker's powerful statement about her own status as a successful director in Hollywood – even if this message might be considered somewhat attenuated by the fact that it is articulated by Ben, and not Jules herself:

> Tough? Jules? She's a total badass. Guess that's how she became an internet sensation. [He sees the other mothers becoming uncomfortable because of their previous biting remarks about Jules]. Must make you proud, huh? One of your own out there every day crashing the glass ceiling of the tech world. So – bravo! Good for her. Right?

The filmmaker herself indicated in reference to *The Intern* that, as 'a working grandmother', she wanted to 'put that character of the working mother out there again, and to show that her daughter is not suffering because her mother works' (in Freeman 2015).

In this context, and without neglecting Meyers's biographic details – often used in critical discourses to disparage her work as trivial or falling short in terms of representing women's experiences – I want to stress the manifold ways in which *The Intern* offers a meta-aware reflection on women directors' position in the Hollywood film industry and their struggles to assert their creative, professional and authorial agency. In one scene Jules goes to see one of the prospective CEO candidates for her company. She is visibly nervous, as if she is the one being interviewed. The rhetoric of high- and low-angle shots firmly establishes the power relations.

In the next scene we see her walking angrily out of the building, the camera rushing to keep up with her. She sits in the backseat of her car and catches her breath. In response to Ben's remark 'that was fast', she responds, exasperated:

GENRE, AUTHORSHIP AND CONTEMPORARY WOMEN FILMMAKERS

Figure 6.3 Jules's eyes track up to the top of the skyscraper in front of her, she then looks to Ben, communicating her unease about the forthcoming interview.

> Not fast enough. [. . .] I thought he was a condescending sexist know-it-all who did not seem to get what we do, *at all*, and honestly, I think he'd run our company in a completely inorganic way that would lose us all the customers we've killed ourselves to get.

In view of the fact that Meyers's romantic comedies have often been described as 'organic' (Nochimson 2010), *The Intern* becomes an apt metaphor for her authorial brand within the mainstream film industry. Even more revealing is a scene that was only included in the script, but which draws many parallelisms between Jules and Meyers as a Hollywood director:

> Jules follows an Assistant down a long corridor. She's nervous, her palm hitting the side of her leg, heart pounding. The Assistant shows her into a large office where Eric Sheekey stands with his back to the door. He hangs up from a call and turns in Jules's direction. Jules catches Eric's ready smile and dimples he's a bit too proud of. [. . .] Jump cuts tell the story.
>
> Eric: Congratulations. You are a great merchant and a passionate visionary. [Jules forces a smile]. But let's look at where you are from 30,000 feet, shall we? [Jules is finding it hard to swallow]. You've had your arms wrapped around the business really well – until the last two quarters. But what everyone wants is a long term sustainable business and at this point, we still need hyper-growth. [. . .] We both know 90% of all tech companies fail so you're going to need me, or someone like me to get you over this hump. We also know mobile is the future . . . you need a plan for that and you needed it six months ago. [Hands Jules the glass of water]. You have relentless perseverance, Jules, I'll give you that, but that's not enough to get you where you need to be. My role will be to keep my head out of the cyclone, provide insight, direction and stability. I've been right here before. [Jules shifts her position]. Now I have some great people I'd like to bring over with me – very smart, very pedigree'd. Different level. [Jules wipes her upper lip – different level???] I guarantee you by next quarter we will do far more than make the trains at [ATF] run on time. [. . .] I've watched what you're doing Jules and it's exciting. Your *obsessive focus on the customer* serves you well, I see it in all the data, but the *money's never there until it's there*. So, take the next step, strengthen your infrastructure and make some changes – and next year at this time, you'll be killing it and right where you should be – hangin' with the *big boys*. That's a promise.
>
> As Eric ends his speech his eyes land on Jules's thigh – her skirt has hiked up a little too far. Jules catches his look. He doesn't have the decency to look away. (Meyers 2014: 41–3 [emphasis added])

This fragment throws into sharp relief the prevailing sexism in big corporations and the mechanisms of disempowering women who struggle to succeed.[36] Jules is perfectly aware that, should she go ahead with hiring a CEO, she would be forced to run every idea she has by this same CEO. She denounces the double standards that undermine women's hard work and creativity, astutely observing: 'Mark Zuckerberg never brought in a CEO. And he was a teenager'. In a subsequent scene, when referring to another meeting with a possible candidate, she bitterly relates: 'Was going well until he called us, I believe the term he used was a "chick site". Then I didn't hear anything he said after that. Apparently selling "clothes" makes us a chick site. I mean, really? How is this not legit?'. When Ben says that 'he couldn't agree more' and that he 'finds that surprising', she replies: 'Really? Sexism in business?'

The exchanges between Jules and the potential CEOs quoted above attest to not only the glass ceiling that remains in place in most creative industries, but also to Meyers's authorial brand as the director of 'chick flicks', the problems of financing and her awareness of the cultural value of romantic comedy. Meyers, who has been working in Hollywood for nearly her entire adult life and, undoubtedly, has thus gained the ability to control the development of her career, has nonetheless routinely condemned the problem of sexism in the film industry, which is still heavily dominated by men. When she started working on *Private Benjamin*, the studio specified in her contract that 'she must never be alone on set without her male co-producers' (in Freeman 2015). In her 2015 *Guardian* interview, 'Nancy Meyers: "I don't see a lot of movies about complicated women . . . I think it's gotten worse"', she made reference to this experience, saying: '[T]hings have moved on from then. But do women have equal rights in Hollywood? No' (in Freeman 2015). The 'female' genres she works with are not the easiest to obtain money for: 'My kind of movie is not the kind of film that studios have wanted to make for a while now. Instead, it's been all comic-book movies, gigantic action movies and guy comedies' (in Freeman 2015). Finally, the scene mentioned above throws into relief the idea (much debated in feminist criticism) that the fashion industry – as part of the broader chick culture, to which Meyers's films are usually ascribed – is not highly ranked in the hierarchy of culture (perhaps except when men themselves are the designers). As Tania Modleski has observed, women's professional and personal involvement with fashion is often denigrated and ridiculed by men, thus putting women in 'a familiar double bind by which they are first assigned a restricted place in patriarchy and then condemned by occupying it' (2016: 73). This, of course, returns us to the tensions that exist at the intersection between women's creativity and mass culture in a wider sense: like most women filmmakers doing genre films associated with 'female' pursuits, Meyers has been largely ignored or treated as a manufacturer of highly formulaic goods.

It is important, however, not to overlook Meyers's concern with the feminised sphere of fashion – and, as already mentioned, with mise-en-scène and commodity cultures more broadly – but rather to consider the ways in which this concern works within the film. Much has been written about how the filmmaker's astonishing visual environments should be read as fundamental to her authorial style. According to Radner, for the filmmaker 'cinema is not merely a shop window; the goods that it displays are crucial to its art' (2011: 179). In this sense, similarly to Sofia Coppola's films, in Meyers's oeuvre the 'surface' décor is also substance. As the filmmaker herself stated, she sees a house 'as a lead character in a movie' (in Abramovitch 2012).[37] For Radner, Meyers's preoccupation with mise-en-scène, which is compatible with the developments and demands of consumer culture, works as an extension of the makeover of her protagonists, who are always defined through their environment. The makeover trope is transformed, thus, 'into a continuous regime of renovation and self-improvement, which extends into home-decorating and language acquisition' (2011: 179).[38] Interestingly, according to Radner, this emphasis on the cultivation of 'an autonomous self that seeks its own fulfilment as its primary goal, ultimately challeng[es] the notion of a natural order associated with the traditional romance' (2011: 180).

Inscribing *It's Complicated* within the 'well-worn postfeminist terrain', Schreiber (2014: 155), in turn, pays attention to Meyers's reliance on the conflation of romance and the vocabulary of consumption: consumerism is inextricably linked to both female autonomy and love. Drawing on Eva Illouz's reflection on the 'romanticization of commodities', a process in which objects gain 'a romantic aura', and the 'commodification of romance' that 'concerns the ways in which romantic practices increasingly interlocked with and became defined as the consumption of leisure goods and leisure technologies offered by the nascent mass market' (Illouz in Schreiber 2014: 147), Schreiber convincingly argues that these two processes intersect in Meyers's entire oeuvre: '[T]he goods that fill Meyers's mise-en-scène provide the landscape for, and become intertwined with, the requisite romance narrative structure' (2014: 147). Put simply, the filmmaker depicts romance as a desirable commodity in itself or, more precisely, 'as one of the many commodities in [the] broader hyper-aestheticised mise-en-scène' (2014: 147). I further contend, however, that the lavish attention paid to the sumptuous goods and luxurious interior designs also offers a self-conscious take on both the genre of the romcom and Meyers's authorship, which is expressed, as with Coppola's authorship, through the language of commodity fetishism. This is evidenced, for instance, in several playful references to Meyers's own preoccupation with interior spaces – which, as already hinted, are styled as though they have sprung directly from the pages of a design magazine, and, in fact, they are often featured in such publications. 'I love this house. It just looks happy to me. Like if it was in a kid's book, it would make you feel good when you turned the page and saw it. Know what I mean?', Jules ruminates, as Ben drops her off after work.[39] Later in the film, when Jules intrudes in Ben's home (the scene which mirrors Ben's similar intrusion into Jules's house earlier in the film) and when, significantly, the film reaches its emotional climax, the mise-en-scène comes to the fore again. In this scene, which resembles the romantic moment when the characters confess their 'true' feelings, Ben tells Jules how he admires what she does:

> Ben: I never had something like this in my career. Not many people do. This big, beautiful, intricate thing that you created – it's *a dream* isn't it? And you're going to give that up in the hopes that your husband will stop having an affair? I don't see how that adds up. You should feel nothing but great about what you've done. Don't let anybody take that away from you. [Jules wipes a tear from her cheek]. I guess you came over here 'cause you wanted to hear some of this . . .
> Jules: Yeah, I did. And maybe also 'cause you're my . . .
> Ben: Intern.
> Jules: I was going to say . . . Intern/Slash/Best friend, but no need to get all sentimental [. . .]. I think it's moments like this when you need someone who you know you can count on. So thank you for that. [Ben nods] I like your *house* so much by the way. [emphasis added]

It is significant that this emotionally intense reconciliation finishes with the self-conscious appreciation of the furnishings in Ben's house. As it turns out, not only romance, but also relational affect in a wider sense, is represented in Meyers's films through the focus on hyper-aestheticised mise-en-scène. But, perhaps most interestingly, this scene also points to the metatextual comment on romantic comedy as fantasy-making: the dream of having (if not buying) it all, the dream of power reversal in a male-dominated world, the dream of happy endings. Schreiber points to the frequent slippage between reality and fantasy typical of Meyers's films, in which 'life imitates art, and then vice versa' (2014: 147). This happens in two ways: through the female characters' self-referential careers – most of them work in creative industries that 'contribute to the culture in which fantasy and reality are interchangeable' – and her films' happy endings, which have a performative function – the protagonists are aware of participating in discourses of love, instead of 'realistically' representing genuine emotional attachment (2014: 147–8). *The Intern* seems to support both points argued by Schreiber. Despite their age difference, Jules can be easily compared to playwright Erica in *Something's Gotta Give*, wedding-dress designer Elisabeth in *The Parent Trap*, advertising executive Darcy in *What Women Want*, movie trailers producer Amanda in *The Holiday* and gourmet food store owner Jane in *It's Complicated*, whose jobs mostly involve, albeit in different ways, selling women commodities by creating fantasies (Schreiber 2014: 148). Almost all of these characters achieve creativity and artistry by exploiting the space codified as feminine, similarly to Meyers, who offers the promise of a happy ending through a markedly feminised genre. If Meyers's typical denouements 'do not just feature the formation of a heterosexual couple but hyper-aestheticise this connection to such an extent that they call attention to their own fiction-based fantasy' (2014: 148), then *The Intern* pushes this feature to its limit. Nowhere is it more conspicuous than in the film's more 'conventional' romantic climax, which seals the heterosexual romance. Just when Jules decides not to hire the CEO – she had previously agreed to this to save her marriage – her husband unexpectedly drops in at her office and urges her to 'do what is right' for her, saying that he is willing to make their marriage work. The fantasy of a 'full-time Dad' who 'had a really good job in marketing', but decided to stay home and support Jules's career, as well as the quintessentially romantic Hollywood image of heterosexual union in a wider sense, is 'on' again. In this context, it could be argued that the film upholds a conservative reading of gender and of the family, conforming to a 'natural order'. However, drawing on Jermyn's reflection on the climax in *What Women Want*, which the scholar reads in a manner akin to Douglas Sirk's penchant for the 'false happy ending', one could consider the reconciliation between Matt and Jules as 'self-consciously artificial or otherwise unconvincing, thus drawing attention to the conflicts [...] and refusing to embed comfortable reassurance at the film's close' (Jermyn 2018: 68).

Schreiber, in contrast, points to the problematic aspects of Meyers's endings, which make her films so 'intoxicatingly pleasurable'. In reference to *It's Complicated* she writes:

> On one hand, it is an incredibly satisfying, well-acted romance film, with the central conflicts resolved and a promise of a happy ending between Jane and a man who respects and admires her success. On the other hand, the film transparently satisfies another kind of desire, which is that of commodity fetishism enabled by the film's significant production budget. To have love alongside a beautiful home and fantastic food without having to consider the costs of such an arrangement is the pleasurable fantasy that Meyers's films offer. But one does wonder whether the desire generated by this intensified mise-en-scène of wealth exceeds that generated by the characters' emotional connection. (2014: 155)

Interestingly, while *The Intern*'s 'romantic' (false) resolution between Jules and Matt also offers a prevalence of mise-en-scène, it takes place not in the house, but in the office – the décor of which is as awe-inspiring as the interior design of the homes shown earlier – which throws into stark relief the tensions between the domestic and the public sphere dramatised throughout the film. Indeed, I propose that this is Meyers's way of commenting on the historical transformations in cultural conceptions of female identity, employment and professional aspirations in the twenty-first century, providing an aesthetic framework that encompasses both the old and the new preoccupations present in different cycles of romantic comedies.

In light of this, the fact that the 'desire generated by this intensified mise-en-scène' – which can be paralleled, as I suggested above, with Meyers's creativity – 'exceeds that generated by the characters' emotional connection' (Schreiber 2014: 155), might be seen as potentially political, as it destabilises the traditional heteronormative assumption that women's ultimate fulfilment is marriage. It is also significant that the apparent capitulation to monogamy is only partial in *The Intern*, as the film concludes with Jules reuniting with Ben, shifting the emphasis in the narrative from romance to friendship, consciously exposing the conventions of the traditional romcom as focused on the former. Meyers sets out to explore and test the contours of the genre by repositioning the centre, while at the same time employing most of the generic basics. Thus, *The Intern* demonstrates the romantic comedy's potential to respond to social and cultural shifts, although, as Christine Gledhill reminds us, genres

> do not reflect or misrepresent gender as it 'really' exists in social world; rather the practices and cultural imaginaries through which gender emerges as a set of widely shared social conventions provide materials to the dramatic purposes of film and television genre fictions. In media genres, the genericity of social gender is put to fictional and dramatic use, making its aporias and contests visible and opening up multiple possibilities of generic-gender play and transformation. (2018: x)

The multiple possibilities of generic-gender transformation in *The Intern*, based on the play of similarities between Jules and Meyers, is further complicated by also making Ben responsible for creating this fantasy. Returning to Garrett's (2007) argument about the coexistence of emotional intensity and affect associated with older forms on the one hand, and a critical attitude towards romance on the other, I argue in the following section that Ben is a mediator between these two modes, offering a self-conscious reflection on past and present cinematic gender/power relations.

Robert De Niro: 'Experience never goes out of fashion'

Stars, as a number of scholars have argued, bring a web of expectations to bear on the film experience, and, in this sense, they work like genre. Mary Harrod observes that, 'as with genre, the extent to which this may be understood to function as pastiche depends on the exact balance of signification between these associations and the character's role in the film' (2010: 32). In what follows I contend that Robert De Niro's star persona is 'redolent of certain feelings and perceptions' (Dyer 2007: 130) and, in this sense, can be read through Dyer's notion of pastiche.

Throughout his career, De Niro has incarnated a number of different roles, while maintaining a persona that suggests a high degree of continuity. This long-established star with a track record over a period of almost five decades brought to *The Intern* a series of associations on which the film plays. As previously mentioned, the film draws predominantly on two major trends in his career: his ventures into dramatic performance – for instance, in Martin Scorsese's *Mean Streets* (1973), *Raging Bull* (1980) and *Taxi Driver* (1976) – and his later comic persona in box office hits such as *Analyze This* (Harold Ramis, 1999), *Meet the Parents* (Jay Roach, 2000) and the romantic comedy-drama *Silver Linings Playbook* (David O. Russell, 2012).

These associations are repeatedly brought up in *The Intern*. The long, impassive stares that Ben gives Matt recall his performance as a hostile father-in-law in *Meet the Parents*, suspicious of his daughter's fiancé, the male nurse Greg (note that Matt stands for the nurturing father, taking care of his daughter in *The Intern*). De Niro's portrayal as a professional bank robber in *Heat* (Michael Mannis, 1995) is evoked in the hilarious scene in which Ben and his co-workers break into Jules's mother's house to delete an embarrassingly nasty email that Jules inadvertently sent. The alarm sounds, and Ben announces that they have thirty seconds to get out – a nod to De Niro's character in *Heat*, who states in one scene: 'Don't let yourself get attached to anything you are not willing to walk out on in 30 seconds flat if you feel the heat around the corner'.[40] What is more, *The Intern* clearly references the protagonist of *Taxi Driver*, who – in analogy to Ben saving Jules from a chauffeur with a drinking problem earlier in the film – rescues a child prostitute, Iris, from her pimp. Both films stress the age difference between the characters, the non-sexual bond between a man and a woman and De Niro's status as a 'fixer of other people's problems' or even a sort of 'vigilante'. But, most importantly, the two films underscore the performative nature of their male protagonists. There is no better example of this than the memorable scene from *Taxi Driver*, in which Travis practices drawing his weapons and repeating the phrase 'you talkin' to me?' to threaten the imaginary 'bad guy' in the mirror. We can find a humorous allusion to this scene in *The Intern*: Ben, in his pyjamas, stands in front of the mirror and dumps out all the pills in the 'Monday' compartment of his seven-day pill organiser. He catches his reflection and decides to practice blinking, saying 'Hi' to himself. The editing, jump cuts and repetitions clearly evoke the scene in *Taxi Driver*.

Blinking is important to Ben, because as he is informed by his colleagues, Jules hates people who never blink. At some point in the film Jules mentions that one of the candidates for CEO 'never blinked. An Olympian non-blinker', suggesting lack of sincerity or integrity, features which De Niro's character possesses in spades (the scene in which he is unable to lie to Jules, sweating and avoiding her gaze, is a perfect example of this). Like other film stars, such as Jack Nicholson, who managed careers that continued through many decades, De Niro's star persona might be described as embodying a recognisable, 'old-style' type of masculinity, although based on different features than that of Nicholson's.[41] As Ben describes himself in the film:

> I've been a company man all my life. I'm loyal, I'm trustworthy and I'm good in a crisis. [. . .] I read once, musicians don't retire. They stop when there's no more music in them. Well, I still have music in me. Absolutely positive about that.

Given the intertextual dimension of these revelations, one can read *The Intern* as a nostalgic tribute to, and at the same time rejuvenation of, De Niro's biographic legend.[42] Rather than focusing on the representation of Ben as yet another example of Meyers's ageing protagonists, however, I want to emphasise the performative aspects of the masculinity that he embodies, already hinted at in my discussion of the blinking scene. There are many moments in *The Intern* that support this contention – for example, when Ben is about to start his first day at work. The viewer sees him sitting in a chair, fully dressed, ready to go. Finally, he rises, saying 'Let's make it happen!'. This crucially performative and meta-aware statement could be understood as a *leitmotiv* for the whole movie.

From the very beginning, the film draws our attention to its self-conscious features. After the fade in, we are faced with a camera shot of trees. The camera movement then leads us down, and we see a group of people of different ages in rows performing t'ai chi. They all move gracefully through their meditative poses. We hear Ben's voice-over, which establishes the main themes of the film: 'Freud said: "Love and work, work and love. That's all there is". Well, I'm retired and my wife is dead. As you can imagine, that has given me some time on my hands'. The camera focuses on Ben, in a funny pose. His movements are clearly not as synchronised as those of the other students. He looks directly at the viewer.

What follows is a scene that resembles a TV interview, but turns out to be a job application in the form of a video.[43] Ben is wearing a suit and tie, sitting in an upright chair and talking to the camera:

> My wife has been gone for 3 and half years. I miss her in every way. And retirement, that is an on-going relentless effort in creativity. I enjoyed the novelty of it. Sort of felt like I was playing hooky [. . .].

The film then cuts to a coffee shop, crowded with men on their way to work. Ben sits on a stool at a corner table with a bagel and the morning's newspaper. Two male executives in their forties ask Ben if they can share his table. Ben is obviously delighted, and he moves his things to make room for them. The men take the two remaining stools, turn them away from Ben and begin an

Figure 6.4 Ben invades the feminised space of 'pink girlhood'.

impromptu meeting, as if Ben is not even there: 'Come rain or shine, I'm at my Starbucks by 7:15. Can't explain it, but it makes me feel part of something'. Ben again looks at the audience with a knowing look. Thinking back to Schreiber's (2014) ideas on Meyers's illusory happy endings, in *The Intern* the opening is also a form of illusion: Ben *pretends* to be someone else so that he can be part of something.

In this sense, from the beginning of the film Ben is signalled as a sort of intruder, not only in the masculinised terrain of considerably younger executives, but also in the feminised space of his granddaughter's bedroom, who he visits when he goes to San Diego, where his family lives now. The scene starts with a shot of a ceiling filled with golden stars that glow in the dark. The camera tilts down past the stars and centres on a little girl asleep in the top bunk, then it continues to tilt down and we see Ben wide awake in the bottom bunk under Dora the Explorer sheets. In a similar way, Ben later invades the feminised space of 'pink girlhood' when he takes Jules's daughter, Paige, to a birthday party in a park.

Not only is he an intruder, but he is also an onlooker – a common trait in Meyers's oeuvre.[44] His subtle glimpses into the camera, and the reason Jules wants to transfer him to a different department (he is 'too observant'), clearly situate him in an 'external' position from which he humorously comments on both gender roles and the genre of romantic comedy. However, while he clearly mobilises the distanced, 'masculine' pleasures of self-conscious looking, he also embodies the sentimentalism associated with the older forms of the genre and closely bound to the cultural perception of female viewing pleasure.

This aspect is immediately clear in reference to his role exposing contemporary romcom masculinity, as discussed before. In contrast to the other men in the office – 'unshaven piles of wrinkles', as the *Jezebel* writer Bobby Finger (2015) jokingly dubs them – Ben insists on wearing a suit and tie, even though Jules tells him 'he didn't have to, it's all casual'. He does not own a pair of jeans, let alone the hoodie almost all of his co-workers wear to work. The filmmaker leaves no doubt about what sort of masculinity she feels nostalgic about, commenting on the changing gender roles through a witty tirade delivered by a half-tipsy Jules, who comes clean about what she *really* thinks about her young workmates:

> Boys, what can I say? Sorry, didn't mean to call you boys. No one calls men 'men' anymore. Have you noticed? Women went from Girls to Women and men went from Men to Boys. This is a problem. [. . .] Yup. Here's my theory about this – we all grew up during the 'Take your Daughter to Work Day' thing, right? So we were always told we could do anything, be anything. And I think somehow the guys got, maybe not left behind but not quite as nurtured. We were the generation of 'you go, girl'. We had Oprah. I wonder sometimes how guys fit in . . . they seem to still be trying to figure it all out. Still dressing like little boys, still playing video games. [. . .] How in one generation have men gone from guys like Jack Nicholson and Harrison Ford to . . . [she pauses as she indicates the guys who look as if they wish they weren't standing there in T-shirt and hoodies]. Take Ben here. A dying breed . . . Look and learn 'cause if you ask me . . . [she points to Ben]. This is what cool is.

Without neglecting the troubling aspect of this nostalgic celebration of an 'old-school' gentleman, it is fair to say that Meyers's film provides timely comments on the type of masculinity that is represented in contemporary Hollywood romcoms. As one of the reviewers aptly observes, the film asks: '[W]hat happens when Raging Bull is 70, and there's no one to pick up the gloves?' (Saltsman 2015). In this way, *The Intern* registers certain changes in gender politics, or even suggests, it might be argued, a possible conservative turn towards more traditional models of masculinity. But it also references affect and masculinity associated with the older cinematic forms, which might be a source of pleasure for (male and female) audiences.

If we accept that the film is nostalgic about past forms of masculinity, it is also nostalgic about romance as represented in older variants of the genre. The business trip sequence to San Francisco illustrates this point. While on the trip, Jules invites Ben up to her hotel suite. 'Do you want to see my room'?, she asks him, using a well-worn cliché. He lies awkwardly on her bed, but, needless to say, nothing 'sexual' happens (similar to the iconic bed scene in *Lost in*

Translation). Jules reveals that she knows about Matt's affair, but she did not confront him about it, because she blamed herself for not spending enough time with him:

> It's classic, though, isn't it? The successful wife's husband feels ignored, his manhood is threatened so he acts out. The girlfriend I guess makes him feel more like a man. Sometimes I think maybe I don't know how to do the – *make him feel like a man* thing, you know? And anyway, is that even what I'm supposed to do? I mean, that's an exhausting endeavour [...]. I'm sure this is why I'm even entertaining this whole CEO thing... thinking maybe it will let me get my life back on track but...

Ben dissuades her from taking responsibility for this situation: 'I hate to be the feminist here [...], but you should be able to have a huge career and be brilliant without having to accept your husband is having an affair as some kind of payback'. He is not as forgiving as Jules, and he expresses anger towards Matt. Jules, in turn, confesses that she 'could potentially be forgiving' and that what really terrifies her is the possibility of being alone:

> I know if we got a divorce, he'd remarry, not necessarily to this girl, but someone and we know I'm not easy, so I could be like single forever which means and forgive me but I think about this sometimes in the middle of the night... [...] That I don't want to be buried alone. Paige will be with her husband, Matt will be with his new family and I'll be buried with strangers. I'll be in the single strangers section of the cemetery.

Ben, acting in the role of the 'Mr Fix It' that he is, immediately offers an easy solution: 'Okay, let's take that one off your plate. You can be buried with me and Molly. I happen to have room'.

This is when Jules, finally comforted, picks up the remote, clicks around and is relieved to land on a Gene Kelly and Debbie Reynolds performance of 'You Were Meant For Me' from *Singin' in the Rain*. As we can read in the script: 'They watch in silence at the optimism, innocence and youthful beauty on the screen. Ben turns to Jules, sees her eyes are shutting. Ben watches the movie alone, happy to be lost in another world' (Meyers 2014: 114). In the movie, we see the protagonist shedding a tear. Some moments before, he was telling Jules about his thirty-eight years of marriage, how he and his wife grew old together and how they loved each other. The romance onscreen seems to parallel Ben's own experience. Yet, the scene holds a sense of the lost pastness. As Mary Harrod suggests in her analysis of empathetic engagement in Heckerling's films:

Figure 6.5 Happy to be lost in another world: Ben shedding a tear over Gene Kelly and Debbie Reynolds's performance of 'You Were Meant For Me'.

> [L]oss is surely the catalyst for the most extreme emotional states, demanding the most radical shifts in psychic energies and thus eliciting that familiar sensation of sadness, yet simultaneously a pleasurable, inspirational feeling of opening up to the outside world and others in it. (2016: 68)

This opening up to the world 'applies whether the other subjectivities concerned are constructed as fictional (onscreen) or notionally implied through a sense of shared collective identity that transcends textuality to encompass interactive engagement, including fan cultures' (2016: 68). As with Ben, who relives the past romance, we inhabit these feelings 'with a simultaneous awareness of their historical constructedness' (Dyer 2007: 130).[45]

In foregrounding prior cinematic codes and conventions, Meyers clearly eulogises this past form of romance, but with her postmodern 'knowingness' she emphasises that it does not really exist. Going back to Schreiber's point, romance 'does not just have meaning as the narrative framework for Meyers's films [. . .], but is elevated to such a level of excess and meaning so hyper-aestheticised that it becomes performative' (2014: 147).[46] Its performative character is manifested earlier in the film in a conversation between Ben and Fiona, after Ben has taken her to a funeral for their first date. Fiona complains about the conventionality of the 'dinner date' and what she dubs the 'why aren't you married' conversation. Thus, they decide to fast-track the convention by describing themselves in under ten seconds each:

> Ben: I can do me in ten seconds. Ready? Widower. One son. Two grandkids. Spent my life manufacturing phone books which now no longer have a function. I'm currently working as an intern, havin' a ball and best news is, I have a crush on a girl I met at work. [. . .]
> Fiona: Divorced. Three beautiful daughters. One grandchild, a boy, on the way. I was sick a few years back. I'm not anymore. I'm an in-house e-commerce masseuse. Love my job and I finally met a man I actually want to hang out with.

This is precisely where the emotional intensity associated with 'woman's film' is 'juxtaposed with a sceptical attitude towards romance and a critique of past cinematic gender relations' (Garrett 2007: 11). Needless to say, for many feminist critics this desire to revisit old genres is deeply disturbing, as it is, at least partially, motivated by the nostalgic appreciation of the traditional gender roles associated with them. As Yvonne Tasker and Diane Negra warn us (2007), self-consciousness or irony cannot entirely obliterate the problematic emphasis on love and marriage in romcoms. But, while mainstream romantic comedies are predisposed to focus on heterosexual coupling and/or white, upper-middle class femininities – aspects which can be disempowering for a wide range of audiences – I would suggest, following Garrett (2007), that the distance placed between old, cinematically familiar notions of gender and contemporary sexual and social mores in *The Intern* inevitably undercuts, rather than reinforces, the patriarchal rationale of their antecedents. Not only does the film emphasise the broader shifts in sociocultural trends and perceptions of gender and power relations, but it also points to the

> inadequacy of a debate which is framed only in terms of postmodernist cinema as an aesthetic mode which either fails to engage with the past in any meaningful way or does so only in order to haul the generically based androcentrism associated with certain past styles back into the domain of popular contemporary cinematic representation. (Garrett 2007: 128)

'This big, beautiful, intricate thing that you created – it's a dream isn't it?' muses Ben, in a self-conscious allusion to Meyers's cinematic oeuvre. And, despite its 'default endings', there is a political hope in this Dream/Factory, to reuse Gaines's (2011) evocative formulation. Janice Radway's groundbreaking work on Harlequin novels argued that romance readers engage in a fantasy world 'to imagine a more perfect social state as a way of countering despair' (1984: 222). Radway encourages the cultural resistance implied in romance reading and argues that we should treat this form seriously: 'If we do not, we have already conceded the fight and, in the case of the romance at least, admitted the impossibility of creating a world where the vicarious pleasure supplied by its reading would be unnecessary' (1984: 222). Romantic comedy operates in a similar way, providing us with utopian longing, but also urging us to imagine social realities in which these fantasies would no longer be needed.

It's All 'About the Fit'

The study of *The Intern* as a (non-)romantic comedy reveals that Meyers rehearses a number of significant genre themes, as delineated by Radner in her study of the neo-feminist chick flick: the affective 'belonging together', the do-over, the double ending, the striver ethos, as well the emphasis on consumer culture and its importance in achieving self-fulfilment (2011: 143). The film is a good example of how this seemingly conservative terrain of the romcom can open up questions that disrupt such traditional interpretations: the possible disillusionment with postfeminist values, the unmasking of the prevailing sexism in the industry and of the return of the backlash against working mothers, as well as underscoring the performative nature of heterosexual coupling. Significantly – even if *The Intern* is very much of its time – it playfully invokes prior cinematic codes and conventions, clearly addressing what has been dubbed in discussions on postmodernism an 'informed viewer'. In pointing to past trajectories and possible future paths for romance films, it comments on changing gender roles, while continuing to provide the pleasures found in the genre of the romcom. Particularly interesting is the way in which the film destabilises the conventional gendered genre address, bridging 'masculine' and 'feminine' postmodernist cinematic codes: *The Intern* combines affect and the more 'cerebral' pleasures of reference-spotting – notably, channelling this affect in the male character played by De Niro. His status as an onlooker might seem patronising in many ways, but if we move beyond the oversimplified notion of gender-to-gender cinematic identification, and accept the mutability of gendered identities, then such a move might lead to more radical readings, not only in relation to image consumption, but also in relation to image-making – that is, the question of authorship. In fact, not only Jules – a professional women who works in a creative industry stigmatised as 'feminine' – but also Ben – who arguably stands for the conventions of classical Hollywood[47] – is a marker of Meyers's brand authorship within the romcom. The filmmaker creatively combines the 'old ways' with 'the new ways', and just like Ben, who needs to adapt to the new business, Meyers also needs to adapt to the constantly changing landscape of romantic comedy – for example, by including bromantic elements (however, as previously hinted, returning these features *with difference*). But, for all its self-awareness and revisions, *The Intern* feels like a classically constructed mainstream Hollywood genre film. While the film is permeated with some specific allusions, it also provides moments of 'diffuse generic referentiality', for which reason Harrod's proposed term of 'heightened genericity', rather than 'metagenericity', seems more apt here. The latter, explains Harrod,

> seems to imply self-awareness – initially on the part, as it were, of the film and ultimately in the mind of the viewer it addresses – given the literal meaning of *meta* as *post*, here suggesting less an affective 'feeling shape', than a later stage in cognitive processing. (2016: 55)

When Jules asks Ben if it was 'weird being back here' – referring to the refurbished warehouse where her company, About the Fit, is now situated and where Ben was previously in charge of overseeing the printing of phone books – he answers without hesitation: 'No, feels like home. Remodelled but home'. If we read this comment in a self-conscious manner, *The Intern* can be considered Meyers's creative statement about her skilful command of the romcom: far from *undoing* 'a tired and predictable genre' (Abbott and Jermyn 2009: 2), the filmmaker updates, revisits and comments on past and today's romantic comedies, proving their status as a remarkably generative and a continually regenerating film form.

Notes

1. Meyers began her career in the 1980s, when she co-wrote and co-produced films such as *Private Benjamin* (Howard Zieff, 1980) and *Baby Boom* (Charles Shyer, 1987) with her now ex-husband, Charles Shyer. Her first produced screenplay won her an Oscar nomination. Meyers's *Something's Gotta Give* (2003), with an US$80 million budget, and *The Holiday* (2006) and *It's Complicated* (2009), with an US$85 million budget each, all broke the US$200 million barrier (Box Office Mojo). *The Intern* is not far behind, as it has earned US$194,564,672 worldwide so far, against a budget of US$35 million. Needless to say, looking at box office performance is not the only way of evaluating the 'success' and 'popularity' of women filmmakers (see Jermyn 2017: 158).
2. For a discussion of Radner's definition of neo-feminism, see her 2011 book, *Neo-Feminist Cinema: Girly Films, Chick Flicks and Consumer Culture*.
3. In this context, it is worth mentioning that Meyers struggled to obtain financing for *The Intern*, as she explained in a number of interviews.
4. A few book chapters and articles should also be mentioned, including, notably, Wiggers (2010), Glitre (2011), Radner (2011), Schreiber (2014) and Sims (2014).
5. This is not to imply that Meyers's position as part of the dominant film industry does not pose challenges for feminist criticism. An unconditional celebration of her merits above other women's work risks reinforcing the discourse of 'exceptionality' (as discussed in the Introduction): similarly to other 'exceptional' women filmmakers studied in this volume, Meyers has frequently been perceived as 'an anomaly' or 'an aberration' in the business (Freeman 2015), while, to be sure, one could easily compare her work to that of Nora Ephron in Hollywood or Nicole Holofcener in the independent sector, just to give a few examples. In reference to the latter, see Schreiber's (2014) comparative analysis of Meyers's *It's Complicated* and Holofcener's *Friends with Money* (2006).
6. See: http://jezebel.com/which-nancy-meyers-kitchen-are-you-1733023749; http://

www.vogue.com/article/nancy-meyers-movie-interiors-shop-the-looks; http://www.architecturaldigest.com/gallery/intern-movie-set-design/all (accessed 20 May 2017).

7. Interestingly, Jermyn points to the idea of 'spaces of wonder' in Meyers's films – self-conscious moments when characters step back to appreciate their settings (2017: 154–8). According to Jermyn, Meyers 'understands her interior design to be both an important part of audience pleasure in her films and, linked to this, a cornerstone of her particular brand of Hollywood spectacle' (2017: 155).
8. Meyers herself confessed: 'I used to not want to talk about this. [Because] I thought that it takes away from us as filmmakers to talk about this' (in Larocca 2015).
9. As Radner observes, feminism produced 'a discourse that was both hostile to, and critical of, consumer culture and its ancillary industries' (2011: 196).
10. Critical discourse tends to conflate the chick flick and romcom labels. The term 'chick flick' refers to the most recent female-orientated cycles of romantic comedy, and other genres, dating from the mid-1990s. It is frequently understood as only one form of a popular phenomenon that has been described as 'chick culture', which also includes chick lit (associated with widely popular Helen Fielding's 1996 novel *Bridget Jones's Diary*) and chick TV (for example, the series *Sex and the City*, based on the book by Candace Bushnell), among others. In general terms, 'the chick culture boom both reflected and promoted the new visibility of women in popular culture' (Ferriss and Young 2008: 2), and was linked with the deliberate address to female audiences. In fact, as Ferriss and Young clarify, the term 'chick flick' dates back considerably further than the 1990s and used to be applied in a derogatory manner 'by unwilling male theatergoers to their girlfriends' film choices' (2008: 2).
11. See also Glitre (2011: 26).
12. For a historical overview of the genre, see Jeffers McDonald (2007).
13. This was not the case, however, with historical predecessors such as the screwball comedy, which has received the greatest volume of scholarly attention. In fact, as Mary Harrod shows (2015: 18), earlier comedy in general has been the subject of considerably more literature than more recent romcoms.
14. As Harrod astutely observes, paradoxically, 'second-wave feminism has been pivotal in shaping critical attitudes to the romance genre for several decades in the postwar period, condemning narratives which tend to idealise the heterosexual couple as a tool of patriarchal oppression' (2015: 16).
15. This incompatibility can be illustrated by their brief exchange at the end of their first two-minute meeting. Ben asks: 'Would you like the door open or closed?', to which Jules responds: 'Doesn't matter'. Ben exits, closing the door behind him, and Jules changes her mind: 'Open. Actually'.
16. As Jeffers clarifies: '[F]emale concerns, female stars and female audiences are all implicit in the term "chick flick," and a glance at the majority of romcoms available in cinemas and for home viewing bears out the dominance of women within the narratives and marketing' (2009: 147).
17. Jeffers traces this tendency in the 1970s/1980s 'Animal Comedy' – in particular, its 'gross-out' moments, such as *Animal House* (1978) and *Porky's* (1982). She argues that the homme-com blends these types of 'gross-out' moments with the romance plot of the standard romcom in order to appeal to male audiences.
18. The 1970s radical romantic comedies' focus on sex has been firmly eradicated since the rise of the Ephronesque romcom, according to Jeffers. 'Films like *Annie Hall* were aware of the importance of fulfilling sex to the success of the couple, and indeed to the well-being of both its members' (2009: 155). For the contrasting view, see, for example, Celestino Deleyto's (2011) article on the complexities of desire, space and sexual discourses in contemporary romcoms. On the other hand,

it should be acknowledged that 'gross-out' body humour is nowadays also found in 'female-oriented' narratives that include romcom elements, such as *Bridesmaids* (Paul Feig, 2011).
19. For example, the oft-commented 'sex' moments between Keaton and Nicholson in *Something's Gotta Give*. In Ephron's films, sex happens off-screen or, mostly, 'it just does not happen' (Jeffers 2009: 150).
20. It is true, however, that we do not see the sexual act, only the beginning of it.
21. Meyers herself is utterly convinced that her films are watched by both men and women. When she comments on the frequently pejorative use of the term 'chick flick', she says: '[T]here's a judgment attached to it, and that judgment is never applied to films that men also go to, though I don't think my movies are just attended by women' (in Larocca 2015).
22. As Glitre argues, this is a common trope for postfeminist chick flicks: '[P]ost-Ally McBeal, the career woman is increasingly imagined as a *fragile* figure, anxiously struggling to maintain (the facade of) success' (2011: 24 [emphasis in original]).
23. Janet McCabe (2009) gives some more examples of the post-classical romcom protagonists that learn sensitivity over the course of the film: Nicholas Cage in *Moonstruck* (Norman Jewison, 1987), Billy Crystal in *When Harry Met Sally* (Rob Reiner, 1989), Richard Gere in *Pretty Woman* (Garry Marshall, 1990), Al Pacino in *Frankie and Johnny* (Garry Marshall, 1991) and Tom Hanks in both *Sleepless in Seattle* (Nora Ephron, 1993) and *You've Got Mail* (Nora Ephron, 1998).
24. This connection between film and fashion is of long-standing. See Hilary Radner's (2011) analysis of *The Devil Wears Prada*.
25. For a discussion of the role of the makeover in contemporary 'chick flicks', see Suzanne Ferriss (2008).
26. In the case of this second film, Hathaway had to undergo an actual transformation in real life, enduring a gruelling diet to slim down. In an interview with *Us Weekly*, the actress discussed the weight loss regimen she and co-star Emily Blunt followed for the film, stating: 'I basically stuck with fruit, vegetables and fish [to slim down]. I wouldn't recommend that. Blunt and I would clutch at each other and cry because we were so hungry'. Available at: http://www.contactmusic.com/anne-hathaway/news/hathaway-starved-on-devil-wears-prada_1070987 (accessed 20 May 2017).
27. Andy only puts up with Miranda's excessively demanding treatment in hopes of getting a job as a journalist somewhere else.
28. It is worth noting here that, more recently, the actress has been a subject of harsh criticism and aggressive anti-fandom practices that popularised the term 'Hathahate' – especially during the 2013 Academy Awards season when she picked up a Best Supporting Actress Oscar for her role in *Les Misérables* (Tom Hopper, 2012). One might speculate that such phenomena attest to a recent backlash against successful women and/or their discursive visibility in the postfeminist media culture.
29. This location is important. As Deborah Jermyn has demonstrated, the Hollywood romcom constantly returns to New York as 'cinema's romantic playground' (2009: 12). Its romanticism can be partly linked to 'the city having fostered the figure of the "independent woman" and mass immigration in the late nineteenth to mid-twentieth century' (2009: 4). However, while most chick flicks are set in Manhattan – such as *Maid in Manhattan* (Wayne Wang, 2002), *How to Lose a Guy in 10 Days* (Donald Petrie, 2003) and *Confessions of a Shopaholic* (P. J. Hogan, 2009), which clearly underscore the glamour of the New York fashion scene and strengthen the links between the chick flick and the fashion industry (Radner 2011: 144) – *The Intern* is located in Brooklyn, which suggests some changes from the previous variants of the romcom.

30. Many thanks to Deborah Jermyn for this insightful comment.
31. Interestingly, in contrast to Jules and Becky, 'the boys' do interact in the office, which points to the gendered dimension of this shift.
32. For a contrasting view, see Jermyn (2018).
33. I would like to thank Andrea Ruthven for this interesting remark.
34. What is more, Jules can be easily compared with other, although much older, heroines in Meyers's romcoms. Katharina Glitre (2011) compares *Private Benjamin*, *Baby Boom* and *What Women Want*, reading them as 'a condensation of the historical trajectory of Hollywood's representation of independent women': 'Act 1, a woman breaks free of patriarchal oppression, proving her self-worth by becoming independent; Act 2, she discovers the difficulty of having it all; Act 3, lonely and frustrated, she decides the cost of independence is too high, settling down with a nice "new man" for a happily-ever-after ending' (2011: 19). We could trace some interesting comparisons between *Baby Boom* and *The Intern*, especially in terms of motherhood and professional careers. In the former, the career promotion of the protagonist (played by Diane Keaton) is suddenly jeopardised when she becomes the caretaker of her cousin's baby. For Giltre, *Baby Boom* is an example of the post-feminist 'retreatist' narrative and, in fact, all Meyers's films are conservative: 'All too often, postfeminist culture represents (white, middle-class) women's achievement of social and economic independence as being at the expense of femininity, relationships, and happiness' (2011: 21). Although I do not necessarily agree with this reading, it is highly illustrative of how Meyers's films present an astute social commentary on changing gender roles in contemporary romcoms.
35. Available at: http://www.bafta.org/media-centre/transcripts/bafta-bfi-screenwriters-lecture-series-nancy-meyers (accessed 20 May 2017).
36. If a demonstration of this were needed, at the time of completing this book the scandal surrounding Hollywood producer Harvey Weinstein burst into the headlines, exposing a history of sexual harassment allegations and legal settlements that concealed the assault claims. In this context, it is telling that this explicit scene denouncing sexism did not make it to the final version of the film.
37. Indeed, as Deborah Jermyn observes, 'the entire premise of *The Holiday* is built around the concept of two women, Iris (Kate Winslet) and Amanda (Cameron Diaz) swapping their homes for the Christmas holidays, where the women are able to get to know something of one another without ever meeting precisely through what their homes say about them' (2018: 63).
38. Radner focuses on Erica in *Something's Gotta Give* – in particular, her dedication to redoing her houses. 'This expansion of the self to its surroundings mimics the evolution of makeover culture extending through the various parts of the body to the body's environment as the required arenas of cultivation, manifest in the proliferation of makeover programming on television, covering the body, clothing, cooking, gardening, home improvement, etc.' (2011: 180).
39. There is another nod to Meyers's concern with interior design when Davis comments on Ben's impeccable bedroom: 'I like that you do the throw pillow thing'.
40. Ben has been told that the key is 'under the flower pot', but when they arrive they discover countless flower pots – a similar situation to the one where Andy, in *The Devil Wears Prada*, has to leave 'The Book' on the 'table with the flowers', encountering many different 'tables with flowers' in her boss's house.
41. Nicholson's masculinity is represented as 'something that must be tamed or even surmounted if the neo-feminist heroine is to reach her goals' (Radner 2011: 177). Ben, in turn, does not evolve significantly in the story. As Meyers explained: 'I change every man I've ever written. I'm always working them into getting it. I don't change this man' (in Keegan 2015).

42. Interestingly, the mobilisation of the mid-life crisis as a frame of reference does not suggest a significant departure in Meyers's work, but it was read as such, as several reviews of the film demonstrate. 'One of the biggest problems with *The Intern* is that she abandons what is so vital to her success – talking about older women', writes Melissa Silverstein in *IndieWire* (2015). These comments testify to the prevalence of the paradigm of 'images of women' in the critical circulation of women's work and the type of expectations that are placed on women filmmakers.
43. Ben's confession recalls many of the scenes in *Analyze This* – a gangster comedy about a psychiatrist whose 'number one' patient is an insecure mob boss played by De Niro.
44. At the beginning of *It's Complicated*, for example, the protagonist, Jane, is more observer than participant (see Schreiber 2014: 149).
45. On nostalgia for 'the golden age' and cinephilia in Meyers's work, see also Jermyn (2017: 23–4).
46. There is no better example of this than 'the memorable sequence from *Something's Gotta Give* in which a heartbroken Erica sobs uncontrollably and unpredictably while she writes her play amid the backdrop of her exquisitely adorned Oceanside Hamptons house, accompanied by the sounds of Edith Piaf' (Schreiber 2014: 147).
47. Jules hates people who do not speak fast enough, and Ben significantly teaches her how to 'slow down' (for instance, in the final park scene). Ben, who has 'some time on his hands', stands for the classical form in terms of its more leisurely pace. In fact, Meyers's films have often been accused of being excessively long or languorous, which Meyer herself recognises: 'I've always made movies in a sort of classic form, the way people have done it for a long time' (in Dawes 2009).

AFTERWORD: DESPERATELY SEEKING WONDER WOMEN

In 'Women's Cinema as Counter-Cinema' ([1973] 2000a) – one of the founding documents of feminist film studies – Claire Johnston suggests, assuming the political 'we' typical of the 1970s, that 'in order to counter our objectification in the cinema, our collective fantasies must be released' (2000a: 32). The word 'counter' – also very much of its moment – clearly announces her oppositional stance; yet, in contrast to Mulvey's model of negative aesthetics, which precipitated the later frequent privileging of 'counter' (namely, art-house or experimental) cinema, Johnston insists that women filmmakers should work on film language *in* mainstream narratives. At the same time that Johnston makes a powerful argument for looking back on the work of women directors in studio-era Hollywood, in particular Dorothy Arzner and Ida Lupino – raising the issue of 'authorship versus genre' in films made by women and anticipating the later debates on contradictions displayed by classical Hollywood cinema – her project is also future-oriented. As Patricia White observes in her useful account of the status of this essay in the genealogy of feminist film studies, Johnston's category of women's cinema is an emergent one, 'to be illuminated and shaped by critical and curatorial as much as by artistic/activist practice' (White 2015: 9; see also White 2006).

In retrospect, it is perhaps not surprising that Johnston's model was overshadowed by that of Mulvey's, which turned out to be much more influential in shaping critical frameworks for thinking about women's cinema and feminist film practice, and was probably more appropriate with regards to the directions that women's filmmaking has often taken in the intervening years. However, the overwhelming diversity of forms and concerns in films made by women today exceeds even the most flexible conceptualisations of counter-cinema (Butler 2002: 21). In the first decade of the twenty-first century, multiple factors came together that force us to theorise about genre, authorship and women's cinema in new ways. Due to the expansion of training possibilities, transnational financing and the reduction of film production costs thanks to digital technologies, many more women have access to the tools of narrative filmmaking, which defines the format of entertainment film. At the same time, as White observes, 'women and girls became targets of national and international development discourses, affecting the content of films as well as opportunities for women in media making' (White 2015: 199).

The period has witnessed significant changes in terms of the discursive visibility of women's embrace of mainstream genre production, as well as the critical and industrial recognition of some of these filmmakers – Bigelow's Best Director Oscar win for *The Hurt Locker* and Coppola's recent triumph at the Cannes Film Festival for what she considers to be her first 'properly' genre film, Southern Gothic thriller *The Beguiled*, epitomise this phenomenon. No less significant is the unprecedented visibility of other texts partly or wholly authored by women – if we adopt an extended concept of authorship – such as *The Hunger Games*, *Twilight* and *Fifty Shades of Grey* franchises, the recent reboots of traditionally male-focused and -oriented sagas and films, such as *Mad Max: Fury Road* (George Miller, 2015), *Ghostbusters* (Paul Feig, 2016) and *Rogue One: A Star Wars Story* (Gareth Edwards, 2016), which displaced the typically male protagonists in favour of female leads (and which open up questions, rarely examined in film theory, of how performance tracks issues of genre and actors as producers of underlying texts); and the women-dominated practices of rewriting and reappropriation such as fanfiction and fanvids, which attest to the important role of the Internet in widening the accessibility and reach of women's audio-visual creativity. Furthermore, over the last couple of decades, there has been a remarkable growth of conferences, festivals and film courses devoted to women's participation in cinema and television,[1] which are also gradually starting to acknowledge the recalibrations of the nature of women's involvement across the spectrum of popular cultural production. Perhaps the most telling example of this trend is a new film festival devoted to female directors of genre films which was run at Film Forum (New York) in June 2016. Evocatively named 'Genre is a Woman', the festival showcased a wide selection of works, ranging from pre-Code to contemporary era filmmakers: Alice Guy-Blaché, Ida Lupino, Stephanie Rothman, Doris Wishman, Sondra Locke, Katt Shea, Penelope Spheeris, Mary Harron, Kathryn Bigelow, Ana Lily Amirpour and Kelly Reichardt. As the festival's official announcement explains, women film directors, 'often typed as the purveyors of domestic melodramas and romantic comedies, have, from cinema's very beginnings, embraced what's thought to be an all-male preserve: the so-called "genre picture"'.² Spanning the length of film history, the festival featured genres as diverse as film noir, horror, science fiction, Westerns and 'no-budget sexploitation' flicks, combining art-house and B-movies, independently shot genre films and commercial Hollywood hits, such as *American Psycho* (Mary Harron, 2000) and *Fast Times at Ridgemont High* (Amy Heckerling, 1982). The two-week event was curated by Giulia D'Agnolo Vallan – a New York-based journalist, film historian and US programmer for the Venice Film Festival – who told *Women and Hollywood*:

> I have done books on John Carpenter, George Romero, Walter Hill, John Landis, and Clint Eastwood: genre is my passion. And I always found it interesting to see the distinctive perspective women filmmakers bring to what is still considered a 'man's world.' Violence, sex, crime, and the darkness in the human soul are the texture of genre cinema. They are all part of our collective experience – not just the male one. The vision, the style, the depth, the humor, and the subversive spirit that the directors in this series have brought to their representation proves it. Still, while genre has often been a stepping stone in the career of male directors, it has proved a less easy path for women, which I find interesting. (in Cipriani 2016)

Her comments – even if they might confirm, rather than shift, the inherent male-gendering of certain genres and, possibly, the marginalisation of 'domestic melodramas and romantic comedies' in the public consciousness – are highly illuminating, as they point to the difficulties that women filmmakers face when stepping into forms that are culturally considered 'off-limits'. If, as I noted in Chapter 1, genre cinema was traditionally seen as a form of a feminised culture, and men were those who were notoriously elevated as genre auteurs, both in the sphere of the more 'legitimate' male-orientated forms and in the contemptible realm of melodramas and romcoms, then Vallan's revisionist project of recuperating female genre auteurs offers multiple feminist potentialities for thinking about women's cinema. It also proves that women's penetration of mainstream fiction is not new, suggestively pointing to an 'incursion [. . .] into a discourse that belongs to them' (Zecchi 2018: 95).

'Genre is a Woman' indexes emerging critical perceptions regarding genre and women's cinema, which can have decisive implications for women's careers in Hollywood. At the time of writing this Afterword, *Wonder Woman* (2017) – the first superhero DC Comic film directed by a woman, Patty Jenkins – has officially become the highest grossing live-action film directed by a female filmmaker and the second-highest grossing film of 2017 behind *Beauty and the Beast* (Bill Condon, 2017).³ With its US$713,900,000 total earnings at the worldwide box office, it took over Phyllida Lloyd's musical *Mamma Mia!* (2008), which grossed US$609,800,000 and, according to industry claims, is 'holding better than any superhero movie in 15 years' (McClintock 2017). For Melissa Silverstein, its success could herald a new era in the Hollywood film industry in terms of female characterisation (in Malo 2017) and, I would add here, also in terms of hiring opportunities for women, especially in directorial roles. *Wonder Woman* makes history as only the fourth women-directed film to be released with a budget over US$100 million. The first was Kathryn Bigelow's 2002 thriller *K-19: The Widowmaker*, followed by the Wachowskis' *Cloud Atlas* (2012) and *Jupiter Ascending* (2015). Sony and Marvel have already announced major superhero films featuring female lead characters (Silver Sable and Black Cat) that are to be directed or co-directed by women.

However, it is also important to point to the risks and challenges of such newly gained visibility. As Sophie Mayer aptly observes: 'Authorship, like box-office success, is at once crucial to coverage and circulation for feminist cinema, and deeply problematic, invoking Default Man models of solitary genius' (2016: 16). While *The New York Times* reports that Patty Jenkins 'just broke Hollywood's superhero glass ceiling' (Barnes 2017), the ceiling remains firmly in place for most female directors, as demonstrated by Martha Lauzen, who since 1998 has been tracking the number of women employed on top-grossing films annually. In fact, Jenkins herself has experienced considerable difficulties in making films throughout her career. Fifteen years ago, she wrote and directed *Monster* (released in 2003, her only feature film before *Wonder Woman*), a critically acclaimed indie biopic about a female serial killer that earned Charlize Theron an Oscar for Best Actress. Following this success, Jenkins worked in television – directing the pilot of *The Killing* and other high-profile TV shows – and in 2011 she was hired to shoot the sequel to the superhero blockbuster *Thor*. However, she left the project before it came to fruition – with Marvel citing 'creative differences' as the reason, and Jenkins herself explaining years after:

> There have been things that have crossed my path that seemed like troubled projects [...] And I thought, 'If I take this, it'll be a big disservice to women. If I take this knowing it's going to be trouble and then it looks like it was me, that's going to be a problem. If they do it with a man, it will just be yet another mistake that the studio made'. (in Siegel 2017)

While Jenkins, similarly to Bigelow, repeatedly downplays the centrality of gender to her style and position within Hollywood cinema, the critical circulation of her film is inevitably marked by discourses that celebrate an individual filmmaker (female auteur, as unique among the men) and the empowering potential of the female action heroine, both of which are narratives of female progress, symptomatic of a neoliberal and postfeminist climate. While some scholars consider the general rise in popularity of these new 'action chicks' as more or less straightforward evidence of women's increased power and status – 'a sign of the different roles available to women in real life' (Inness 2004: 6) – other writers have been more sceptical about the progressive potential of such representations. Lisa Coulthard, for instance, points to the 'apolitical, individualistic, and capitalistic [. . .] celebration of the superficial markers of power', which – for all its irony and pastiche that underpin these texts – is, in fact, not transgressive at all, as it returns these action heroines to a normative femininity or a fantasy of individualised violence (2007: 173).[4] The difficulty in thinking about a heroine's (individual) quest for power echoes the complex, fraught and ambivalent terrain for conceptualising the woman filmmaker,

> whose exceptional status marks her out as exemplary of feminist success for individual women and the exception that proves the rule of women's 'normal' choices made in general (for example, the idea that 'normal' women would choose motherhood over a high-powered career). (Cobb 2015: 50)[5]

The debates concerning the rare presence of female auteurs in Hollywood are confirmed, and additionally fuelled, by statistics, usually quoted on the occasion of such events. Nevertheless, as White rightly observes in drawing on Kathleen McHugh's critique of the prevalent models of scholarship on women directors, an excessive focus on statistics 'amounts merely to a tally of "exceptional anomalies"', for which reason the scholar posits that 'attending to the discourses that support the visibility of women filmmakers [. . .] and dismantling their exceptional and anomalous status through close reading, helps reveal an incipient redistribution of image-making power' (2015: 41). Even though her comments refer to the context of international festivals and the art-house sector – a commercialised niche market of women's cinema where female filmmakers are steadily growing in numbers – they can be easily applied to the Hollywood context. Given women's increased visibility in the mainstream turf of genre production, and precisely because they are particularly underrepresented among directors of the world's 'best' films, it is imperative to address and challenge the 'auteurist discourses of exceptional individual achievement' to reveal and stimulate 'an incipient redistribution of image-making power' (White 2015: 41) within the commercial global media sphere.

What I have attempted in this book, then, is the critical interrogation of the issues inherent in questions regarding what happens when women do genre films in Hollywood or at the penumbra of Hollywood, focusing on a selection of films through which these questions can be traced. Without diminishing the significance of the breakthrough that these films represent for the filmmakers under discussion, the close reading of these texts through the optics of genre problematises the authorial or female exemplariness, while also – with its attention not only on what they 'undo', but also focused on what they 'do' with genre – proves their undeniably unique talents. In acknowledging their skilful command or interpretation of genre, in which they often pursue cultural commentary on the gendered power relations, I have tried to avoid the common fallacy of subversion, starting from the premise that genre films typically lend themselves to multivalent tensions in their political possibilities – 'seemingly reactionary one moment, but able to surprise us the next' (Jermyn 2018: 70). Johnston ([1973] 2000a: 23) famously argues that Myth – or ideology – operates through 'icons', but these 'icons' are also Myth's weakest point: they can be rewritten, reappropriated or denaturalised. 'Yet if "icons" are saturated with the history of their previous usages, then they can also be reworked in less overtly dislocating ways', observes Sue Thornham (2012: 33). This is where Meaghan Morris's formulation of women's cinema as a 'minor cinema', taken up by Alison Butler (2002), is particularly apt. If 'gaps, fissures and ruptures' (Bergstrom 1979: 21) are integral to the operation of the major language of genres, then their generative power should be acknowledged in this wider project of the recuperation of women genre auteurs.

But, as Deborah Jermyn argues in reference to the critical reception of Meyers's work, it is striking and significant how 'much more tremendously vocal the critical voices pointing to conservative readings of her films have been to date, so that attention has barely been paid to any potential to locate other, more textured [...] commentary at work in her oeuvre' (2018: 70) – an observation that could be extended to other filmmakers under discussion. This 'outright resistance to the possibility she could have anything more than one-dimensional vision' (Jermyn 2018: 70), often manifested not only in the mainstream press but also in feminist scholarly writing, is embedded within the complex processes of the gendering of genres, as well as the uneasy status of women's film authorship in the postfeminist context. Perhaps one of the most perturbing aspects is how little has changed since the publication of *How to Suppress Women's Writing* (1983) by Joanna Russ more than three decades ago. The same sexist stereotypes and gender-based assumptions which many women writers were subjected to continue to surround contemporary filmmakers, even though they are sometimes expressed in more subtle ways:

> She didn't write it. (But if it's clear she did the deed . . .) // She wrote it, but she shouldn't have. (It's political, sexual, masculine, feminist.) // She wrote it, but look what she wrote about. (The bedroom, the kitchen, her family. Other women!) // She wrote it, but she wrote only one of it. ('Jane

Eyre. Poor dear, that's all she ever . . .') // She wrote it, but she isn't really an artist, and it isn't really art. (It's a thriller, a romance, a children's book. It's sci-fi!) // She wrote it, but she had help. (Robert Browning. Branwell Brontë. Her own 'masculine side.') // She wrote it, but she's an anomaly. (Woolf. With Leonard's help. . . .) // She wrote it BUT. . . . (Russ 1983: book cover)

As Jermyn's analysis of a repeated derision of Meyers as a *woman* director shows, it is still urgent to unpack, scrutinise and rebuke these acutely gendered discourses. Equally timely is White's call to question the myth of isolated achievement and anomalousness – that is, seeing a woman filmmaker as 'the sole *femme* – not one woman (director) among many' (White 2015: 32).

This is not to suggest that the critical reception of the films studied in this book was necessarily one-dimensional or unproblematic. The constructed opposition between women's culture and men's culture had a profound impact on how these works were read and points to the several critical strategies employed to make sense of these particular examples of women's cinema: celebration of films as 'universal' and assimilation of them into a cinematic canon; rejection as anti-feminist because of their reiteration of generic codes and the assumed complicity with patriarchal ideology; and acclamation of some of the films as feminist subversion of 'male' genres.

The five chapters in this book work in conjunction with one another to provide contrasting examples of a woman filmmaker's brand image and suggest that her gender and the genre in which she chooses to work can be utilised by studios, critics and spectators to isolate her as a novelty or an oddity, or to reaffirm gender stereotypes – for example, because her film represented scenes of a violent or sexual nature (Bigelow, Cody and Kusama), because she was not particularly interested in depicting women's stories (Bigelow), or completely the opposite (Meyers), because her film subverted forms codified as male (Reichardt) or because it displayed her authorial, recognisable style (Coppola, Bigelow and Reichardt). Labelling women filmmakers in certain ways might help Hollywood executives, journalists and film theorists to account for the female 'intruders' within the predominantly male industry. However, I contend that the discourses around 'exceptional achievement', 'authorial subversion', 'authenticity' and, in some cases, 'masculinity' that surround these women filmmakers tend to obscure other possible dimensions of their films: the popularity among a wide range of audiences, engagement with sexism or racism filtered through the generic and intertextual connections with other women's work, to give only some examples.

This book also shows a variety of ways in which women filmmakers negotiated within these terms and dealt with this reality, illustrating the complex, multilayered nature of their authorship: as a celebrity director, as an auteur, as a marketing tool, as the industry outsider who works at the margins of the dominant system, as a feminist icon and as a filmmaker who resists the horizon of expectations generated by the stereotypical conception of feminism.[6] Rather than providing definitive answers, I have sought to raise some questions about women authorship in the contemporary global media sphere: what expectations did her gender bring to bear on the kinds of films she made? How did she negotiate these expectations in relation to her public persona? How did reviewers interpret women's films? It is this complex network of discourses that future work on women filmmakers needs to scrutinise, so that we can offer a more complex understanding of this production than characterising it, as Johnston herself did, as 'simply films made by women in a man's cinema' (in White 2006: 147). Equally urgent is the reconfiguration of the equation of authorship with the director and the acknowledgement of the myriad of often invisible roles involved in genre making, such as production, costume design, writing, performance and the role of audience and fan rewriting of shared generic materials (see Harrod and Paszkiewicz 2018) – practices that make evident the role of women in the publicness of genre, and cinema, in a wider sense. The insistently individualist nature of film authorship might prove uncomfortable for some women directors and their film practice, especially as regards genre-oriented projects which do not fit easily within traditional auteurist discourses of exceptionality and ownership. On the other hand, I am convinced that the study of female directors in a wider variety of contexts is vital for feminist film theories. Broadening our research to the use of genres in non-US contexts, transmigration of genres between national cultures, intersections of gender with race, nationality and class in and beyond dominant industries might help denounce, as Christine Gledhill observes, 'the limitation of genre theory to Hollywood and of gender as a totalising identity' (2012: 1), as well as allow for a transnational theorisation of women's cinema that would challenge the traditional approaches based on Western frameworks, methodologies and film texts (see White 2015).

As I have shown in this book, the benefits of considering the mode of generic production not as an obstacle, but as a resource for creative imagining, are multiple. Gledhill convincingly argues that

> acknowledging the malleability of genre conventions and the fluidity of their boundaries opens the way for innovative 're-writing' by women media makers of the tropes of violence, uncanny terror, romantic yearning and reversal that lie latent within the aesthetic and emotional storehouse of Hollywood's genres. (2018: xii)

Genres provide not only repertoires of cultural materials, but also 'concrete possibilities for intervention through generic renewal, re-inflection and contestation' (2018: xi). Women have a crucial role in this public social vision, both as impactful producers and media consumers.

Ultimately, genre has the potential to reposition women filmmakers as female auteurs on several levels. It urges us to shift from romantic fictions of 'autonomous' being to the sociality of 'genre's generative powers' (Dyer 2007: 176);[7] from desperately seeking a Wonder Woman to 'accepting that you are in the realm of the already said [. . .] within the limits and potentialities of the cultural construction of thought and feeling' (Dyer 2007: 180). According to Richard Dyer, pastiche (and thereby genre) can 'allow us to feel our connection to the affective frameworks, the structures of feeling, past and present, that we inherit and pass on. That is to say, it can enable us to know ourselves affectively as historical beings' (2007: 180). Given the inspirational influence exerted on this project by Gaines's stimulating theorisation of the women filmmakers' role in 'ingenuities of cultural recombination' (2012: 20), it is apt to close this book with acknowledgment of my own connection to the framework I inherited and now pass on:

> The generosity of film genre is its assumption that all know and feel – no privileged auteur knows and feels more than an audience member or any of the other creative personnel on the motion picture production set [. . .]. The director and the actors step into the genre which, like a ready-made, takes over and generates the work we have historically designated as 'theirs.' If genre is the locus of genius, however, is not 'theirs' more properly 'ours'? (2012: 27)

This eloquent formulation conveys my own sense of the 'generous' and 'generative' work of genre, which I strived to reflect in this book. I believe that situating women's embrace of popular forms within this potentially positive and appropriative framework of interpretation poses compelling questions about the future of the intersections between gender, genre and women's film authorship and the degree to which female-authored films can align with political discussions around feminism and women's capacity to challenge traditional industry boundaries.

Notes

1. For instance, the Console-ing Passions, Women and the Silent Screen and Doing Women's Film and Television History conferences, the International Women Film Pioneers Project at Columbia University and the British-based Women's Film and Television History Network – UK/Ireland.
2. Available at: http://filmforum.org/series/genre-is-a-woman-series (accessed 20 May 2017).
3. In terms of a movie by female and male co-directors, Jennifer Lee and Chris Buck's *Frozen* (2013) is currently at the top of the box office list with US$1.28

billion of total earnings worldwide. See: www.boxofficemojo.com/ (accessed 20 June 2017).
4. See also Andrea Ruthven (2015) on representing heroic women in contemporary popular culture.
5. This reflects what Diane Negra labels 'a platitudinous postfeminist culture that continually celebrates reductions and essentialisms [. . .] and [. . .] fetishizes female power and desire while consistently placing these within firm limits' (2009: 4).
6. Some filmmakers, such as Meyers or Cody, consciously use feminism as a part of their commercial identity. Arguably, feminism has become visible and saleable material in Hollywood over the last couple of years (for example, Emma Watson's 2014 speech on feminism at the UN Women's HeforShe launch event; Patricia Arquette's speech about equal pay at the Oscars in 2015; Meryl Streep starting a screenwriting workshop for women; and recent initiatives such as 'The Women of Hollywood Speak Out' [Dowd 2015]). These initiatives bring much-needed attention to the problem of gender inequality, but at the same time they undoubtedly contribute to the commodification of feminism, as observed by a number of commentators.
7. As Dyer observes: 'Contemporary cultural values for the past couple of centuries put a premium on thinking and feeling autonomously out of the inner imperatives of the self' (2007: 180).

BIBLIOGRAPHY

Abbott, Stacey and Deborah Jermyn (eds) (2009), *Falling in Love Again: Romantic Comedy in Contemporary Cinema*, New York: I. B. Tauris.
Abramovitch, Ingrid (2012), 'An exclusive Q&A with Nancy Meyers', *Elle Décor*, 2 July, http://www.elledecor.com/celebrity-style/celebrity-homes/news/a5373/an-exclusive-qa-with-nancy-meyers-a/ (accessed 20 May 2017).
Abu-Lughod, Lila (2013), *Do Muslim Women Need Saving?*, Cambridge, MA, and London: Harvard University Press.
Adorno, Theodor and Max Horkheimer (1979), *Dialectic of Enlightenment*, London: New Left Books.
Alleva, Richard (2011), 'Departures "Jane Eyre" & "Meek's Cutoff"', *Commonweal*, 3 June, pp. 19–20.
Altman, Rick (1999), *Film/Genre*, London: British Film Institute.
Andrew, Dudley (1984), *Concepts in Film Theory*, London: Oxford University Press.
Andrew, Geoff (1962), 'Editorial', *Movie*, no. 5, pp. 6–7.
Ang, Ien (1985), *Watching Dallas: Soap Opera and the Melodramatic Imagination*, London: Methuen.
Angelo, Megan (2011), 'From stripper to screenwriting star: how Diablo Cody's sharp tongue conquered Hollywood', *Business Insider*, 8 December, http://www.businessinsider.com/diablo-cody-young-adult-2011-12?op=1 (accessed 20 May 2017).
Backman Rogers, Anna (2012), 'The historical threshold: crisis, ritual and liminality in Sofia Coppola's *Marie Antoinette* (2006)', *Relief: Révue Électronique de Littérature Française*, vol. 6, no. 1, pp. 80–97.
Backman Rogers, Anna (2016), '"A market of the senses; your relations are of power": the female body as decorative object and commodity in Sofia Coppola's *Marie Antoinette* (2006)', Film-Philosophy Conference, http://www.film-philosophy.com/conference/index.php/conf/FP2016/paper/view/1276 (accessed 20 May 2017).
Badley, Linda (2016), 'Down to the bone: neo-neorealism and genre in contemporary women's indies', in Linda Badley, Claire Perkins and Michele Schreiber (eds), *Indie*

Reframed: Women's Filmmaking and Contemporary American Independent Cinema, Edinburgh: Edinburgh University Press, pp. 121–37.

Badley, Linda (2018), 'Performance and gender politics in Mary Harron's female celebrity anti-biopics', in Mary Harrod and Katarzyna Paszkiewicz (eds), *Women Do Genre in Film and Television*, New York and London: Routledge, pp. 23–40.

Baldwin, Sarah (2010), 'Sigourney Weaver: James Cameron lost out on Oscar because he "didn't have breasts"', *The Guardian*, 14 April, http://www.theguardian.com/film/2010/apr/14/sigourney-weaver-james-cameron-oscars-breasts (accessed 20 May 2017).

Barker, Jennifer M. (2009), *The Tactile Eye: Touch and The Cinematic Experience*, Berkeley: University of California Press.

Barker, Martin, Ernest Mathijs and Xavier Mendik (2006), 'Menstrual monsters: the reception of the *Ginger Snaps* cult horror franchise', *Film International*, vol. 4, no. 21, pp. 68–77.

Barnes, Brooks (2017), '*Wonder Woman* deflects doubt to win battle at the box office', *The New York Times*, 4 June, https://www.nytimes.com/2017/06/04/movies/wonder-woman-deflects-doubt-to-win-battle-at-the-box-office.html?mcubz=0 (accessed 20 May 2017).

Barthes, Roland ([1967] 1984), 'La mort de l'auteur', in *Le Bruissement de la langue*, Paris: Seuil, pp. 61–7.

Baudrillard, Jean (2001), 'The Gulf War did not take place', in Mark Poster (ed.), *Jean Baudrillard: Selected Writings*, Cambridge: Polity Press, pp. 231–53.

Baudry, Jean-Louis (1975), 'Le dispositif: approches métapsychologiques de l'impression de réalité', *Communications*, vol. 23, no. 1, pp. 56–72.

Baxter, Charles (1997), *Burning Down the House: Essays on Fiction*, St Paul: Graywolf Press.

Bazin, André ([1958–62] 2008), *¿Qué es el cine?*, Madrid: Rialp.

Benjamin, Walter ([1931] 1972), 'A short history of photography', *Screen*, vol. 13, no. 1, pp. 5–26.

Benjamin, Walter ([1936] 2008), *The Work of Art in the Age of Mechanical Reproduction*, London: Penguin, Kindle Edition.

Bennett, Bruce and Bülent Diken (2011), '*The Hurt Locker*: cinematic addiction, "critique," and the War on Terror', *Cultural Politics*, vol 7, no. 2, pp. 165–88.

Benson-Allott, Caetlin (2010), 'Undoing violence: politics, genre, and duration in Kathryn Bigelow's cinema', *Film Quarterly*, vol. 64, no. 2, pp. 33–43.

Berardinelli, James (2015), '*The Intern*', *Reel Views*, 24 September, http://www.reelviews.net/reelviews/intern-the (accessed 20 May 2017).

Berenstein, Rhona J. (1996), *Attack of the Leading Ladies: Gender, Sexuality, and Spectatorship in Classic Horror Cinema*, New York: Columbia University Press.

Bergstrom, Janet (1977), '*Jeanne Dielman, 23 Quai du Commerce, 1080 Bruxelles* by Chantal Akerman', *Camera Obscura*, no. 2, pp. 114–18.

Bergstrom, Janet (1979), 'Rereading the work of Claire Johnston', *Camera Obscura*, no. 3–4, pp. 21–31.

Berlant, Lauren (2007), 'Nearly utopian, nearly normal: post-Fordist affect in *La Promesse* and *Rosette*', *Public Culture*, vol. 19, no. 2, pp. 273–301.

Berlant, Lauren (2011), *Cruel Optimism*, Durham: Duke University Press.

Berlant, Lauren (2015), 'Structures of unfeeling: mysterious skin', *International Journal of Politics, Culture and Society*, vol. 28, pp. 191–213.

Beugnet, Martine (2007), *Cinema and Sensation: French Film and the Art of Transgression*, Edinburgh: Edinburgh University Press.

Bingham, Dennis (2010), *Whose Lives Are They Anyway? The Biopic as Contemporary Film Genre*, New Brunswick, NJ: Rutgers University Press.

Bingham, Dennis (2013), 'The lives and times of the biopic', in Robert A. Rosenstone and Constantin Parvulescu (eds), *A Companion to the Historical Film*, Malden, MA: Wiley-Blackwell, pp. 233–54.

Biskind, Peter (2004), *Down and Dirty Pictures: Miramax, Sundance and the Rise of Independent Film*, New York: Simon & Schuster.

Blakeley, Kiri (2010), 'Kathryn Bigelow vs. James Cameron: an Oscar-themed battle of the exes', *Forbes*, 2 February, http://www.forbes.com/2010/02/02/james-cameron-avatar-kathryn-bigelow-hurt-locker-forbes-woman-time-oscar-nominations.html (accessed 20 May 2017).

Blanchot, Maurice (1987), 'Everyday speech', *Yale French Studies*, vol. 73, pp. 12–20.

Bloch, Ernst (1986), *The Principle of Hope*, vol. I, Oxford: Basil Blackwell.

Bordwell, David (1981), *The Films of Carl-Theodor Dreyer*, Berkeley: University of California Press.

Bordwell, David and Kristin Thompson (2011), 'Good and good for you', *Observations on Film Art*, http://www.davidbordwell.net/blog/2011/07/10/good-and-good-for-you/ (accessed 20 May 2017).

Bradshaw, Peter (2015), '*The Intern* review – a too-sucrose Ephron-lite cringe-fest', *The Guardian*, 28 August, http://www.guardian.co.uk/film/2009/aug/28/the-hurt-locker-review (accessed 20 May 2017).

Braidotti, Rosi (1991), *Patterns of Dissonance. A Study of Women in Contemporary Philosophy*, Cambridge: Polity Press.

Brinkema, Eugenie (2014), *The Forms of the Affects*, Durham: Duke University Press.

Bruno, Giuliana (2002), *Atlas of Emotion: Journeys in Art, Architecture, and Film*, London: Verso.

Brunsdon, Charlotte (1997), *Screen Tastes: Soap Opera to Satellite Dishes*, London: Routledge.

Buhrmester, Jason (2009), 'Diablo Cody says no', *Inked*, 2 September, http://www.inkedmag.com/features/article/diablo-cody-says-no/page/1/ (accessed 20 May 2017).

Burgoyne, Robert (2008), *The Hollywood Historical Film*, Oxford: Blackwell.

Burgoyne, Robert (2012), 'Embodiment in the war film: *Paradise Now* and *The Hurt Locker*', *Journal of War & Culture Studies*, vol. 5, no. 1, pp. 7–19.

Burgoyne, Robert (2013), 'Somatic war: re-enchantment and the body at risk in the new war films' [conference paper], University of St Andrews, 21 February.

Buscombe, Edward (1970), 'The idea of genre in the American cinema', *Screen*, vol. 12, no. 2, pp. 33–45.

Bussmann, Kate (2009), 'Cutting edge: Mary Harron', *The Guardian*, 6 March, http://www.theguardian.com/lifeandstyle/2009/mar/06/mary-harron-film (accessed 20 May 2017).

Butler, Alison (2002), *Women's Cinema: The Contested Screen*, London: Wallflower.

Butler, Judith (1988), 'Performative acts and gender constitution: an essay in phenomenology and feminist theory', *Theatre Journal*, vol. 40, no. 4, pp. 519–31.

Butler, Judith (1993), *Bodies That Matter: On the Discursive Limits of 'Sex'*, New York: Routledge.

Butler, Judith (1999), *Gender Trouble: Feminism and the Subversion of Identity*, New York: Routledge.

Butler, Judith (2004a), *Undoing Gender*, New York: Routledge.

Butler, Judith (2004b), *Precarious Life: The Powers of Mourning and Violence*, London: Verso.

Butler, Judith (2014), 'Vida precaria, vulnerabilidad y ética de cohabitación', in Begonya Saez Tajafuerce (ed.), *Cuerpo, memoria y representación. Adriana Cavarero y Judith Butler en diálogo*, Barcelona: Icaria, pp. 47–79.

Carlson, Erin (2008), 'Diablo Cody pays the price of fame too', *Breitbart*, 26 February, http://www.breitbart.com/article.php?id=D8V2BKHO5&show_article=1 (accessed 20 May 2017).

Caughie, John (ed.) (1981), *Theories of Authorship*, London: Routledge.

Cavarero, Adriana (2014), 'Inclinaciones desequilibradas', in Begonya Saez Tajafuerce (ed.), *Cuerpo, memoria y representación. Adriana Cavarero y Judith Butler en diálogo*, Barcelona: Icaria, pp. 17–38.

Cawelti, John G. (1976), *Adventure, Mystery and Romance: Formula Stories as Art and Popular Culture*, Chicago: Chicago University Press.

Cherry, Brigid (2002), 'Refusing to refuse to look: female viewers of the horror film', in Mark Jancovich (ed.), *Horror, the Film Reader*, London: Routledge, pp. 169–78.

Cheshire, Ellen (2015), *Bio-pics: A Life in Pictures*, London and New York: Wallflower.

Chitwood, Adam (2013), 'Producer Kevin Misher talks finding the right cast, keeping a well-known story suspenseful, committing to an R rating, and more on the set of *Carrie*', *Collider*, 16 July, http://collider.com/kevin-misher-carrie-interview/ (accessed 12 February 2017).

Cipriani, Casey (2016), 'Genre is a Woman festival will highlight female directors of genre films', *Woman and Hollywood*, 31 May, https://blog.womenandhollywood.com/genre-is-a-woman-festival-will-highlight-female-directors-of-genre-films-5504635d816a (accessed 12 February 2017).

Clover, Carol J. (1992), *Men, Women, and Chain Saws: Gender in the Modern Horror Film*, Princeton: Princeton University Press.

Clúa, Isabel (2011), 'Las chicas sólo quieren divertirse: mujeres y géneros populares', in Helena González Fernández and Isabel Clúa (eds), *Máxima audiencia. Cultura popular y género*, Barcelona: Icaria, pp. 31–52.

Cobb, Shelley (2015), *Adaptation, Authorship, and Contemporary Women Filmmakers*, London: Palgrave.

Cody, Diablo (2006), *Candy Girl: A Year in The Life of an Unlikely Stripper*, New York: Gotham Books.

Colaizzi, Giulia (ed.) (1995), *Feminismo y teoría fílmica*, Valencia: Episteme.

Colaizzi, Giulia (2001), 'El acto cinematográfico: género y texto fílmico', *Lectora: revista de dones i textualitat*, no. 7, pp. v–xiii.

Colaizzi, Giulia (2007), *La pasión del significante. Teoría de género y cultura visual*, Madrid: Biblioteca Nueva.

Colangelo, Brittney Jade (2009), 'Feminism does exist in horror films whether you see it or not', *Day of the Woman*, 13 September, http://dayofwoman.blogspot.com/2009/09/feminism-does-exist-horror-films.html (accessed 12 May 2017).

Cole, Susan G. (2010), 'Kathryn Bigelow, the absentee feminist', *Now Toronto*, 11 March, http://www.nowtoronto.com/daily/story.cfm?content=174034 (accessed 20 May 2017).

Collins, Luke (2012), '100% pure adrenaline: gender and generic surface in *Point Break*', in Christine Gledhill (ed.), *Gender Meets Genre in Postwar Cinemas*, Urbana: University of Illinois Press, pp. 54–68.

Comolli, Jean-Louis and Jean Narboni (1971), 'Cinema/Ideology/Criticism', *Screen*, vol. 12, no. 1, pp. 131–44.

Cook, Pam (1988), 'Women in the Western', in Edward Buscombe (ed.), *The BFI Companion to the Western*, London: British Film Institute, pp. 240–3.

Cook, Pam (1996), *Fashioning the Nation: Costume and Identity in British Cinema*, London: British Film Institute.

Cook, Pam (2006), 'Portrait of a lady: Sofia Coppola', *Sight and Sound*, vol. 16, no. 11, pp. 36–40.

Cook, Pam (2012), 'No fixed address: the women's picture from *Outrage* to *Blue*

Steel'*, in Christine Gledhill (ed.), *Gender Meets Genre in Postwar Cinemas*, Urbana: University of Illinois Press, pp. 29–40.
Cook, Pam (2014), 'History in the making: Sofia Coppola's *Marie Antoinette* and the new auteurism', in Tom Brown and Belén Vidal (eds), *The Biopic in Contemporary Film Culture*, London: Routledge, pp. 212–26.
Coppa, Francesca (2018), 'A Hollywood of our own: media fandom as female art-world', in Mary Harrod and Katarzyna Paszkiewicz (eds), *Women Do Genre in Film and Television*, New York and London: Routledge, pp. 213–30.
Corrigan, Timothy (1991), *A Cinema Without Walls: Movies and Culture After Vietnam*, New Brunswick, NJ: Rutgers University Press.
Coulthard, Lisa (2007), 'Killing Bill: rethinking feminism and film violence', in Yvonne Tasker and Diane Negra (eds), *Interrogating Postfeminism: Gender and the Politics of Popular Culture*, Durham and London: Duke University Press, pp. 153–75.
Craig, Pamela and Martin Fradley (2010), 'Teenage traumata: youth, affective politics and the contemporary American horror film', in Steffen Hantke (ed.), *American Horror Film: The Genre at the Turn of the Millennium*, Jackson: University Press of Mississippi, pp. 77–102.
Creed, Barbara (1986), 'Horror and the monstrous-feminine: an imaginary abjection', *Screen*, vol. 27, no. 1, pp. 44–71.
Creed, Barbara (1993), *The Monstrous-Feminine: Film, Feminism, Psychoanalysis*, London: Routledge.
Cunningham, Douglas A. (2010), 'Explosive structure: fragmenting the new modernist war narrative in *The Hurt Locker*', *CineAction*, no. 81, pp. 2–10.
Custen, George Frederick (1992), *Bio/pics: How Hollywood Constructed Public History*, New Brunswick, NJ: Rutgers University Press.
Dargis, Manohla (2006), '*Marie Antoinette*: best or worst of times?', *The New York Times*, 25 May, http://www.nytimes.com/2006/05/25/movies/25fest.html (accessed 20 May 2017).
Dargis, Manohla (2010a), 'How Oscar found Ms. Right', *The New York Times*, 10 March, http://www.nytimes.com/2010/03/14/movies/14dargis.html (accessed 20 May 2017).
Dargis, Manohla (2010b), 'The work of war, at a fever pitch', *The New York Times*, 7 January, http://www.nytimes.com/2010/01/10/movies/awardsseason/10darg.html?_r=0 (accessed 20 May 2017).
Dargis, Manohla (2015), 'Review: in "The Intern," she's the boss, but he's the star', *The New York Times*, 24 September, https://www.nytimes.com/2015/09/25/movies/review-the-intern-proves-experience-doesnt-have-to-start-at-the-top.html?mcubz=0 (accessed 20 May 2017).
Dargis, Manohla and A. O. Scott (2011), 'In defense of the slow and the boring', *The New York Times*, 3 June, http://www.nytimes.com/2011/06/05/movies/films-in-defense-of-slow-and-boring.html?_r=0 (accessed 20 May 2017).
Dawes, Amy (2009), 'Head of the table', *DGA Quarterly*, Spring, http://www.dga.org/Craft/DGAQ/All-Articles/0901-Spring-2009/Interview-Nancy-Meyers.aspx (accessed 20 May 2017).
De Lauretis, Teresa (1984), *Alice Doesn't: Feminism, Semiotics, Cinema*, Bloomington: Indiana University Press.
De Lauretis, Teresa (1987a), 'Rethinking women's cinema: aesthetics and feminist theory', in *Technologies of Gender: Essays on Theory, Film, and Fiction*, Bloomington: Indiana University Press, pp. 127–48.
De Lauretis, Teresa (1987b), *Technologies of Gender: Essays on Theory, Film, and Fiction*, Bloomington: Indiana University Press.

De Lauretis, Teresa (1990), 'Guerilla in the mist: women's cinema in the 80s', *Screen*, vol. 31, no. 1, pp. 6–25.

De Luca, Tiago (2011), 'Realism of the senses: a tendency in contemporary world cinema', in Lucia Nagib (ed.), *Theorising World Cinema*, New York: I. B. Tauris, pp. 183–206.

Degli-Esposti, Cristina (1996), 'Sally Potter's *Orlando* and the neo-baroque scopic regime', *Cinema Journal*, vol. 36, no. 1, pp. 75–93.

Del Rio, Elena (2008), *Deleuze and the Cinemas of Performance: Powers of Affection*, Edinburgh: Edinburgh University Press.

Deleuze, Gilles (1985), *Cinéma 2: L'image-temps*, Paris: Éditions de Minuit.

Deleuze, Gilles (1994), *Difference and Repetition*, trans. Paul Patton, New York: Columbia University Press.

Deleuze, Gilles (2005), *Cinema 2: The Time Image*, trans. Hugh Tomlinson and Robert Galeta, London and New York: Continuum.

Deleuze, Gilles and Félix Guattari (1975), *Kafka: pour une littérature mineure*, Paris: Éditions de Minuit.

Deleuze, Gilles and Félix Guattari (1987), *A Thousand Plateaus: Capitalism and Schizophrenia*, trans. Brian Massumi, Minneapolis: University of Minnesota Press.

Deleyto, Celestino (2003), 'Between friends: love and friendship in contemporary romantic comedy', *Screen*, vol. 44, no. 2, pp. 167–82.

Deleyto, Celestino (2009), *The Secret Life of Romantic Comedy*, Manchester: Manchester University Press.

Deleyto, Celestino (2011), 'The comic, the serious and the middle: desire and space in contemporary film romantic comedy', *Journal of Popular Romance Studies*, vol. 2, no. 1, http://jprstudies.org/2011/10/the-comic-the-serious-and-the-middle-desire-and-space-in-contemporary-film-romantic-comedy-by-celestino-deleyto/ (accessed 20 May 2017).

Denby, David (2011), 'Strange trips', *The New Yorker*, 11 April, https://www.newyorker.com/magazine/2011/04/11/strange-trips (accessed 20 May 2017).

Denny, David (2011), 'On the politics of enjoyment: a reading of *The Hurt Locker*', *Theory & Event*, vol. 14, no. 1, http://muse.jhu.edu/ (accessed 20 January 2016).

Derrida, Jacques (1980), 'The law of genre', *Critical Inquiry*, vol. 7, no. 1, pp. 55–81.

Derrida, Jacques (1986), 'La loi du genre', in *Parages*, Paris: Galilée, pp. 251–87.

Devin, Gordon (2001), 'She's getting the royal treatment. A face to watch: Anne Hathaway', *Newsweek*, 6 August, https://www.highbeam.com/doc/1G1-76875223.html (accessed 20 May 2017).

Doane, Mary Ann (1990), 'Film and the masquerade: theorising the female spectator', in Patricia Erens (ed.), *Issues in Feminist Film Criticism*, Bloomington, Indiana University Press, pp. 41–57.

Donato, Matt (2015), 'Exclusive interview with director Karyn Kusama on *The Invitation*', *We Got This Covered*, http://wegotthiscovered.com/movies/exclusive-interview-director-karyn-kusama-invitation/2/ (accessed 22 May 2017).

Dowd, Maureen (2015), 'The women of Hollywood speak out', *The New York Times*, 20 November, www.nytimes.com/2015/11/22/magazine/the-women-of-hollywood-speak-out.html?_r=0 (accessed 5 April 2017).

Duboff, Josh (2010), 'Rachel Maddow questions G4's "real-life *Hurt Locker*" TV series', *New York Magazine*, 26 August, http://nymag.com/daily/intelligencer/2010/08/rachel_maddow_questions_g4s_re.htm (accessed 20 May 2017).

Dyer, Richard (1997), *White: Essays on Race and Culture*, London and New York: Routledge.

Dyer, Richard (2002), *The Culture of Queers*, London and New York: Routledge.

Dyer, Richard (2007), *Pastiche*, London: Routledge.

Dyer, Richard and Ginette Vincendeau (eds) (1992), *Popular European Cinema*, London: Routledge.
Ebert, Roger (2007), *Roger Ebert's Movie Yearbook 2007*, Kansas City: Andrews McMeel Publishing.
Ebert, Roger (2009), '*It's Complicated*', rogerebert.com, 23 December, http://www.rogerebert.com/reviews/its-complicated-2009 (accessed 20 May 2017).
Ebert, Roger (2012), *Roger Ebert's Movie Yearbook 2012*, Kansas City: Andrews McMeel Publishing.
Eberwein, Robert (2010), *The Hollywood War Film*, London: Wiley-Blackwell.
Elsaesser, Thomas and Malte Hagener (2010), *Film Theory: An Introduction Through Senses*, New York and London: Routledge.
Erbland, Kate (2017), 'Karyn Kusama on making horror films and fighting evil in the age of Trump', *IndieWire*, 15 February, http://www.indiewire.com/2017/02/karyn-kusama-horror-films-donald-trump-xx-1201783181/ (accessed 7 December 2017).
Faludi, Susan (2006), *Backlash. The Undeclared War Against American Women*, New York: Three Rivers Press.
Ferriss, Suzanne (2008), 'Fashioning femininity in the makeover flick', in Suzanne Ferriss and Mallory Young (eds), *Chick Flicks: Contemporary Women at the Movies*, New York: Routledge, pp. 41–57.
Ferriss, Suzanne and Mallory Young (eds) (2008), 'Introduction: chick flicks and chick culture', in Suzanne Ferriss and Mallory Young (eds), *Chick Flicks: Contemporary Women at the Movies*, New York: Routledge, pp. 1–25.
Fielding, Helen (1996), *Bridget Jones's Diary*, London: Picador.
Fine, Marshall (2009), 'Interview: Diablo Cody dishes *Jennifer's Body*', *Huffington Post*, 18 September, http://www.huffingtonpost.com/marshall-fine/iinterviewi-diablo-cody-d_b_291525.htmlhttp://www.huffingtonpost.com/marshall-fine/iinterviewi-diablo-cody-d_b_291525.html (accessed 20 May 2017).
Finger, Bobby (2015), 'In *The Intern*, Anne Hathaway & Robert De Niro explore an unlikely bromance', *Jezebel*, 25 September, http://themuse.jezebel.com/in-the-intern-anne-hathaway-robert-de-niro-explore-a-1732385323 (accessed 20 May 2017).
Fischer, Lucy (1989), *Shot/Counter Shot: Film Tradition and Women's Cinema*, Princeton: Princeton University Press.
Flanagan, Michael (2008), 'Towards an aesthetic of slow in contemporary cinema', vol. 16: 9, no. 29, November, http://www.16-9.dk/2008-11/side11_inenglish.htm (accessed 20 May 2017).
Flynn, Peter (1998), 'The silent western as a mythmaker', *Images*, vol. 3, http://www.imagesjournal.com/issue06/infocus/silentwesterns.htm (accessed 20 May 2017).
Ford, Rebecca (2017), '*The Beguiled*: Sofia Coppola on taking on a genre movie and why it's not a remake (Q&A)', *The Hollywood Reporter*, 16 May, http://www.hollywoodreporter.com/news/beguiled-sofia-coppola-taking-a-genre-movie-why-not-a-remake-q-a-1004173 (accessed 20 May 2017).
Foucault, Michel (1969), 'Qu'est-ce qu'un auteur?', *Bulletin de la Société française de philosophie*, no. 3, pp. 73–104.
Foucault, Michel ([1969] 1984), 'What is an author?', in Paul Rabinow (ed.), *The Foucault Reader*, New York: Pantheon, pp. 101–20.
Fradley, Martin (2013), '"Hell is a teenage girl"?: postfeminism and contemporary teen horror', in Joel Gwynne and Nadine Muller (eds), *Postfeminism and Contemporary Hollywood Cinema*, New York: Palgrave Macmillan, pp. 204–21.
Francke, Lizzie (1994), *Script Girls: Women Screenwriters in Hollywood*, London: British Film Institute.
Fraser, Antonia (2001), *Marie Antoinette: The Journey*, London: Phoenix.
Freeman, Hadley (2015), 'Nancy Meyers: "I don't see a lot of movies about complicated

women . . . I think it's gotten worse"', *The Guardian*, 1 October, https://www.theguardian.com/film/2015/oct/01/nancy-meyers-the-intern-interview-women-hollywood (accessed 20 May 2017).

Freer, Ian (2006), 'Q&A Sofia Coppola', *Empire*, November, pp. 150–1.

Fuller, Graham (2011), 'The Oregon trail', *Sight and Sound*, vol. 21, no. 5, pp. 38–42.

Gaines, Jane M. (1990), 'White privilege and looking relations', in Patricia Erens (ed.), *Issues in Feminist Film Criticism*, Bloomington: Indiana University Press, pp. 197–214.

Gaines, Jane M. (1992), 'Dorothy Arzner's trousers', *Jump Cut*, no. 37, July, pp. 88–98, http://www.ejumpcut.org/archive/onlinessays/JC37folder/ArznersTrousers.html (accessed 1 September 2015).

Gaines, Jane M. (2002), 'Of cabbages and authorship', in Jennifer Bean and Diane Negra (eds), *A Feminist Reader in Early Cinema*, Durham: Duke University Press, Kindle Edition.

Gaines, Jane M. (2011), 'Dream/Factory', in Christine Gledhill and Linda Williams (eds), *Reinventing Film Studies*, London and New York: Bloomsbury Academic, pp. 100–13.

Gaines, Jane M. (2012), 'The genius of genre and the ingenuity of women', in Christine Gledhill (ed.), *Gender Meets Genre in Postwar Cinemas*, Urbana: University of Illinois Press, pp. 15–28.

Galt, Rosalind (2011), *Pretty: Film and the Decorative Image*, New York: Columbia University Press.

Garrett, Roberta (1995), 'Costume drama and counter memory: Sally Potter's *Orlando*', in Jane Dowson and Steven Earnshaw (eds), *Postmodern Subjects, Postmodern Texts*, Amsterdam: Rodopi, pp. 89–99.

Garrett, Roberta (2007), *Postmodern Chick-Flicks: The Return of the Woman's Film*, London: Palgrave Macmillan.

Geraghty, Christine (1991), *Women and Soap Opera: A Study of Prime Time Soaps*, Cambridge: Polity Press.

Gillett, Sue (1999), 'More than meets the eye: the mediation of affects in Jane Campion's *Sweetie*', *Senses of Cinema*, 5 December, http://sensesofcinema.com/1999/feature-articles/sweetie/ (accessed 20 May 2017).

Gledhill, Christine (1987), 'Introduction' and 'The melodramatic field: an investigation', in Christine Gledhill (ed.), *Home Is Where the Heart Is: Studies in Melodrama and the Woman's Film*, London: British Film Institute, pp. 1–4; pp. 5–39.

Gledhill, Christine (1994), 'Images and voices: approaches to Marxist feminist film criticism', in Diane Carsonet, Linda Dittmar and Janice R. Welsch. (eds), *Multiple Voices in Feminist Film Criticism*, Minneapolis: University of Minnesota Press, pp. 109–23.

Gledhill, Christine (2006), 'Pleasurable negotiations', in John Storey (ed.), *Cultural Theory and Popular Culture: A Reader*, vol. I, New York: Pearson Education, pp. 111–23.

Gledhill, Christine (2011), 'Rethinking genre', in Christine Gledhill and Linda Williams (eds), *Reinventing Film Studies*, London and New York: Bloomsbury Academic, pp. 221–43.

Gledhill, Christine (ed.) (2012), *Gender Meets Genre in Postwar Cinemas*, Urbana: University of Illinois Press.

Gledhill, Christine (2018), 'Preface', in Mary Harrod and Katarzyna Paszkiewicz (eds), *Women Do Genre in Film and Television*, New York and London: Routledge, pp. ix–xiv.

Gleiberman, Owen (2006), '*The Holiday*', *Entertainment Weekly*, 8 December, http://edition.cnn.com/2006/SHOWBIZ/Movies/12/08/ew.mov.diamond/ (accessed 20 May 2017).

Glitre, Katharina (2011), 'Nancy Meyers and "popular feminism"', in Melanie Walters (ed.), *Women on Screen: Feminism and Femininity in Visual Culture*, Basingstoke: Palgrave Macmillan, pp. 17–30.

Godwin, Fay (1985), *Land*, London: Heinemann.

Golubov, Nattie (2015), 'Del anonimato a la celebridad literaria: las figuras autoriales de la teoría literaria feminista', *Mundo Nuevo. Revista de Estudios Latinoamericanos*, vol. 16, pp. 29–48.

Gorfinkel, Elena (2012), 'Weariness, waiting: *enduration* and art cinema's tired bodies', *Discourse: Journal for Theoretical Studies in Media and Culture*, vol. 34, no. 2, http://digitalcommons.wayne.edu/discourse/vol34/iss2/8 (accessed 20 May 2017).

Gorfinkel, Elena (2016), 'Exhausted drift: austerity, dispossession and the politics of slow in Kelly Reichardt's *Meek's Cutoff*', in Tiago de Luca and Jorge Nuno Barradas (eds), *Slow Cinema*, Edinburgh: Edinburgh University Press, pp. 123–36.

Grant, Catherine (2001), 'Secret agents: feminist theories of women's film authorship', *Feminist Theory*, vol. 2, no. 1, pp. 113–30.

Gray, Brandon (2009), 'Weekend report: moviegoers feast on "Meatballs", slim pickings for "Jennifer"', *Box Office Mojo*, 21 September, http://boxofficemojo.com/news/?id=2615&p=.htm (accessed 20 May 2017).

Gross, Terry (2011), 'Going west: the making of *Meek's Cutoff*', *Fresh Air*, National Public Radio, 4 April, www.avclub.com/article/kelly-reichardt-and-jon-raymond-55095 (accessed 20 May 2017).

Guillen, Michael (2010), 'Midnites for maniacs: Diablo Cody on *Jennifer's Body* (2009)', *Twitch Film*, 22 June, http://twitchfilm.com/2010/06/midnites-for-maniacs-diablo-cody-on-jennifers-body-2009.html (accessed 20 May 2017).

Gunning, Tom (1994), 'Bodies and phantoms: making visible the beginnings of motion pictures', *Binocular*, pp. 84–99.

Gwenllian Jones, Sara (2003), 'Vampires, Indians, and the queer fantastic: Kathryn Bigelow's *Near Dark*', in Deborah Jermyn and Sean Redmond (eds), *The Cinema of Kathryn Bigelow: Hollywood Transgressor*, London: Wallflower, pp. 57–71.

Hahn, Robert (2006), 'Dancing in the dark', *Southern Review*, no. 42, pp. 153–65.

Halberstam, Judith (1993), 'Imagined violence/queer violence: representation, rage, and resistance', *Social Text*, no. 37, pp. 187–201.

Halberstam, Judith (1995), *Skin Shows: Gothic Horror and the Technology of Monsters*, Durham and London: Duke University Press.

Hall, E. Dawn (2014), *American Independent Female Filmmakers: Kelly Reichardt in Focus*, Doctoral Dissertation, Middle Tennessee State University.

Hall, E. Dawn (2018), 'Gender politics in Kelly Reichardt's feminist western *Meek's Cutoff*', in Mary Harrod and Katarzyna Paszkiewicz (eds), *Women Do Genre in Film and Television*, New York and London: Routledge, pp. 138–46.

Hall, E. Dawn (forthcoming), *ReFocus: The Films of Kelly Reichardt*, Edinburgh: Edinburgh University Press.

Hall, Stuart (1980), 'Encoding/Decoding', in Centre for Contemporary Cultural Studies (ed.), *Culture, Media, Language*, London: Hutchinson, pp. 128–38.

Handyside, Fiona (2015), 'Girlhood, postfeminism and contemporary female art-house authorship: the "nameless trilogies" of Sofia Coppola and Mia Hansen-Løve', *Alphaville: Journal of Film and Screen Media*, vol. 10, http://www.alphavillejournal.com/Issue10/PDFs/ArticleHandyside.pdf (accessed 20 May 2017).

Handyside, Fiona (2017), *Sofia Coppola: A Cinema of Girlhood*, London: I. B. Tauris.

Harper, Sue (1994), *Picturing the Past: The Rise and Fall of the British Costume Film*, London: British Film Institute.

Harrod, Mary (2010), 'The aesthetics of pastiche in the work of Richard Linklater', *Screen*, vol. 51, no. 1, pp. 21–37.

Harrod, Mary (2015), *From France with Love: Gender and Identity in French Romantic Comedy*, London: I. B. Tauris.
Harrod, Mary (2016), '"As if a girl's reach should exceed her grasp": gendering genericity and spectatorial address in the work of Amy Heckerling', in Frances Smith and Timothy Shary (eds), *ReFocus: The Films of Amy Heckerling*, Edinburgh: Edinburgh University Press, pp. 53–72.
Harrod, Mary (forthcoming 2017), 'From the city of love to romantic playground: Paris in recent US and French rom-coms', in Ginette Vincendeau and Alastair Phillips (eds), *Paris in the Cinema: Beyond the Flâneur*, London: BFI Palgrave.
Harrod, Mary (forthcoming), *Genre, Pastiche and Women's Filmmaking in Hollywood*, London: Palgrave.
Harrod, Mary and Katarzyna Paszkiewicz (eds) (2018), *Women Do Genre in Film and Television*, New York and London: Routledge.
Haskell, Molly (1974), *From Reverence to Rape: The Treatment of Women in the Movies*, Chicago: University of Chicago Press.
Hayt, Anthony (2017), 'Moving past the trauma: feminist criticism and transformations of the slasher genre', in Kristin Lené Hole, Dijana Jelača, E. Ann Kaplan and Patrice Petro (eds), *The Routledge Companion to Cinema & Gender*, New York: Routledge, pp. 131–40.
Hedges, Chris (2002), *War is a Force That Gives Us Meaning*, New York: Anchor Books/Random House.
Heller, Nathan (2010), 'Sofia Coppola: you either love her or hate her. Here's why', *Slate*, 28 December, http://www.slate.com/articles/news_and_politics/assessment/2010/12/sofia_coppola.html (accessed 20 May 2017).
Heller-Nicholas, Alexandra (2011), *Rape-Revenge Films: A Critical Study*, Jefferson: McFarland.
Henderson, Eric (2015), '*The Intern*', *Slant Magazine*, 24 September, https://www.slantmagazine.com/film/review/the-intern (accessed 20 May 2017).
Hess, Judith (1974), 'Genre films and the status quo', *Jump Cut: A Review of Contemporary Media*, no. 1, http://www.ejumpcut.org/archive/onlinessays/JC01folder/GenreFilms.html (accessed 20 May 2017).
Higson, Andrew Douglas (1993), 'Re presenting the national past: nostalgia and pastiche in the heritage film', in Lester Friedman (ed.), *Fires Were Started: British Cinema and Thatcherism*, Minneapolis: Minnesota University Press, pp. 109–29.
Hillier, Jim (1993), *The New Hollywood*, London: Studio Vista.
Hjort, Mette (2005), *Small Nation, Global Cinema: The New Danish Cinema*, Minneapolis: Minnesota University Press.
Hohenadel, Kristin (2006), 'French royalty as seen by Hollywood royalty', *The New York Times*, 10 September, http://www.nytimes.com/2006/09/10/movies/moviesspecial/10hohe.html (accessed 20 May 2017).
Holloway, David (2008), *9/11 and the War on Terror*, Edinburgh: Edinburgh University Press.
Hollows, Joanne (2000), *Feminism, Femininity and Popular Culture*, Oxford and Manchester: Manchester University Press.
Hollows, Joanne (2003), 'The masculinity of cult', in Mark Jancovich, Antonio Lazaro Reboll, Julian Stringer and Andrew Willis (eds), *Defining Cult Movies: The Cultural Politics of Oppositional Taste*, Manchester: Manchester University Press, pp. 35–53.
Holmlund, Chris (2005), 'Postfeminism from A to G', *Cinema Journal*, vol. 44, no. 2, pp. 116–21.
hooks, bell (1992), 'The oppositional gaze: Black female spectators', in *Black Looks: Race and Representation*, Boston: South End Press, pp. 115–31.
Hutchings, Peter (1993), 'Masculinity and the horror film', in Pat Kirkham and Janet

Thumim (eds), *You Tarzan: Masculinity, Movies and Men*, New York: St Martin's Press, pp. 84–94.

Huyssen, Andreas (1986), 'Mass culture as woman: modernism's other', in *After the Great Divide: Modernism, Mass Culture, Postmodernism*, Bloomington: Indiana University Press, pp. 44–62.

Ince, Kate (2017), *The Body and the Screen: Female Subjectivities in Contemporary Women's Cinema*, London, Delhi, New York and Sydney: Bloomsbury.

Inness, Sherrie (ed.) (2004), *Action Chicks: New Images of Tough Women in Popular Culture*, New York: Palgrave Macmillan.

Jameson, Fredric (1979), 'Reification and utopia in mass culture', *Social Text*, vol. 1, pp. 130–48.

Jameson, Fredric (2000), 'Postmodernism or the cultural logic of late capitalism', in Michael Hardt and Kathi Weeks (eds), *The Jameson Reader*, Oxford: Blackwell, pp. 188–232.

Jancovich, Mark (ed.) (2002), *Horror, the Film Reader*, London: Routledge.

Jay, Martin (1993), *Downcast Eyes: The Denigration of Vision in Twentieth-Century French Thought*, Berkeley: University of California Press.

Jeffers McDonald, Tamar E. L. (2007), *Romantic Comedy: Boy Meets Girl Meets Genre*, London: Wallflower.

Jeffers McDonald, Tamar E. L. (2009), 'Homme-com: engendering change in contemporary romantic comedy', in Stacey Abbott and Deborah Jermyn (eds), *Falling in Love Again: Romantic Comedy in Contemporary Cinema*, London: I. B. Tauris, pp. 146–59.

Jeffords, Susan (1993), *Hard Bodies: Hollywood Masculinity in the Reagan Era*, New Brunswick, NJ: Rutgers University Press.

Jermyn, Deborah (2003), 'Cherchez la femme: *The Weight of Water* and the search for Bigelow in a "Bigelow film"', in Deborah Jermyn and Sean Redmond (eds), *The Cinema of Kathryn Bigelow: Hollywood Transgressor*, London: Wallflower, pp. 125–44.

Jermyn, Deborah (2009), 'I love NY: the rom-com's love affair with New York', in Stacey Abbott and Deborah Jermyn (eds), *Falling in Love Again: Romantic Comedy in Contemporary Cinema*, London: I. B. Tauris, pp. 9–24.

Jermyn, Deborah (2014), 'Nancy Meyers: the wrong kind of woman filmmaker?' [conference paper], University of East Anglia, 11 April.

Jermyn, Deborah (2017), *Nancy Meyers*, New York: Bloomsbury Academic.

Jermyn, Deborah (2018), 'The contemptible realm of the romcom queen: Nancy Meyers, cultural value and romantic comedy', in Mary Harrod and Katarzyna Paszkiewicz (eds), *Women Do Genre in Film and Television*, New York and London: Routledge, pp. 57–71.

Jermyn, Deborah and Sean Redmond (eds) (2003), *The Cinema of Kathryn Bigelow: Hollywood Transgressor*, London: Wallflower.

Johnston, Claire ([1973] 2000a), 'Women's cinema as counter-cinema', in E. Ann Kaplan (ed.), *Feminism and Film*, Oxford: Oxford University Press, pp. 22–33.

Johnston, Claire ([1975] 2000b), 'Dorothy Arzner: critical strategies', in E. Ann Kaplan (ed.), *Feminism and Film*, Oxford: Oxford University Press, pp. 139–48.

Kamber, Michael (2010), 'How not to depict a war', *Lens: The New York Times*, 1 March, http://lens.blogs.nytimes.com/2010/03/01/essay-15 (accessed 20 May 2017).

Kaplan, E. Ann (1988), *Women and Film: Both Sides of the Camera*, New York: Methuen.

Kaplan, E. Ann (2012), 'Troubling genre/reconstructing gender', in Christine Gledhill (ed.), *Gender Meets Genre in Postwar Cinemas*, Urbana: University of Illinois Press, pp. 71–83.

Keegan, Rebecca (2015), 'Fall Movie Guide. Anne Hathaway, Nancy Meyers say *The Intern* evolved from "baby boom"', *Los Angeles Times*, 3 September, http://www.latimes.com/entertainment/movies/la-ca-mn-sneaks-the-intern-20150906-story.html (accessed 20 May 2017).

Kennedy, Todd (2010), 'Off with Hollywood's head: Sofia Coppola as feminine auteur', *Film Criticism*, vol. 35, no. 1, https://www.thefreelibrary.com/Off+ with+Hollywood's+head%3A+Sofia+Coppola+as+feminine+auteur.-a0241514974 (accessed 20 May 2017).

King, Geoff (2005), *American Independent Cinema*, London and New York: I. B. Tauris.

King, Geoff (2009), *Indiewood, USA: Where Hollywood Meets Independent Cinema*, London and New York: I. B. Tauris.

King, Geoff, Claire Molloy and Yannis Tzioumakis (eds) (2013), *American Independent Cinema: Indie, Indiewood and Beyond*, London: Routledge.

Kitses, Jim (1969), *Horizons West*, Bloomington: Indiana University Press.

Klinger, Barbara (1986), 'Cinema/Ideology/Criticism revisited: the progressive genre', in Barry K. Grant (ed.), *Film Genre Reader III*, Austin: University of Texas Press, pp. 75–91.

Klinger, Barbara (1994), *Melodrama and Meaning: History, Culture, and the Films of Douglas Sirk*, Bloomington: Indiana University Press.

Kois, Dan (2011), 'Eating your cultural vegetables', *The New York Times*, 29 April, http://www.nytimes.com/2011/05/01/magazine/mag-01Riff-t.html?pagewanted=all&_r=0 (accessed 20 May 2017).

Kooyman, Ben (2012), 'Whose body? Auteurism, celebrity and feminism in *Hostel Part II* and *Jennifer's Body*', *The Australasian Journal of Popular Culture*, vol. 1, no. 2, pp. 181–96.

Krämer, Peter (2013), 'The limits of autonomy: Stanley Kubrick, Hollywood and independent filmmaking, 1950–1953', in Geoff King, Claire Molloy and Yannis Tzioumakis (eds), *American Independent Cinema*, London: Routledge, pp. 153–64.

Kristeva, Julia (1982), *Powers of Horror: An Essay on Abjection*, New York: Columbia University Press.

Kuhn, Annette (1994), *Women's Pictures: Feminism and Cinema*, London and New York: Verso.

Lane, Christina (2000), *Feminist Hollywood: From Born in Flames to Point Break*, Detroit: Wayne State University Press.

Lane, Christina (2003), 'The *Strange Days* of Kathryn Bigelow and James Cameron', in Deborah Jermyn and Sean Redmond (eds), *The Cinema of Kathryn Bigelow: Hollywood Transgressor*, London: Wallflower, pp. 178–97.

Lane, Christina (2005), 'Just another girl outside the neo-indie', in Chris Holmlund and Justin Watts (eds), *Contemporary American Independent Film: From the Margins to the Mainstream*, New York: Routledge, pp. 193–209.

Lane, Christina and Nicole Richter (2011), 'The feminist poetics of Sofia Coppola: spectacle and self-consciousness in *Marie Antoinette*', in Hilary Radner and Rebecca Stringer (eds), *Feminism at the Movies: Understanding Gender in Contemporary Popular Cinema*, New York: Routledge, pp. 181–202.

Larocca, Amy (2015), 'In conversation: Nancy Meyers', *Vulture*, 7 September, www.vulture.com/2015/09/nancy-meyers-amy-larocca-in-conversation.html# (accessed 20 May 2017).

Lattimer, James (2011), 'Beyond neo-neo realism: reconfigurations of neorealist narration in Kelly Reichardt's *Meek's Cutoff*', *Cinephile*, vol. 7, no. 2, pp. 37–41.

Lauzen, Martha M. (2009), 'The celluloid ceiling: behind-the-scenes employment of women on the top 250 films of 2008', San Diego: Center for the Study of Women in

Television and Film, http://womenintvfilm.sdsu.edu/files/2008_celluloid_ceiling.pdf (accessed 20 May 2017).

Lauzen, Martha M. (2010), 'The celluloid ceiling: behind-the-scenes employment of women on the top 250 films of 2009', San Diego: Center for the Study of Women in Television and Film, http://womenintvfilm.sdsu.edu/files/2010_Celluloid_Ceiling.pdf (accessed 20 May 2017).

Lauzen, Martha M. (2016), 'Independent women: behind-the-scenes representation on festival films', San Diego: Center for the Study of Women in Television and Film, http://womenintvfilm.sdsu.edu/files/2016%20Independent_Women_Report.pdf (accessed 20 May 2017).

Lauzen, Martha M. (2017), 'The celluloid ceiling: behind-the-scenes employment of women on the top 100, 250, and 500 films of 2016', San Diego: Center for the Study of Women in Television and Film, http://womenintvfilm.sdsu.edu/wp-content/uploads/2017/01/2016_Celluloid_Ceiling_Report.pdf (accessed 20 May 2017).

Lenihan, John H. (1980), *Showdown: Confronting Modern America in the Western Film*, Urbana: University of Illinois Press.

Lever, Évelyne (2006), 'Marie-Antoinette revue et corrigée par Hollywood', *L'Internaute*, May, http://www.linternaute.com/savoir/interview/evelyne-lever/chat-evelyne-lever.shtml (accessed 20 May 2017).

Limerick, Patricia Nelson (1987), *The Legacy of Conquest: The Unbroken Past of the American West*, New York: Norton.

Limerick, Patricia Nelson (2000), *Something in the Soil: Legacies and Reckonings in the New West*, New York: Norton.

Lodge, Guy (2015), 'Film review: *The Intern*', *Variety*, 21 September, http://variety.com/2015/film/reviews/the-intern-review-anne-hathaway-robert-de-niro-1201596471/ (accessed 20 May 2017).

Longworth, Karina (2011), 'Kelly Reichardt explains *Meek's Cutoff*, her latest road movie', *San Francisco Weekly*, 4 May, http://www.sfweekly.com/2011-05-04/film/kelly-reichardt-interview-meeks-cutoff-karina-longworth/ (accessed 20 May 2017).

Macon, Alexandra (2015), 'Is Nancy Meyers's new movie *The Intern* sexist?', *Vogue*, 5 October, http://www.vogue.com/article/nancy-meyers-the-intern-sexist (accessed 20 May 2017).

Malo, Sebastien (2017), '*Wonder Woman* conquering Box Office a sign Hollywood sexism outdated?', *Reuteurs*, 7 June, http://www.reuters.com/article/us-film-sexism-wonderwoman-idUSKBN18Y052 (accessed 20 May 2017).

Margulies, Ivone (1996), *Nothing Happens: Chantal Akerman's Hyperrealist Everyday*, Durham and London: Duke University Press.

Marks, Laura U. (2000), *The Skin of the Film: Intercultural Cinema, Embodiment, and the Senses*, Durham: Duke University Press.

Marks, Laura U. (2002), *Touch: Sensuous Theory and Multisensory Media*, Minneapolis and London: University of Minnesota Press.

Martin, Angela (2008), 'Refocusing authorship in women's filmmaking', in Barry Keith Grant (ed.), *Auteurs and Authorship: A Film Reader*, Malden: Blackwell Publishing, pp. 127–34.

Martin-Márquez, Susan (1999), *Feminist Discourse and Spanish Cinema: Sight Unseen*, Oxford: Oxford University Press.

Martinuzzi, Heidi (2009), '"Since when is there feminist horror?": articles like this are why *Pretty/Scary* exists', *Pretty/Scary*, 13 September, http://www.fangirltastic.com/content/when-there-feminist-horror-articles-are-whyprettyscary-exists (accessed 20 May 2017).

Massumi, Brian (2002), *Parables for the Virtual: Movement, Affect, Sensation*, Durham: Duke University Press.

Mathijs, Ernest and Jamie Sexton (2012), *Cult Cinema: An Introduction*, Malden, MA: Wiley-Blackwell.
Matin, Samiha (2012), 'Private femininity, public femininity: tactical aesthetics in the costume film', in Christine Gledhill (ed.), *Gender Meets Genre in Postwar Cinemas*, Urbana: University of Illinois Press, pp. 96–110.
Mayer, Sophie (2016), *Political Animals: The New Feminist Cinema*, London: I. B. Tauris.
Mayne, Judith (1990), *The Woman at the Keyhole: Feminism and Women's Cinema*, Bloomington: Indiana University Press.
Mayne, Judith (1994), *Directed by Dorothy Arzner*, Bloomington: Indiana University Press.
Mayne, Judith (1995), 'Paradoxes of spectatorship', in Linda Williams (ed.), *Viewing Positions: Ways of Seeing Film*, New Brunswick, NJ: Rutgers University Press, pp. 155–83.
McCabe, Janet (2009), 'Lost in transition: problems of modern (heterosexual) romance and the catatonic male hero in the post-feminist age', in Stacey Abbott and Deborah Jermyn (eds), *Falling in Love Again: Romantic Comedy in Contemporary Cinema*, London: I. B. Tauris, pp. 160–75.
McCarthy, Todd (2006), '*Marie Antoinette*', *Variety*, 24 May, http://variety.com/2006/film/awards/marie-antoinette-4-1200515977/ (accessed 20 May 2017).
McClain, William (2010), 'Western, go home! Sergio Leone and the "death of the Western" in American film criticism', *Journal of Film and Video*, vol. 62, no. 1–2, pp. 52–66.
McClintock, Anne (1995), *Imperial Leather: Race, Gender, and Sexuality in the Colonial Contest*, New York: Routledge.
McClintock, Pamela (2017), 'Box office: *Wonder Woman* holding better than any superhero movie in 15 years', *The Hollywood Reporter*, 13 July, http://www.hollywoodreporter.com/heat-vision/wonder-woman-box-office-superhero-movies-1020621 (accessed 20 May 2017).
McHugh, Kathleen (2009), 'The world and the soup: historicising media feminisms in transnational contexts', *Camera Obscura*, no. 72, pp. 110–51.
McRobbie, Angela (2004), 'Post-feminism and popular culture', *Feminist Media Studies*, vol. 4, no. 3, pp. 255–64.
Mellencamp, Patricia (1995), *A Fine Romance: Five Ages of Film Feminism*, Philadelphia: Temple University Press.
Meyers, Nancy (2014), *The Intern* [script], http://www.ivanachubbuck.com/wp-content/uploads/2012/02/The-Intern-Ben-Patty-Entire-Screenplay.pdf (accessed 20 May 2017).
Miller, Jenni (2009), '*Jennifer's Body* is strong enough for a man, but made for a woman', *MTV Movies Blog*, 18 September, http://moviesblog.mtv.com/2009/09/18/jennifers-body-is-strong-enough-for-a-man-but-made-for-a-woman/ (accessed 20 May 2017).
Miller, Nancy K. (1988), *Subject to Change: Reading Feminist Writing*, New York: Columbia University Press.
Modleski, Tania (1982), *Loving with a Vengeance: Mass Produced Fantasies for Women*, New York and London: Routledge.
Modleski, Tania (1998), *Old Wives' Tales and Other Women's Stories*, London and New York: I. B. Tauris.
Modleski, Tania ([1988] 2016), *The Women Who Knew Too Much: Hitchcock and Feminist Theory*, New York and London: Routledge.
Monk, Claire (1995), 'Sexuality and the heritage film', *Sight and Sound*, vol. 5, no. 10, pp. 32–4.

Morris, Wesley (2006), '*Marie Antoinette*: movie review', *Boston Globe*, 20 October.
Morrison, Susan (2010), 'In transit: Kelly Reichardt's *Meek's Cutoff*', *CineAction*, no. 82–3, pp. 40–4.
Mottram, James (2006), *The Sundance Kids: How the Mavericks Took Back Hollywood*, London: Faber.
Muir, Kate (2010), 'Kathryn Bigelow's great leap forward – or was it?', *The Times*, 12 March, http://www.thetimes.co.uk/tto/arts/film/article2464415.ece (accessed 20 May 2017).
Mulvey, Laura (1975), 'Visual pleasure and narrative cinema', *Screen*, vol. 16, pp. 6–18.
Mulvey, Laura (1989a), 'Film, feminism and the avant-garde', *Visual and Other Pleasures*, Bloomington: Indiana University Press, pp. 111–26.
Mulvey, Laura (1989b), *Visual and Other Pleasures*, Bloomington: Indiana University Press.
Murnane, Jamie (2009), 'Diablo Cody didn't do the same-sex kiss in "Jennifer's Body" for publicity', *AfterEllen.com*, 8 September, http://www.afterellen.com/blog/jamiemurnane/diablo-cody-didnt-do-the-same-sex-kiss-in-jennifer-body-for-publicity (accessed 20 May 2017).
Murray, Rona (2011), 'Tough guy in drag? How the external, critical discourses surrounding Kathryn Bigelow demonstrate the wider problems of the gender question', *Networking Knowledge: Journal of the MeCCSA Postgraduate Network*, vol. 4, no. 1, pp. 1–22.
Naficy, Hamid (2001), *An Accented Cinema: Exilic and Diasporic Filmmaking*, Princeton: Princeton University Press.
Neale, Steve (1980), *Genre*, London: British Film Institute.
Neale, Steve (1981), 'Art cinema as institution', *Screen*, vol. 22, no. 1, pp. 11–40.
Neale, Steve (1993), 'Melo talk: on the meaning and use of the term "melodrama" in the American trade press', *Velvet Light Trap*, Autumn, pp. 66–89.
Neale, Steve (2000), *Genre and Hollywood*, London: Routledge.
Negra, Diane (2009), *What a Girl Wants: Fantasising the Reclamation of Self in Postfeminism*, London: Routledge.
Neumaier, Joe (2013), '*The Bling Ring*: movie review', *New York Daily News*, 13 June, http://www.nydailynews.com/entertainment/tv-movies/bling-ring-movie-review-article-1.1371518 (accessed 20 May 2017).
Newitz, Annalee (2009), 'Did stupid marketing kill *Jennifer's Body*?', *io9*, 10 September, http://io9.com/5376462/did-stupid-marketing-kill-jennifers-body (accessed 20 May 2017).
Newman, Michael Z. (2011), *Indie: An American Film Culture*, New York: Columbia University Press.
Nielsen, Bianca (2004), '"Something's wrong, like more than you being female": transgressive sexuality and discourses of reproduction in *Ginger Snaps*', *Thirdspace*, vol. 3, no. 2, pp. 55–69.
Nochimson, Martha (2010), 'Kathryn Bigelow: feminist pioneer or tough guy in drag?', *salon.com*, 24 February, http://www.salon.com/2010/02/24/bigelow_3 (accessed 20 May 2017).
O'Hagan, Sean (2006), 'Sofia Coppola', *The Guardian*, 8 October, https://www.theguardian.com/film/2006/oct/08/features.review1 (accessed 20 May 2017).
Orange, Michelle (2009), 'Taking back the knife: girls gone gory', *The New York Times*, 3 September, http://www.nytimes.com/2009/09/06/movies/06oran.html?_r=4&hpw (accessed 20 May 2017).
Orsman, Harry (1997), *The Dictionary of New Zealand English*, Auckland: Oxford University Press.

Ortner, Sherry B. (2013), *Not Hollywood: Independent Film at the Twilight of the American Dream*, Durham: Duke University Press.

Oughton, Karen (2014), 'The home, the body and otherness: Canadian representations of identity and feminism in Mary Harron's *American Psycho*, Sarah Polley's *Away from Her* and the Soska Sisters' *American Mary*', in Gabrielle Kelly and Cheryl Robson (eds), *Celluloid Ceiling: Women Film Directors Breaking Through*, Twickenham: Supernova Books, pp. 54–76.

Paszkiewicz, Katarzyna (2015), 'Hollywood transgressor or Hollywood transvestite? The reception of Kathryn Bigelow's *The Hurt Locker*', in Christine Gledhill and Julia Knight (eds), *Doing Women's Film History: Reframing Cinemas, Past and Future*, Urbana: Illinois University Press, pp. 166–80.

Paszkiewicz, Katarzyna (2018), 'When the woman directs (a horror film)', in Mary Harrod and Katarzyna Paszkiewicz (eds), *Women Do Genre in Film and Television*, New York and London: Routledge, pp. 41–56.

Paszkiewicz, Katarzyna (forthcoming), '"She looks like a little piece of cake": Sofia Coppola and the commerce of auteurism', *Interférences littéraires*, vol. 21, pp. 107–28.

Pérez Fontdevila, Aina and Meri Torras Francès (2015), 'La autoría a debate: textualizaciones del cuerpo-corpus (una introducción teórica)', *Tropelías. Revista de Teoría de la Literatura y Literatura Comparada*, vol. 24, pp. 1–16.

Perkins, Claire (2004), 'This time it's personal: *Touch: Sensuous Theory and Multisensory Media* by Laura U. Marks', *Senses of Cinema*, vol. 33, October, http://sensesofcinema.com/2004/book-reviews/touch_laura_marks/ (accessed 20 May 2017).

Perkins, Claire (2014), 'Beyond Indiewood: the everyday ethics of Nicole Holofcener', *Camera Obscura*, vol. 29, no. 1, pp. 137–59.

Perkins, Victor (1992), 'The Atlantic divide', in Richard Dyer and Ginette Vincendeau (eds), *Popular European Cinema*, London: Routledge, pp. 194–205.

Pidduck, Julianne (1997), 'Travels with Sally Potter's *Orlando*: gender, narrative, movement', *Screen*, vol. 38, pp. 172–89.

Pidduck, Julianne (2004), *Contemporary Costume Film: Space, Place and the Past*, London: British Film Institute.

Pilger, John (2010), 'Why the Oscars are a con', *New Statesman*, 11 February, http://www.newstatesman.com/film/2010/02/pilger-iraq-oscar-american-war (accessed 20 May 2017).

Pinedo, Isabel Cristina (1997), *Recreational Terror: Women and the Pleasures of Horror Film Viewing*, Albany: State University of New York Press.

Pisters, Patricia (2003), *The Matrix of Visual Culture: Working with Deleuze in Film Theory*, Stanford: Stanford University Press.

Pisters, Patricia (2010), 'Logistics of perception 2.0: multiple screen aesthetics in Iraq War films', *Film-Philosophy*, vol. 14, no. 1, pp. 232–52.

Phillips, Michael (2009), '*The Hurt Locker*', *Chicago Tribune*, 9 July, http://featuresblogs.chicagotribune.com/talking_pictures/2009/07/the-hurt-locker-3-12-stars.html (accessed 20 May 2017).

Poirier, Agnès (2006), 'An empty hall of mirrors', *The Guardian*, 27 May, https://www.theguardian.com/commentisfree/2006/may/27/comment.filmnews (accessed 20 May 2017).

Potter, Claire (2010), 'Don't ask, don't tell: gendering war in *The Hurt Locker*', *The Chronicle: Blog Network*, 20 March, http://chronicle.com/blognetwork/tenuredradical/2010/03/dont-ask-dont-tell-hurt-locker-writes/ (accessed 20 May 2017).

Powell, Anna (2006), *Deleuze and Horror Film*, Edinburgh: Edinburgh University Press.

Powers, Nicole (2009), 'Diablo Cody: *Jennifer's Body*', *Suicide Girls*, 15 September, https://www.suicidegirls.com/members/nicole_powers/blog/2680164/diablo-cody-jennifers-body/ (accessed 20 May 2017).

Projansky, Sarah (2007), 'Mass magazine cover girls: some reflections on postfeminist girls and postfeminism's daughters', in Diane Negra and Yvonne Tasker (eds), *Interrogating Postfeminism: Gender and the Politics of Popular Culture*, Durham: Duke University Press, pp. 40–72.

Purse, Lisa (2011), *Contemporary Action Cinema*, Edinburgh: Edinburgh University Press.

Purse, Lisa (2016), 'Affective trajectories: locating diegetic velocity in the cinema experience', *Cinema Journal*, vol. 55, no. 2, pp. 151–7.

Quart, Leonard (2011), 'The way west: a feminist perspective. An interview with Kelly Reichardt', *Cineaste*, vol. 36, no. 2, pp. 40–2.

Rabinovitz, Lauren (1991), *Points of Resistance: Women, Power & Politics in the New York Avantgarde Cinema, 1943–71*, Champaign: University of Illinois Press.

Radner, Hilary (2011), *Neo-feminist Cinema: Girly Films, Chick Flicks and Consumer Culture*, New York: Routledge.

Radway, Janice (1984), *Reading the Romance: Women, Patriarchy, and Popular Literature*, Chapel Hill: University of North Carolina Press.

Rassos, Effie (2005), *Everyday Narratives: Reconsidering Filmic Temporality and Spectatorial Affect Through the Quotidian*, Doctoral Dissertation, University of New South Wales.

Rea, Steven (2006), '*Marie Antoinette*: a sugar rush that goes pop', *Philadelphia Inquirer*, 10 October, http://www.philly.com/philly/entertainment/movies/MovieReviewID_20061020_inq_weekend_SRAMAR.html (accessed 20 May 2017).

Read, Jacinda (2000), *The New Avengers: Feminism, Femininity, and the Rape-Revenge Cycle*, Manchester and New York: Manchester University Press.

Ringrose, Jessica (2006), 'A new universal mean girl: examining the discursive construction and social regulation of a new feminine pathology', *Feminism & Psychology*, vol. 16, no. 4, pp. 405–24.

Robé, Chris (2009), 'Taking Hollywood back: the historical costume drama, the biopic, and popular front US film criticism', *Cinema Journal*, vol. 48, no. 2, pp. 70–87.

Rogers, Anna (2007), 'Sofia Coppola', *Senses of Cinema*, vol. 45, http://sensesofcinema.com/2007/great-directors/sofia-coppola/ (accessed 20 May 2017).

Romney, Jonathan (2006), '*Marie Antoinette*', *Independent on Sunday*, 21 October, http://www.independent.co.uk/arts-entertainment/films/reviews/marie-antoinette-12a-6230488.html (accessed 20 May 2017).

Romney, Jonathan (2010), 'In search of lost time', *Sight and Sound*, vol. 20, no. 2, pp. 43–4.

Rose, Steve (2009), 'Kathryn Bigelow: back in the danger zone', *The Guardian*, 19 August, https://www.theguardian.com/film/2009/aug/19/kathryn-bigelow-iraq-hurt-locker (accessed 7 December 2017).

Rosen, Marjorie (1973), *Popcorn Venus: Women, Movies, & The American Dream*, New York: Coward, McCann & Geoghegan.

Rowe Karlyn, Kathleen (1995), *The Unruly Woman: Gender and the Genres of Laughter*, Austin: University of Texas Press.

Rowe Karlyn, Kathleen (2011), *Unruly Girls, Unrepentant Mothers: Redefining Feminism on Screen*, Austin: University of Texas Press.

Rozen, Leah (2006), 'Kirsten's Marie Antoinette fizzles at Cannes', *People*, 30 May, http://people.com/celebrity/kirstens-marie-antoinette-fizzles-at-cannes/ (accessed 20 May 2017).

Rushing, Robert A. (2016), 'Skin flicks: haptic ideology in the peplum film', *Cinema Journal*, vol. 56, no. 1, pp. 88–110.

Russ, Joanna (1983), *How to Suppress Women's Writing*, Austin: University of Texas Press.

Ruthven, Andrea (2015), *Representing Heroic Figures and/of Resistance: Reading Women's Bodies of Violence in Contemporary Dystopic Literatures*, Doctoral Dissertation, University of Barcelona.
Saltsman, Peter (2015), 'The *Intern*'s Nancy Meyers teaches you how to be a man', *Sharp Magazine*, 24 September, http://sharpmagazine.com/2015/09/24/the-interns-nancy-meyers-teaches-you-how-to-be-a-man/ (accessed 20 June 2017).
Sandhu, Sukhdev (2012), '"Slow cinema" fights back against Bourne's supremacy', *The Guardian*, 9 March, http://www.theguardian.com/film/2012/mar/09/slow-cinema-fights-bournes-supremacy (accessed 20 May 2017).
Sarris, Andrew (1968), *The American Cinema: Directors and Directions, 1929–68*, New York: Da Capo Press.
Sarris, Andrew (1976), 'Towards a theory of film history', in Bill Nichols (ed.), *Movies and Methods*, vol. I, Berkeley: University of California Press, pp. 237–51.
Sarris, Andrew (1981), 'Notes on auteur theory in 1962', in John Caughie (ed.), *Theories of Authorship*, London: Routledge, pp. 62–7.
Schatz, Thomas (1981), *Hollywood Genres: Formulas, Filmmaking and the Studio System*, New York: Random House.
Schoonover, Karl (2012), 'Wastrels of time: slow cinema's laboring body, the political subject and the queer', *Framework: The Journal of Cinema and Media*, vol. 53, pp. 65–78.
Schreiber, Michele (2011), 'Independence at what cost? Economics and female desire in Nicole Holofcener's *Friends With Money* (2006)', in Hilary Radner and Rebecca Stringer (eds), *Feminism at the Movies: Understanding Gender in Contemporary Popular Cinema*, New York and London: Routledge, pp. 177–88.
Schreiber, Michele (2014), *American Postfeminist Cinema: Women, Romance and Contemporary Culture*, Edinburgh: Edinburgh University Press.
Schwarzbaum, Lisa (2009), '*The Hurt Locker*', *Entertainment Weekly*, 17 June, http://www.ew.com/ew/article/0,,20285519,00.html (accessed 20 May 2017).
Scott, A. O. (2006), 'Holding a mirror up to Hollywood', *The New York Times*, 25 May, http://www.nytimes.com/2006/05/25/arts/movies/cannes-journal-marie-antoinette-best-or-worst-of-times-holding.html (accessed 20 May 2017).
Scott, A. O. (2009a), 'Hell is other people, especially the popular girl', *The New York Times*, 17 September, http://www.nytimes.com/2009/09/18/movies/18jennifer.html?_r=0 (accessed 20 May 2017).
Scott, A. O. (2009b), 'Neo-neo realism', *The New York Times Magazine*, 17 March, http://www.nytimes.com/2009/03/22/magazine/22neorealism-t.html?pagewanted=all (accessed 20 May 2017).
Scribe, Scarlet (2009), 'The problem with arguing feminism in *Jennifer's Body*', *I Went There*, 25 September, http://iwentthere.wordpress.com/2009/09/25/the-problem-with-arguing-feminism-in-jennifers-body/ (accessed 20 October 2016).
Segarra, Marta (2011), 'El abismo del sexo: la *vagina dentata* en la cultura contemporánea', in Helena González Fernández and Isabel Clúa (eds), *Máxima audiencia: Cultura popular y género*, Barcelona: Icaria, pp. 173–92.
Shaviro, Steven (1993), *The Cinematic Body*, Minneapolis and London: University of Minnesota Press.
Shaviro, Steven (2003), 'Straight from the cerebral cortex: vision and affect in *Strange Days*', in Deborah Jermyn and Sean Redmond (eds), *The Cinema of Kathryn Bigelow: Hollywood Transgressor*, London: Wallflower, pp. 159–77.
Shaviro, Steven (2008), 'The cinematic body REDUX', *Parallax*, vol. 14, no. 1, pp. 48–54.
Shaviro, Steven (2010), 'Slow cinema vs. fast films', *The Pinocchio Theory*, 12 May, http://www.shaviro.com/Blog/?p=891 (accessed 20 May 2017).

Siegel, Tatiana (2017), 'The complex gender politics of the *Wonder Woman* movie', *The Hollywood Reporter*, 31 May, http://www.hollywoodreporter.com/features/complex-gender-politics-wonder-woman-movie-1008259 (accessed 20 May 2017).

Silverman, Kaja (1990), 'Dis-embodying the female voice', in Patricia Erens (ed.), *Issues in Feminist Film Criticism*, Bloomington: Indiana University Press, pp. 309–29.

Silverstein, Melissa (2009), 'Sexism alert: the catfight begins', *Women and Hollywood*, 24 September, http://womenandhollywood.com/2009/09/24/sexism-alert-the-catfight-begins/ (accessed 20 May).

Silverstein, Melissa (2012), 'What Bigelow effect? Number of women directors in Hollywood falls to 5 percent', *IndieWire*, 24 January, http://www.indiewire.com/2012/01/what-bigelow-effect-number-of-women-directors-in-hollywood-falls-to-5-percent-240868/ (accessed 20 May 2017).

Silverstein, Melissa (2015), 'The contradictory feminism of Nancy Meyers's *The Intern*', *IndieWire*, 28 September, http://www.indiewire.com/2015/09/the-contradictory-feminism-of-nancy-meyers-the-intern-213252/ (accessed 20 May 2017).

Sims, Deborah M. (2014), 'Genre, fame and gender: the middle-aged ex-wife heroine of Nancy Meyers's *Something's Gotta Give*', in Aaron Barlow (ed.), *Star Power: The Impact of Branded Celebrity*, Westport: Praeger, pp. 191–205.

Skinner, Marjorie (2016), 'Kelly Reichardt's unearthed *River of Grass*', *The Portland Mercury*, 11 May, http://www.portlandmercury.com/film/2016/05/11/18043652/kelly-reichardts-unearthed-river-of-grass (accessed 20 May 2017).

Slotkin, Richard (1992), *Gunfighter Nation: The Myth of the Frontier in Twentieth-century America*, New York: Atheneum.

Smaill, Belinda (2013), 'Sofia Coppola: reading the director', *Feminist Media Studies*, vol. 13, no. 1, pp. 148–62.

Smelik, Anneke (1998), *And the Mirror Cracked: Feminist Cinema and Film Theory*, London: Palgrave.

Smith, Frances and Timothy Shary (eds) (2016), *ReFocus: The Films of Amy Heckerling*, Edinburgh: Edinburgh University Press.

Smith, Henry Nash (1950), *Virgin Land: The American West as Symbol and Myth*, Cambridge, MA: Harvard University Press.

Smith, Stacy, Katherine Pieper and Marc Choueiti (2013), 'Exploring the barriers and opportunities for independent women filmmakers', Sundance Institute and Women in Film Los Angeles–Women Filmmakers Initiative, Annenberg School for Communication & Journalism: University of Southern California.

Sobchack, Vivian (1992), *The Address of the Eye: A Phenomenology of Film Experience*, Princeton: Princeton University Press.

Sobchack, Vivian (2004), *Carnal Thoughts: Embodiment and Moving Image Culture*, Berkeley: University of California Press.

Soloway, Jill (2009), 'The prime of Miss Diablo Cody', *Bust*, no. 58, pp. 38–45, http://issuu.com/celinahex/docs/issue_58_100dpi_flipbook (accessed 20 May 2017).

Spivak, Gayatri (1998), 'Can the subaltern speak?', in Cary Nelson and Lawrence Grossberg (eds), *Marxism and the Interpretation of Culture*, Urbana and Chicago: University of Illinois Press, pp. 271–313.

Stacey, Jackie (1994), *Star Gazing: Hollywood Cinema and Female Spectatorship*, New York and London: Routledge.

Stacey, Jackie (2015), 'Crossing over with Tilda Swinton – the mistress of "flat affect"', *International Journal of Politics, Culture, and Society*, vol. 28, no. 3, pp 243–71.

Staiger, Janet (1992), *Interpreting Films: Studies in the Historical Reception of American Cinema*, Princeton: Princeton University Press.

Staiger, Janet (2000), *Perverse Spectators: The Practices of Film Reception*, New York: New York University Press.

Staiger, Janet (2011), 'The first Bond who bleeds, literally and metaphorically: gendered spectatorship for "pretty boy" action movies', in Hilary Radner and Rebecca Stringer (eds), *Feminism at the Movies: Understanding Gender in Contemporary Popular Cinema*, New York and London: Routledge, pp. 13–24.
Staiger, Janet (2013), 'Independent of what? Sorting out differences from Hollywood', in Geoff King, Claire Molloy and Yannis Tzioumakis (eds), *American Independent Cinema*, London: Routledge, pp. 15–27.
Stam, Robert (2000a), *Film Theory: An Introduction*, Oxford: Blackwell.
Stam, Robert (2000b), 'Beyond fidelity: the dialogics of adaptation', in James Naremore (ed.), *Film Adaptation*, London: Athlone, pp. 54–76.
Stevens, Dana (2006), 'Queen bees: Sofia Coppola and Marie Antoinette have a lot in common', *Slate*, 19 October, http://www.slate.com/id/2151855/# (accessed 20 May 2017).
Stobo, Matt (2010), 'In-depth analysis: *The Hurt Locker*', *Film Trout*, 5 June, http://filmtrout.com/mattsblogs.html (accessed 20 May 2017).
Tarkovsky, Andrey ([1986] 2012), *Sculpting in Time: Reflections on the Cinema*, Austin: University of Texas Press.
Tasker, Yvonne (1991), 'Having it all: feminism and the pleasures of the popular', in Sarah Franklin, Celia Lury and Jackie Stacey (eds), *Off-Centre: Feminism and Cultural Studies*, New York: HarperCollins Academic, pp. 85–96.
Tasker, Yvonne (1993), *Spectacular Bodies: Gender, Genre and the Action Cinema*, London and New York: Routledge.
Tasker, Yvonne (1999), 'Bigger than life', *Sight and Sound*, vol. 9, no. 5, pp. 12–15.
Tasker, Yvonne (2010), 'Vision and visibility: women filmmakers, contemporary authorship and feminist film studies', in Vicky Callahan (ed.), *Reclaiming the Archive: Feminism and Film History*, Detroit: Wayne State University Press, pp. 213–30.
Tasker, Yvonne (2011), '*Enchanted* (2007) by postfeminism: gender, irony, and the new romantic comedy', in Hilary Radner and Rebecca Stringer (eds), *Feminism at the Movies: Understanding Gender in Contemporary Popular Cinema*, New York and London: Routledge, pp. 67–79.
Tasker, Yvonne (2017), 'Contested masculinities: the action film, the war film, and the western', in Kristin Lené Hole, Dijana Jelača, E. Ann Kaplan and Patrice Petro (eds), *The Routledge Companion to Cinema & Gender*, New York: Routledge, pp. 111–20.
Tasker, Yvonne and Eylem Atakav (2010), '*The Hurt Locker*: male intimacy, violence, and the Iraq War movie', *Sine/Cine: Journal of Film Studies*, vol. 1, no. 2, pp. 57–70.
Tasker, Yvonne and Diane Negra (eds) (2007), *Interrogating Postfeminism: Gender and the Politics of Popular Culture*, Durham: Duke University Press.
Thompson, Anne (2009), 'Trailer watch: *Jennifer's Body*', *IndieWire*, 6 July, http://blogs.indiewire.com/thompsononhollywood/trailer_watch_jennifers_body (accessed 20 May 2017).
Thornham, Sue (2012), *What If I Had Been the Hero? Investigating Women's Cinema*, London: Palgrave Macmillan.
Thornham, Sue (2016), '"Not a country at all": landscape and *Wuthering Heights*', *Journal of British Cinema and Television*, vol. 13, no. 1, pp. 214–31.
Threadgold, Terry (1989), 'Talking about genre: ideologies and incompatible discourses', *Journal of Cultural Studies*, vol. 3, no. 1, pp. 101–27.
Tudor, Andrew (1973), *Theories of Film*, New York: Viking Press; London: British Film Institute.
Tulard, Jean (2010), 'Marie-Antoinette, la reine de l'écran', *Le Figaro*, 14 September, http://www.lefigaro.fr/cinema/2010/08/14/03002-20100814ARTFIG00004-marie-antoinette-la-reine-de-l-ecran.php (accessed 20 May 2017).

Tzioumakis, Yannis (2006), *American Independent Cinema: An Introduction*, Edinburgh: Edinburgh University Press.
Tzioumakis, Yannis (2013), '"Independent", "Indie" and "Indiewood": towards a periodization of contemporary (post-1980) American independent cinema', in Geoff King, Claire Molloy and Yannis Tzioumakis (eds), *American Independent Cinema*, London: Routledge, pp. 28–40.
Valby, Karen (2007), 'Diablo Cody: from ex-stripper to a-lister', *Entertainment Weekly*, 5 November, http://www.ew.com/ew/article/0,,20157948,00.html (accessed 20 May 2017).
Vidal, Belén (2005), 'Playing in a minor key: the literary past through the feminist imagination', in Mireia Aragay (ed.), *Books in Motion: Adaptation, Intertextuality, Authorship*, Amsterdam: Rodopi, pp. 263–84.
Vidal, Belén (2012), *Heritage Film: Nation, Genre, and Representation*, London and New York: Wallflower.
Vidal, Belén (2014), 'Introduction: the biopic and its critical contexts', in Tom Brown and Belén Vidal (eds), *The Biopic in Contemporary Film Culture*, London: Routledge, pp. 1–32.
Wakeman, Jessica (2009), 'Exclusive Q&A: Diablo Cody talks Megan Fox, therapy, and doing "The View" with Courtney Love', *The Frisky*, 8 September, http://www.thefrisky.com/2009-09-08/diablo-cody-interview/ (accessed 20 May 2017).
Wallace, Amy (1997), 'Shooting for a role in a male film genre', *Los Angeles Times*, 25 September, http://articles.latimes.com/1997/sep/25/news/mn-35944 (accessed 20 May 2017).
Walton, Saige (2016), *Cinema's Baroque Flesh: Film, Phenomenology and the Art of Entanglement*, Amsterdam: Amsterdam University Press.
Warshow, Robert (1964), *The Immediate Experience: Movies, Comics, Theatre and Other Aspects of Popular Culture*, New York: Anchor Books.
Warshow, Robert ([1954] 1999), 'Movie chronicle: the western', in Gerald Mast, Leo Braudy and Marshall Cohen (eds), *Film Theory and Criticism: Introductory Readings*, Oxford: Oxford University Press, pp. 605–17.
Waxman, Sharon (2006), *Rebels on the Backlot: Six Maverick Directors and How They Conquered the Hollywood Studio System*, New York: Harper Perennial.
'Wendy and Lucy: Press Notes' (2008), *Wendy and Lucy Official Website*, http://www.wendyandlucy.com/press_images/wal_pressnotes.pdf (accessed 20 May 2017).
White, Patricia (2006), 'The last days of women's cinema', *Camera Obscura*, vol. 63, pp. 145–51.
White, Patricia (2008), 'Lesbian minor cinema', *Screen*, vol. 49, no. 4, pp. 410–25.
White, Patricia (2009), 'Watching women's films', *Camera Obscura*, no. 72, pp. 152–62.
White, Patricia (2015), *Women's Cinema, World Cinema*, Durham and London: Duke University Press.
White, Patricia (2017), 'Pink material: white womanhood and the colonial imaginary in world cinema authorship', in Kristin Lené Hole, Dijana Jelača, E. Ann Kaplan and Patrice Petro (eds), *The Routledge Companion to Cinema & Gender*, New York: Routledge, pp. 215–26.
Wiggers, Darryl (2010), 'Enough already: the wonderful, horrible reception of Nancy Meyers', *CineAction*, vol. 81, pp. 65–72.
Williams, Linda (1991), 'Film bodies: gender, genre, and excess', *Film Quarterly*, vol. 44, pp. 2–13.
Williams, Linda (1998), 'Melodrama revised', in Nick Browne (ed.), *Refiguring American Film Genres: Theory and History*, Berkeley: University of California Press, pp. 42–88.

Williams, Linda (2002), 'When the women looks', in Mark Jancovich (ed.), *Horror, the Film Reader*, London: Routledge, pp. 61–6.
Williams, Rachel (2001), *No Job for a Lady: Women Directors in Hollywood*, Doctoral Dissertation, University of Nottingham.
Wiseman, Rosalind (2002), *Queen Bees and Wannabes*, New York: Three Rivers Press.
Wood, Robin ([1977] 2012), 'Ideology, genre, auteur', in Barry K. Grant (ed.), *Film Genre Reader IV*, Austin: University of Texas Press, pp. 78–92.
Wood, Robin (1986), *Hollywood from Vietnam to Reagan*, New York: Columbia University Press.
Wortel, Elise and Anneke Smelik (2013), 'Textures of time: a becoming-memory of history in costume film', in Liedeke Plate and Anneke Smelik (eds), *Performing Memory in Art and Popular Culture*, New York: Routledge, pp. 185–200.
Wright, Will (1975), *Sixguns and Society: A Structural Study of the Western*, Berkeley: University of California Press.
Wright, Will (1982), 'The Empire bites the dust', *Social Text*, no. 6, pp. 120–5.
Zecchi, Barbara (2011), '¿Qué es el GYNOCINE?', *Gynocine: History of Spanish Women's Cinema*, http://digitalhumanities.umass.edu/gynocine/node/31 (accessed 20 May 2017).
Zecchi, Barbara (2014), *Desenfocadas. Cineastas españolas y discursos de género*, Barcelona: Icaria.
Zecchi, Barbara (2018), 'Comedy as a feminist strategy: Spanish women filmmakers reclaim laughter', in Mary Harrod and Katarzyna Paszkiewicz (eds), *Women Do Genre in Film and Television*, New York and London: Routledge, pp. 91–105.

INDEX

40 Days and 40 Nights, 222
40-Year-Old Virgin, The, 222, 225
9/11, 98n, 132n
  post-9/11, 32n, 112, 150, 154

Abbott, Stacey, 22, 215–19, 249
abjection, 65, 77, 80, 88, 126, 206n
Academy Awards, The, 1–2, 7, 31n, 67, 100, 102, 176, 206n, 251n; *see also* Oscars
action cinema, 3–4, 9, 24, 26, 28, 31–3n, 48, 81, 98n, 108,122, 130, 132n, 212, 236, 256, 258
Adams, Robert, 162
adaptation, 32n, 54, 61, 64, 175, 187, 191, 197, 205–6n
address, 3, 12, 13, 23, 28, 30, 74, 83, 104
  embodied, 33n
  female, 71–4, 83, 97n
  gendered (genre), 6, 62, 70–5, 78, 226, 248
  male, 72
  mode of, 23, 25, 117, 191–2
Adorno, Theodor W., 43, 46, 49
Æon Flux, 63
aesthetic(s)
  materialist, 208
  minimalistic, 158
  of austerity, 134, 159
  of generic cross-referencing, 114
  of pastiche, 56, 166
  post-heritage, 186
  realistic, 107, 141, 156
  see also heritage film, pastiche and realism

affect, 13, 24–30, 33n, 54, 92, 118, 123, 156, 160–1, 166, 185, 187, 194, 198, 227, 240, 244, 248
  flat, 160–1, 172n
  relational, 238
  sensorial, 117
age, 24–5, 223, 231
  difference, 238, 241
  ageing protagonists, 211, 242
agency, 7, 10, 35, 37–40, 60, 83, 95, 135, 147, 188, 201, 205n, 211, 219, 233
  female, 5, 37, 184, 193
agent-hood, 10, 37–8, 55, 68
Akerman, Chantal, 5, 12, 31n, 156–7, 207
All the Boys Love Mandy Lane, 65, 88
Allen, Woody, 216
allusionism, 228
Along Came Polly, 222
alterity, 130, 148
alternative genealogies, 162
Altman, Robert, 48
Amadeus, 185
America's Army (videogame), 124
American dream, 45
American freedom, 165
American Mary, 61, 97n
American Psycho, 28, 61, 66, 97n, 256
American West, 151, 162
Amirpour, Ana Lily, 61, 97n, 255
anachronism, 182, 186
Analyze This, 241, 253n
Anderson, Paul W. S., 133n

286

INDEX

Anderson, Wes, 67, 139, 178
androcentrism, 247
Animal House, 250
Annie Hall, 216, 250n
Annie Get the Gun, 145
Apatow, Judd, 212, 222, 224
Apocalypse Now, 111, 117
apparatus theory, 30, 107, 118
appropriation, 13, 17, 54, 60, 87, 90, 125, 132n, 181, 203, 227
  feminist, 13, 88
  re-, 57, 255
Apted, Michael, 196
Aquamarine, 90
Argento, Dario, 75, 79
Arnold, Andrea, 162–3
Aronofsky, Darren, 178
Arzner, Dorothy, 12, 31n, 36, 53, 55, 105, 192, 254
Attic, The, 61
audience, 13, 23, 38, 40, 44–4, 51, 55–7, 62, 67, 71, 77, 82–4, 91, 107, 129, 136, 138, 151, 192–3, 200, 226, 261; see also spectator, the public
austerity, 159, 162, 168
auteur, 5, 8, 10, 15, 17–19, 21, 24, 67–8, 103–6, 136–7, 171n, 177, 182–3, 194, 201–2, 205n, 209, 211, 213–15, 257, 260, 262
  auteur cinema, 17, 24, 34–5, 40, 217
  auteur-star, 39
  auteur-structuralism, 47
  politique des auteurs, 18, 34, 43, 68, 140
  progressive auteur, 50, 217
  subversive auteur, 34–59
  see also authorship
authentication, 21, 170, 173
  de-, 21, 139, 173
authorial figure(s), 6, 38, 40, 55, 67
authorisation, 5
  de-, 5, 49
authorship
  as a commercial brand, 214
  as a commercial performance, 209
  collective, 62, 69

Babadook, 61
Backman Rogers, Anna, 183, 194, 200
Bad Girls, 160, 167
Bahrani, Ramin, 150
Ballad of Little Jo, The, 32n, 145
Barker, Jennifer, 25–6, 33n, 39n, 129, 172n
Barry Lyndon, 175, 185
Barthes, Roland, 38, 51, 56
Baudrillard, Jean, 123, 128
Baudry, Jean-Louis, 107
Bay, Michael, 71, 132n
Bazin, André, 31n, 53, 151, 156
Beauty and the Beast, 256

Beguiled, The, 204n, 255
Benjamin, Walter, 127–8, 153, 163
Berenstein, Rhona J., 74
Bergstrom, Janet, 53
Berlant, Lauren, 159–60
Beugnet, Martine, 164
Bingham, Dennis, 21, 174–5, 195–9, 204n, 207n
biography, 67, 174, 195, 199, 207n
biographic legend, 62, 98n, 102, 105, 184, 194, 228, 242
biopic, 6, 7, 21–2, 57, 173–208, 257
Black Cat, 257
Black Swan, 178
Blade Runner, 108
Blanchot, Maurice, 157
Bling Ring, The, 21, 178–81
Bloch, Ernst, 46, 56
Blood Diner, 61
Blue Steel, 108, 110, 113, 132n
body, the, 70, 82, 119, 121, 125–31, 162–3, 225, 252n
  female, 62, 64, 69, 70, 75, 77, 85, 98n, 161–2, 189, 203
  lived-, 25
  monstrous, 89
  of film, 26, 130
  of the cultural other, 162
body genre, 20, 70, 82, 118–31
Bordwell, David, 38
Boxing Helena, 66
boxing picture, 14, 89
Braidotti, Rosi, 162
brain-body dualism, 27
Brontë, Emily, 162
Bruno, Giuliana, 25
Burgoyne, Robert, 20, 108–9, 117, 119, 126, 129
bush, 163
Bush, George W., 122, 143–5, 163, 168
Butler, Alison, 16–17, 69, 259
Butler, David, 145, 160
Butler, Judith, 10, 37, 46, 81–2, 96, 126

Cahiers du cinéma (magazine), 5, 34–5
Calamity Jane, 145, 160
Cameron, James, 20, 33n, 102–4, 131–2n, 178, 212, 220
Campion, Jane, 5, 27, 31n, 101, 104, 162–3, 174, 187, 193
Cannes Film Festival, 101, 131n, 136, 175, 204n, 255
carnivalesque, the, 75, 80–1, 122
Carpenter, John, 256
Carrie, 61, 81, 83, 91, 97–8n
Casino Royale, 24
Cassavetes, John, 156
Cat Ballou, 145
Cattle Queen of Montana, 145
Caughie, John, 34

celebrity, 39, 67, 177, 181, 194, 260
Certain Women, 135
Chained, 66
chick culture, 219, 236, 250n
chick-flick, 215, 218–19, 222, 227, 229–32, 236, 248, 250–1n
cine-psychoanalysis, 11, 32n
Clockwork Orange, A, 108
Cloud Atlas, 257
Clover, Carol J., 19, 66, 70, 76, 90–3, 132n
Cobb, Shelley, 11, 54, 101, 206n
Coen brothers, 140–1
colonial fictions, 148
colonialism, 148
colonisation, 135, 143, 162–3
comedy
  bromantic, 22, 222–6, 248
  nervous, 216, 218
  non-romantic, 218–28
  of remarriage, 218
  physical, 26
comic-book movies, 236
commodity cultures, 179, 182, 189, 194, 199–202, 211, 236
conquest narrative, 160
consumerism, consumption, 38, 46, 50, 51, 81, 88, 173, 178, 182, 184, 187, 193–4, 196, 201, 203, 211, 214, 228, 230–2, 237, 248
contact theory, 33n, 119
Cook, Pam, 25, 103, 183, 199, 204–5n
Coolidge, Martha, 3
Coppola, Francis Ford, 39, 111, 177
corporal excess, 70
corporeal self-sufficiency, 126, 130
Corrigan, Timothy, 19, 21, 38–40, 67, 105, 209, 214
costume film, 6, 85, 183, 184–96, 199, 200, 202, 203
counter-cinema, 50, 82, 102, 136, 139, 141, 170n, 199, 254–5
cowboy, 50, 114, 142, 144
Cracked Earth, 162
Creed, Barbara, 19, 66, 76–80, 88–9, 92
crime fiction, 24
Cronenberg, David, 24
culinary metaphors, 182, 214
cult cinema, 24, 75

Dance, Girl, Dance, 192
Dans ma peau, 61
Dardenne brothers, 158–9
Dargis, Manohla, 1, 103, 115, 132n, 171n, 175, 213, 224, 230
Davis, Geena, 36
Day, Doris, 160
De Lauretis, Teresa, 12, 32n, 55, 87, 166
De Niro, Robert, 22, 220, 226, 228, 232, 240–8, 253n
De Palma, Brian, 75, 79, 83, 91, 112, 124

De Sica, Vittorio, 150, 157
De Van, Marina, 61
Dead Hooker in a Trunk, 61
death of the author (Barthes), the, 18, 36–7, 59n
Deleuze, Gilles, 16–17, 25, 32n, 53–4, 96, 118, 120, 128, 133n, 155–6, 169
Denis, Claire, 5, 31n, 61, 148, 162
Deren, Maya, 12, 36
Derrida, Jacques, 41, 58n
desert, the, 113, 119, 124, 127, 151, 159–60, 165–7
deterritorialisation, 169
Devil Wears Prada, The, 92, 228–32, 251–2n
Dibb, Saul, 183, 193
Die Hard, 28
Doane, Mary Ann, 87
docudrama, 175
dream-factory, 46, 233–40, 247
Duchess, The, 183, 193–4
Dulac, Germaine, 12, 36
Dunst, Kirsten, 187
Duras, Marguerite, 12
duration, 123, 151, 153–60
Dwan, Allan, 145
Dyer, Richard, 51–5, 59n, 95, 136, 142, 167–8, 171n, 240, 246

Easton Ellis, Bret, 61, 98n
Ebert, Robert, 62, 217
economic crisis, 159
economic precariousness, 168
Edison, Thomas, 142
Edwards, Gareth, 255
embodied memory, 29, 187
embodiment, 25, 27, 76, 82, 119, 163, 220, 230
  disembodied look, 85
  disembodied voice, 84–5
emotional overload, 28–9, 118–20
emotions, 27, 29, 161
empathy, 148, 158, 206n
empowerment, 63, 72, 88–9, 95, 149, 194, 203, 230, 232
endurance, 158–60, 172n
enduration *see* endurance
Ephron, Nora, 3, 5, 14, 27, 176, 225, 231, 249n, 251n
epic films, 112
Evil Dead, The, 81, 89, 99
exceptionalism, 5, 10, 58n, 136, 249n, 261
exceptionality *see* exceptionalism
Exorcist, The, 80–1, 89
eye, 84, 107–8, 110, 118, 122, 125, 129–30, 154, 162, 182
eye/I (Descartes), 108

failure, 72, 82, 116, 119, 122, 130, 143–4, 167, 179, 195–7

fame, 174, 180–1, 194, 198
fan(s), 13, 15, 32n, 60, 62, 65, 97n 246, 251n, 255
Fanon, Frantz, 108
Far West, 48, 113
fashion, 176, 179, 181, 193–4, 205n, 229–32, 236, 240, 251n
Fast Times at Ridgemont High, 256
fatherhood, 111, 117
fatigue, 151, 155–9
Fawcett, John, 80, 88
fear, 45, 49, 77, 93, 95, 147–9, 195
Feig, Paul, 251n, 255
femininity, 7, 12, 21, 33n, 49–50, 81, 83, 91, 94, 103, 105, 140, 165, 179, 194, 201, 214, 227, 258
  bourgeois, 178, 182, 193
  heterosexual, 88
  individualist, 102
  middle-class, 87, 231
  monstrous, 65, 81, 87
  neoliberal, 21, 88, 91
femme castratrice, 77–8, 88, 92
femme fatale, 45, 197
fetishism, 110, 213, 237, 239
fetishistic scopophilia, 72, 77
Fifty Shades of Grey, 51, 255
film noir, 14, 24, 33n, 45, 53, 58n, 140, 256
Final Girl, 69, 76, 90–7
Fincher, David, 28
Fiske, John, 23
Fog, The, 61
Ford, John, 24, 133n, 143, 147, 171n, 195
Forman, Miloš, 185
formula, 16, 18, 43, 45, 52, 58–9n, 140, 174, 217, 222
Foucault, Michel, 55, 59n,138
Fox, Megan, 62–3, 69, 71–3, 77, 97n
Fradley, Martin, 66, 83, 88, 91–5, 99n
Frankfurt School, 43, 46
Fraser, Antonia, 174–5
fraternity, 116
Freddy's Dead, 61
Freud, Sigmund, 107, 242
Friedkin, William, 80
friendship, 22, 64, 219–22, 240
frivolity, 7, 179, 187, 203
frontier, 113, 142–50, 167, 171n
Frozen River, 140, 172n
Fujiwara, Kei, 61
Fuller, Sam, 48
Funny Face, 229

Gaines, Jane, 15, 19, 46, 52–7, 69, 96, 262
gangster films, 45, 253n
Garbo, Greta, 195
Garland, Judy, 160
Garrett, Roberta, 27–9, 33n, 141, 185–6, 193, 205–7n, 219, 227–8, 240, 247

gaze, 72, 77, 84–7, 103, 108, 110, 115–16, 118–31, 147–50, 161, 163, 186, 192, 198
genericity, 8, 14, 21, 29, 39, 152, 172n, 240, 249
genre
  as a cycle, 195
  as a formula, 43, 45, 53, 59n, 217
  as a structure, 47
  as process, 16, 52–3, 217
  author-genre, 52, 185
  gendered, 23–30, 32n
  gendering of, 3, 22, 24, 27, 30, 184–5, 215, 225–6, 259
  genre auteur, 6, 18–23, 256, 259
  progressive, 53
  transmigration of, 261
Gentlemen Prefer Blondes, 48
Ghost in the Machine, 61
Ghostbusters, 255
Ginger Snaps, 65, 80–1, 88–9, 99n
girl
  culture, 194, 203
  hero, 90, 99n
  mean girl, 85–7, 99n
  popular, 85–8, 92
  power, 65, 89, 91, 94, 98n, 194
Girl Walks Home Alone at Night, A, 61
Girlfight, 62
girlhood, 182, 194, 228, 231–2, 243
glass ceiling, 233, 236, 257
Gledhill, Christine, 13–15, 23, 30, 32n, 40, 45, 57, 59n, 95, 106, 240
Godard, Jean-Luc, 156
Gordimer, Nadine, 51
gore, 71, 74, 89, 204n
Gorfinkel, Elena, 134–5, 148, 152–60, 165–8, 171–2n
Gorillas in the Mist, 195
Granik, Debra, 14, 20, 140, 172n
Grant, Catherine, 10, 37, 176
Great Man, the (genre), 195, 198, 201, 207n
Great Train Robbery, The, 142
Greenwald, Maggie, 32n, 145
Guattari, Félix, 16–17, 32n, 96, 133n, 169
Guy-Blaché, Alice, 69, 255

Haas, Philip, 112
Haggis, Paul, 67, 112, 124
Halberstam, Jack, 76–8, 82–3, 93–5
Hall, Stuart, 74
Halloween (1978), sequel (1981), 61
happiness, 159, 252n
happy ending, 86, 207n, 216, 219, 238–9, 243
haptic, the, 25–6, 33n, 129, 165, 206n
Hard Body, 20, 130, 133n
Hardwicke, Catherine, 14, 97–8n
Harrod, Mary, 13–14, 27, 29–30, 56, 152, 166, 216, 219, 221, 240, 245–9
Harron, Mary, 15, 28, 61, 66, 97n, 198, 204n, 255–6

Harvey Girls, The, 160
Hathaway, Anne, 22, 220, 228–33, 251n
Hawks, Howard, 48
Haynes, Todd, 174
Heat, 241
Heckerling, Amy, 14, 27, 29, 152, 172n, 245, 256
Hepburn, Katharine, 58, 195
Her Only Living Son, 97
heritage film, 10, 185–7, 189, 194, 206n
hero, 9, 44, 76, 90, 92, 99n, 112, 113–17, 122, 130, 144, 166, 170, 188, 216, 227
heroine, 13, 24, 33n, 58n, 89, 94, 98n, 132n, 150, 193, 198, 205–6n, 252n, 257–8
heroism, 9, 20, 31n, 107, 114–17, 130
Hess, Judith, 44
heteronormativity, 10, 105, 240
Higson, Andrew, 185
Hill, Debra, 61
Hilton, Paris, 181
His Girl Friday, 48
historical accuracy, 175
historical film, 21, 175, 184–5, 207n
history, 37, 41, 52, 61, 66, 80, 87, 138, 143–5, 174–5, 183, 186–9, 256–7
Hitch, 222
Hitchcock, Alfred, 24, 75
Holden Jones, Amy, 61
Holiday, The, 209, 215, 238, 249n, 252n
Hollows, Joanne, 4, 31n, 70, 75
Holofcener, Nicole, 20, 140–1, 249n
homme-com, 222–6, 250n; see also comedy
hooks, bell, 108
hope, 46, 56, 58n, 247
Horkheimer, Max, 43, 46
horror film, 6, 8, 60–99
Hostel Part II, 65
House of Wax, 88
How to Lose a Guy in 10 Days, 251
Hunger Games, The, 51, 255
Hunt, Courtney, 14, 20, 140, 172n
Hutchings, Peter, 84
Huyssen, Andreas, 49, 182, 217
hyper-aestheticisation, 152, 238
hypertrophy of the visual, 107–18

identification, 3, 9, 14, 19, 25–6, 29–30, 33n, 76, 93, 97n, 114, 122, 132n, 152, 164–5, 192, 199, 248
ideology, 5, 32n, 44–6, 50, 178, 219, 259
  bourgeois, 12, 50
  conservative, 129, 219
  dominant, 44, 73, 185
  nation-sate, 117
  of progress, 160
  patriarchal, 5, 260
image
  authorial, 63

brand, 178–9, 201, 260
positive image criticism, 31–2n
immobility, 108, 153, 159, 165
imperialism, 6, 101, 171n
In the Valley of Elah, 112, 124
independence, 135, 138, 140, 170n, 204n, 219, 229–312, 252n
  discourse of, 8, 168, 173
independent film, 8, 20, 29, 62, 136–41, 170n, 227
  American independent cinema, 20–1, 134, 136–7, 150, 178
  indie cinema, 8, 20, 28, 62, 138, 140, 173, 176, 220, 257
intersectionality, 31n, 231
intersubjectivity, 38, 165
intertext, 16, 28, 29, 32n, 54, 76–83, 162, 184, 212
intertextuality see intertext
Iscove, Robert, 86
It's Complicated, 209, 212, 217, 237–9, 249n, 253n
Italian neorealists, 134, 156–7

Jameson, Fredric, 46, 59n, 185–6
Jarmusch, Jim, 140
Jay, Martin, 118
Jeanne Dielman, 23, Quai du Commerce, 1080 Bruxelles, 156–7, 207n
Jeffers McDonald, Tamar, 219, 222–5, 250n
Jenkins, Patty, 14, 256, 258
Jermyn, Deborah, 14, 22, 24, 31n, 59n, 103n, 105–6, 210–19, 226, 239, 250–3n, 259–60
Joffé, Roland, 88
Johnny Guitar, 31n, 145
Johnston, Claire, 12–13, 16, 17, 46, 55, 142, 192
Jonze, Spike, 177–8
Juno, 63, 67
Jupiter Ascending, 257

K-19: The Widowmaker, 106, 257
Kaufman, Charlie, 67, 139
Keaton, Buster, 26
Keaton, Diane, 211, 252n
Kelly, Gene, 245–6
Kent, Jennifer, 61
Khouri, Callie, 36
Kill Bill (Vol. 1 and 2), 81, 94, 177
Killing, The, 257
Kitses, Jim, 47, 58–9n, 114
Klinger, Barbara, 50–6
Kluge, Alexander, 39
Kracauer, Siegfried, 163
Kristeva, Julia, 77, 126
Kubrick, Stanley, 108, 170n, 175, 185

LaBute, Neil, 139
Ladri di biciclette, 150

Lambert, Mary, 61
land, 114, 161–9
landscape, 98n, 103, 112–14, 128, 135, 142, 146, 152–5, 160, 248
Lane, Christina, 11, 35, 100, 102, 104, 141, 201–2
Lauzen, Martha, 2, 4, 139, 257
Legally Blonde, 232
lesbian vampire, 79
Lessing, Doris, 50
Lévi-Strauss, Claude, 47
Lichtenstein, Mitchell, 78, 88
Lincoln, 174
Lloyd, Phyllida, 257
Locke, Sondra, 255
loss, 82, 117, 126, 129
Lost in Translation, 32n, 141, 176–7, 187, 203, 204n, 206
love, 62, 220, 222, 228, 231, 237–8
Loveless, The, 106, 123, 131n
Lupino, Ida, 12, 254–5
Lynch, David, 28
Lynch, Jennifer, 66

Mackie, Anthony, 111
Mad Max: Fury Road, 255
Madness of King George, The, 175
Mae Brown, Rita, 61
Maguire, Sharon, 27
majors, 71, 138, 170n
makeover, 92, 191, 205n, 228–33, 237, 251–2n
Mamma Mia!, 257
Mamoulian, Rouben, 195
Manifest Destiny Doctrine, 142–3, 171n
Mannis, Michael, 241
Marks, Laura, 25–6, 33n, 128–9, 133n, 164–5
marriage, 29, 44, 104, 132n, 177, 181, 193, 196–7, 218, 227, 239–40, 245, 247
Marshall, Garry, 86, 228–9, 251
masculinity, 2–3, 7–9, 45, 90, 103, 106, 115–16, 122, 124, 135, 144, 147, 166, 201, 227, 232, 242–4, 252n, 260
  abstract, 114, 125
  heroic, 107, 115, 126, 130
  mythical, 20, 130
mass-culture, 19, 22, 43, 47, 49–51, 140, 175, 181–2, 214–15, 217, 236
masses, the, 43, 49–50, 128, 186
Massumi, Brian, 117, 133n
materiality, 21, 26, 29, 124–5, 130, 163, 167, 169, 183, 189–90
Mayne, Judith, 5, 16, 31n, 36–7, 73, 105
McLaglen, Andrew V., 171n
Mean Girls, 71, 85–6, 99n
Mean Streets, 241
Meet the Parents, 241
melodrama, 4, 8, 13–14, 23–6, 32n, 42, 50, 53, 69–70, 83, 104, 119, 140, 145, 186, 198, 215–17, 255–6

menstrual witch, 79
Merleau-Ponty, Maurice, 26, 33n, 163
meta-cinematic approach, 20, 107, 115, 123
metagenericity, 20, 28, 152, 249
migration, 146, 172n
Miller, George, 255
Ming-liang, Tsai, 134
Minority Report, 108
Mirkin, David, 229
mise-en-scène, 21–4, 50, 79, 112, 121, 126, 159, 185–7, 190, 194, 210–13, 236–9
misogyny, 24, 49, 69, 98n
Miss Congeniality, 219
mobility, 9, 111, 135, 159, 165, 188, 193, 206n
modernism, 49, 51, 160 182
Modleski, Tania, 236
Monster, 257
monster, 73, 76–7, 82, 84, 88–9, 90, 92, 98n
monstrosity, 72, 77–8, 80, 82–3, 87, 94–5
monstrous-feminine, the, 76–82, 87–8
Moonstruck, 229, 251n
Morricone, Ennio, 114, 121
Morris, Meaghan, 17, 259
motherhood, 29, 196, 252n, 258
Mulvey, Laura, 11, 17, 32n, 72, 82, 84, 107, 115
Munro, Alice, 51
Murray, Bill, 219
musicals, 26, 45
My Big Fat Greek Wedding, 229

Naficy, Hamid, 129
nationalism, 117
nature, 9, 44, 114, 124, 143–4, 206n, 211, 231
Neale, Steve, 15, 24–5, 41, 53, 56
Near Dark, 61, 106, 113, 131–2n
Negra, Diane, 39, 65, 88, 178, 232, 247, 263
neoliberal individualism, 5, 88, 231, 258
New Love and The Old, The, 69
New York, 66, 102, 170n, 181, 251n, 255–6
New Zealand, 163
Newman, Michael, 173, 205
Nichols, Mike, 232
Nicholson, Jack, 241, 244
Nicolodi, Daria, 61
Night Moves, 135
nostalgia, 46, 73, 185–6, 206n, 244, 247, 253n
Notorious Bettie Page, The, 198

objectification, 12, 69, 128–9, 191–3, 254
ocularcentrism, 107–8, 118
Office Killer, The, 61
Old Joy, 135
opacity, 165–6
operations of suture, 82
optical images, 26, 128–30
Organ, 61
Orlando, 183, 187–8, 193, 199, 206–7n

291

Oscars, 6, 32n, 58n, 67, 104, 106, 263n
Other, the, 126–30, 147–8, 162

Paradise, 67
Parent Trap, The, 238
Passion Fish, 141
Passion of Jeanne d'Arc, The, 185
pastiche, 141, 166–7, 172n, 185–6, 240, 258, 262
Pattinson, Robert, 62, 97n
Peeping Tom, 108
Peirce, Kimberly, 14, 31n, 61, 97–8n
perception, 25–6, 101, 118, 123, 127–8, 165–6
   embodied, 118, 129, 133n
performance, 60, 86, 160, 255, 261
   as an auteur, 177
   authorial, 5, 7, 10, 105, 182
   commercial, 67, 141, 209
   dramatic, 228, 241
performativity, 96, 186, 190
period film, 29, 186–7; *see also* costume film
persona, 32n, 105, 141, 177, 219, 240–1
   authorial, 8, 18, 102, 175, 177, 201, 228
   public, 5–6, 38–9, 63, 67 196, 261
Pet Sematary, 61
phenomenology, 25–7, 29–30, 33n, 118, 133n, 135, 152–3, 156, 162–6, 190, 200
photograph, 35, 38, 127, 153, 162, 199
photography *see* photograph
Piano, The, 163–4, 187–8, 193
Pidduck, Julianne, 188, 205n
Pisters, Patricia, 25, 108, 123–4
Point Break, 106, 113, 123, 131–2n, 202–3
Polk, Mimi, 36
Popcorn Venus, 58
pornography, 9, 24, 70, 119
Porter, Edwin S., 142
postfeminism, postfeminist discourse, 5–6, 10, 12, 19, 21, 65, 88–9, 91–4, 98n, 101–2, 184, 193–4, 219, 232–3, 237, 248, 251–2n, 258–9, 263n
postmodern nostalgia film, 185
Potter, Sally, 5, 12, 27, 31n, 183, 187
Powell, Michael, 108
Pretty Woman, 229, 251n
Princess Diaries, The, 86
Private Benjamin, 236, 249n, 252n
privilege, 7–11, 71, 73, 148, 177–81, 184, 186, 194, 203, 205n, 211, 213, 225
progress, 44, 153, 160–1, 171n, 257–8
prom queen, 91–2
prom scene, 86, 91
Propp, Vladimir, 47
psychoanalysis, 46, 165
public, the, 44, 56
   adolescent, 73
   expectations of, 52–3, 57
   female, 49

homogenising of, 24
see also: audience, spectator

Queen Christina, 197
Quick and the Dead, The, 176

race, 24–5, 35, 76, 172n, 261
racism, 95, 132n, 142–5, 147, 260
Radner, Hilary, 209, 211, 229, 236–7, 248, 250n, 252n
Radway, Janice, 247
Raging Bull, 241
Raimi, Sam, 89, 167
Ramsay, Lynne, 162
rape-revenge, 63, 77–8, 92, 97n; *see also* revenge
Ray, Nicholas, 31n, 145
reader-response theory, 73
Reagan, Ronald, 144
realism, 29, 135, 141, 151, 155–7, 178
Redacted, 112, 124
Reddy, Helen, 100
reference-spotting, 29–30, 248
Reiner, Rob, 225, 251n
relationality, 31n, 148, 164, 172n
Renoir, Jean, 205
repetition, 10, 15, 18–19, 40–2, 45, 49, 52–3, 56, 57, 59n, 69, 81–2, 96, 201–2, 207n
revenge, 63, 72, 88, 90, 93, 97n
Reynolds, Debbie, 245
River of Grass, 135
Rivette, Jacques, 35, 156
Roach, Jay, 241
road movie, 1, 8, 134–5, 150
Rocky Horror Picture Show, 89
Rogue One: A Star Wars Story, 255
romance, 4, 8, 13, 22–3, 29, 50, 171n, 193, 210, 215, 218–20, 224, 226–31, 237, 239–40, 244–8, 250n, 260
romantic comedy, 8–9, 13, 22, 24, 59n, 92, 103, 209–253
romantic drama, 4
Romanticism, 41
romcom *see* romantic comedy
Romy and Michele's High School Reunion, 229
Rosebud syndrome, 44
Rosetta, 158
Rossellini, Roberto, 157
Rothman, Stephanie, 255
Rowe Karlyn, Kathleen, 83–4, 89–90, 94–5, 227
Ruiz, Raoul, 39
Russ, Joanna, 259

Sarandon, Susan, 36
Sarris, Andrew, 43, 49
Sayegh, Christopher, 111
Schatz, Thomas, 41

Schreiber, Michele, 139–40, 209–12, 219, 230–1, 238–9
science fiction, 8, 33n, 42, 44, 63, 71, 108, 212, 256
Scorsese, Martin, 28, 58n, 204n
Scott, A. O., 75, 150, 171–2n
Scott, Ridley, 1, 36, 108
Scream (saga), 83, 99n
screwball comedy, 218, 250n
Searchers, The, 147
self-awareness *see* self-consciousness
self-consciousness, 11, 27–8, 53, 59n, 78, 89, 140, 167, 186, 247–9
self-reflexivity *see* self-consciousness
sentimentalism, 28, 222, 228, 243
Set-Up, 108
Sex and the City: The Movie, 92
Sex and the City (television series), 230, 250n
sex comedies, 218
sexism, 2–3, 81, 95, 142–3, 218, 235–6, 248, 250, 252n
Seyfried, Amanda, 63, 71–4, 86
Shane, 53
Sharman, Jim, 89
Shaviro, Steven, 25, 107, 110, 118–19, 155
She's All That, 86, 229
Shea, Katt, 255
Sherman, Cindy, 61
Shyer, Charles, 233, 249n
Sidney, George, 145, 160
Silver Linings Playbook, 241
Silverman, Kaja, 82, 84
Silverstein, Elliot, 145
Sirk, Douglas, 50, 213, 216–17, 239
Situation, The, 112
slasher film, 32n, 61, 76, 90–2, 99n
Sleepless in Seattle, 225, 251n
Slotkin, Richard, 143
slow cinema, 8, 154–60, 169, 171–2n
Slumber Party Massacre, 61
Snow White, 79
soap opera, 13, 23, 66, 83, 215
Sobchack, Vivian, 25–7, 33n, 133n, 163–4
Soderbergh, Steven, 198
Solaris, 42
Solondz, Todd, 139–41
Something's Gotta Give, 209–11, 238, 249n, 251–3n
Somewhere, 178, 181, 204–5n
Soska Sisters, 61, 97n
spectacle, 70, 72, 77, 80, 115, 117, 184–6, 192, 201–2, 205–6n, 211
spectator, 4, 9, 16, 25, 33n, 60, 73, 76, 83–4, 103, 117–18, 122, 146, 156, 159, 164–5, 184–5, 191, 197, 220, 260; *see also* audience, the public
spectatorship, 13, 19, 26–7, 30, 62, 73, 82, 95, 130, 159; *see also* audience, the public, spectator

Spheeris, Penelope, 255
Spielberg, Steven, 108, 174
stardom, 67, 228
Stevens, George, 53, 133n
stillness, 119, 193
Stone, Oliver, 28, 204n
Stop Loss, 31
Strange Days, 108, 132n
Streep, Meryl, 229, 263n
Streisand, Barbra, 2, 100
subversion, 5, 19–20, 32n, 47–59, 64, 81, 93, 95, 145, 184, 195, 198, 215, 217, 259–60
Superbad, 224
superhero film, 256–7
surface, 21, 82, 116, 118, 128, 130, 164, 167, 179, 182–3, 186–7, 200–3, 212, 231, 237
surgeon-cameraman (Benjamin), 127
Surveillance, 66
Suspiria, 61, 79
Swinton, Tilda, 192
Szymborska, Wisława, 51

tactile visuality, 125–31
Talalay, Rachel, 61, 98n
Tarantino, Quentin, 2, 28, 81, 139–41, 170n, 177–8
Tarkovsky, Andrei, 42
Tarr, Béla, 134
Tasker, Yvonne, 9, 23, 48, 81, 88, 104, 135, 144, 213, 219, 247
Taxi Driver, 241
teen film, 14, 19, 72–6, 83, 85–6, 88, 90, 92, 99n
Teeth, 65, 78, 81, 88, 92
temporality, 120, 122, 150–61
Tennant, Andy, 222
Terminator, 104
Texas Chainsaw Massacre 2, The, 82
Thelma and Louise, 1, 35
Theron, Charlize, 63, 257
Thor, 257
Thornham, Sue, 55, 162
thriller, 24, 75, 108, 255, 257, 260
time, 21, 120–3, 133n, 135, 151–60, 165, 171–2n, 206n
to-be-looked-at-ness, 71, 77, 115
trailer, 72–3, 75, 97n, 228
Transformers, 71, 132n
transvestism, 2, 100, 171n, 199
trauma, 98n, 111, 129
Trouble Every Day, 61
Turner, Frederick Jackson, 165
Twilight, 51, 62, 97–8n
Tzioumakis, Yannis, 135, 137

Umberto D., 150
United States of Tara, The, 67
Urban Legends: Bloody Mary, 61
utopian, the, 46, 54, 56, 141, 248

vagina dentata, 78, 92
Van Dyke, W. S., 197, 205n
velocity, 111, 135, 160
Verfremdungseffekt (Brecht), 95
victimhood, 94–5, 198
victimisation, 70, 195, 198, 207n
Vidal, Belén, 174–5, 186, 187, 193–4
viewer *see* spectator, audience
vigilantism, 149, 241
violence, 9, 19, 24, 28, 35, 62, 66, 69–70, 82, 85, 90–6, 98n, 111, 119, 122–5, 132n, 147, 256, 258, 261
virginity, 83, 87
voyeurism, 108, 110, 117
vulnerability, 9, 117, 126

Wachowski brothers, The, 257
Wagon Master, 143, 172n
Walking and Talking, 141
Wall Street, 150
Walt Disney, 79
war
  Cold War, 45, 145
  film (genre), 1, 3, 6, 8, 9, 13, 31n, 100–33
  First Gulf War, 112, 123, 133n
  Iraq War, 20, 24, 26, 29, 57, 101, 107, 112, 114, 124, 143–4
  Vietnam War, 111
  World War II, 45, 112, 150–1, 158, 204n
Warshow, Robert, 42, 149
Waters, Mark, 85
Wayne, John, 114, 133n, 150, 153
Weaver, Sigourney, 104
Wedding Crashers, 220, 222, 225
Weight of Water, The, 103, 132n
Welcome to the Dollhouse, 141
Wendy and Lucy, 135–6, 150, 158–9, 161
Western, the, 1, 3, 6, 8–9, 13, 21, 24, 29, 31–2n, 42, 45, 48, 53, 59n, 61, 87, 107, 110, 113–16, 118, 122, 126, 128, 134–73, 256, 261

classical, 24, 145, 150, 165
hero, 9, 24, 107, 110, 116, 126, 130, 144, 147
non-American, 51, 114, 121–2, 167
Weston, Edward, 162
What Women Want, 209, 226–7, 238–9, 252n
When Harry Met Sally, 225, 251n
White Material, 148
White, Patricia, 4–6, 11, 148, 169n, 254
Wild West, 21, 29, 113, 114, 147, 153, 165
wilderness, 44, 114, 143–5, 167
Williams, Linda, 26, 29, 70, 84, 119
Williams, Michelle, 160
Williams, Raymond, 56
Winter's Bone, 140, 172n
Wishman, Doris, 15, 255
woman
  as myth, 156
  as spectacle, 192
  independent, 230, 233, 251n
  phallic, 84
  possessed, 80
  voice, 106
  with glasses, 87
  woman-snake, 79
  writer as a celebrity, 51
women's cinema, 106, 139, 168–9n, 176, 183, 210, 254–61
Wonder Woman, 256–7
Wood, Robin, 43
Woolf, Virginia, 191, 199
Working Girl, 232
working mothers, 233, 248
writer, 36, 51, 169
Wuthering Heights, 162–3

Young Adult, 67

Zavattini, Cesare, 157
Zero Dark Thirty, 101, 132n

EU representative:
Easy Access System Europe
Mustamäe tee 50, 10621 Tallinn, Estonia
Gpsr.requests@easproject.com

www.ingramcontent.com/pod-product-compliance
Lightning Source LLC
Chambersburg PA
CBHW052152300426
44115CB00011B/1640